Moon in Eclipse

Moon in Eclipse

A Life of Mary Shelley

Jane Dunn

Weidenfeld and Nicolson   London

To Philip

Copyright © by Jane Dunn 1978

First published in Great Britain in 1978 by
George Weidenfeld and Nicolson Ltd
91 Clapham High Street, London SW4 7TA

Second impression 1978

All rights reserved. No part of this
publication may be reproduced, stored in
a retrieval system, or transmitted, in
any form or by any means, electronic,
mechanical, photocopying, recording or
otherwise, without the prior permission
of the copyright holder.

ISBN 0 297 77383 6

Printed in Great Britain by
Butler & Tanner Ltd, Frome and London

Contents

	Illustrations	vii
	Preface	1
1	Inheritance	5
2	Books and Daydreams	16
3	Enter Shelley	36
4	Renaissance	53
5	Vagabondage through France	64
6	Honeymoon's End	84
7	A Runaway Dormouse	100
8	Birth of a Son	114
9	Frankenstein and the Villa Diodati	124
10	Two Suicides	144
11	Italian Exile	166
12	My Lost William	193
13	Rumours and Blackmail	206
14	Pisan Acquaintances	222
15	Presentiments of Evil	238
16	Lost in Darkness	251
17	A Funeral Pyre	256
18	The Lonely Survivor	271
19	Some Clever Men	278
20	Love's Sacrifice	298
21	Counting the Blessings	312
22	Dust Claims Dust	319
	Afterword	327

Notes	330
Bibliography	355
Acknowledgements	358
Index	360

Illustrations

1 William Godwin by James Northcote, 1802
2 Mary Wollstonecraft by John Opie
3 Putative portrait of Mary Shelley by S. J. Stump, 1831
4 Shelley by Amelia Curran, 1819
5 Mary Shelley by Rothwell, 1841
6 Sir Percy Florence Shelley, photographed about 1880
7 William Shelley by Amelia Curran, 1819
8 Claire Clairmont by Amelia Curran, 1819
9 Jane Williams by George Clint
10 Byron by Richard Westall, 1813
11 Trelawny by Joseph Severn, 1838
12 Casa Magni, Lerici
13 Field Place, 1812

Art thou pale for weariness
Of climbing heaven and gazing on the earth,
Wandering companionless
Among the stars that have a different birth,
And ever changing, like a joyless eye
That finds no object worth its constancy?

To the Moon, Percy Bysshe Shelley

Preface

There is plentiful evidence throughout Mary's journal and letters of her modesty, her recoil from any exposure of her private life to the inquisitive world. This fear of disclosure reached a peak during the times when she was most desperate to be accepted by 'society'. '... all I ask is obscurity', she wrote when she was preoccupied in easing her son Percy into university. She wrote to Thomas Medwin, who intended to publish an unauthorized life of Shelley, 'In modern society there is no injury so great as dragging private names and private life before the world.' Mary was certainly a shy and private person, but this natural reticence was exaggerated by her loneliness after Shelley's death and by fear of rejection and censure for the irregularities in her own life with him. But she also wished above all to protect her son Percy from any calumny that, through her, might slur his name.

The present world is more tolerant of human frailty and individual gratification; today it is hardly worth the mention that a literary lady in her youth ran off with a married man. Times have changed, Percy Florence Shelley is long dead; perhaps with these conditions Mary would have been less chary of the prospect of a biography than she was a hundred and fifty years ago when she wrote to a magazine who requested a memoir, 'I do not see what the public have to do with me – I am a great enemy to the prevailing custom of dragging private life before the world, taking the matter generally – and with regard to myself there is no greater annoyance than in any way to be brought out of my proper sphere of private obscurity.'

Her wish for personal obscurity in a strange way has been fulfilled. The whole world knows about her creation, Frankenstein, or rather Frankenstein's monster, largely through the recent dissemination of cinema, but few know her as the author of that universal myth, or realize that she wrote subsequent novels, one of which at least is worthy of interest today. Of the few people who recognize her name, still fewer know much about her other than her illustrious parentage and union with Shelley. This lack of celebrity is partly due to the fact that she was Shelley's wife. In life his distinct and eccentric genius eclipsed her quieter character, her more modest talents. It is easy to forget that she was extraordinary too. In death, the roller-coaster of Shelley's reputation, given impetus by Mary, grew up, oblivious of the small but indomitable figure by his side.

Perhaps, too, fame passed her by because ultimately her ambitions were modest and domestic; the committed love of family and friends was all she really desired. The folly of worldly ambition and the value of the affections of the heart were recurring and powerful themes in her fiction.

After Shelley's death there was very little pleasure left for Mary in writing anything except the biographical sketches commissioned for Lardner's *Cyclopaedia*. Sheer necessity was the driving force, her pen was the only means by which she could secure a precarious future for herself and her son and help for her friends. She explained to her step-sister, Claire, 'I own myself I am sorry I am writing – but I feel that I shall save poor G [a Carbonaro exiled in Paris] from starvation – from desperation & the lowest depths of misery – I know this – & write when otherwise I never would – that never my name might be mentioned in a world that oppresses me....' It is not surprising that such eschewal of public notice in her lifetime should mean that after death she is remembered merely through her relationships with names less wary of the headlines: daughter of Wollstonecraft and Godwin, wife of Shelley, 'author of Frankenstein', creator of that hideous progeny, the man-made monster. The essential elusive Mary, passionate and controlled, reserved and melancholy, yet ready to give everything for those she loved; the studious intellectual and loving mother, the working writer, the reluctant solitary, all this makes her a sympathetic and remarkable woman, and her life surely, as she herself realized, 'a tale romantic beyond romance'.

Probably for the same reasons that eclipsed her in life, Mary has been neglected recently by biographers. Mrs Marshall's two-volume *Life and Letters* was published in 1889 under the aegis of Lady Jane Shelley. Lucy Madox Rossetti worked largely from this for her slim *Mrs Shelley*, published the following year in Allen & Company's Eminent Women Series. In 1928 Richard Church published his sympathetic and slight *Mary Shelley*, followed ten years later by Rosalie Grylls's carefully researched, generous and sympathetic biography. Since that date Mary's letters and most of her journal have been published, excellently edited by the illuminating scholar, Frederick L. Jones.

This was followed in 1951 by a reassessment of Mary by Muriel Spark, entitled *Child of Light*. Here Miss Spark writes an elegantly wise and witty life which is inevitably contracted by her intention of including an abridged version of *The Last Man* and discussing this and *Frankenstein* in detail. From America there came studies of Mary's work, amongst the most notable being Elizabeth Nitchie's *Mary Shelley*, published in 1953.

In the extraordinarily fertile field of Shelley research, dramatic discoveries are a rare and almost arbitrary thing. I cannot claim that my research has led me to any startlingly 'new' facts, but to expect them is to misunderstand, to some extent, this kind of biography and my aim in writing the book. I wished primarily to draw Mary from her obscurity, to rescue her from the brilliance of her husband and the force of Shelley biography which has too often kept her in the shadows. I have sought to give her a justly independent and vivid existence beside her famous relations, to trace her life of extraordinary and romantic extremes and give due credit to her talents, her sometimes faltering courage and her enduring generosity of spirit. In doing so I have drawn together various important threads which have been given little or no attention in her previous biographies and have reviewed the wealth of existing information in the light of Mary's life, at times revealing completely fresh perspectives and emphases.

As Mary was particularly veracious and lacking in self-delusion, I have relied heavily on her own accounts of herself, her condition and her feelings, including previously unpublished portions of her later journals, now lodged in the Bodleian Library, Oxford. As her fiction was so often a dramatization of parts of her own life and the personalities and situations that distinguished it, sometimes even premonitory of what was to come (a characteristic she clearly recognized), I feel justified in including excerpts of that fiction as oblique but vivid mirrorings of the facts. I have not set out to examine in detail her works, nor to assess conscientiously her place in literature. I chose to write primarily a life of Mary. Her writing is discussed in that context; as her livelihood, as illumination of something of her motives and emotions and attitude to life, even as an attempt to win the affection and approval of friends, as she admitted in an unpublished portion of her journal for 1822: 'I once dreamt that the thoughts labouring this brain might shape themselves to such words as might weave a chain to bind the thoughts of my fellow creatures to me in love and sympathy ...'

It was Mary Shelley that I set out to discover. I hope that in these pages she is sometimes herself, a fallible, feeling woman who illustrated amply the Burke quotation with which she closed her last journal:

'Preserve always a habit of giving....'

1
Inheritance

> 'They say that thou wert lovely from thy birth,
> of glorious parents, thou aspiring Child.'
>
> Dedication to Mary, *The Revolt of Islam*,
> Percy Bysshe Shelley

Mary Shelley was a woman of quiet but compelling influence. It was appropriate that even before she was born she should precipitate a momentous and heretical union between the two most renowned radicals of her parents' day.

Such pre-natal disruption was only to be expected from this extraordinary woman whose life was so filled with passion and tragedy that it outplayed her own distinctive fiction.

So it was that on 29 March 1797 her mother and father stepped out from the gloom of old St Pancras church into the spring air. Mary Wollstonecraft, celebrated feminist and author of *A Vindication of the Rights of Woman*, had married William Godwin, the illustrious novelist, philosopher and author of *Political Justice*, handbook for every young radical of the day.

As they walked down through the churchyard and across the fields into Somers Town they looked an odd couple. Mary Wollstonecraft was nearly thirty-eight, tall and handsome with soft, mouse-brown hair, light eyes and fair, clear skin. Her body was plump and burgeoning with a four months' pregnancy. Beside her Godwin at forty-one was of smaller build, sharp-featured, with large striking eyes and a nose so distinctive as to effect an outburst from the poet Southey, 'Oh most abominable nose! Language is not vituperatious enough to describe the effect of its downward elongation.'[1]

However, the fact of their marriage was stranger still. Mary's disapproval of marriage was well-known; she hated this 'legalized prostitution', where a woman, and her offspring, became the property of her husband, economically, physically and socially dependent on him, encouraged to be a domestic slave and vapid ornament. Godwin, bleakly rational about the subject, was equally opposed to the institution. 'Marriage is law, and the worst of all laws',[2] he stated in *Political Justice*. He wished for man and woman to be wholly guided by reason, to be educated towards the ideal where everyone would act in a rational desire for the good, and laws, marriage amongst them, would become obsolete.

So, irrationally united, they walked home together across fields damp and clumped with primroses and cowslips, for the River Fleet still flowed past the church from the heights of Hampstead and Highgate ponds. Mary Wollstonecraft returned to her lodgings in Judd Place West in the lower reaches of Somers Town. There waiting for her was her three-year-old daughter Fanny Imlay, with Marguerite, her French maid. Her house was intentionally convenient to Godwin's abode at 7 Evesham Buildings. Within days they moved into a new house, 29 the Polygon, which faced Evesham Buildings, still retained for Godwin as a bolt-hole and for work. Somers Town was a newly-built but uncompleted garden suburb of London, a healthier place in which to bring up young children than the seething, cramped and dirty lanes of the City, stacked a couple of miles to the south.

During the eighteenth century the movement of families out of these narrow, tumbledown and frequently dangerous city streets meant that new housing developments advanced in surges across the fields and villages surrounding London. War stemmed the flow while peace brought a flood of new building. Somers Town was one of the victims of this stop/go expediency.

Mary and Godwin were nervous at breaking the news of their marriage to some of their friends. They were sheepish at such blatant apostasy. However, the best took it well. Johnson, Mary's trusty and long-suffering publisher, was enthusiastic and probably relieved. Thomas Holcroft, novelist and translator, although regretting not having been told earlier, warmly responded: 'From my very heart & soul I give you joy. I think you the most extraordinary married pair in existence. May your happiness be as pure as I firmly persuade myself it must be.'[3] Godwin's mother, long-suffering over his atheism, replied to the news, 'Your broken resolution in regard to matrimony encourages me to hope that you will ere long embrace the Gospel ... all your friends and mine wish you happiness, and shall be glad to see you and your wife in Norfolk, if I be spared...."[4] And Maria Reveley, a friend of Godwin's who was to become a lasting friend and mother-figure of sorts to their unborn baby, reported to that daughter Mary many years later, 'instead of losing one she had secured two friends, unequalled, perhaps, in the world for genius, single-heartedness, and nobleness of disposition...'[5] Apart from some ridicule and acrimony from a few of their friends, in particular Mrs Inchbald, actress and beauty, who had cherished some hopes in Godwin's direction, most of their contemporaries considered their marriage a 'matchless union'. Such a co-operation between two of the leading radicals of the age, a marriage of Mary's passion and Godwin's logic, promised great things, not least the unborn baby who had already disconcerted her mother's feminism and her father's rational principles.

Mary and Godwin certainly felt they had to justify their marriage to their friends, and perhaps to themselves too. Mary wrote a long apologia in a letter to Amelia Alderson: 'The wound my unsuspecting heart formerly received is not healed. I found my evenings solitary, and I wished, while fulfilling the duty of a mother, to have some person with similar pursuits, bound to me by affection....'[6] However, she omitted to say that she was pregnant again and was quite grateful to have the law on her side providing a little belated respectability, along with the shell of security. Godwin was more theoretical in a letter to his friend Thomas Wedgwood: 'Nothing but a regard for the happiness of the individual, which I have no right to injure, could have induced me to submit to an institution which I wish to see abolished....'[7]

Although in some ways it was a marriage of convenience there was undoubted mutual affection and admiration. Their unorthodox living arrangements, with Godwin walking over from Evesham Buildings to join Mary and Fanny at the Polygon for meals or for bed, as they decided, provided a wealth of notes penned from one to the other; intimate, hurried letters, some wry, some ill-tempered; certainly most of Mary's were provocative, but all were affectionate and revealing.

The spontaneous expressiveness of this letter written before they were married was characteristic of Mary Wollstonecraft, although the contentment was rare:

'I would describe one of those moments, when the senses are exactly tuned by the rising tenderness of the heart, and according reason entices you to live in the present moment, regardless of the past or future – It is not rapture. – It is a sublime tranquillity. I have felt it in your arms – Hush! Let not the light see, I was going to say hear it – These confessions should only be uttered – you know where, when the curtains are up – and all the world shut out....'[8]

But equally can the lady project an irritated and injured air as in this note written on 11 April, a few weeks after their wedding:

'I wish you would desire Mr Marshall to call on me. Mr Johnson, or somebody, has always taken the disagreeable business of settling with trades and people off my hands – I am, perhaps as unfit as yourself to do it – and my time appears to me, as valuable as that of any person's accustomed to employing themselves. Things of this kind are easily settled with money, I know; but I am tormented by the want of money – and feel, to say the truth, as if I was not treated with respect, owing to your desire not to be disturbed....'[9]

Independent as she could be and professed to be, she still liked to be protected from some of the chores of life.

This over-sensitive and emotionally insecure woman was a trial at times to Godwin who was used to a calm and ordered life. His puzzlement and affection were clear in this note sent the following day: 'The sole principle of conduct of which I am conscious in my behaviour to you, has been in every thing to study your happiness. I found a wounded heart, &, as that heart cast itself upon me, it was my ambition to heal it. Do not let me be wholly disappointed.'[10]

The 'wounded heart', of which Mary's friends had heard much, dated back to two unhappy love affairs that deeply hurt and humiliated her. The story of Mary's life, as she saw it, would have been very familiar to her second daughter, Mary. She read and re-read both *Mary*, an autobiographical novel by her mother, and *Memoirs*, a tender eulogy by Godwin written rapidly in the months following his wife's death. Mary Wollstonecraft had not had a harsh childhood by most standards of the day but felt herself unloved and unappreciated by her family, and lacked money and any real education.[11] She managed through her wits and perseverance to support herself and a few hangers-on by various teaching ventures and writing and translating work for her publisher, Johnson. Then in 1788, when she was twenty-nine, she met Fuseli through Johnson and fell in love with him on sight.

Fuseli, scholar and painter, was then middle-aged, his name made by his famous picture, *The Nightmare*, shown in 1782. He was small, delicate-featured and dapper, while Mary was large, untidy and going through a plain feminist stage. Surprisingly, the attraction was mutual, although the passion seemed to be a one-way affair. Fuseli married, Mary wrote and published *A Vindication of the Rights of Woman* in 1792. Muddled and passionately subjective, it nevertheless echoed the revolutionary ardour of the time and was felt by radical intellectuals of the day to be a distinctive blow for freedom. For a time, according to Godwin, this made her the most famous woman in Europe.

Partly to recover from the disappointment and humiliation of Fuseli's rejection, partly due to her commitment along with every other radical of the day to the principles of the French Revolution, she went to Paris at the end of 1792 to report on the situation there. In 1793 life was becoming more difficult and unpredictable for everyone, not least the English who were regarded less warmly now that France and England were at war. During this unsettled time Mary met Gilbert Imlay, an American in Paris. Charming and slippery, pretentious and unprincipled, she disliked him initially but grew to love him, or her idea of him. He quickly tired of her; she became pregnant; he was continually away dealing with business or women, leaving Mary alone in a hostile Paris. Menaced by the sickening progress of The Terror, her sense of dependence increased. She escaped into a fantasy of domestic longings; she would live with Imlay and their baby in productive tranquillity, perhaps settling somewhere in America. She gave birth to Fanny on 14 May 1794 and was greatly delighted with her small daughter. Imlay visited them fleetingly but was always off again.

Finally returning to London in 1795 Mary was forced to accept that Imlay had replaced her with another woman, this time a blowzy actress, and that he was probably never going to return to her and Fanny. With this brutal fact came the more painful realization that her relationship with Imlay had only really lasted a few months and that its very worth and substance, in which she had so fervently believed, was little more than fiction. Humiliated by such self-delusion, Mary's natural melancholy and dramatic temperament combined in a determination to end her life by jumping off Putney Bridge into the wintery Thames. Choking and half-drowned, she eventually lost consciousness and was picked up by some watermen as she floated downstream. Revived in a disreputable riverside tavern, collected and cherished by friends, she resiliently lived to re-enter the intellectual circles and to meet for a second time the great philosopher William Godwin.

It was this doubly-bruised heart that he inherited and had to handle so very carefully. Temperamentally, Godwin hardly seemed an ideal spouse for the emotional and demanding Mary Wollstonecraft. He had been trained at the famous Dissenters' College at Hoxton for the Presbyterian ministry, but had transferred the allegiance of his puritanical vigour from God to Reason. Reason, if clearly heeded, would never betray; reason alone would lead individuals to make the right political decisions. Fame and the radical cause were all Mary and Godwin shared. Mary met him at the height of this fame – 'he blazed as a sun in the firmament of reputation'[12] was how Hazlitt remembered him – still riding high on the success of *An Enquiry Concerning Political Justice*, published in 1793.

Despite his lack of contact with women, despite his entrenched bachelor ways, Godwin managed remarkably well with this new, womanly intrusion into his life. Loving and steadfast, reasonable and pragmatic, he was everything that Fuseli and Imlay were not. He may have lacked glamour and practised charm but, as his relationship with Mary expanded, their love and delight in their coming baby, 'little William', grew too. Fanny was blossoming in the general security and happiness of life at 29 the Polygon, with a father-figure more reliable and thoughtful than the last one. Godwin, on a trip to Etruria to see his old friend Thomas Wedgwood, wrote at the end of a letter, 'Kiss Fanny for me; remember William, but (most of all) take care of yourself. Tell Fanny, I am safely arrived in the land of mugs.'[13]

This short separation warmed the hearts of both of them to the advantages of their marriage. Mary wrote with newly-acquired circumspection: 'A husband is a convenient part of the furniture of a house, unless he be a clumsy fixture. I wish you, from my soul, to be rivetted in my heart; but I do not desire to have you always at my elbow – though at this moment I did not care if you were.'[14] Equally circuitious was Godwin's reply: 'You cannot imagine how happy your letter made me. No creature expresses, because no creature feels, the tender affections, so perfectly as you do; &, after all one's philosophy, it must be confessed that the knowledge, that there is someone that takes an interest in our happiness something like that which each man feels is his own, is extremely gratifying.'[15]

In any event it sounded distinctly as if the bleakly rational philosopher, the crusty middle-aged bachelor, was embracing happily enough his role of soft-hearted family man. While the independent and prickly Mistress Wollstonecraft was with equal alacrity playing the part of a loving, wifely Mrs Godwin.

However, Mary's wounded heart was bruised again by Godwin's prolonged absence, compounded by his professed wish to see at the Coventry fair a lady dressed down to resemble Lady Godiva. All the old insecurity and fears, memories of Imlay's absences and deceits, as well as his predilection for other women, crowded back to unsettle her. And always one to blurt it out she wrote: 'Certainly at first my affection was increased; or rather was more alive – But now it is just the contrary. Your latter letters might have been addressed to any body – ... Whatever tenderness you took away with you seems to have evaporated in the journey, and new objects – and the homage of vulgar minds, restored you to your icy Philosophy.' With a dig at the Lady Godiva incident and a further chastisement she signed off, very icily, with 'I am afraid to add what I feel – Good-night.'[16]

However, Godwin returned and life continued, everything leading up inexorably to the birth of their baby. This event was expected in August and Mary approached it with cheerfulness and practicality. At a time when death in or as a result of childbirth was commonplace, the greatest occupational hazard in being a woman, Mary was courageous and sensible in advocating that women in labour should be free from ignorance and fear, trusting in their bodies. Fanny's birth had been hard work but straightforward and satisfactory. She had left her bed after only a week and scoffed at the French women (and English) who made themselves invalids for a full month.

This birth was going to be even better; she was experienced, she was in her own home, she had a husband who loved her and was as eager to see 'little William' as she was. The saddest irony of it all was that no amount of sensible attitudes and felicitous surroundings could save her when things went badly wrong. As it was, Mary's labour started on 30 August. The baby was to be born at home with only a senior midwife, Mrs Blenkinsop, in attendance. Fanny and the maid Marguerite were to spend the day with friends. On this day Mary wrote her last three notes to Godwin, optimistic and matter of fact as they were. The first:

> 'I have no doubt of seeing the animal today; but must wait for Mrs Blenkinsop to guess at the hour – I have sent for her – Pray send me the news paper – I wish I had a novel, or some book of sheer amusement, to excite curiosity & while away the time – Have you anything of the kind?'[17]

She could hardly settle to anything, full of the restlessness, that apprehensive excitement, at the prospect of giving birth to her familiar yet unknown child. Mary's last note to Godwin in the afternoon was to the point; she was promised a safe delivery but 'I must have a little patience',[18] a coincidental echo of her mother's dying words, 'a little patience, and all will be over'.[19] But all was not yet over for Mary.

Her labour continued through the afternoon and into the evening. It was protracted and painful. Mary did not want Godwin to come to her room. She could be strangely prudish about some things and had not wanted a doctor to attend her because she felt a male presence was unseemly. Perhaps she was still insecure of Godwin's love, afraid of disillusioning him in her dishevelled state, reduced as she was to the common lot of womankind, labouring in childbirth. Banished from this woman's work, he had supper with friends at Evesham Buildings then returned to the Polygon to wait.

Finally at twenty minutes past eleven on that Wednesday evening, 30 August, the precious child was born. A good-sized and good-looking baby, she was not the 'little William' they had joked about but a second Mary. Godwin heard the news of her safe delivery with relief but was not yet allowed up to see either of the Marys. The placenta, which within minutes should have followed the infant Mary into the world, had not been delivered. This is the final and essential stage of any satisfactory labour and in 1797, when bacteriology was in the Dark Ages and gross ignorance about the basics of cleanliness and the transmission and nature of puerperal fever menaced every woman in childbirth, a retained placenta was critical. Antibiotics were a century and a half away. Haemorrhage and infection, that almost inevitably ensued, were a prelude to death.

But hope for Mary had not expired. After she had cuddled and cursorily examined her baby, the little girl was swaddled and put aside while Mrs Blenkinsop attempted to detach the placenta from the wall of Mary's womb by tugging on the cord, pummelling Mary's stomach, exhorting her to cough or bear down. Perhaps little Mary was put to her mother's breast in the hope that her suckling would stimulate the uterine contractions and help expel the placenta.

But all was to no avail. The chief obstetrician, Dr Poignard, had to be fetched by a frightened Godwin from the Westminster Lying-in. It was early morning as he climbed the stairs to find Mary exhausted, battered and bleeding. Godwin accompanied him and turned away, alarmed by such a transformation from the healthy and confident woman he had seen the day before.

Poor Mary then had to submit to Dr Poignard's attempts to extract every bit of the placenta by hand, and without the aid of anaesthetic to block the pain. Almost without doubt it was this operation which introduced the deadly infection into Mary's womb. Unknowingly Dr Poignard worked until daylight, and left satisfied that he had removed every fragment. At last Mary and Godwin fell asleep. She was herself again, smiling and happy. Her survival of the pain and the peril of the previous day heightened their feelings for each other and for their new baby. The remaining hours of Thursday and most of Friday were spent in a warm post-natal glow, with Fanny joining them to examine the strange and noisy addition to her family.

These two days were full of pleasure in the present and hope for the future. They were the last that they were to enjoy, for on Saturday Mary was racked by two terrible and prolonged shaking fits. The doctors who came to her must have immediately recognized the common and dreaded symptoms. There was little hope, for she had puerperal fever and nothing now could halt the spreading infection.

The newborn Mary was still being fed at her mother's breast; she had a few more days of security in that familiar voice and warm smell, so sharply distinctive to a baby even from birth. But the infection was irresistible in its progress from Mary's womb into her circulation, and this security was not to last. After only four days' acquaintance with her mother, Mary was banned from her breast by the doctors, for Mary Godwin was dying and they feared that her baby, too, would die, poisoned by her milk.

This baby was now taken to the house of Maria Reveley where Fanny and Marguerite were staying. A wet-nurse would have to be found to feed her, for little Mary was already motherless, a harsh deprivation that was to shadow her life with a sense of solitariness and loss.

Godwin and Mary now had to cope together with the individual terms of death. Mary was in pain, at times incoherent, but her will resisted the inevitable end. Having attempted negligently to apprehend death twice before, having been dragged back, not altogether willingly, to life, here she was refusing to die for the sake of Godwin and her children and the promise of her own life. This life ebbed gradually and tragically and she died on Sunday, 10 September. Godwin in his diary, always so tersely and precisely kept, simply wrote the time and drew three straight lines, to close the chapter.

He had found it impossible to accept throughout that long nightmare week that Mary was really dying; he called in doctors, grasping hope from every slight improvement. Having rediscovered forgotten emotions, having, through the intervention of such a woman, unwrapped his heart, he could not face the fact that death senselessly should take her from him.

Amongst Mary's last words were, 'He is the kindest, best man in the world.'[20] Now that kindest of men was left with two small daughters, pressured by ever-present debts and nonplussed with hopeless despair at his loss. That same day he wrote to his old friend Thomas Holcroft to tell him of Mary's death. He added, 'I firmly believe that there does not exist her equal in the world. I know from experience we were formed to make each other happy. I have not the least expectation that I can now ever know happiness again.'[21] In a way his gloomy prognostication was fulfilled. The late flowering of his deepest affections had been blighted by Mary's death and never were to recover. They lay as dead wood in his personality. He became immersed once again in joyless study and writing, imprisoned in a spiral of financial anxiety and familial responsibility. In the following letter to Mrs Cotton, an old friend of Mary's, this sense of his melancholy and depression freezing him into inaction is clearly seen in his escape from everyday responsibilities towards his children:

'I partook of happiness, so much the more exquisite, as I had a short time before had no conception of it, and scarcely admitted the possibility of it. I saw one bright ray of light that streaked my day of life only to leave the remainder more gloomy, and, in the truest sense of the word, hopeless.... The poor children! I am myself totally unfitted to educate them. The scepticism which perhaps sometimes leads me right in matters of speculation, is torment to me when I would attempt to direct the infant mind. I am the most unfit person for this office; she was the best qualified in the world.'[22]

The poor children indeed. The loss of a sensible, affectionate and talented mother and the failure of the future Mrs Godwin to fulfil in any way the emotional needs of these two girls was destructive in different ways to both. Godwin's position as Fanny and Mary's only parent and his abdication of any real domestic involvement with them characterized his strong but faulty paternity. If he had been able to lavish on his two daughters something of the warmth and demonstrative affection that he had managed to tap for his wife's needs, it would have endowed them both with a more secure and optimistic view of life. But his more tender emotions had withdrawn into the philosopher's shell. He was always concerned and kind enough, but his aloofness, his self-centred preoccupation with work and money, precluded the everyday intimacies on which children's lives are founded.

The postscript to this domestic tragedy took place on Friday 15 September, when Mary Wollstonecraft Godwin was buried in Old St Pancras churchyard. She returned to the green hill whence she had walked with Godwin on that spring day only six months earlier. But this time Godwin was too distraught to attend. And the new baby Mary, having lost her close safe universe, was learning to adjust to the cold and confusion of the real world.

2
Books and Daydreams

> 'As I grew older books in some degree supplied the place of human intercourse....'
> *Mathilda*, Mary Shelley

Life at 29 the Polygon gradually resumed. Fanny returned from Mrs Reveley's care on the following Saturday evening, a bemused and unhappy little girl. At three years she was quite old enough to be desolated by the mysterious loss of her mother. She was doubly abandoned, for Marguerite, the French maid with whom she had grown up, also disappeared from her life, probably making the upheaval and her mistress's death a good enough reason to return home. Mary was carried back to the Polygon on Sunday. Godwin moved his books and papers and scanty belongings over the road from his old lodgings in Evesham Buildings and took what had been Mary's room as his study. Life was never again to be simple and straightforward. His two little daughters needed a sensible woman to look after them and to keep the household running. This unenviable job was accepted by a Miss Louisa Jones, a friend of Hannah, Godwin's sister. She became increasingly unhappy with the arrangement; being part servant, part friend was difficult enough without the added aggravation of Godwin's open house and undomesticated habits.

Friends called round frequently, a few of whom were keen to help and take the children on outings, providing some relief for Miss Jones. There was a good deal of interest in Mary, the only fruit of a 'matchless union' abruptly curtailed. Just two and a half weeks after her birth Godwin asked a neighbour and friend, William Nicholson, to practise his theories of physiognomy, inspired by Lavater's *Speculations*, and give him a character reading of the singular baby. The inconclusive speculations were:

'1. The outline of the head viewed from above, its profile, the outline of the forehead, seen from behind and in its horizontal positions, are such as I have invariably and exclusively seen in subjects who possessed considerable memory and intelligence.
2. The base of the forehead, the eyes and eyebrows, are familiar to me in subjects of quick sensibility, irritable, scarcely irascible, and surely not given to rage. The part of the outline of the forehead, which is very distinct in patient investigators, is less so in her. I think her powers, of themselves, would lead to speedy combination, rather than continued research....
6. The mouth was too much employed to be well observed. It has the outlines of intelligence. She was displeased, and it denoted much more of resigned vexation than either scorn or rage. On this imperfect sight it would be silly to risk a character; for which reason I will only add that I conjecture that her manner may be petulant in resistance, but cannot be sullen....'[1]

All this promise of intelligence and memory boded well for the future but the present was pretty grim. The most economical and satisfactory way of providing a permanent housemaid and housekeeper would be for Godwin to marry again. He was feeling bereft and lonely. Bothered by money problems, frequently supporting members of his own importunate family and burdened with responsibility, a wife seemed an attractive answer to most of these ills. Mary, years later, explained his motives in notes she made for a projected biography of her father:

'The happiness he had enjoyed, instilled the opinion that he might, at least in a degree, regain the blessing he had lost, if he married a woman of sense, and of amiable disposition. Instead of, as heretofore, guarding himself from the feelings of love, he appears rather to have laid himself open to them. The two orphan girls left in his charge of course weighed much in the balance; he felt his deficiency as the sole parent of two children of the other sex.'[2]

So in the following spring, Godwin went courting with a will. His choice of wife was of crucial importance to the future of his two small daughters. His first candidate was a literary lady, Miss Harriet Lee of Bath. She was co-author with her sister of *Canterbury Tales* and ran a school in the town. He bombarded her with letters but she resolutely refused all attempts to persuade her into marriage, admitting only 'regard and esteem'. This left Louisa Jones still reluctantly in charge of the domestic arrangements. She had hoped that Godwin would regularize her position and promote her to being his wife, but with his precipitate pursuit of Miss Lee that hope foundered.

Godwin was still at the height of his fame. Hazlitt, writing twenty-five years later, remembered, 'No one was more talked of, more looked up to, more sought after, and wherever liberty, truth, justice was the theme, his name was not far off.'[3] His fame had been reinforced by his novel, *Caleb Williams*, published in 1794, heavy with unmitigated injustice and nightmare pursuit; Mrs Inchbald and many others found it quite 'sublimely horrible – captivatingly frightful'.[4] But his reputation was more firmly built on his *Enquiry Concerning Political Justice*, published the previous year, of which Hazlitt claimed, 'No work in our time gave such a blow to the philosophical mind of the country.'[5] With ruthless logic and a pen of steel Godwin pursued his arguments to extremity, drawing to him like a flame the young, the radical and the revolutionary.

Despite these intellectual distinctions, he was not of the stuff of which ideal husbands were made. Lacking in charm and outwardly cool, his atheism and radical principles alarmed many, but it was probably his material circumstances which most effectively discouraged future wives. It was a time when there was no real opportunity for women to earn a living except in the appalling conditions of industry or in the underprivileged twilight of a governess post. It would take a determined woman to throw in her lot with a middle-aged widower who had two very young daughters, who had always been impecunious and would in fact stumble on the brink of financial ruin for most of the rest of his life.

The next lady he approached was his long-time friend, Maria Reveley. Her husband died unexpectedly and traumatically of a brain tumour in July 1799. His death had an alarming effect on Maria, who spent a week closeted in an empty attic room 'in a state bordering on frenzy'.[6] Maria Reveley was an interesting woman. She had spent an exotic youth with her father in Constantinople. She grew up with few of the restraints of an English girlhood and married, very young, Mr Reveley, an English architect, and returned with him to England. Their liberal politics eventually brought her into contact with Godwin and Thomas Holcroft and the friendship developed from there.

Mary Shelley noted years later that 'Maria Reveley had been a favourite pupil, a dear friend, a woman whose beauty and manners he ardently admired'.[7] She was a prize indeed and Godwin did not see any point in wasting time. She probably would have refused to marry him anyway, but his want of sensibility and tact in writing to her on the matter less than a month after Mr Reveley's death meant his attentions from the very beginning were unwelcome and duly rebuffed. His perseverance, his faultless logic, even an air of desperation were all present in his letters, but they were not love letters, they lacked personality and subjectivity; as Mary Wollstonecraft had complained two years before, 'Your ... letters might have been addressed to any body.'[8] Poor Godwin, his feelings were real enough but they shrank from the paper. This typical extract from one of his letters to Maria was singularly unseductive:

> 'You have it in your power to give me new life, a new interest in existence, to raise me from the grave in which my heart lies buried. You are invited to form the sole happiness of one of the most known men of the age, of one whose principles, whose temper, whose thoughts, you have long been acquainted with, and will, I believe, confess their universal constancy. This connection, I should think, would restore you to self-respect, would give security to your future peace, and insure you no mean degree of respectability.'[9]

Resolutely refused for a second time, Godwin retired demoralized and hurt. The next time he saw Mrs Reveley she was with Mr Gisborne, whom she married a short time later.

But how different life for Godwin and his children might have been if this high-spirited lady had consented to become the second Mrs Godwin. As it was the domestic life at 29 the Polygon continued joylessly. Coleridge remarked after one of his visits, 'the cadaverous Silence of Godwin's Children is to me quite catacomb-ish: & thinking of Mary Wollstonecraft I was oppressed by it...'[10]

Fanny at five was particularly affectionate and over-sensitive. Mary was a toddler of two years, walking and talking and demanding her share of Godwin's affections. Both girls lacked a constant and secure love relationship with one person. Godwin was there but greatly preoccupied in his studies and numerous literary projects. He socialized a good deal and certainly did not have the time and inclination to play games regularly with them, read stories and submit to childish demands and routines. Louisa Jones had moved out of the house but, with the kindly but detached help from friends like Mrs Fenwick and Mr Marshall, was responsible still for the practical side of the household and children.

Somers Town was a pleasant, countrified place. Behind the Polygon the fields and trees stretched west to what would become Regent's Park and east to the St Pancras workhouse and on to where the houses and spires of Islington blurred in the distance. To the north it was still quite rural with open country rolling up to the hills of Hampstead and Highgate and on through what was once the old county of Middlesex. Here the children would be taken on walks, collecting flowers in the fields, stumping in the mud and investigating the River Fleet which flowed at the foot of Old St Pancras churchyard.

Godwin's terse and factual diary made little mention of his children in the early years, but during the summer of 1800 his letters from Ireland to Mr Marshall, whom he had left in charge of children and home, were full of fond references and notes to them.

'Their talking about me, as you say they do, makes me wish to be with them ... it is the first time I have been seriously separated from them since they lost their mother.... I hope you have got Fanny a proper spelling-book.... Tell Mary I will not give her away, and she shall be nobody's little girl but Papa's.'[11] He promised to return and, from the coach stop at Camden Town, see the Polygon two fields away. It was under the trees that Mary and Fanny and Mr Marshall were to wait for him in a month's time. Three-year-old Mary's doubt that she would ever see her father again and be given to someone else was probably a lurking fear for the whole of his absence. However his letters gave the two sisters something to smile about:

> 'I depute to Fanny and Mr Collins, the gardener, the care of the garden. Tell her I wish to find it spruce, cropped, weeded, and mowed at my return; and if she can save me a few strawberries and a few beans without spoiling, I will give her six kisses for them. But then Mary must have six kisses too....'[12]

He was always careful to be fair in his treatment of both; there was a glimpse of Mary's more determined character in his last letter: 'Would pretty little Mary have apprehension enough to be angry if I did not put in her name?'[13]

After Godwin's return, life continued at the Polygon much as before with Godwin as busy as ever, visiting and being visited. The children were growing up and becoming more interesting to him as he supervised their early education, listened to Fanny's reading, checked her spelling book and began to teach Mary to read a few words too. In *Political Justice* he wanted education to be less structured and formal, encouraging a child's enthusiasm for learning rather than forcing it with demands for progress or stifling it in a strait-jacket of convention and regime. As with most excellent theories the reality was more of a compromise and Godwin certainly did not spend as much time and effort in answering questions, kindling childish curiosity and establishing natural learning patterns as his philosophy would have required. Nevertheless, this enlightened view of education meant that both Fanny and Mary were saved much of the deadly learning by rote which oppressed their less fortunate contemporaries, and were liberated from the confines of a stuffy nursery in the charge of an ignorant or tyrannous nursemaid; more free to watch and learn from the adult activities around them, to play in the garden and explore the fields beyond the house. As their reading became proficient they had access to Godwin's library and all the wealth of ideas and knowledge that lay therein. Girlish arts and social graces were not imposed from an early age on these two girls. Mary as a young woman discovered this to be something of a mixed blessing, for she found that many men of her acquaintance, too often accustomed to prescribed femininity, were disconcerted by a woman who was intense and seriously intellectual, and they sought to mitigate their unease by labelling her mind 'masculine' and therefore acceptable and free from threat.

During the next year, 1801, Godwin's friendship with Coleridge flourished. Coleridge wrote frequently suggesting that Godwin come to stay in his lovely house in Keswick in Cumberland: 'I have house-room & heart-room for you, and you must come & write your next work at my house.'[14]

Most of the letters contained fond references to Fanny and Mary and kisses were frequently posted to them from the Coleridge family entrenched in the poets' country of wooded hills and water. 'My youngest is a fat little creature, not unlike your Mary. God love you & S T Coleridge',[14] he wrote, while not at all well and plagued by boils behind his ear, one of which he christened 'Captain Robert', after Defoe's Captain Robert Boyle.

The following year began inauspiciously for Godwin. The failure of his tragedy *Antonio* was not only a great personal disappointment; its hoped-for success would have given the Godwin household a surer financial footing. As it was, there was little money and multiplying debts. Godwin's utilitarian approach to money was very important if we are to understand his continual demands on Shelley's inconsiderable means in later years. One of the most important parts of his argument in *Political Justice* was that relating to property. Property should be redistributed in proportion to each person's reasonable needs, a principle which he did not fail to put into practice. He supported, as best he could, various members of his family when they were all too frequently unemployed or insolvent, and equally he requested money for himself from friends when he was particularly needy. Of all his creditors only Shelley really understood and accepted this as a working principle and, although he eventually became bitterly disillusioned with the old man who had plagued him and Mary through their tragedies and crises, his irritation and anger were provoked more by Godwin's self-righteous manner and insensitivity to the problems of others than by these persistent demands.

Pressured by money worries, lacking in confidence, having been flatly refused by the two women he wanted to marry, and idealizing married life as a panacea for life's problems, he was easy prey to the determined woman who chose him for a husband.

Mrs Mary Jane Clairmont and her two children, Charles, the elder, and Jane, a few months younger than Mary Godwin, had moved into the house next to the Godwins. She was middle-aged, plump and handsome, a shrewd woman but lacking subtlety and sensibility. Her wooing of Godwin relied heavily on flattery and was initiated with admirable boldness; she called out from her balcony to his, 'Is it possible that I behold the immortal Godwin?' Godwin obviously found this approach irresistible for his diary noted on 5 May 1801, 'Meet Mrs Clairmont'[16] and from then on her name occurred frequently and the relationship flourished. In December of that year they married, in Shoreditch church.

The second Mrs Godwin has been severely criticized by Godwin's friends, by his children, by biographers past and present. She was certainly not a remarkable woman cast in the mould of a Mary Wollstonecraft or even a Maria Reveley, but she loyally and industriously took on the Godwin household with all its inherent problems. Their financial troubles were never resolved and the stresses and bitterness they engendered were to reverberate through the three daughters' lives for years to come. However, Mrs Godwin was a good business manager and an adequate wife to Godwin. He never recaptured that good-humoured, loving tone that characterized his letters to Mary Wollstonecraft. But then Mrs Godwin's lot was not easy running a large and motley family on a fluctuating and seldom adequate income, while working alongside Godwin in the publishing business they were to start together. Godwin was still lauded and applauded and sought by young disciples, while she was ignored or criticized for failing to fill the former Mrs Godwin's famous shoes.

Where the second Mrs Godwin failed tragically was in her relationship with her step-children, Fanny and Mary. Again it was as much circumstances as her own emotional inadequacies that conspired against her. By marrying Godwin she inevitably trespassed on the delicate and indivisible territory of Fanny and four-year-old Mary, who until then had been the only loved ones in their father's life. Adoring him and idolizing the memory of their mother, they could only look with intense dislike and suspicion on this strange insensitive woman who, with her own children in tow, had so trespassed on their home, upset the fine balance of their lives and assumed control. A difficult situation was exacerbated by Mrs Godwin's obvious and natural preference for her own children. The birth of a Godwin son in 1803 probably put a seal on the two sisters' sense of having been cruelly usurped. Sweet, pliable, affectionate Fanny learnt to compromise for the sake of peace and what affection she could scrounge. She was naturally domesticated and helpful, and as she was the eldest girl many of the household chores fell to her. Mary was altogether different. Rebellious and intolerant, never domesticated, aware that she was the unique daughter of an exceptional mother and a beloved and genius father, she chose to remain apart and, in rejecting her step-mother, turned all the more to her father for intellectual, if not physical and emotional, comfort.

In her writing, Mary's fictional characters were drawn very much from life. In one of her short stories, 'The Elder Son', she described the heroine's father and their relationship and could have been talking as easily about her own feelings for her father.

'He was . . . a venerable-looking man; for he was thin and pale, and he was partly bald. His manners were cold and reserved; he seldom spoke, and when he did it was in such measured phrase, in so calm and solemn voice, and on such various topics, as resembled rather oracular enunciation than familiar conversation.' These characteristics were confirmed by other more direct accounts of Godwin's character and mien, but the suspicion that Mary's childhood lacked much physical expression of affection was vividly evoked as she continued, 'He never caressed me; if ever he stroked my head or drew me on his knee I felt a mingled alarm and delight difficult to describe. Yet, strange to say, my father loved me almost to idolatry; and I knew this and repaid his affection with enthusiastic fondness, notwithstanding his reserve and my awe. He was something greater, wiser, better, in my eyes, than any other human being.'[17]

Mary had never known a mother. Neither had she known a permanent motherly figure who would take her into her warm lap for consolation and affection. There was no admired woman to watch, from whom to learn; no motherly presence always there to make sense of experience and centre the world. Sadly, the antipathy between Mary and Mrs Godwin, together with the intrinsic difficulties of step-parenthood, had robbed Mary of her last chance of growing up less deprived.

Another contemporary writer, Mrs Gaskell, who suffered the same deprivation, wrote with hindsight: 'I think no one but one so unfortunate as to be early motherless can enter into the craving one has after the lost mother.'[18] In Mary, this craving became a desperate longing to love and be loved, while her emotional loss was manifested in an inability to express spontaneously her deep sensibilities and warm heart. To her chagrin she was misunderstood and so many times accused of coolness and emotional detachment. Under the enlightened eye of her father, her admirable intellect flourished but her heart had little but itself, her ideas, idealizations and fantasies, to feed on.

Life at the Polygon was crowded and noisy. It rocked with the arguments and play of five young children and frequently was not a very happy place. Mrs Godwin was hard-worked and short-tempered and Godwin self-absorbed with his literary efforts and money problems; it was not surprising that their relationship was more fractious than contented. The patronizing tone of the last paragraph of one of Godwin's letters to his *'chère amie'* before they were married was probably all the more in evidence after they were legally bound together and no longer on best behaviour:

'My dear love, take care of yourself. Manage and economise your temper. It is at bottom most excellent: do not let it be soured and spoiled. It is capable of being recovered to its primaeval goodness, and even raised to something better. Do not however get rid of all your faults. I love some of them. I love what is human, what gives softness, and an agreeable air of frailty and pliability to the whole....'[19]

In an attempt to augment and formalize the family's income, Mrs Godwin suggested they start a publisher's and bookshop together, producing books 'for the use and amusement of children'. In 1805 the business was modestly established in Hanway Street, a small inlet running between the two main thoroughfares of Oxford Street and Tottenham Court Road. Their books were distinctive and well produced. Both Godwin and his wife worked hard, he writing *Fables* and potted histories under the pseudonym of Baldwin and she translating some tales from the French. The stories and histories were all tested on their children at home, who remarked, much to Godwin's relief, 'How easy this is! Why, we learn it by heart almost as fast as we read it!'[20]

The business did well, and in order to expand they moved in 1807 to a much larger building at 41 Skinner Street. It made economic sense for the family to move too and live above the shop. Not everyone can have been happy about such a move. Fanny was thirteen and Mary a studious girl of ten. They were leaving behind the house they had lived in for all of Mary's life, exchanging the airy rural suburbs for the busy heart of London. Today Skinner Street has long gone, flattened and gouged to become a part of the Holborn Viaduct. Then it ran between Holborn and Newgate Street, a busy thoroughfare uncomfortably close to Smithfield market and Newgate prison. Some of the surrounding roads were notorious for squalor and iniquity, their dim stinking alleys harbouring thieves and prostitutes, vagabonds and brawlers. Smithfield itself was a suspect district for typhus, a sure sign of an area's poverty and neglect.

It was both exciting and alarming for the Godwin children to move into the midst of this seething populace. Early in the mornings Mary may well have been awoken by the clattering hooves, the lowing of animals and the shouts and curses of the herdsmen taking them to market. When there was to be an execution at Newgate, Skinner

Street was thronged with a rough-necked crowd determined to enjoy themselves while regaled with tripe and ginger-pop from the street sellers who moved in for the kill.

Mary's education continued informally. Charles Clairmont was at the local Charter House School and the remaining children had short daily lessons with Godwin and various visiting tutors and governesses. They were largely undirected, however, and were expected to pursue their own trains of learning, or not, as they so chose. Mary's love of reading and study was largely inherited from and influenced by Godwin who was an exacting and thorough scholar, but it was also encouraged by her domestic circumstances. She was often at variance with Mrs Godwin, feeling ill-used for being expected, with Fanny, to help out with domestic chores while Jane Clairmont, a few months younger, was excused for singing lessons or other cultivations. Reading was the great escape from the imperfect reality of her home life. Her learning was mostly self-taught and her naturally eager and penetrating brain was unfettered by so much of the prejudice and poppycock that stupefied many of her female contemporaries. She wrote years later in her autobiographical novel, *Lodore*, 'There is a peculiarity in the education of a daughter, brought up by a father only, which tends to develop early a thousand of those portions of mind, which are folded up, and often destroyed, under mere feminine tuition',[21] although she would not be referring to Mary Wollstonecraft with that damning final phrase.

Godwin set out in a letter to a friend his theories on the education of children which doubtless were practised on his own. It was a delightful letter full of sentiments which are whole-heartedly supported by most educationalists today:

'I make no difference between children male and female.... I am most peremptorily of opinion against putting children extremely forward. If they desire it themselves, I would not baulk them, for I love to attend to these unsophisticated indications. But otherwise *festina lente* is my maxim in education.... We should always remember that the object of education is the future man or woman; and it is a miserable vanity that would sacrifice the wholesome and gradual development of mind to the desire of exhibiting little monsters of curiosity.... Without imagination there can be no genuine ardour in any pursuit, or for any acquisition, and without imagination there can be no genuine morality, no profound feeling of other men's sorrow, no ardent and persevering anxiety for their interests. This is the faculty which makes the man, and not the miserable minutenesses of detail about which the present age is so uneasy. Nor is it the only misfortune that these minutenesses engross the attention of children: I would proscribe them from any early share, and would maintain that they freeze up the soul, and give a premature taste for clearness and exactness, which is of the most pernicious consequence.... I would undoubtedly introduce before twelve years of age some smattering of geography, history, and the other sciences; but it is the train of reading I have here mentioned which I should principally depend upon for generating an active mind and a warm heart.'[22]

Although propagated by a man famous for his clearness and exactness, it is a refreshingly child-centred philosophy and one which would have made Mary Wollstonecraft happy.

Apart from books, there were many compensations for Mary. Her father's friends became more interesting to her as she grew up and came to listen, fascinated by their conversations. They were interested in her, too, for she was the only child of that remarkable Wollstonecraft/Godwin union, a distinction that helped her retain some specialness in a household in which she was neither the oldest nor youngest, without either privilege or position. When she could get her father to herself they would gaze at John Opie's portrait of Mary Wollstonecraft, warm and motherly and out of reach, looking down at them from the study wall. Then she would begin to understand her inheritance and gradually make sense of her own self.

Charles Lamb, whose book *Tales from Shakespeare* had been published by the Godwins, and kindly Coleridge were frequent visitors to Skinner Street. There is a story that Mary and Jane hid behind a sofa to hear Coleridge recite his *Rime of the Ancient Mariner*. In the candlelight the mesmerizing verses intoned by the poet himself thrilled the two girls crouched together in the shadows.

> 'I closed my lids and kept them close,
> And the balls like pulses beat;
> For the sky and the sea, and the sea and the sky
> Lay like a load on my weary eye,
> And the dead were at my feet.'

In the middle of the saga, Mrs Godwin discovered the girls. Breaking the dream, she was determined to bundle them off to bed until Coleridge begged that they be allowed to stay to the end. The poem, whether recited by Coleridge or re-read many times by Mary, had a lasting effect on her. Her novel *Frankenstein* was to echo some of its atmosphere in the last despairing pursuit of the monster through the snowy wastes of the North Pole.

Perhaps with a vivid apprehension of Coleridge's nightmare, Mary went up to bed that night to meet her own. Throughout her youth she indulged in daydreams and fantasies, and spent what time she could writing them down, experimenting with thoughts and words. She wrote in her introduction to *Frankenstein*, 'It is not singular that, as the daughter of two persons of distinguished literary celebrity, I should very early in life have thought of writing. As a child I scribbled; and my favourite pastime during the hours given me for recreation was to "write stories".'[23]

There were outings, too, for the family which relieved some of the pressures of city life. In summer they would go for the day to Hampstead Heath and swim in the ponds there. There were also their old haunts in Somers Town, with St Pancras churchyard a favourite pilgrimage for Mary where she would go and read under the willow tree by her mother's grave.

London became more noisome during the hot summer months. Rubbish was dumped in the streets with impunity and householders added to the garbage by chucking their domestic waste out through windows and doors. Slaughterhouses still existed alongside dwelling houses in overcrowded districts; animals were killed at Smithfield market and the offal and blood left to putrefy in the open gutters. The stench of animals alive and dead frequently tainted the literary air in 41 Skinner Street, associated by name with the slaughterhouses of neighbouring Smithfield. In the early part of the nineteenth century efforts were being made to clean up the city by paving and guttering the streets, providing sewers and clearing and demolishing the worst rookeries.[24] However, beyond the streets in narrow alleys, desperately overcrowded slums were commonplace, with one family to a bed and ten beds to a room, in buildings four or five storeys high. The narrow sunless courtyards contoured with years of rubbish and human and animal excrement festered, frequently resounding with violent brawls and always threatening an epidemic of the dreaded typhus.

It was from these miasmas of summertime London that Mrs Godwin, young William, Charles and Mary escaped in May 1811 to Ramsgate for a short holiday by the sea. Mary had some sort of muscular weakness in her arm and was prescribed sea-bathing as a therapy. Fanny seemed to be happy enough to stay behind and look after Godwin. Charles Clairmont wrote in a letter to a friend, 'I am quite delighted with Ramsgate. There are the most beautiful fields of barley, corn and tares that you can imagine – high cliffs, and sea, to a person who never saw it before.'[25] Mary enjoyed the open rolling countryside and the freedom to wander and dream. She certainly agreed to stay on and board at Mrs Petman's school from June, when Mrs Godwin returned to London, through to December. Beyond the cliffs there was a profusion of wild flowers amongst the corn and in the shade of the trees sprouted the delicate fronds of wild orchids. A good walk away along the cliffs of Pegwell Bay and then inland a couple of miles was one of the three massive forts built by the Romans against Saxon invaders. Stout walls, a watchtower and part of an amphitheatre stood sturdily against the east winds.

Some interesting letters passed between Mrs Godwin and her husband during this respite. Godwin wrote, 'I am delighted with the cheerfulness that pervades your letter of yesterday. Fanny conducts herself delightfully, and I am what you call comfortable.'[26] Fanny was always a favourite of Godwin's with her amenable and placid disposition. Just seventeen, it was probably enjoyable for her to have charge of the house and responsibility for the care of a much-loved father, without the demands and interference of her imperious, serious and self-willed sister Mary.

This self-willed girl was obviously still chafing Mrs Godwin even while away from home and in congenial surroundings, for Godwin had written in an earlier letter to his wife, 'Tell Mary that, in spite of unfavourable appearances, I have still faith that she will become a wise and, what is more, a good and happy woman'[27] – a long-suffering parent's response to adolescent perversity.

Mrs Godwin and her children returned to London in June, leaving Mary in residence at Mrs Petman's school in Ramsgate. Mary was to write only three years later, 'I detest Mrs G. She plagues my father out of his life.'[28] With the hostility of ten years of sharing a home and a father with Mrs G this short separation from her family provided some relief for both Mary and those at home in Skinner Street.

Nevertheless it must have heightened her feelings of isolation and solitariness. She was not the sort of person to endear herself easily to a school full of girls, already established in their adolescent coteries, more willing to ostracize than include. Mary was a reserved and scholarly young girl of nearly fourteen whose very qualities made her appear aloof and superior when really she longed to be part of some friendship, probably envying the girls their easy familiarity and apparent facility with relationships.

All her novels were to deal in varying degrees with loneliness and isolation. The pulse that quickened and sustained *Frankenstein* through novelty and into myth was the ineluctable pathos of the monster, sentenced to blunder through life in utter isolation, rejected by his maker, denied even the humblest society, denied love. Desolation of landscape and spirit pervade this *tour de force*. There was much speculation then, and wonder still, as to how so young a woman could engender such a story. But the monster was of her life, a dramatic symbol of her own alienation and separateness, rooted within her long before she had to endure the further deprivation and tragedies to come.

In December, Mary returned to Skinner Street to find that the Godwin household had a new and almost daily visitor in the expansive personage of Aaron Burr. The following spring was to see the end of his four years' exile from the United States, during which time he committed much of his European experience to his private journal and to letters to his daughter back home. He noted Mary's return, 'looks very lovely but has not the air of strong health',[29] and was amused to witness the didactic spirit predictably strong in Godwin's children. William, at nine years, would deliver from a little wooden pulpit a weekly lecture written by fourteen-year-old Mary. The lecture Burr attended on 15 February 1812 was entitled 'The Influence of Governments on the Character of the People' and was delivered with 'great gravity and decorum'.[30]

Despite these sober entertainments, Mary found herself once more ensnared in the emotional claustrophobia and domestic uneasiness of Skinner Street. Out of place and unappreciated, Mary felt there was little to keep her there, and when an admirer of Godwin's, a wealthy merchant called William Baxter, invited her for a prolonged stay with his family at their home near Dundee, there was a general sigh of relief in the Godwin household. Mary was not to leave until June 1812 and as the day approached she probably had mixed feelings about the whole enterprise. Although she was pleased to be free of her step-mother and Skinner Street with all its frictions, she would miss her father. She felt, too, that she was being cast adrift from the family and from him, sent off to a bunch of indifferent strangers who lived practically at the North Pole, a seasick seven days away by packet boat up the east coast to Scotland. Her sisters also had second thoughts: Fanny, concerned for her safety and happiness, hoping her departure would restore some measure of tranquillity to the household and more than grateful that it was not her having to journey into the unknown; and Jane, wishing she could go on an adventure like that, for anything was more exciting than life at home when you were talented and vivacious and wanted to be an actress.

Godwin was full of misgivings. His letter to Mr Baxter written the day after Mary had sailed on 7 June gave a reliably objective view of his daughter and some indication of his feelings of having failed to be a real friend and confidant to her through his own preoccupations and tendency to authoritarianism:

'I have shipped off to you by yesterday's packet, the *Osnaburgh*, Captain Wishart, my only daughter. I attended her, with her two sisters, to the wharf, and remained an hour on board, till the vessel got under way. I cannot help feeling a thousand anxieties in parting with her, for the first time, for so great a distance, and these anxieties were increased by the manner of sending her, on board a ship, with not a single face around her that she had ever seen till that morning. She is four months short of fifteen years of age....

'I daresay she will arrive more dead than alive, as she is extremely subject to sea-sickness, and the voyage will, not improbably, last nearly a week. Mr Cline, the surgeon, however, decides that a sea-voyage would probably be of more service to her than anything.

'I am quite confounded to think what trouble I am bringing on you and your family, and to what a degree I may be said to have taken you in when I took you at your word in your invitation upon so slight an acquaintance. The old proverb says, 'He is a wise father who knows his own child,' and I feel the justness of the apothegm on the present occasion.

'There never can be a perfect equality between father and child, and if he has other objects and avocations to fill up the greater part of his time, the ordinary resource is for him to proclaim his wishes and commands in a way somewhat sententious and authoritative, and occasionally to utter his censures with seriousness and emphasis.

'It can, therefore, seldom happen that he is the confidant of his child, or that the child does not feel some degree of awe or restraint in intercourse with him. I am not, therefore, a perfect judge of Mary's character. I believe she has nothing of what is commonly called vices, and that she has considerable talent. But I tremble for the trouble I may be bringing on you in this visit. In my last I desired that you would consider the first two or three weeks as a trial, how far you can ensure her, or, more fairly and impartially speaking, how far her habits and conceptions may be such as to put your family very unreasonably out of their way; and I expect from the frankness and ingenuousness of yours of the 29th inst. (which by the way was so ingenuous as to come without a seal) that you will not for a moment hesitate to inform me if such should be the case. When I say all this, I hope you will be aware that I do not desire that she should be treated with extraordinary attention, or that any one of your family should put themselves in the smallest degree out of their way on her account. I am anxious that she should be brought up (in this respect) like a philosopher, even like a cynic. It will add greatly to the strength and worth of her character. I should also observe that she has no love of dissipation, and will be perfectly satisfied with your woods and your mountains. I wish, too, that she should be *excited* to industry. She has occasionally greater perseverance, but occasionally, too, she shows a great need to be roused...In all other respects except her arm she has admirable health, has an excellent appetite, and is capable of enduring fatigue....'

In another illuminating letter, in answer to an enquiry earlier in the year about the Wollstonecraft girls' education, Godwin was similarly rather shamefaced, aware that he had slipped from his and the famous Wollstonecraft ideals of parenthood:

'They are neither of them brought up with an exclusive attention to the system and ideas of their mother. I lost her in 1797 and 1801 I married a second time. One among the motives which led me to choose this was the feeling that I had in myself of an incompetence for the education of daughters. The present Mrs Godwin has great strength and activity of mind, but is not exclusively a follower of the notions of their mother ... nor have I leisure enough for reducing novel theories of education to practice ... my own daughter is considerably superior in capacity to the one her mother had before. Fanny, the eldest, is of a quiet, modest, unshowy disposition, somewhat given to indolence, which is her greatest fault, but sober, observing, peculiarly clear and distinct in the faculty of memory, and disposed to exercise her own thoughts and follow her own judgements. Mary, my daughter, is the reverse of her in many particulars. She is singularly bold, somewhat imperious, and active of mind. Her desire of knowledge is great, and her perseverance in everything she undertakes almost invincible. My own daughter is, I believe, very pretty; Fanny is by no means handsome, but in general prepossessing.'[31]

This very pretty daughter was nearly fifteen and growing into a woman. The most striking thing about her youthful looks was the aureole of soft pale auburn hair that seemed to reflect a light of its own. 'She wore it in its natural state, flowing in gauzy wavings around her face and throat, and upon her shoulders, and it was so fine the slightest wind or motion tangled it into a golden network,'[32] was how Jane described it in years to come. Trelawny, when he first met her in Italy in 1822, mentioned her fairness and her calm grey eyes, eyes which by their largeness and the cool intentness of their gaze added singularity to her otherwise quiet good looks. She was small and slight with a delicate oval face, a particularly wide forehead and a distinctive nose, luckily a ladylike version of her father's proboscis, so impugned by Southey all those years ago. Trelawny's description raised the spectre of her loneliness, 'witty, social and animated in the society of friends, though mournful in solitude'.[33]

As a young woman Mary could be infectiously spontaneous and enthusiastic, sometimes quite dizzy with high spirits. But she was dogged by fits of melancholy, possibly inherited from her mother and certainly exacerbated by her loss. Godwin, who prided himself on his cheerfulness in adversity, called her a Wollstonecraft for suffering so.

Mary arrived in Dundee and met the Baxters. There were two daughters, Christy, and Isabel who was to become the first real friend that Mary had ever had. The house was situated just east of the town at Broughty Ferry, overlooking the dark expanse of the Tay estuary and surrounded by well-treed grounds. A near contemporary of Mary's gave an account of her immediate environment:

> 'A bold promontory crowned with an ancient castle jutting far out into the Tay, which here broadens into the arm of the ocean – a beach in part smooth with sand, and in part paved with pebbles – cottages lying artlessly along the shore, clean as if washed by the near sea – sandy hillocks rising behind – and westward, the river, like an inland lake stretching around Dundee, with its fine harbour....'[34]

Here, living closely with the Baxters in a familial cosiness that sadly had been lacking in her home all the fifteen years of her life, she found security and freedom. Her time was spent studying, writing stories and declamations which were invariably shared with Isabel. No doubt she went sea-bathing too, for there is no further mention of her afflicted arm, although possibly that was a psychosomatic response to the unhappiness at home and her antagonism for Mrs Godwin. Her most memorable times were spent in flights of fancy or, as she described them in her introduction to *Frankenstein* in the Standard Novels edition of 1831, 'castles in the air – indulging in waking dreams – the following up of trains of thought, which had for their subject the formation of a succession of imaginary incidents. My dreams were at once more fantastic and agreeable than my writings ... my dreams were all my own; I accounted for them to nobody; they were my refuge when annoyed – my dearest pleasure when free.'[35]

The stark river banks and the bleak mountains beyond became her 'aerie of freedom', sustaining her daydreams. But unlike most adolescent fantasies these were not self-centred. Mary judged herself and her life to be too commonplace for her to become in any way, even in fantasy, a romantic heroine, meeting the prince of her dreams, travelling to far-away places; her sufferings noble, her pleasures sublime. She wrote years later in ironical reminiscence, 'I could not figure to myself that romantic woes or wonderful events would ever be my lot.'[36]

This lack of confidence in herself, despite a clear awareness and pride in her famous parentage, may have been in part an expression of an innately modest and pessimistic character, but it was equally a sad reminder of the lack of cherishing in her childhood. As children are prone to blame themselves for unhappy or unsatisfactory aspects of their family life, Mary almost certainly was burdened by guilt for the death of her idealized mother. Although blaming Mrs Godwin for her maternal and conjugal deficiencies, at times she was nagged by the thought that she herself was unlovable and unlovely and that this was as likely a cause of her fractured family relationships.

She was always perceptive and shrewd in her estimations of character and was particularly critical of her own. Her family and friends were submitted to this keen appraisal and the most charmed of them, particularly Shelley and Byron, peopled her novels and stories in varying degrees of vividness and reality. But as yet her stories were imitative, 'rather doing as others had done, than putting down the suggestions of my own mind'.[37]

This fundamental peace and security that the Baxters provided left her free to study, something she loved to do, to indulge her daydreams and the stirrings of her literary creativity; free to let loose some of the pent-up emotion and invest her active affections in her best friend Isabel. Mary was at last beginning to feel a sense of belonging, learning the rules of happy families that were to make her long, when she was a mother, for the orthodox unit: man, woman and children.

3
Enter Shelley

'He was a Poet ... whom the muses had crowned in his cradle, and on whose lips bees had fed....'

Mathilda, Mary Shelley

In the meantime an insignificant event occurred which was nevertheless the precursor of an episode that was to rock Godwin's complacency and revolutionize his daughter's existence. Godwin's diary, characteristically laconic, noted under the date 6 January 1812, 'write to Shelly'. Misspelling his name, he had immediately answered an enthusiastic introductory letter from the nineteen-year-old Percy Bysshe Shelley which had begun: 'You will be surprised at hearing from a stranger.... The name of Godwin has been used to excite in me feelings of reverence and admiration, I have been accustomed to consider him a luminary too dazzling for the darkness which surrounds him.' Godwin still attracted young idealistic men alight with enthusiasm for the philosophical principles of his *Political Justice*. He was always helpful and interested and enjoyed their attentions. Certainly Shelley's genuine flattery would have warmed the old philosopher's heart. He was now nearly fifty-six and, to paraphrase Hazlitt, the blazing sun was sinking below the horizon; once inflexible and captious he had now become 'as easy as an old glove'.[1]

Shelley's letter continued, mentioning their mutual endurance of prejudice and persecution, and ending with a promise of future persistence: 'I pray you to answer this letter. Imperfect as may be my capacity, my desire is ardent and unintermitted – Half an hour would be at least humanely employed in the experiment – I may not in fine have an answer to this letter. If I do not when I come to London I shall seek for you.'[2]

At this time Shelley was a hot-headed, susceptible and fundamentally unstable young man. Tall and slightly built with a scholar's stoop, he had an air of dishevelment though always fashionably dressed. His face was soft and clear-skinned, almost girlish, with bright eyes and fair unruly hair. To many, especially women, he was irresistible, charming them with his provocative eloquence and disarming them with his apparent vulnerability and artless other-worldliness. But he was not all he seemed. Still an adolescent jumble of undirected and uncoordinated passions and philosophies, he was highly impressionable and sensitive, a vivid fantast and idealistic humanitarian. Yet he was, too, a political revolutionary and active propagandist as well as a redoubtable and largely self-taught scholar. Quixotic and at times strangely ruthless, he was about to disrupt the predictable existence of the Godwins of Skinner Street and the reverberations were to shake, even shatter, the lives of at least four of that family in the years to come.

It began quietly enough. Godwin's reply asking for less generalization and more specifics was quickly countered by Shelley with a naturally biased résumé of his life so far. He conjured up a picture of a repressed and emotionally arid childhood: 'Passive obedience was inculcated and enforced in my childhood; I was required to love because it was my *duty* to love.... I was haunted with a passion for the wildest and most extravagant romances ... my sentiments were unrestrained by anything within me; external impediments were numerous, and strongly applied – their effects were merely temporary....'[3] In fact he was born into a family of Whig aristocrats. His father was an MP, his mother was a beautiful and efficient lady of the manor and he lived with them and his two younger sisters (a third sister and a brother were born later) at the big house, Field Place, in the little village of Warnham near Horsham in Sussex. His early childhood there was free and uninhibited; he ranged over his father's land, splashing stones and sailing sticks on Warnham pond beyond the orchard. He loved intensely his mother and his sisters, particularly Elizabeth who was only two years his junior. His father was benign and pedestrian, preoccupied with his own pursuits and maintaining his position in the world.

From the beginning Percy was an exceptional and extraordinary child. As he said in his letter to Godwin, he was dominated by his teeming imagination but it produced as many nightmares as it did childish fancies. His sisters would relate how he entranced and terrorized them with his stories of ghosts in the attics and ghouls and the Great Snake who lived in the woods. For ten years he revelled in his rural domain, indulged by his parents, adored by his sisters and excelling at the rudiments of a classical education offered to him by the kindly local vicar. When he was ten years old this idyll was disenchanted by his surrender of a Sussex childhood for the grown-up world of preparatory school, and then Eton. These years were a torment to him. The boys, brutalized by the system, hated his singularity and bullied him mercilessly; they mocked his uncommon looks and his unathletic build. Yet in many ways the attacks were in part provoked. Shelley was uncompromising and arrogant. For the best reasons, but quite foolhardily, he refused to fag at Eton. He was naturally eccentric, a gifted scholar and wild romancer. He eschewed the compromises and toadying that were essential to survival in a boys' school. He hated violence and tyranny the whole of his life but while at school and baited by a ferocious mob of boys he discovered his own weapon. He had a murderous temper and could himself be spontaneously violent. Mary wrote in 1825, 'I have often heard our Shelley relate the story of stabbing an Upper Boy with a fork.... He always described it in my hearing as being an almost involuntary act, done on the spur of anguish, and that he made the stab as the boy was going out of the room....'[4] This was one of many agonized retaliations and this stain of violence in his own nature was always a source of pain to him.

He felt threatened and besieged, abandoned by his family when he most needed them. He had been ejected from Paradise. Even in school holidays back at Field Place it could never be the same again. He became more uncontrollable and perverse. Fascinated by science, the occult and alchemy, he experimented with gunpowder, blowing up an old tree stump, and with sorcery and incantations to the devil. His fantasies became more persistent and macabre. He alarmed his parents with his hare-brained expeditions involving even his young sisters, but apparently they still treated him benevolently. However his father, Timothy, orthodox and jealously maintaining his family status, must have been disappointed and vexed by his bizarre and unreliable son. Certainly his solid Whig senses could not approach an understanding of Shelley's quivering sensibilities and tenuous grasp of reality.

When he was seventeen Shelley became infatuated with his cousin

Harriet Grove; she looked remarkably like him, and he fell in love with the idea of love. In 1810 his Gothic romance, *Zastrozzi*, was published. Adolescent, imitative and rather bad, it was however revealingly full of his own fantasies. It was interestingly psychoanalysed as dream material by Dr Eustace Chesser* as suggesting extreme narcissism with a predilection for falling in love with projections of himself, a passivity in sexual relationships and an inability to sustain them.

Regardless of any deeper meaning, the publication of *Zastrozzi* allowed him to leave Eton, if not in a blaze of glory, at least with a flicker of hard-won esteem.

Neither was the university of Oxford the place for Shelley. Intellectually null and inspirationally void, it was a circumspect, prejudiced finishing school for aristocratic and moneyed sons. Here he published his second Gothic novel, *St Irvyne, or The Rosicrucian*, no better than the first. Here he met Thomas Jefferson Hogg, his first real love outside his family. Together they shared a scorn for Oxford poppycock, a zest for radicalism and a dangerous atheism. It was this atheism and an attempt to disseminate their heretical views through a pamphlet, *The Necessity of Atheism*, flaunted in the window of the local bookshop, that effected their expulsion from Oxford.

This expulsion was a dreadful disappointment to his father. It also alarmed him, for the disgrace and the behaviour that prompted it threatened his own and his family's good name and vulnerable status. Sadly, after hurt letters at crossed purposes had fleeted between father and son, Timothy Shelley in frustration and fear put all further communication in the hands of his solicitor, Whitton. This dry old stick was to remain wholly unsympathetic to Shelley, and then to Mary for years to come. With this move a temporary alienation between father and son became irreparable.

Shelley was in London, very lonely, vaguely fearful and miserably lacking in direction. He began spending time with the Westbrook sisters, Eliza, ten years his senior, broodingly dark and scheming, and Harriet, a mere sixteen, extremely fair and sweet. Unfortunately she was immature and compliant too, excessively dependent on her subtly imperious sister who was out to make a match for her with this heir to a baronetcy.

* Dr Eustace Chesser, *Shelley & Zastrozzi: self-revelation of a neurotic* (London, 1965).

Shelley was charmed by Harriet and increasingly became enthused with the idea of liberating her from parental, educational and religious tyranny. 'Yet *marriage* is hateful detestable, – a kind of ineffable sickening disgust seizes my mind when I think of this most despotic most unrequired fetter which prejudice has forged to confine its energies.'[5]

During this early summer of 1811 he also met and began corresponding with a Miss Elizabeth Hitchener. She, like Eliza Westbrook, was dark-skinned and twenty-nine, but was in charge of a school in Sussex. She was lonely, liberal and intellectually curious and Shelley set out zealously to further enlighten and spiritually nurture her. With their long letters brim-full of intellectual discourse and candid emotional self-analysis, she gradually assumed a position of confidante and soul-mate, though at a distance.

After an uneasy few weeks' kicking his heels in his cousin's remote house in Wales, Shelley rushed back to London at the beginning of August to save and protect Harriet Westbrook from tyranny. Both Harriet and Eliza had written to him. He had written to Hogg, '... if I know anything about *Love* I am *not* in love. I have heard from the Westbrooks, both of whom I highly esteem.'[6] Harriet was then writing unhappy letters on the stirring subject of her cruel father's insistence that she return to school; she mentioned suicide and called upon Shelley for help. All of this was irresistible stuff and certain to inflame Shelley's quixotic temperament.

He arrived at Harriet's side but could not persuade her, as she was strongly supported by Eliza, to elope with him on a basis of free love. But to him marriage was 'hateful'. For two weeks the negotiations went on, Eliza no doubt holding out for this socially elevating marriage for her sister, reminding her, quite rightly, that without that legality she was jeopardizing her family ties, her honour, any future children and her future marriage prospects. Harriet would probably have gone with Shelley on his terms for she was pliant, trusting and unaware of life's realities.

At the end of August, Shelley capitulated and on borrowed money fled with Harriet to Scotland. He married her there. Within days Hogg had joined them in Edinburgh.

They studied and talked and walked together, an inseparable threesome, Shelley just nineteen and Harriet only sixteen. But lack of money was a growing apprehension. His father's unresponsiveness and withdrawal of his allowance on hearing of the elopement reawakened in Shelley the old feelings of rejection and despondency.

All three of them moved to York, impecunious and unsettled. Shelley held on firmly to Hogg, diluting the concentrated intimacy of the early days of marriage. He also renewed his correspondence with Miss Hitchener, inviting her to join them, reviving his abiding interest in founding a community of radical intellectuals, soul brothers – or more to the point, sisters. Miss Hitchener enthusiastically answered, 'Harriet ... shall have a Sister's affection, for are you not the Brother of my soul.'[7]

In October Shelley left Harriet with Hogg to go on a fleeting visit to Field Place to demand his allowance in person. He failed and left the poorer, having intimidated and insulted his father and mother and frightened his sisters. He returned to York to find Eliza Westbrook *in situ* and busy regularizing her sister's life. There was coldness, too, between Hogg and Harriet. Eventually it was revealed to Shelley that Hogg had attempted some sexual intimacy with Harriet which had upset her and prompted her to remonstrate; 'Harriet talked to him much of immorality ... and Hogg confessed to her his conviction of having acted wrong....'[8] The amiable *ménage à trois* was now dramatically imbalanced, swung by the considerable weight of authority in the form of the interfering Eliza.

Under her auspices and with her financial help, they left Hogg behind in York to suffer his ignominy alone and settled in Keswick in the Lake District. Shelley was tormented by the loss of his friend; having little compunction in sharing Harriet with Hogg, he was nevertheless distraught at having had to share Hogg with Harriet. It was Harriet and her wishes, and probably Eliza's, which prevented their reunion: 'If I were free I were yours.... But I *am* Harriet's.'[9]

At this time Miss Hitchener and her sympathetic philosophizing became especially important to him. Pages of Shelleyan doubts and dialectic were answered with even greater prolixity, brimming with kindness, flattery and a gentle insidiousness. 'Your letters are like angels sent from heaven on missions of peace,' Shelley began one of many letters, 'they assure me that existence is not valueless, they point out the path which it is Paradise to tread.'[10]

Although Elizabeth Hitchener was fulfilling a role akin to mother confessor, providing some sort of necessary catharsis for Shelley's turbulent emotions at this time, sadly for her she was becoming more deeply involved and most certainly infatuated with and flattered by this emotionally restless young man. Shelley's relationship with her was yet another distraction from the development of a real intimacy between himself and Harriet.

Living in Wordsworth, Coleridge and Southey country, he only met the latter and they, predictably, clashed. Shelley was becoming enamoured of this beautiful land of lakes and mountains. Alongside the enchantment with his wish to establish some sort of community of friends, was a growing political awareness. Here he began to study seriously Godwin's writings. At this time, too, he began to think of going to Ireland to propagate his views and to help enlighten the people to their rights to 'freedom'.

It was while in this uneasy state, living with both Eliza and Harriet, but feeling emotionally uncommitted to his child-wife, alienated from his family and to a lesser extent from Hogg, that Shelley sat down to compose that first circumspect letter to his new-found hero, William Godwin.

Mary and Shelley were growing up in very different circumstances; nevertheless the first link of the chain of cause and effect that was to bring them together had been forged. In Shelley's short life there had been an excess of drama and hysterical agitation and there was to be more before Mary's understanding and whole-hearted support helped ward off the worst of his nervous turmoils and lapses into self-destruction.

His emotions, he admitted in that second letter to Godwin, were unconstrained, inflamed by his wild imaginings and fears. Mary's emotions had suffered fifteen years of control and sublimation. But her intellect had been nurtured in similar though narrower study and her imagination, less wild than Shelley's, was as great a resource and as free. Trelawny, meeting her when she was twenty-four, was struck by the keenness and command of her language: '... like Shelley, though in a minor degree, she had the power of expressing her thoughts in varied and appropriate words, derived from familiarity with the works of our vigorous old writers.' This was all the more impressive when contrasted with the limited vocabulary of the average lady of the day, 'in which a score of poor hackneyed phrases sufficed to express all that is felt or considered proper to reveal'.[11]

Her father had always tried to instil the maxim that emotions should be tempered by reason. Mary's keen intelligence and eagerness to learn had made her a good and willing pupil of this and other Godwinisms. Although she was outwardly reserved and shy, her Scottish home gave her a freer and easier outlook on life, a growing confidence that was to surprise the Skinner Street family when she returned.

In November of the same year, 1812, Mary went home for Christmas, taking Christy Baxter with her, to show her country friend the sights and the mixed attractions of the great city. Mary was more poised and independent, delighted to see her father again, although noticing, with the shock of objectivity, that he had grown older, increasingly careworn and preoccupied. Now that Mary was no longer under her step-mother's roof and control, Mrs Godwin seemed less of an ogre as she and Fanny set about the preparations for Christmas. She looked older too, her plump body slacker, the robust bloom of her skin fading. London's smoke and the toils of an ailing business were exacting their price. Fanny as ever was wistful and self-sacrificing, doing all she could to help, and particularly attentive towards Godwin. It seems probable that she still did not know the full circumstances of her birth and believed herself to be Godwin's daughter. This meant that he and the rest of the family and their friends must have been involved in some protective conspiracy, made all the more difficult by Mary Wollstonecraft's fame and the general cognizance of the irregularities of her love life, thanks to Godwin's frank *Memoirs* published the year after her death. Certainly, when Christy Baxter was an old lady she recalled, when talking to Mrs Marshall,[12] that she realized on this trip to London that Fanny was not aware of her illegitimacy; a factor that may well have contributed to her tragic death.

The Godwin parents made a good impression on Mary's Scottish friend. She was surprised by the independence of each member of the household; they all went their own ways, only gathering together for lunch and then separating again. Godwin was the most remote; 'he lives so much from his family, only seeing them at stated hours',[13] as Harriet was also to remark to a friend.

The excitement of Mary and Christy's arrival from Scotland was sustained the next day by a special lunch party at Skinner Street. The assembled Godwin family were joined by their new friends, Shelley, Harriet and her sister Eliza. The Godwin girls were plainly dressed for they were encouraged to eschew materialism and worldliness, their dark silks a perfect foil to Harriet's radiant blonde beauty and purple satin dress, truly *bon ton*. Shelley, too, was handsomely dressed and full of excited talk. He was delighted with these new friends but, although he was always to admire the principles of *Political Justice*, his extravagant enthusiasm for Godwin was as self-generating and unreal as his later hatred of Miss Hitchener. Both were extreme and subjective expressions of his emotional instability at the time.

Christy Baxter described Mary as she remembered her at this time as 'agreeable, vivacious, and sparkling; very pretty, with fair hair and complexion and clear, bright white skin'.[14] However, her quiet beauty would never outshine Harriet's distinctive prettiness, even had Shelley been less interested in his own news and discussions with Godwin to take particular notice of this fifteen-year-old and her friend.

Harriet related her youthful enthusiasm for the Godwin family when they had met for the first time a month previously:

'We have seen the Godwins. Need I tell you that I love them all? His manners are so soft and pleasing that I defy even an enemy to be displeased with him. . . . There is one of the daughters [Fanny] of that dear Mary Wolstoncroft [sic] living with him. She is 19 years of age, very plain, but very sensible. The beauty of her mind fully overbalances the plainness of her countenance. There is another daughter of hers [Mary] who is now in Scotland. She is very much like her mother, whose picture hangs up in his study. She must have been a most lovely woman. Her countenance speaks her a woman who would dare to think and act for herself. . . . The many trials that Mrs Godwin has had to encounter makes me very much inclined to believe her a woman of great fortitude and unyielding temper of mind. There is a very great sweetness marked in her countenance. In many instances she has shown herself a woman of great magnanimity and independence of character. . . . It gives me very great pleasure to sit and look at him [Godwin]. Have you even seen a bust of Socrates, for his head is very much like that?'[15]

Harriet's letters during her few happy years with Shelley were characterized by their simplicity, intelligent observation and good nature. Having at long last met the acclaimed philosopher and his family it was only natural that she, influenced too by Shelley's hero-worship, should be fulsome in her praise, although her enthusiasm was to fade as the relationship progressed.

However, that other Wollstonecraft daughter, at this her first meeting with the revolutionary poet and polemicist, sat back, quietly watching and listening. She had heard snippets of information from her father and especially from Fanny who had become particularly interested in the romantic Mr and Mrs Shelley. As his high melodic voice dominated conversation at the table she learnt more.

The year for Shelley had been an eventful and disturbing one. Since his first letters to Godwin at the beginning of January he had been frightened by an attack on him at his cottage at Keswick by unknown, possibly politically-inspired assailants. He, Harriet and Eliza had then embarked hastily on an ill-conceived and worse-fated expedition to Ireland, to help 'Catholic emancipation'. Here their eagerness to do their share for the common good was only equalled by their naïvety, impracticality and ineffectual idealism. The horror of the plight of the poor and starving of Dublin slowly filtered through Shelley's high-minded rhetoric. He left Dublin having completely failed in his mission. An attempt to set up a rural commune in Wales was thwarted and Shelley and Harriet and Eliza eventually moved to Lynmouth in Devon. By now the Home Office had been alerted to Mr Shelley's subversive outbursts and the unorthodox household was being 'watched' by a government agent. Local speculation must have become rife as this outrageous coven was joined by yet another female, Miss Hitchener, with Shelley attempting to persuade Godwin to let Fanny join them too. Godwin refused. 'I have never seen your face. ... Until I have seen a man's face ... I do not know him.'[16] Shelley settled down to intensive study, literary projects and disseminating propaganda. With wonderful and characteristic extravagance he rolled up sheets of his 'Declaration of Rights', and posted them into bottles and then, with arms full and pockets bulging, cast them into the sea. He wrote a sonnet on it, *On Launching some bottles filled with Knowledge into the Bristol Channel.*

It was their more pedestrian methods of distribution which caught them out. Dan, their servant, was apprehended while pasting up copies of the 'Declaration' and the authorities were alerted. Once again it was time for the Shelleys to be up and away. They came to rest in the Welsh village of Tremadoc and set their hearts on leasing an imposing new house with an impressive view, Tan-yr-allt. But before they could possess it, financial and legal complications had to be tackled and once more they were on the move, arriving on 4 October in London, and visiting the Godwins nearly every day of the six weeks they were there.

During this time Godwin was enthusiastically propounding to Shelley the same advice he had given Mary on a comprehensive course of reading and study, all of which was eagerly noted and duly embarked upon when Shelley returned to Tan-yr-allt in the middle of November. The early meetings at Skinner Street developed into lively discussions either in the study or at family mealtimes. Shelley, who was vegetarian and uninterested in food, would pick at the bread, choosing to talk rather than eat. These debates ranged over the merits and demerits of such literati as Ben Jonson, Spenser, Donne, Bacon, Milton and Izaak Walton, with Godwin exhorting Shelley to entrench himself in 'a breastwork of books'. 'It is for boarding school misses to read one book at a time.'[17] Mary knew well this enthusiastic and didactic side of her father; he enjoyed nothing more than discoursing with and advising a young and able disciple. In his solitary profession these were fertile interludes of wit-sharpening and ego-boosting. Leavening the intellectual contest was the gossip. Shelley always had a good tale to tell, he courted the bizarre and extraordinary. Before this visit to London both he and Harriet had become increasingly irritable, even antagonistic, towards Miss Hitchener. Harriet anyway had found her rather odd and overbearing in the flesh; the main contention seemed to have been a sexual one, for Harriet's amused and tolerant voice rapidly became a jealous and injured one: 'She built all her hopes on being able to separate me from my dearly beloved Percy, and had all the artfulness to say that Percy was really in love with her, and [it] was only his being married that could keep her within bounds now.'[18] Shelley's defection from the 'sister of my soul' was more extreme and cruel and in this letter to Hogg there is a real sense of sexual revulsion:

> 'The Brown Demon as we call our late tormentor and school mistress, must receive her stipend. I pay it with a heavy heart and unwilling hand; but it must be so. She was deprived by our misjudging haste of the situation, where she was going on smoothly: and now she says that her reputation is gone, her health ruined, her peace of mind destroyed by my barbarity – ... She is an artful,

superficial, ugly, hermaphroditical beast of a woman, and my astonishment at my fatuity inconsistency, and bad taste was never so great, as after living four months with her as an inmate.'[19]

Of course the admiring Godwin circle took Shelley's side against this interloper, but Shelley had ruthlessly denied Miss Hitchener her promised renaissance and left her hard-won career and small-town respectability in ruins.

Of all the Godwin daughters, Fanny was the best acquainted with Shelley and Harriet, and on their unexpectedly hasty removal from London and return to Wales she wrote a letter to Shelley. It lacked confidence and was tentatively flirtatious, gently admonishing him for having left without saying good-bye and adding rather wistfully, even with a trace of Godwinian disapproval, that Harriet was 'such a fine lady'. Shelley's answer must have been pored over many times by Fanny, Jane and Mary too. It arrived before Christmas and was jokey, condescending and kind:

'So you do not know whether it is *proper* to write to me. – Now one of the most conspicuous considerations that arise from such a topic is who & what am I? I am one of those formidable & long clawed animals called a *Man*, & it is not until I have assured you that I am one of the most inoffensive of my species, that I live on vegetable food, & never bit since I was born that I venture to intrude myself on your attention.'[20]

All good flirtatious stuff designed to increase the pulses of the young women of Skinner Street. Once again he had established an admiring sisterhood. Godwin wrote in a letter to him in the spring, 'You cannot imagine how much all the females of my family, Mrs G. and three daughters, are interested in your letters and your history',[21] and no wonder, for he could be dazzling: he idealized and needed women, he was practised in appealing to their sensibilities and was by far the most exciting and prepossessing young man to have come within the portals of Skinner Street. Something of Mary's first impressions of him can be gleaned from her fiction. Mary's novels and stories were largely autobiographical, and she freely used her experiences either as a purge for her own powerful and unexpressed emotions, or to work out interrelationships which intrigued her in life, or simply as fuel for a good romantic plot. Her memory and acute perception never let her down.

Even in middle age she could recall events and impressions with such clarity that frequently she was overwhelmed with a sense of living it all again. Her novel *Mathilda*, remaining unpublished until recently,* incorporated a distinct portrait of Shelley in the role of poet and friend. Mary drew an unflattering picture of herself, written as it was in 1819 after compounded tragedies and ill-health had brought her to a nadir in her relationship with Shelley and the world.

Mathilda's reminiscence of her meeting with the poet Woodville was as equally Mary's unfailing memory of her fateful meeting seven years before: 'I was struck by his exceeding beauty ... the sweet but melancholy cadence of his voice brought tears into my eyes ... his conversation which glowed with imagination and sensibility; the poetry that seemed to hang upon his lips and to make the very air mute to listen to him were charms that no one could resist.'[22] Although idealized, this was essentially how an impressionable and romantic fifteen-year-old would have responded to the charisma that was so much a part of Shelley when on his best behaviour. His voice, too, was to become for Mary, whose ear was acute, as distinctive as his face; even after his death, the conversation of friends like Byron and Coleridge would remind her poignantly of what she had lost: 'I would endure ages of pain to hear one tone of your voice strike on my ear!'[23]

Shelley, his pregnant wife Harriet and Eliza were back in Wales for Christmas. The Godwin family were gathered. Charles Clairmont had left Charter House School and was now worthily employed as a clerk with Constables, the publishers. His sister Jane, nearly fifteen, was as high-spirited as ever but silly and temperamental too, full of extravagant ideas for her future and prone to sulk when life did not go her way. Domestic drudgery and minding the shop, or helping her mother with accounts and the copying of letters, were all too much of a drag on her volatile nature. Mary found her caprices irritating; nevertheless she was more interesting and better company than eighteen-year-old-Fanny, who had grown over-responsible, was not very imaginative or adventurous and too busy anyway, doing her share of running the home and business, to indulge in romantic speculation and philosophy. William was nine, a brattish age as far as his older half-sisters were concerned, and doubly so for he was spoilt and doted on by his mother and indulged by his father.

* Mary Wollstonecraft Shelley, *Mathilda*, edited by Elizabeth Nitchie (Chapel Hill, 1959).

This mother and father fell from Shelley's grace during the spring and early summer of the following year, 1813. Harriet, in her revealing letters to her Irish friend Mrs Nugent, chattered on: 'Godwin, he, too, is changed, and [filled] with prejudices, and besides, too, he expects such universal homage from all persons younger than himself, that it is very disagreeable to be in company with him on that account, and he wanted Mr Shelley to join the Wig [sic] party and do just as they pleased, which made me very angry, as we know what men the Wigs are now.' She then sounded the death knell for the old fuddy-duddy: 'He is grown old and unimpassioned, therefore is not in the least calculated for such enthusiasts as we are.'[24] Mrs Godwin, too, was exposed to the disenchanted gaze of the young Shelleys: '... his wife is so dreadfully disagreeable that I could not bear the idea of seeing her. Mr S. had done that away tho', by telling G. that I could not bear the society of his darling wife. Poor man, we are not the only people who find her troublesome.'[25] Harriet's intolerance of Mrs Godwin could well have been aggravated by her discomfort and anxiety as she approached the last weeks of her pregnancy. By the time Harriet had been delivered of a little daughter, Eliza Ianthe, at the end of June 1813, Mary and Christy Baxter had sailed back in the packet boat to Dundee.

It was summertime and, amongst the trees and the mountains or on the bleak shore of the Tay estuary, Mary was remote from the quibbles and crises of Skinner Street. She had brought one particular image with her, something real to dominate the visions and imaginings that filled her girlhood which now suddenly was slipping away. At last she had a real romantic hero in Percy Shelley; his eyes bright in a flushed face, his zealous talk in the study at home, his letters to her father bursting with ideas and political idealism, his dashing and courageous attempts at setting men free and easing their burdens of poverty and exploitation. Regardless of Mary's father's opinion of these crusades, Shelley was a man of action while other radicals sat at home and discussed and wrote and complained. Besides, Shelley was young and strikingly good-looking; he was the stuff of which young girls' dreams were made. Thus idealized, his attractions were undeniable. No doubt in Mary's imagination Shelley did set the world to rights, was lauded as a Saviour and a Poet and, dare she think it, came to carry her away to be his helpmate, inspiration and lover.

The reality was as always very different. Shelley had returned to Tan-yr-allt for the winter and spring. Both he and Harriet were delighted with the house and its situation. 'I continue vegetable. Harriet means to be slightly animal until the spring. – My health is much improved by it. Tho partly perhaps by my removal from your nerve racking & spirit quelling metropolis',[26] he wrote to Hogg.

Incensed by the sight of the local starving poor, often cheated and ill-treated by their bosses, Shelley turned once again to political polemic and pamphleteering, and in his usual inflammatory way succeeded in blowing an already ugly local discontent into a threatening and explosive situation. This culminated in an alarming incident at Tan-yr-allt, that has been a point of endless controversy: what was real and what Shelleyan persecution mania?[27] He claimed, and there was much evidence at the time to support it, that he was attacked at night by a sinister assassin who shot at him with a gun, then escaped having threatened ghastly revenge. Whatever the events, they so frightened and disturbed the household, and Shelley in particular, that they determined to leave Wales as soon as he was recovered.

In March they travelled to Dublin and on into the wilds of Killarney. But by the beginning of April they were back in London again. Shelley had finished his first major poem, *Queen Mab*, and it was about to be printed. They were afraid of its subversive content, propagating atheism and free love, and intended to distribute it privately amongst friends.

However, the summer brought anxieties and frustrations. The baby Ianthe was born and responsibility and disagreements with Harriet's ideas on child-rearing accompanied her. Reconciliations with Field Place were thwarted. Their finances were increasingly precarious. By November Shelley and Harriet had left London in search of a more permanent home for the winter, eventually ending up in Windsor. The winter and spring of 1814 was a time of emotional stress and upheaval for Shelley. His sister-in-law Eliza had always been an insidious influence on Harriet and was a considerable inhibitor in her relationship with Shelley. Now that their baby was born Eliza became overtly managing and interfering, ensuring Harriet was treated 'properly', and generally assuming control of little Ianthe. Shelley's seething resentment of this familial invasion and his own exiling burst into a vituperative attack on Eliza, reminiscent of his abhorrence of the unfortunate Miss Hitchener. In March he wrote to

Hogg, 'I certainly hate her with all my heart and soul. It is a sight which awakens an inexpressible sensation of disgust and horror, to see her caress my poor little Ianthe, in whom I may hereafter find the consolation of sympathy. I sometimes feel faint with the fatigue of checking the overflowings of my unbounded abhorrence for this miserable wretch. But she is no more than a blind and loathsome worm, that cannot see to sting.'[28]

He had at this time, and had increasingly during the last months, taken refuge in the home of the Boinvilles at Bracknell – a few miles from the house at Windsor where Harriet, Ianthe and Eliza were residing. Mrs Boinville was prepossessing and prosperous, her daughter Cornelia young and cultured and extremely pretty. There was no mention at all of Harriet in this letter to Hogg but ominous references to the transitory 'paradise' and 'delightful tranquillity of this happy home – for it has become my home'.[29] Emotionally overwrought and spiritually and physically estranged from Harriet, it was little wonder that he should nurture a half-suppressed passion for the undemanding Cornelia. In a notebook he had written at this time this line from St Augustine's *Confessions*: 'I was not yet in love, but I was in love with love itself; and I sought for something to love, since I loved nothing.'[30]

This period with the Boinvilles was for Shelley a time of painful reassessment of her personal life; the realization of his sexual revulsion for Harriet was the vortex to which all his thoughts were drawn.

> 'I saw the full extent of the calamity which my rash & heartless union with Harriet: an union over whose entrance might justly be in[s]cribed
>
> Lasciate ogni speranza voi ch'entrate*
>
> had produced. I felt as if a dead & living body had been linked together in loathsome & horrible communion'[31]

he wrote to Hogg the following October in a résumé of the events of the previous six months.

Throughout the May days in the heat of that early summer Shelley, not yet twenty-two, was suffering a disorientation and a kind of emotional breakdown. He was also longing for emotional fulfilment and in a daze of sexual desire, of which Cornelia was only a temporary

---

* 'Abandon hope all ye who enter here', Dante's *Inferno*, Canto III.

embodiment. In the letter to Hogg he went on to explain 'a train of visionary events in which this longing was implicit and which, more importantly, preceded by a month or more Mary's fateful re-acquaintance with him. In this extraordinary letter, it was obvious that Shelley considered these visions to be a premonition of his discovery of her and his embrace of this most important relationship in both of their lives:

> 'I wandered in the fields alone. The season was most beautiful. The evenings were so serene & mild – I never had before felt so intensely the subduing voluptuousness of the impulses of spring. Manifestations of my approaching change tinged my waking thoughts, & afforded inexhaustible subject for the visions of my sleep. I recollect that one day I undertook to walk from Bracknell to my father's, (40 miles). A train of visionary events arranged themselves in my imagination till ideas almost acquired the intensity of sensations. Already I had met the female who was destined to be mine, already had she replied to my exhalting recognition, already were the difficulties surmounted that opposed our entire union. I had even proceeded so far as to compose a letter to Harriet on the subject of my passion for another. Thus was my walk beguiled, at the conclusion of which I was hardly sensible of fatigue.'[32]

This evocative paragraph illustrated just how delicate were his susceptibilities at this time, just how ready he was to be inspired and enthralled by a young woman like Mary Wollstonecraft Godwin, herself so young and longing for love, yet exalted by her parentage and distinguished beyond most women by her intellect and education.

4
Renaissance

'... [he] caused me to walk as one, not in eclipse, not in darkness and vacancy – but in a new and brilliant light, too novel, too dazzling for my human senses....'

The Last Man, Mary Shelley

In the spring of 1814 Mary Godwin said her farewells to the Baxter family. She was particularly sad to be leaving Isabel, her first real friend. They had often gone rambling together amongst the rugged hills and mysterious caves that gave the Baxters' house and grounds, perched beside the Firth of Tay, its special atmosphere of wildness and freedom. But Mary was sixteen and a half now, grown and more confident than the displaced and unhappy girl who had first sailed for Scotland two years before. London beckoned her. The house at Skinner Street was cramped, there were few luxuries like those she had known with the Baxters; she was exchanging the fresh Scottish breezes for the smoky stacks and stench of London streets, but her father was there and around him the glamour of intellectual friends and acquaintances, not least the blazing Mr Shelley. The close, affectionate family and the massive Highland landscape had fortified Mary's spirit. It had given her security and peace to work out her feelings and personality away from the nonconformity and friction of her own family life.

Mary arrived back in London on 30 March. Everything seemed smaller and dirtier than she had remembered. Her father looked older and noticeably balding; he was nearing sixty but was as astute as ever and keen to quiz her on her studies. They were delighted to be reunited, although Godwin must have been a little disconcerted by his unfamiliar, grown-up and good-looking daughter. She had always been clear-sighted and perspicacious about the personalities and motivation of herself and others, and realized the intensity of her love for her father. She wrote to her dear friend Jane Williams in 1822, 'Until I met Shelley I [could] justly say that he [Godwin] was my God – and I remember many childish instances of the [ex]cess of attachment I bore him.'[1] It seemed that, secretive as she thought she was, Mrs Godwin had nevertheless discovered early on Mary's 'excessive and romantic attachment to my Father'.[2]

She was well aware of his greatness and his failings and portrayed aspects of his character and of their relationship in some of her fiction. In *Mathilda*, the heroine's father, who suffers an incestuous passion for her which is implicitly and tragically reciprocated, was at times clearly Godwin. Their relationship, too, was strongly autobiographical, although fond reminiscence and the demands of plot no doubt added a dramatic glow:

'... we removed to London where I was led by my father to attend to deeper studies than had before occupied me. My improvement was his delight.... We saw a great deal of society, and no day passed that my father did not endeavour to embellish by some new enjoyment. The tender attachment that he bore me and the love and veneration with which I returned it cast a charm over every moment.'[3]

Mary was well back into the intellectual swing; always a voracious reader her studies would once again be directed by her father with probably much the same advice as he had given Shelley the previous year. He felt strongly that one should only 'select and dwell upon the best' in literature. 'Put a new book into my hands, and the first question I shall ask you, if I question you wisely, is: What are its excellencies? Does it exhibit any grand views? Does it contain any beautiful passages? Here all the good and all the honour lies.'[4] The gist of his advice to both Mary and Shelley had been to surround themselves with good books, never to read one at a time, and always in reading history to avoid derivative works in favour of contemporary narrations. So with these Godwinian maxims Mary ably and keenly set to work on further studies of such pinnacles of English literature as Shakespeare, Bacon, Milton, no doubt spiced with a few Gothic fantasies like M. G. Lewis's *The Monk* or Mrs Radcliffe's popular terror stories.

Mr Shelley, in whom she, Fanny and Jane were reputedly so interested, was not in town during that month of April, but there were his letters to Godwin and to Fanny to read and bits of gossip about his political escapades, disposal of the 'Brown Demon' and the birth of his daughter, which would all have been well worth discussing.

Jane was very pleased to have Mary back. They were almost the same age, although Mary was very much the elder in nature for she was intellectually mature beyond her years and had a quality of stillness and strength which made the impressionable Jane admire and seek to imitate her. She could be high-spirited and exuberant, too, especially with people she liked who were responsive to her. However, Mary's was essentially a personality in which the intellectual and analytical Godwinian exterior was more frequently the victor over the strong emotions and clear intuitions of her inner life; where outbursts of Wollstonecraft melancholy or enthusiasm, flights of morbid and sometimes inspired fantasy, could play havoc with her usually composed and thoughtful demeanour. Physically, Mary and Jane were opposites. Mary was day to Jane's night. She was all light and gold, her fine translucent skin and gauzy auburn hair emphasized the intensity of her grey eyes; while Jane's Latin good looks, her thick dark hair and darker eyes, her olive skin, made her seem distinctly foreign beside the English fairness of her step-sister.

Jane had just returned home from a boarding school run by a French lady; she had a good singing voice and had intermittently had lessons, but above all she favoured the idea of becoming an actress and bemoaned the burden of being just plain Jane. Within the next few months, after she had left home, she was to succeed in changing her name in everyday use to the more evocative 'Claire', although her mother and Godwin refused to call her anything but Jane for the rest of their lives. She hated housework and could be generally obstructive and petulant. Mrs Godwin was already harassed and overworked and her spirits surely flagged further on the return of these two adolescent girls: her own daughter self-willed and temperamental, and Mary disapproving and aloof.

The weather improved and, as an escape from the cramped quarters and domestic frictions of Skinner Street, Mary began to walk regularly to Old St Pancras churchyard. There she sat against her mother's gravestone to read and dream. She might love her father intensely with an awareness of his failings but her mother was essentially unknown. The patchy image of her was romanticized and adored but the reality was painfully missed. It was difficult to persuade Godwin to talk about her, Fanny had dim memories, and old family friends like Marshall and Maria Gisborne probably were the best sources of anecdote and information. Years later, in her fiction, she was particularly astute at relating the emotional deprivation involved in being motherless or orphaned. Lionel Verney, who was the last man on earth (as Mary, when she wrote it, felt herself to be too) in the novel *The Last Man*, grew up uncared for and solitary. Mathilda of course lost her talented and loving mother in exactly the same way as did Mary, and Elizabeth Raby of *Falkner* was very much alone and made daily visits to her mother's grave.

As Mary sat in the peace of her own mother's graveyard, under the weeping branches of the two willows her father had planted, perhaps she felt she had some contact with this remarkable woman who had died in giving her life. Mary was certainly very proud of her mother and distinctly aware of her achievements and reputation. In the subsequent years she, with Shelley, who was an ardent upholder of the Wollstonecraft memory and principles, read and re-read all her works, no doubt fortified with long discussions, speculations, and enthusiastic eulogy. She was to write years later in notes for a biography of her father,

> 'Mary Wollstonecraft was one of those beings who appear once perhaps in a generation, to gild humanity with a ray which no difference of opinion nor chance of circumstances can cloud. Her genius was undeniable.... Her sound understanding, her intrepidity, her sensibility and eager sympathy, stamped all her writings with force and truth, and endowed them with a tender charm that enchants while it enlightens. She was one who all loved who had ever seen her....'[5]

She was talking of a stranger; it was all impersonal praise. Certainly if Mary had known her she would not always have loved her so unfalteringly, but she would have been much better equipped for the emotional demands and crises in her own life.

It was probably of this nebulous personification of humanized intellectual, fascinating woman and loving mother that Mary dreamed as she sat in the spring sunshine, her mother's books in her lap and her ring on her hand.

The fifth of May was an important day. Shelley was due to dine with Godwin to discuss money. He had been ensconced in Bracknell with the seductive Boinvilles and this was the first time for quite a few months that he had come to Skinner Street. It was not a family meal but the young women of the house made sure they caught at least a glimpse of him and he of them. Shelley was under increasing financial pressure from Godwin and his own creditors and had come to London to arrange a further crippling loan to pay off his most threatening debts and to further subsidize Godwin. Although this one-way cash flow was quite consistent with the principles of both of them – that those who have should distribute the surplus amongst the deserving have-nots – it was only human of Shelley to resent increasingly the ruinous debts he had to incur in order to keep his own and Godwin's head above water.

It is unlikely that Shelley, harassed by grave money problems, his emotions in ferment, would have taken much notice of the three hovering girls. However, he did call the next day and he and Mary probably saw each other again. Mary's interest was already established. But by Shelley's own admission it was June before the full force of her charms assailed him:

'The originality & loveliness of Mary's character was apparent to me from her very motions & tones of voice. The irresi[s]tible wildness & sublimity of her feelings shewed itself in her gestures and her looks – Her smile, how persuasive it was & how pathetic! She is gentle, to be convinced & tender; yet not incapable of ardent indignation & hatred. I do not think that there is an excellence at which human nature can arrive that she does not indisputably possess, or of which her character does not afford manifest intimations.'[6]

Here was a girl who was quite different from any Shelley had known before. She had not the striking prettiness of Harriet but rather a strange unearthly beauty, a watchful, tranquil quality that was balm to his troubled spirit. She had the intelligence and intuition to be that 'sister to my soul' which Miss Hitchener's philosophizing temporarily had fulfilled. But for Shelley, Mary's intellectuality was united with passion, her sexuality with a sense of the unobtainable; the whole illuminated by the nimbus of Wollstonecraft and Godwin glory in irresistible combination.

Certainly Shelley could not resist. Mary understood those feelings too complex for words and answered his unspoken thoughts. She was a narcissist's dream, a rosy mirror to his soul: '... so intimately are our natures now united, that I feel whilst I describe her excellencies as if I were an egoist expatiating upon his own perfections.'[7]

Suddenly his visits to Skinner Street became more frequent. Between 19 and 29 June he dined there every day. Hogg recalled with characteristic colour and humour a visit he paid with Shelley to see Godwin:

'... he said "I must speak with Godwin; come in, I will not detain you long." I followed him through the shop, which was the only entrance, and up-stairs. We entered a room on the first floor; it was shaped like a quadrant. In the arc were windows; in one radius a fire place, and in the other a door, and shelves with many old books. William Godwin was not at home. Bysshe strode about the room, causing the crazy floor of the ill-built, unowned dwelling house to shake and tremble under his impatient footsteps. He appeared to be displeased at not finding the fountain of *Political Justice*. "Where is Godwin?" he asked me several times as if I knew. I did not know, and, to say the truth, I did not care. He continued his uneasy promenade; and I stood reading the names of old English authors on the backs of the venerable volumes, when the door was partially and softly opened: A thrilling voice called "Shelley". A thrilling voice answered "Mary!" And he darted out of the room, like an arrow from the bow of the far-shooting king. A very young female, fair and fair-haired, pale indeed, and with a piercing look, wearing a frock of tartan, an unusual dress in London at that time, had called him out of the room. He was absent for a very short time – a minute or two; and then returned.

"Godwin is out; there is no use in waiting." So we continued our walk along Holborn.

'"Who was that, pray?" I asked; "a daughter?"

'"Yes."

'"A daughter of William Godwin?"

'"The daughter of Godwin and Mary."'[8]

There were walks, too. Shelley would join Mary on her pilgrimage to her mother's grave. Jane would sometimes accompany them as a sort of chaperone; not that her presence was any great discouragement as it turned out. She wrote, when very much older, her reminiscences of those days. 'We both used to walk with him in the Wilderness of the Charterhouse and also to Mary Wollstonecraft's tomb – they always sent me to walk some distance from them, alleging that they wished to talk on philosophical subjects and that I did not like or know anything about those subjects – I willingly left. I did not hear what they talked about.'[9] No doubt in the beginning it ranged widely over philosophy, literary speculations, Shelley's own poems and projects; for Mary it was a thoroughgoing emotional and intellectual awakening. Shelley's prodigious imagination and unorthodox mind brought a thrill to learning which Godwin, with his narrower disciplines and more pedestrian ways, rarely managed to impart.

With their growing intimacy Shelley confided his fears and frustrations, his disappointment in Harriet and the betrayal and rejection by his family. Mary unburdened her hatred of her step-mother, her love for Godwin and her lonely childhood, her regrets at never having known her mother whose grave was their destination. As they walked in the hot June days, picking their way through the crowded, littered streets of the city towards St Pancras churchyard, they realized that each could save, protect and succour the other. It was inevitable that their rapt and mutual attraction should flare into passion, exaggerated by the youthful perspective of uniqueness and urgency. Mary was prepared in every way by her upbringing to fall in love with someone like Shelley: an intellectual, a poet, humanitarian and political radical, willing to act on his principles. But most tellingly, and despite her rational upbringing, Shelley's looks appealed; he was so familiarly fair and clear and girlish, with little threat of the beast in man.

The walks and meetings continued, each trying to hide from the other the true nature of their feelings. Until on 26 June by her mother's grave, Mary candidly declared her love for Shelley and offered herself to him on any terms. This simple, straightforward approach amazed and thrilled Shelley and he wrote later to Hogg, 'No expressions can convey the remotest conception of the *manner* in which she dispelled my delusions.'[10] Godwin maintained that Shelley seduced her on her own mother's gravestone but it seems more likely that any seduction was initiated by Mary. The anxieties and guilt, the vacillation and conflict with duty which had been plaguing Shelley, were temporarily washed away. The sky was clear and the sun was shining as they walked back to Skinner Street, their arms intertwined. For Mary then, life and love were simple things.

Full of confidence and hope for the future, Shelley revealed his and Mary's love to Godwin who, contrary to his famous anti-marriage principles, was horrified and alarmed. He argued so passionately in favour of the duty and advisability of patching up the relationship with Harriet that he wrung from Shelley a promise to renounce his passion for Mary.

Mary continued to see him, for he still dined at the Godwins's until the end of the month, both of them trying hard to act the part of friends, not lovers. Mary was closeted in Skinner Street with Mrs Godwin's suspicious eye on her, watching every mood and move. But the constraints intensified the agony and attraction of forbidden love. Godwin's fears were not fully allayed for his diary noted 'Talk with Mary'[11] on 8 July, and the following day he sat down to compose a ten-page letter to Shelley. Mary could tearfully and painfully assure her father that their relationship would continue only as friendship and that she would neither encourage nor entertain anything more. But she confided her real and tumultuous feelings to her copy of *Queen Mab* which had been given to her by Shelley, with this dedication scribbled in pencil, 'You see, Mary, I have not forgotten you'. At the end of the book she herself wrote:

'July 1814

This book is sacred to me, and as no other shall ever look into it, I may write what I please. Yet what shall I write? That I love the author beyond all powers of expression and that I am parted from him. Dearest and only love, by that love we have promised to each other, although I may not be yours, I can never be another's. But I am thine, exclusively thine.'

She then wrote out a modified stanza of Byron's poem *To Thyrza*:

'By the kiss of love, the glance none saw beside,
The smile none else might understand,
The whispered thought of heart allied,
The pressure of the thrilling hand,

I have pledged myself to thee, sacred is the gift. I remember your words, "You are now, Mary, going to mix with many, and for a moment I shall depart, but in the solitude of your chamber I shall be with you." Yes, you are ever with me, sacred vision.'

Then more Byronic adaptation:

> 'But ah! I feel in this was given
> A blessing never meant for me,
> Thou art too like a dream from heaven
> For earthly love to merit thee.'[12]

It was a miserable and overwrought time for everyone. Mrs Godwin had a story to relate which, although coloured with bias against Shelley, nevertheless echoed earlier dramatic and frantic gestures and gave a likely and distinct impression of the extent of Mary and Shelley's distress:

> 'Shelley suddenly entered the shop and went upstairs.... He looked extremely wild. He pushed me aside with extreme violence, and entering, walked straight to Mary "They wish to separate us, my beloved; but Death shall unit us," and offered her a bottle of laudanum. "By this you can escape from tyranny; and this," taking a small pistol from his pocket, "shall re-unite me to you." Poor Mary turned as pale as a ghost, and my poor silly [Jane] who is so timid even at trifles, at the sight of the pistol filled the room with her shrieks ... with tears streaming down her cheeks, [Mary] entreated him to calm himself and go home.... "I won't take this laudanum; but if you will only be reasonable and calm, I will promise to be ever faithful to you." This seemed to calm him, and he left the house leaving the phial of laudanum on the table.'[13]

Shelley had succeeded in enacting the sort of melodramatic gesture of which most adolescents merely dream. It was probably poor Mary's first taste of the extremities of feeling and action to which he could go. One thing was certain: this enforced separation and antagonism to their love only served to determine Mary's emotional commitment and set Shelley's obduracy in the face of yet another case of parental tyranny.

Mary adored and respected her father and had a naturally strong desire to please him, but for the first time in her life she was caught in the mainstream of passion. Shelley had suddenly invaded her life and overcome her will; all her thoughts were for him, all she wanted was him. Moreover, he *needed* her; that age-old hook had become embedded in her heart, for Shelley had revealed to her how vulnerable he was, how ill-used. From his birth he had been misunderstood and rejected, first by his family, tortured at school, now trapped by Harriet into marriage, then let down by her coldness, lack of intellectual application and final apostasy. To Mary he was a prodigy burdened by a world too narrow to contain his genius. Without her his suffering and drive to self-destruction would continue unabated; she alone could secure him with her unfaltering love and salve his spirit with her belief in his genius.

Mary grew paler and more reserved. Jane was her only confidante and she could be flippant and irresponsible, unable to grasp the force of emotions involved. Shelley was distraught and far from resigned to the situation. He wrote summoning Harriet from Bath, where she had been feeling abandoned and alarmed by the lack of communication from him. She came immediately and was appalled to be faced with Shelley's bald announcement that he was passionately in love with Mary. With remarkable sophistry he made it difficult for Harriet to protest without sounding petty and churlish; he still loved her, of course, but theirs had been a relationship based more on friendship and brotherly attachment; she had known that, she knew his views on marriage when they first eloped together. 'It is no reproach to me that you have never filled my heart with an all-sufficing passion – perhaps you are even yourself a stranger to these impulses. . . .' So saying, he added how as brother/father/friend he would love all the more his Harriet and Ianthe, financially he would provide for them and everything would be lovely. She should love Mary too: 'to the most indifferent eyes she would be interesting only from her sufferings, & the tyranny which is exercised upon her'.[14]

Harriet would have time to reflect bitterly that just two years previously her own sufferings from parental opposition were what had roused Shelley's quixotic interest in her. But stunned and shocked she could only be compliant with his wishes, hoping it was merely an infatuation and that eventually he would return to her. Godwin was doing his best to mend the relationship; Mary was confined to the house, he visited Harriet, interviewed Shelley, and enlisted even Mrs Boinville's help.

But Shelley was busy absolving himself of any blame for this desertion of his wife and children – for Harriet was pregnant again – and from any responsibility other than the financial. Mary in her inexperience and youthful idealism spared hardly a thought for Harriet's plight. She had forfeited Shelley's love through her own inadequacies and stupidity and, love being all, it was only right that Shelley should be free to move on and love another. His philosophies, her father's too, supported the principle of individual honesty and choice. Then a mere sixteen, Mary felt no guilt. She was to learn compassion with the years and the loss of her own beloved ones, but was to grieve for Harriet too late, and suffer the stings of unabsolved remorse. 'Poor Harriet, to whose sad fate I attribute so many of my own heavy sorrows, as the atonement claimed by fate for her death',[15] Mary wrote in her journal in 1839.

Although Mary and Shelley were reasoning in the light of Godwin's principles of free love, her father had grown more pragmatic, his critics might say hypocritical, with age. He was fully aware of the social ostracism his daughter faced, of Harriet's despair and loneliness as a discarded wife and mother, for had not he inherited Mary Wollstonecraft's bruised heart, the result of a similar abandonment? He knew Shelley was an unstable young man whose volatile affections could ruin his daughter's life as they threatened to ruin little Harriet's. He was determined to play the heavy father and do all he could to prevent it. However, he did not bargain with his own daughter's strength of mind.

Years later Mary wrote that despite a certain indolence, when she really desired something she 'would go thro' fire and water',[16] and she desired Shelley undoubtedly more than anything else in the world. Rebellion was stirring in her breast. It was oppressive being confined to the small, hot, noisy house; she was tired of the shelves upon shelves of weighty tomes in her father's study which were her sole contact with the outside world – and then it was a dusty, dry and passionless place. The only part of the world she wanted to know was the bright white arc that Shelley inhabited. Neither could Shelley stand passively by and allow anything that even whiffed of proscription or obstruction of his desires and rights to go unchallenged. He had, after all, once before snatched the closeted daughter of the house from under her father's nose. Godwin should have known better what to expect.

5
Vagabondage through France

> 'Mary especially seems insensible to all future evil....'
> Shelley's entry in Mary's journal

Mary and Shelley were determined that their fates were inextricably entwined. He justified his actions by the ill behaviour of others, 'the cruelty & injustice with which we were treated impelled us to disregard, all consideration but that of the happiness of each other'.[1] Mary was more clear-sighted; uneasily ignoring the problem of Harriet's and her children's rights, she was quite aware nevertheless of her abandonment of her beloved father; but Shelley came first and a new and brilliant light beckoned to her from the world beyond Skinner Street.

They had decided to elope to the Continent. At the last moment they agreed that Jane should come as well. From Mary's point of view it was to be a disastrous and far-reaching decision for they were uniting her fate with theirs. But it seemed sensible at the time. She herself begged to be allowed to come; her romanticism and sense of adventure were flying high for she had been involved vicariously in the excitement of Mary and Shelley's affair, fascinated by but excluded from the sexuality that enthralled them. Skinner Street could offer little inducement to stay when the alternative was escape with an admired step-sister and her handsome poet. Vagabondage through France was much more thrilling than plodding the stuffy streets of Smithfield doing the shopping for a cross and philistine mother. They were going to be romantic exiles. Mary was more matter of fact; she was suddenly apprehensive about the journey, perhaps also about Shelley with whom she had yet to spend a whole day, let alone a night. Anyway Jane could speak French and would be useful.

Shelley was never averse to rescuing young women from tyranny, neither was he averse to having two women in his entourage; with Harriet he had always felt happier when the exclusivity of the relationship was diluted by the presence of a third person.

The early morning of Thursday, 28 July, was to be Mary's genesis. She hardly slept. She quickly wrote a letter of explanation and apology to her father. It was terrible to have to steal out of his house like a thief in the night, but for the sake of her love and her Shelley it had to be done. She was fully aware that, being under age, she could be pursued and wrested from her lover's arms. As the night wore on the thought of this and her father's pain and anger, the dark unknown into which she was fleeing, all made her faint with trepidation. Her ears strained to catch the distant rattle of the coach wheels or, God forbid, the creak of her father's or step-mother's door. Jane was dizzy with excitement, neither doubts nor apprehension clouded her gleeful anticipation.

At last St Sephulchre's clock chimed four. It was the hour that Shelley had appointed for their escape. The night was paling into dawn as Mary, followed by Jane, tiptoed into the street. Shelley was nervously waiting, and Mary ran to him, almost collapsing in his arms. Their meagre baggage was quickly loaded on and they clambered in. The coach clattered off over the cobbles. At last they were together, alone except for Jane, her face wide-eyed and flushed as she sat opposite swaying happily to the rhythm of the coach. Mary was less resilient. As the day wore on, she was travel-sick and prostrate with nervous exhaustion and the heat. They travelled under the blazing summer sun, Mary resting at every stage. Shelley too was disquieted, anxious for her comfort, elated at finally possessing 'this inestimable treasure'[2] and fearful of pursuit. They dared not let up their pace and arrived at Dover at four in the afternoon.

Finally, after a meal and haggling with sailors and custom-house officers, they sailed off in a tiny boat with a couple of crew bound for Calais. Shelley wrote in the journal that they decided to keep, 'The evening was most beautiful; the sands slowly receded; we felt safe; there was little wind, the sails flapped in the flagging breeze.'[3] Their tranquillity and sense of safety were not to last long. The breeze stiffened to a gale, a storm broke, lashing the fragile boat which was shipping water at an alarming rate. Luckily Mary was so seasick and emotionally exhausted that she was oblivious of their moments of real peril. She lay in Shelley's arms until, when he was too fatigued to support her, she slipped down to lean between his knees and remained there silent and still. Their clothes were soaked from the spray, their hair and faces stiff with salt. Shelley had time to reflect on death and found it 'rather a thing of discomfort and disappointment than horror to me. We should never be separated, but in death we might not know and feel our union as now.'[4] With Mary's ashen face in his lap, with the running sea threatening to engulf their little craft, this was a strange yet characteristic passivity and resignation in the face of death.

The wind died down and blew them straight into Calais. Jane, who was an excellent sailor anyway, was already enjoying herself, contemplating the fuss at home and the adventures to come. Mary was sleeping as they beached and Shelley woke her to show her the broad sun rising over France.

Mary stumbled stiffly through the sand to an inn where they took a room and had breakfast. In the evening they received the news that they had been expecting for the last twelve hours, that 'a fat lady had arrived'.[5] Mrs Godwin had valiantly and determinedly pursued them across the Channel in an attempt at saving her daughter's virtue, reputation, and possibly her life. Mary, whom she had always thought sly and deceitful, was now quite beyond hope. But her Jane was too innocent, too dutiful to embark of her own free will on such a madcap escapade. What fearful thoughts had crowded poor Mrs Godwin's mind on that long, uncomfortable journey? Perhaps Shelley had seduced her daughter too? Certainly Mary had put her under some sort of duress or tricked her with characteristic duplicity.

Jane spent the night with her mother who appealed directly and emotionally to her to return. She nearly succumbed to her entreaties but at the last moment decided to continue the adventure. Mrs Godwin surprisingly accepted the decision and, with no further admonitions, left to make her return journey unhappily and alone. In fact she had every reason to fear for Jane's future. She became as much a social outcast as Mary and Shelley, yet for eight years she lived in their shadow. Their influence for better or worse affected the whole course of her long life and her spirited and interesting personality was to be unfulfilled and thwarted by early tragedy and the hardship and frustration to come. However, quite unaware of any blots on their horizon, the extremely youthful and bedraggled party set off that

Friday evening for Boulogne on their way to Paris. They travelled all day and sometimes all night and arrived on the Tuesday. Mary was still not very well and the six days they tarried in Paris restored her.

She retrieved from their luggage her precious box of papers, previously kept covertly for no eyes but hers. She had promised that Shelley could read her early writings, her father's letters to her and others from her friends, all carefully stowed therein along with other keepsakes. Mary was intoxicated with love and high on freedom. Europe stretched before her, enticing, dazzling, and nothing could prevent her sharing its treasures with Shelley. Never particularly practical at the best of times, Mary abandoned reason to the emotions that engulfed her. 'Mary especially seems insensible to all future evil. She feels as if our love would alone suffice to resist the invasions of calamity.'[6] She was content to lie in Shelley's arms, hardly bothering to eat. One night they lay awake until the dawn light seeped through the shutters, 'too happy to sleep'.[7] Mary's sixteen years of regulated and repressed affection had found luxurious expression. It was probably during this rapturous week that Mary conceived.

Despite their ecstasy and elation, it must have been at times a trying week. They were attempting unsuccessfully to raise a loan and settle their passports, and Shelley had to sell his watch and chain. They received a cold, disapproving letter from the bookseller, Thomas Hookham; antagonism towards Shelley was brewing at home and the Boinvilles and Hookham had joined the Godwins in denunciation of his character and behaviour. Mary's box of treasures, too, was lost or stolen during these days in Paris.

Amid all this, Shelley had forgotten his twenty-second birthday. When Mary reminded him on 1 August he told her that he thought his birthday had been 27 June, that sunny day by her mother's tomb when Mary had revealed her love for him. She did some sightseeing with Shelley; they were eager to visit the key points of a city which had been the spiritual mecca of every European radical twenty years before. They were delighted to retrace Napoleon's footsteps, for he was another revolutionary hero of theirs, until he too turned to aggrandizement and imperialism. For Mary, seeing Paris was particularly poignant for here her mother was for a time most happy and passionately in love. However, the more orthodox sights got short shrift: the gardens of the Tuileries were 'very formal and uninteresting, without any grass'; the Louvre was rather dull, only one picture was really impressive, otherwise as Shelley remarked, 'There was Hell and Heaven also; the Blessed looked too stupid.'[8]

At long last they managed to raise some £60 and on the following Monday, the eighth, Shelley went with Jane, whose French was just about up to bargaining, to buy a donkey. They intended to walk to Uri on Lake Lucerne and possibly set up a community of soul brothers and sisters to live together in creative harmony and freedom. The mistress of the hotel was horrified at the idea of their walking unprotected through the war-ravaged countryside. France had only just emerged from the Napoleonic wars and the devastation of defeat was everywhere visible. The potential dangers to three naïve English travellers were great. The Shelley party would have been amongst the first tourists into Europe after over a decade of wars. Hordes were to follow their example in the peaceful century to come, but in the meantime these pioneers had to contend with the threat of roving bands of cut-throats and footpads, the odd deserter living on his wits and brutalized by years of privation and killing, the starving uprooted peasants who would hardly welcome well-heeled young English folk with their eyes on the scenery and heads in the clouds.

Nevertheless these three adventurers set off in neither doubt nor trepidation. Mary and Jane were to ride on the donkey but the ass merchant had sold them a lame one and, instead of it carrying them, they ended up having to carry the animal to Charenton where they sold it and bought a mule. Shelley was aware that once again the bargain was not in their favour. Yet it seemed nothing could dampen their high spirits. Mary was to write twelve years later that,

> 'every inconvenience was hailed as a new chapter in the romance of our travels ... we saw with extasy the strange costume of the French women, read with delight our own descriptions in the passport, looked with curiosity on every *plât* fancying that the fried leaves of artichokes were frogs; we saw shepherds in opera-hats, and post-boys in jack-boots; and (*pour comble de merveille*) heard little boys and girls talk French; it was acting a novel, being an incarnate romance.'[9]

This reminiscence captured the ingenuousness and enthusiasm of all three of them on their outward journey. As they travelled further from Paris the only available accommodation became meaner and more repellent. The beds were habitually filthy. Mary specially made the observation that they had discovered with some amazement 'that the inhabitants were not in the habit of washing themselves either when they rose or went to bed'. There were rats to contend with which were bold enough, as Jane claimed, to 'put their cold paws upon her face'.[10] Food was meagre and unappetizing, milk and sour bread one day followed the next by fare at such a loathsome inn that they could hardly force down the little sustenance they were offered. Although Mary, like Shelley, was not particularly interested in food, she must have been permanently hungry and certainly her awareness and emotions were heightened by her semi-fast.

She found the villages they passed through beautiful, despite the fact that as they approached Troyes, every settlement and practically every building had been razed to the ground by the avenging Cossacks. The peasants' homes were destroyed, their animals and poultry taken, and one man they met claimed they had murdered his children. None of these desolate sights and miserable tales seemed to subdue their zest. Jane noted that 'old towns are always dirty'[11] and quite happily would have had them all pulled down and destroyed.

On Saturday, 13 August, they finally reached Troyes. Shelley had sprained an ankle and Mary gave up her place on the mule to him. As they approached the last long haul into the town they were very weary and grey with dust from the dry dirt roads. The countryside had been chalky and uncultivated for miles and the peasants desperately poor. Village upon village was reduced to mounds of white stones and charred timbers. They talked, Jane sang and Shelley told Mary the story of the Seven Sleepers to pass the time. On the outskirts of Troyes the fields were once again cultivated, this time with vines for they were in the heart of champagne country.

They limped into the town. Mary was really flagging by now and they decided then and there to exchange their mule for a cart or carriage of some sort to take them quickly on to Neuchâtel. The filth, misery and grinding poverty of ravaged France made Mary wish to cross the border into Switzerland as quickly as possible. They found it difficult to pity the inhabitants of this devasted countryside because they were 'the most unamiable, inhospitable & unaccommodating of the human race'.[12]

It was from Troyes that Shelley wrote his sincere but blunderingly insensitive letter to Harriet. No doubt Mary and he were utterly engrossed in their own pleasures and emotions, each discovering the other. Harriet's loneliness and dejection all those hundreds of miles away was then quite beyond their understanding and sympathies. Mary must have been very confident of her sexual and emotional hold over Shelley to agree to his invitation to Harriet to join them in a community in the mountains: 'I write to show you that I do not forget you. I write to urge you to come to Switzerland, where you will at least find one firm & constant friend, to whom your interests will always be dear, by whom your feelings will never wilfully be injured. From none can you expect this but me.'[13] Of course it was the last thing Harriet would have wanted or attempted. To drag herself, already swelling with her second pregnancy, together with her fifteen-month-old daughter Ianthe, through a perilous country to join the unpredictable Shelley and his Godwin girls, to live as his rejected sexual partner for ever in the shadow of this paragon of wit and sensibility, who had seduced him away in the first place – it was madness, and insult.

Having secured a *voiture*, Mary, Shelley and Jane rose very early on the Sunday morning and left at four. Mary had become accustomed to the scenes of ruined villages and expanses of unproductive land and it was a pleasure and a surprise to come upon a section of the Aube valley which differed so radically. Steep hills hanging with vines and dark with trees reared up on either side of the narrow valley. As their old vehicle trundled down between them, Mary could see sunny green meadows basking amongst the wooded slopes. With delight she pointed out the spires of village churches amid the trees, the first sign in miles that anything had survived the marauding Cossacks.

Mary had been keeping her and Shelley's journal assiduously, writing it up at night or, if she had a moment, en route. Jane became enthusiastic about the idea and cajoled Shelley into giving her one of his notebooks for the purpose. Her breathless, at times incoherent, but always lively diary started on this Sunday 14 August.

They were in the outlying hills of the Alps. The varied and bold scenery of forest, hill and stream enchanted Mary and filled them all with excited anticipation at seeing the real mountains. On the Tuesday Mary and Shelley met a little girl, Marguerite Pascal, and were so taken with her beauty that they requested that her father allow them to take her with them. Luckily he refused.

During all these days of journeying they were rising at four and travelling through the day until evening. The following day the *voiturier* insisted that they spend the night at Mort. The beds were too filthy to sleep in so Mary and Shelley went out on to the rocks of the Alpine foothills and read her mother's autobiographical novel *Mary* until the light faded. The rest of the night was spent uncomfortably, Mary dozing fitfully by the kitchen fireside, Shelley troubled 'by the creaking door, the screams [of] a poor smothered child & the fille who washed the glasses'.[14]

They were off again at dawn, unrefreshed and fatigued. It was now 18 August, and at last the hills were looming into mountains. Mary's spirit was revived by this spectacular scenery.

> 'From the summit of one of the hills we see the whole expanse of the valley filled with a white undulating mist, over which the piny hills pierced like islands. The sun had just risen, and a ray of the red light lay on the waves of this fluctuating vapour. To the west, opposite the sun, it seemed driven by the light against the rock in immense masses of foaming cloud until it becomes lost in the distance, mixing its tints with the fleecy sky.'[15]

They asked the *voiturier* to wait for them as they walked into the pine forest to gaze at the sentinel trees and breathe the dark, tangy air. On their return he had gone. Shelley had riled and incensed him over the last few days and this request was the last straw. However, in Jane's amended journal, she gave a different explanation for the *voiturier*'s departure. Written a few years later, it was possibly coloured by a bitterness that surfaced when Mary had aggravated her sisterly competitiveness and envy, nevertheless it gave a vivid picture of how Shelley's frolics could force Mary to retreat from natural reserve into false prudery.

> '... we came to a clear running shallow stream, and Shelley entreated the Driver to stop while he from under a bank could bathe himself – and he wanted Mary to do the same as the Bank sheltered one from every eye – but Mary would not – first, she said it would be most indecent, and then also she had no towel and could not dry herself – He said he would gather leaves from the trees and she could dry herself with those but she refused and said how could he think of such a thing....'[16]

Shelley's naked cavortings finally decided the *voiturier* that indeed he was a mad Englishman, and he made all haste to be off. His passengers carried on along the road on foot. He left a message that he would be at Pontarlier on the French side of the border. Mary walked on. The clean smell of pine was in the air. The dark forests shadowed the mountainsides above them and filled the deep valleys below. It was night before they arrived in Pontarlier.

They found their errant *voiturier* who 'makes a thousand excuses – all falsehoods'.[17] As they were about to cross into Switzerland Mary slept in a clean bed for the first time since she had left home, but after her day's walk she was too tired to appreciate the luxury and could only curl up against Shelley in oblivious sleep. Jane's presence and the prevalence of bug-filled beds meant that circumstances were not the most comfortable for Mary and Shelley's sexual discovery – unless, on their long rapturous walks through the woods, passion at times managed to overcome Mary's modesty.

Friday dawned fine and full of promise; all being well, they expected to reach Neuchâtel. They left at three in the morning and on horseback rode to the border and there engaged a more good-natured but garrulous *voiturier*. They trundled slowly through the most breathtaking Alpine scenery, gasping and gaping at the mountains that jutted above them, sunless forests, the slabs of barren rock amid glades so luminously green and fertile that the senses tingled.

Mary expected to see the real Alps at every turn in the track. The *voiturier* was mumbling on about the excellent pasture and the local cheese. These mundanities irritated Jane, distracting her from poetic appreciation of the scene. Mary hardly heard his dairy logic; she had relinquished sense to sensation. To these young travellers it was intensity of experience that mattered and a sight of the Alps was something to be relished and remembered. Her imagination was in flight to something more vivid than anything inspired by the bleaker, humbler landscape of Tayside.

Then suddenly they glimpsed what they had been anticipating for days, the Alps, exalted and timeless, in a turbulent sea of mountains. Shelley cried out, Jane could not believe it: 'I thought they were white flaky clouds.'[18] For Mary it was almost too great an assault on her senses and imagination:

'Hill after hill is seen extending its craggy outline before the other, and far behind all, towering above every feature of the scene, the snowy Alps; they are 100 miles distant; they look like those accumulated clouds of dazzling white that arrange themselves on the horizon in summer. This immensity staggers the imagination, and so surpasses all conception that it requires an effort of the understanding to believe that they are indeed mountains.'[19]

This awesome scenery was to have a lasting effect on both Mary and Shelley; their impressions were to be put to great effect in their literary works, notably Shelley's *Alastor* and *Prometheus Unbound*, and more significantly Mary's *Frankenstein* where the force and menace of the narrative accumulated through Mary's evocation of this overwhelmingly powerful landscape.

They travelled the remaining six miles to Neuchâtel in high spirits and poetizing rhapsody. Jane, less susceptible to landscape than Mary, had noticed with relief and patriotic enthusiasm (as far as we know her father was Swiss) that the Swiss character was a vast improvement on the French:

'The Cottages & people (as if by magic) became almost instantaneously clean & hospitable – The children were rosy & interesting, no sallow care worn looks – in France it is almost impossible to see a woman that looks under fifty – most of them bear marks of advanced age – their cottages are in a horrible state – dirt & ruin seem to have taken up their everlasting abode with them but in Switzerland (which I love to consider my own country) you see cheerful content & smiling healthy faces.'[20]

No doubt this restored something of her sense of importance and identity; many times she had felt excluded by the young lovers who would go off on walks alone and sit into the night reading together, discussing subjects and philosophies considered by them to be far too recondite for her immature understanding. She was half-Swiss after all, she belonged amongst this breathtaking scenery, she felt romantically that she had come home.

They slept in a spick-and-span inn in the town. The following day was a Saturday and Mary and Shelley surveyed their situation. There were no letters at the *bureau de poste* and they were seriously short of money having been cheated on every commercial transaction along the way. Shelley set off to see the town's banker but with little hope of reflation. Having been told to wait for two hours for an answer he was summoned and, to Mary's amazement and delight, returned staggering into their room with a canvas bag bulging with silver. The unexpected sight of so much money sent Mary into a fit of high spirits. But Shelley knew only too well how £38 could be like quicksilver through their fingers.

With money in his pocket Shelley booked three seats the following morning on a *voiture* bound for Lucerne. The morning of Sunday, 21 August, dawned cool and misty. They were off by six and although the Alps were veiled from view there was a lot to see as they travelled through picturesque but more subdued countryside. They exclaimed at the clean towns, the fountains and the scrubbed faces of the people.

The novelty and euphoria of their early elopement was beginning to wear thin. Mary was finding Jane's continual presence at times particularly disruptive. It was difficult enough having to share her honeymoon with a third person, but the fact that the person was Jane compounded the intrusion. Clever as Mary was, she sadly lacked a sense of humour, a buffer against the everyday irritations of life and the extremities of fortune. Living with Jane demanded both humour and tolerance. She would interrupt Mary's intense and idealistic discussions with Shelley with interjections which were often flippant and inappropriate. She could dominate proceedings and turn them her way, especially when Shelley, who seldom could resist the challenge of enlightening the mind of a credulous young woman, broke off to explain a point in eloquent detail. She upset the fine balance of Mary's growing relationship with Shelley. Here the roots of all Mary's future trouble with Jane were being set down firmly.

Jane liked and admired Shelley and with natural adolescent self-interest felt herself to be in some sort of competition with Mary for his affection and attention. It was inevitable that as a child she should have felt a mixture of envy and awe for her slightly older, arrogant and remarkable step-sister. Now that she was growing up, her feelings towards Mary, and Mary's for her, were complicated by the presence of Shelley. Jane was resentful that Mary was yet again the favoured one; she had captured an intellectual, a radical and a poet; to a girl brought up in a Godwin household there could be no more seductive a package than that.

Mary realized this as Jane increased her claims on Shelley. On that Sunday of 21 August resentments reached a head, the first of many, and there was an argument between the two girls. Shelley had a salutary talk 'concerning Jane's character',[21] Mary noted in her journal. Jane later destroyed the page from her own journal which mentioned this talk and her feelings about Shelley and what he had to say. She certainly sulked for the rest of the day and Mary's mood was spoiled too. They arrived in the evening at Soleure and Mary went with Shelley to see the cathedral there. However, its attractions were not such as to revive their low spirits for she damned it in her journal as 'very modern and stupid'.[22]

The next day was as bad. Again they were up early in the bitterly cold morning. Grandiose mountain scenery was becoming monotonous and overbearing. Mary's spirits no longer soared as she surveyed the serried peaks and rock-scarred slopes that closed in around them. She was not feeling well and the motion of the *voiture* increased her queasiness. She was fully a month pregnant and was probably by now aware of her condition. She was not quite seventeen and having a baby by a married man who had deserted his own pregnant wife and his child to be with her. By her precipitate behaviour, its flagrance established beyond doubt by her pregnancy, Mary knew that she had alienated her family and outraged society. But yet she longed to be loved, she needed friends and she still loved her father inordinately. Despite her intellectual unorthodoxy and liberal ideals, in reality she felt some trepidation for the future, especially on the bad days when she felt sick, was irritated by Jane and lost faith in the feasibility of their community of kindred spirits that they hoped to set up on the shores of Lake Lucerne.

Shelley, too, was in a 'jocosely horrible mood'.[23] But on the next day all doubts were dispelled. They arrived at Lucerne in time for a late second breakfast and were once again delighted with the scenery. It was a beautiful day and they embarked on a boat trip down the lake. The towering pine trees grew darkly and closely packed to the water's edge. Rocky outcrops interrupted the flow of the forest and Mary gazed up to the ever-present mountains, their snowcaps invading the sky. During the journey Shelley produced his copy of Barruel's *Histoire de Jacobinism* and they read it together as they passed through the unremittingly grand lakeside scenery on their way to found an enlightened community of their own.

Having arrived at Bressen, Shelley eventually procured a room at nearby Brunnen with terrible beds but a predictably awesome view from the window. Mary stood with Shelley looking out on the choppy lake and the waves that broke insistently on the shore below the house. The next morning the wind was blowing and the lake was still turbulent when Mary awoke. The dirt and dinginess of their little room and the lumpy coarseness of their beds, greasy from the unwashed bodies of the occupants before her, filled her with disgust and despair. She woke Shelley; they had to find a house.

Fired with this resolve they were up and off and, with Jane, began to look for lodgings. After various frustrations and, as Mary was beginning to think they would never find a place of their own, they discovered a small two-roomed apartment in an ugly house called the Château. Lacking the energy to look any further, Mary agreed with Shelley on this compromise. They rented it for six months at the rate of one louis per month. Tired out, resigned but relieved, the three young English travellers returned to their inn. Having eaten supper Mary and Shelley left Jane and went off to sit by the lakeside and read Tacitus's *History of the Siege of Jerusalem* until the distant banks were obscured in the gathering dusk.

The following day was Thursday, 25 August, and, although it was cloudy, Mary's spirits were high. She and Shelley read a bit more of Barruel's *History*. They moved into their lodgings and Mary attempted to make it look cosy while outside the sky darkened and it began to rain. The clouds came rolling down the mountainside enclosing their little house between lake, rock and louring sky. Jane was restless and bad-tempered. She was disillusioned with the Swiss and sat writing in her journal about 'the amazing populousness of the country. The Mountains are covered with cottages – It is impossible to find a wild & entire solitude....' Apart from there being too many of them, the Swiss were no longer the attractive and admirable race embraced so keenly the previous week as her romantic heritage. 'The people are uninteresting for they are most immoderately stupid & almost ugly to deformity – The children beg the moment they see you – not from poverty but merely from habit which I suppose has descended from their ancestors who originally begged from Poverty.'[24] Having vented some of her frustration with the weather and her disappointment that their romantic dash across Europe should end so tamely in boring little Brunnen, Jane decided to go to bed early.

Mary had sat down at a table next to Shelley and together they worked on a new romance entitled *The Assassins*. She contributed directly to this composition as well as assuming what was to become a familiar role as Shelley's amanuensis. This unfinished novel reflected Shelley and Mary's interests and preoccupations during those fleeting summer days. It began with the siege of Jerusalem, from which a revolutionary band of Christians escaped to an Alpine paradise exotically set in the Lebanon. They founded an enclosed community and practised a way of life echoed in every essential a century and a half later by the hippy culture of west-coast America. They were gentle, peace-loving, sexually free and intellectually tolerant; hedonists to whom pleasure was the chief good. It illustrated a timeless urge to return to the simple life, close to nature, but with the benefit of extraordinary awareness, intensified perception and ecstatic appreciation of that nature. Shelley and Mary here were rejecting the sterner stuff of Godwin's Utilitarianism. It was an exciting literary project for them because it was so closely linked to their insubstantial plans for setting up an equally ideal community, equally immune to the canker of the outside world. The idea appealed to them in exile. In such a haven Mary could have her baby and live freely with Shelley; they would be relieved of family pressures and responsibility, free of the censure and antagonism that awaited them in England, free, too, of financial stress, for money like food would most likely grow on the trees. Mary discussed it enthusiastically as outside the rain streamed down from the black sky.

Enthusiasm for *The Assassins* continued and Mary and Shelley worked at it through the following day. Jane was restless and bored. Their return to England was mooted. Jane was keen, she had had enough of adventuring. To Mary the dream of last night's community, happily secured within the Swiss mountains, faded in the reality of day. The apartment was unattractive and unwelcoming, lack of money contracted their freedom, homely England and the English beckoned. Jane was suddenly in no doubt about the superiority of the English: '... dear England. After having travelled & viewed the follies of other nations my own country appears the most reasonable & the most enlightened.'[25]

They decided to leave and, being spontaneous creatures, would have gone immediately if they had not had to wait for their laundry to be returned by the washerwoman. Rapid packing, relieved laughter, jokes about how their perverse behaviour would perplex the stolid citizens of Brunnen – as if that many had even noticed – kept their spirits up. Money was so tight that Shelley decided they would have to make their return journey by the waterways. It was to be a perilous, slow and uncomfortable trip. The passenger boats that plied up and down the great European rivers were often in ill-repair, used only by peasants, students and disreputables who were frequently a rough and smelly crew. Their abusiveness and vulgarity shocked the fresh-faced young English travellers who sat aloof and disdainfully amongst them.

Mary, who found seafaring such an agony, seemed to accept with equanimity this fortnight's hard travel that lay ahead. On Sunday morning they fled from Brunnen without a backward glance. The boat took them across the lake to Lucerne. It rained determinedly all day, the clouds again hanging low over the lake; the weather compounded their relief at leaving.

At Lucerne Mary and Shelley continued work on *The Assassins*. Jane was reading *King Lear* and when she reached the point 'when Cornwall tears out the eyes of the Duke of Gloster'[26] she cried out and could not continue. Soon after retiring to bed, while Mary was still up working and reading with Shelley, Jane came rushing into the room full of horrid and wild imaginings and had to be calmed and reasoned with by Shelley. Mary found she was less patient with her sister but Shelley was good at being reassuring, and anyway was rather intrigued by her horrors for they reminded him of fiendish visions which used to pursue him as a younger man. Jane's horrors were to become a feature of Mary and Shelley's life with her; at times Jane and Shelley would inflame each other's lurid imaginations, each scaring the other so much that Mary had to intervene, to mediate and restore them.

The next day they boarded the boat that sailed the river Reuss to Basle. Again it rained all day into the dark water, broken by stretches of rapids through which the boatload surfed. It was Mary's first acquaintance with the sort of roughnecks who shared their journey. Her natural sensitivity to her surroundings was intensified by her pregnancy, and the ugliness and coarseness of their companions repulsed her; they were 'loathsome creepers' with their 'horrid and slimy faces'. With a surprising illiberality and characteristic lack of compromise she decided that these monsters could never be enlightened or improved and so the best answer was 'to absolutely annihilate such uncleanly animals'.[27] That murderous resolve made her feel better for she did not even mind the rain that drenched every man, woman and beast crouched and steaming in the dirty boat.

Tuesday, 30 August, was Mary's seventeenth birthday. It was to be a happy yet anxious day. Mary recorded in her journal her satisfaction with the present and hopes for the future: 'We expect to be, not happier, but more at our ease before the year passes.'[28] Certainly she had little expectation of less ease; they left Basle on the River Rhine swollen with the past week's rain, heading into a gusting wind that chilled them through and increased the sickening pitch of their boat. Then suddenly this broad, full river was compressed into a narrow channel between the bank and a rocky pine-clad hill and they were precipitated at alarming speed down this watery helter-skelter. When their boat was back on an even keel, Shelley read aloud from Mary Wollstonecraft's *Letters from Norway* and Mary, surrounded by the grand water and mountain scenery that she had loved and lived amongst, felt a close affinity with her mother whose delight in Norwegian landscape and whose strong adventurous spirit enlivened every page of the book. Despite the hazardous journey, Mary felt her imagination soar on the heady mixture of her mother's affective description and the romantic triumph of the landscape around her:

> 'A ruined tower, with its desolated windows, stood on the summit of another hill that jutted into the river; beyond, the sunset was illuminating the mountains and the clouds, and casting the reflection of its hues on the agitated river. The brilliance and colourings in the circling whirlpools of the stream was an appearance entirely new, and most beautiful.'[29]

The rest of the journey down the Rhine followed a similar pattern of discomfort and frustrating delay, elation with the scenery and disgust at the dregs of humanity with which they had to share the diligences. Jane, appalled by the lecherous watermen kissing and embracing each other, spoke for the three of them: 'Never was a more disgraceful set than the Common order of people of Germany. Your soul shrinks back to its inmost recesses when by accident you cast your eye over countenances begrimmed with mental & bodily depravity.'[30] Nothing except the bitterest cold would induce Mary to go down into the cabin and breathe the smoky blue air. Over-friendly approaches were summarily dealt with. Mary recorded in her journal with some amusement how she and Shelley frightened off a man who wanted to practise his English, and whom they disliked, by revolutionary talk of cutting off kings' heads.

Her journal noted more frequently those times when she and Shelley were alone. To Mary at least this privacy was becoming increasingly important. As they neared Bonn and the end of their river journey Mary was sick to death of the river, the water diligences, the infuriating boatmen and their despicable passengers. Nevertheless she was to savour for years the memories of this trip down a great river where ruined castles brooded in the bordering hills.

On the evening of Monday, 5 September, they arrived in Bonn, thankfully disembarked and hired a *voiture* to take them to Cologne and on to Rotterdam. Their postillion, a German, drove maddeningly slowly, 'five times slower than a snail's walk; that is to say, rather more than a mile an hour'.[31] They made their disgruntled way across Holland. Mary was unimpressed by the flat and boring countryside and scornful of the stupidity of the people. They finally arrived in Rotterdam on the Thursday and paid off the *voiturier*. Once again they had been 'horribly cheated'[32] and were left with a mere 28 écus.

That evening Mary and Shelley reminisced on their adventure honeymoon, uneasily aware that the future that lay in wait for them in England was less carefree and less sure. Mary swore everlasting love, loyalty and allegiance to Shelley; had not she promised it in his copy of *Queen Mab* when he had given it to her that age ago? Now that she was his mistress, the undoubted sister of his soul and the mother of his unborn baby, she was all the more deeply committed to him. Just seventeen, she knew with the certainty of youth that she was his for ever, come what may.

The following day Mary left Jane reading and writing her journal and set off with Shelley to find a captain who would undertake to sail them across the Channel to England. Money proved to be a stumbling-block; Shelley bargained and eventually agreed to three guineas for each of them to be paid on arrival. They were one step nearer home. At three in the afternoon they sailed, but as they neared the mouth of the estuary the wind grew stronger and the river more turbulent and they were forced to put into Maarluis and stay the night. This was an added expense and threatened to exhaust the last of their money. The wind blew and buffeted the inn all through the night. The following day it was still too forceful and blowing towards the land. The captain and the other passengers had all decamped to Rotterdam for the day and Mary settled down to write the beginnings of a novel called *Hate*.[33] Shelley and Jane were busy writing too, Shelley working on *The Assassins* and Jane embarking on her own attempt at a Gothic novel, *The Ideot*, about a kind of noble savage.

Overnight the wind turned favourable. In the morning Mary was enthusiastically writing more of *Hate*, until they at last boarded the little boat for England. The wind was very high and the Dutch captains of the packet-boats, huddled in the harbour, called out that they were mad, they were risking their lives and would never get past the hazardous sand bar that straddled the mouth of the estuary. However, their captain was English and said 'he knew well enough what he was about & he was not going to be such a coward as the Dutchman',[34] Jane reported with glee.

The Dutchmen's prophecies were almost proved to be right. It turned out to be a terrible crossing. As they approached the sand bar the river was already running high and in the distance the waves were breaking on the bar in sprays of ominous white. Poor Mary, always pale-skinned, had turned a deathly white. She was crippled with sea-sickness and had to retire to bed amid the tobacco fumes of the other passengers in refuge below deck. This time Shelley was not cradling her in his arms but was sitting on deck with Jane, their faces full of wind and spray, braving the tempestuous crossing of the bar. The great breakers crashed against their fragile boat, some breaking over Shelley and Jane as they huddled together tense with fearful anticipation.

Mary stayed below. The wind, if anything, increased out at sea and she heard the boom break overhead with a terrible heart-stopping crash. She feared she and Shelley were going to die. Still, the gale was at least carrying them home. After the terrible night in which everyone was sick except Jane, much to her delight, Monday was calm and sunny with the distant blur of the Suffolk coast cheering their spirits. Mary was so much recovered that she and Shelley entered into an impassioned argument with a fellow passenger on the iniquities of the slave trade.

The following morning they docked at Gravesend and submitted to the questions and searches of the custom-house officials who came on board. Shelley had almost run out of money and certainly did not have the nine guineas he owed for the crossing. The captain was angry and suspicious. At length Shelley persuaded him to trust them enough to let them disembark and speed post-haste to London to collect his money.

They hired a smaller boat and were rowed by a boatman up the Thames to Blackwall. Here they piled into a coach and made for Shelley's bankers. To his dismay he found his account quite depleted by Harriet to whom he had given free access in his absence. They then rushed off to Thomas Hookham, their once friendly bookseller, but only his brother was there. He was distinctly hostile to Shelley and Mary, looking so much the vagabonds that they were: dishevelled, grubby and tired, and coolly asking for a loan in order to continue their irresponsible behaviour.

It was getting late and Mary was tired and beginning to despair of honouring their debt and finding somewhere to sleep. She could not face going to see her father, knowing how icy would be his displeasure. She was hurt and indignant that her beloved Shelley was considered the instigator of their elopement and was vilified by people who did not understand him and who should have known better. Shelley decided that he had to pay a visit to Harriet at her father's house in Chapel Street, off Grosvenor Square. He directed the coach driver and sat in the back with Mary, who was nervous and miserable about the visit, and Jane, who thought it was all rather amusing.

Shelley bounded in to Harriet whose emotions on seeing him must have been overwhelmingly confused. Hope that he had outgrown his infatuation and was returning to her, surprise at how different he looked, sunburnt and dishevelled, love and resentment and pain for all the hurt he had caused her – a turmoil of such feelings burst through her miserable resignation, to confront Shelley with an indubitable case for his own guilt. It took him two hours to unravel some of the strands, to explain that his love for Mary was not a passing fancy, that he still was his wife's truest friend and wished to support and succour her. He tried fervently to justify his desertion and ended up implying that Harriet was being cruel and unjust by blaming him.

Meanwhile, Mary was still waiting outside in the coach. It was growing darker and colder, the horses were restive, the postillion was grumbling; what was keeping Shelley? Perhaps Harriet had persuaded him to return to her, perhaps she was seducing him there and then. Mary could hardly bear to wait any longer when at last he appeared. He had tried to clarify his relationship with Harriet, and had finally got her to part with some money. Mary was white with fatigue from their travels and from sheer nervous exhaustion. Shelley paid off their debts to the coachman and directed him to drive them to the Stratford Hotel in Oxford Street.

It was an inauspicious beginning to Mary's new life. Her eight years with Shelley were to be closely packed with domestic problems, chastening personal tragedies, yet great intellectual and creative projects too, and a good measure of true understanding and real happiness.

6
Honeymoon's End

> 'We are told by the wisest philosophers of the dangers of the world, the deceits of men, and the treason of our own hearts....'
>
> *The Last Man*, Mary Shelley

Those first few months back in London were unsettling and insecure. Money was the most pressing problem and one which necessitated Mary's first parting from Shelley in two agonized weeks of stolen hours and clandestine meetings under the threat of the bailiffs', and debtors' prison. Mary was isolated, too, unable to go to Skinner Street and see her father who remained inflexible in his censure of them. Friends were aloof, some shocked and reproving. Harriet's status was still not resolved and Jane was being as irritating and childish as ever with her attention-seeking tantrums and the silly games she played with Shelley. Mary's pregnancy was making her all the more tired and less able to participate in the lengthy evening discussions and communal projects on which she and Shelley used to work with such binding pleasure.

Yet despite all these distractions and frustrations Mary embarked on a programme of enthusiastic reading and study. Less than a week after arriving in London, she had her first Greek lesson.

They moved immediately from the Stratford Hotel to cheap and temporary lodgings at 56 Margaret Street, off Regent Street. Shelley was in very frequent contact with Harriet, with a flurry of letters and three visits in those first three days. At first he was friendly and gently chiding, yet uncompromising about the reality and power of his feelings for Mary: 'My attachment to Mary neither could nor ought to have been overcome; our spirits & [blank space] are united. We met with passion; she has resigned all for me.'[1] Yet when it transpired that Harriet had put all details of their separation in the hands of her lawyer, thereby seriously jeopardizing his hopes of raising a loan, his caring tone turned to one of wounded and self-righteous invective. 'I do not know that it is conducive to your interest to injure an innocent man struggling with distress.... If you can represent your conduct to me in a more favourable light than I now behold it I shall rejoice....'[2] Sad Harriet, in Shelley's eyes she was the one who had fallen from grace, she had debased his 'pure & liberal principles' with her 'mean & despicable selfishness' and 'vilest superstitions'.[3] It is no wonder that she was bitterly wounded by these letters and that they should be kept by her family as evidence against Shelley, in the end to be used to defame him in his application for custody of his children after Harriet's tragic death.

Mary knew only Shelley's side of the dispute. She saw him upset and infuriated by Harriet's lack of either understanding or compliance; he was frustrated by the breakdown of his financial negotiations, precipitated by her lack of co-operation, and alarmed by the ever-increasing pressure of pursuing bailiffs. Mary might have felt some sympathy and guilt for his discarded wife, pregnant as she was too, but it would have been quickly submerged by concern for Shelley and for their immediate future. There was even a little condescension expressed towards Harriet, 'certainly a very odd creature',[4] for having slipped from the noble slopes of Shelleyan principle.

During these early weeks Mary and Shelley frequently read aloud to each other in their dingy lodgings. Shelley chose *The Ancient Mariner*, which he read with dramatic relish, and some of Southey's poetry. *Caleb Williams*, Godwin's famous novel of dreadful injustice and deadly pursuit, was another work that they all enjoyed as he intoned its densely wrought plot by the light of the candle in the shadowy room.

Mary was still reading avidly, doing some drawing and applying herself to her Greek lessons. On Friday, 16 September, as Shelley sat writing his first letter since their elopement to Godwin, she suddenly saw Mrs Godwin and Fanny at the window, probably having come to see how she and Jane were. However, they refused to speak to Shelley who ran to meet them and they hurried off down the street. Mary was in the habit of going to bed early and this evening she was woken by the unexpected arrival of her step-brother, Charles Clairmont. She was delighted to see him and to have a chance of questioning him about her father and Skinner Street. The news was not good. Godwin was obdurately set against Shelley, and he was full of reproach and bitter disappointment in Mary. Financially he was as rocky as ever. There were plans afoot, too, to send Jane off to a convent to keep her from Shelley's evil clutches and salvage what was left of her virtue. This piece of information produced hoots of derisive laughter. Yet it also underlined their sense of being under siege. Both Mary and Jane were under age and could legally be snatched by their outraged parents from their life of sin, to be despatched at will to a convent prison or maiden aunt's rural retreat. Shelley's favoured role as champion of tyrannized maidens was etched a little deeper. Charles stayed until three in the morning when Shelley and Mary finally crawled into bed.

Shelley was now having to resort to a rascally trio of moneylenders, the last ditch for desperate men. They had their eyes on the Shelley estate, in return for a pile of ready cash. A man called Ballechy seemed the most promising and, on 24 September, Mary went along with Shelley on one of his numerous visits. Bargaining and discussions continued. To cheer themselves up Mary bought some prints to add life to the dreary walls of their lodgings. They were about to move again. Only three days later she was packing her few belongings and with Shelley and Jane piled into a coach to take them to Somers Town, the suburb where she was born. This time their home was 5 Church Terrace, not the grand Polygon, and Somers Town was already on the road to ruin: first slums and eventually demolition. However, it was still backed by rolling fields that stretched to the uplands of Kentish Town and Hampstead.

This address was known only to a few friends and those were sworn to secrecy. Harriet was not informed of their new abode and was instructed to communicate through Hookham. Despite their unsettled existence Mary's reading and study continued unabated. When Shelley returned from his daily round of moneylenders she would walk with him over the Kentish Town fields or up to Hampstead Heath to sail and set fire to paper boats on the ponds there. It was a beautiful and invigorating walk and these daily excursions in the brisk autumn air cheered them and inspirited their lively discussions. On one such walk, after breakfast on 30 September, Shelley became very enthusiastic about an idea for 'liberating two heiresses',[5] his two younger sisters, Elizabeth and Hellen, who were boarding at a school in Hackney. Mary supported his wild plan, and even level-headed Thomas Love

Peacock, Shelley and Harriet's friend, who spent that evening with them, appeared to accede to it too. His alacrity for the scheme itself, or merely the prospect of witnessing another madcap Shelley escapade, brought him round to Church Terrace the following morning. Having eaten frugally, all four of them then walked over to Hackney and Mary and Jane were sent to spy out the place and talk with Eliza and Hellen. That evening they continued enthusiastically with their plans for the kidnapping. Then, as suddenly as the idea had flared, it faltered and faded away. The liberating of these oppressed girls was never again considered.

The walks on the heath and the sailing of fleets of fire boats continued. These excursions, their reading together, Mary's studying and Peacock's daily visits, all were part of an informal routine during those autumn days. All this activity, however, was a distraction from the real problems of money and Harriet and the domestic friction between Mary and Jane.

Mary was easily tired and had eschewed meat, following the same sort of limited vegetarian diet that Shelley favoured. Neither of them were particularly practical and they had not the knowledge nor the inclination to be sure they ate as nutritiously as possible. Shelley seldom submitted to regular mealtimes; whenever he remembered he was hungry he would buy a loaf of bread and some raisins and eat his way through them. Mary might have been more organized, although in the early nineteenth century a vegetarian did not have a wide choice of food and she, who was neither a keen nor an experienced cook, probably ate bread and cakes more often than not. She certainly grew less well and less strong as her pregnancy advanced and had to spend even more time miserably resting or in bed, while Jane eagerly accompanied Shelley on his walks out and about.

Jane shared another dubious pleasure with Shelley. During these long evenings when Mary was in bed they sat up together and talked, and almost invariably their discussions turned to contemplations of the supernatural, of horror and various other frightful topics. These sessions would often begin with Shelley setting out to frighten Jane by playing on her susceptibilities, much as he used to frighten his young sisters when a boy at Field Place. But often these subtle manipulations would end with Shelley nearly as alarmed as Jane and having to awaken Mary who was expected to soothe them both.

They were emotionally unsettled and fraught times. Jane was bored and dissatisfied. Mary, herself not very well or comfortable, often found it as difficult to tolerate her despondency and sulks as it was to accept her high-spirited intimacy and emotional demands on Shelley. In the first week of October, Jane and Shelley's indulgent morbidity and scare talk reached a peak. After one such midnight discussion, Jane was terrified by what appeared to be some supernatural interference with her pillow which, as she turned her back, was apparently displaced from her bed to the chair. Two nights later, when Mary had gone to bed, she and Shelley were talking again over the fire: 'get rather in a horrid mood – thinking of ghosts cannot sleep all night',[6] she wrote in her journal. Mary would have nothing to do with this late-night ghost-mongering but it was nevertheless a bad week for her too. She was alarmed by a letter from Harriet implying that she was very seriously ill. Mary considered visiting her with Shelley, but when the doctor's more favourable report arrived that crisis was averted.

The alarms and the excursions continued. The following day, the thirteenth, after an unsettled morning when Shelley and Mary resolved to quit London had they the £5 necessary, they ended up at Drury Lane Theatre instead. There the great Edmund Kean was playing Hamlet, not it seemed to the liking of the Shelley party. They stormed out in the middle, Shelley particularly disgusted by the contrivance of the acting and by the depravity of parts of the play. Their nerves had become so strained and emotions so overwrought that on returning to their lodgings in Church Terrace Jane, possibly Mary and Shelley too, were so loath to enter the house and terrified of sleeping there that they all jumped into a coach and spent the night at the Stratford Hotel.

Jane's temper had not improved for the next morning she came down in a black mood and picked a quarrel with Shelley. She immediately felt better, despite being lectured on her faults, and walked back to Church Terrace through Regent's Park. Shelley rather self-consciously committed his feelings to his and Mary's journal:

'Jane's insensibility and incapacity for the slightest degree of friendship. . . . Beware of weakly giving way to trivial sympathies. Content yourself with one great affection – with a single mighty hope; let the rest of mankind be the subjects of your benevolence, your justice, and, as human beings, of your sensibility; but, as you value many hours of peace, never suffer more than one even to approach the hallowed circle.'[7]

It was wise enough advice to himself but equally it proved impossible for him to follow. However, it did reassure and please Mary when she read it that evening. Through experience and hardship, her love for Shelley was growing from its romanticized, unreal beginnings into something more substantial and enduring. Shelley was always more self-centred, even narcissistic, in his appreciation of Mary's love; how much better she made *him*. In his long and revealing letter to Hogg explaining the events of the previous months he wrote with amazement and delight of his discovery of the fusion in Mary of a formidable intellect and healthy sexuality. She was the only woman of Shelley's intimate acquaintance with the ability to fulfil both the carnal and spiritual sides of his nature, and as such centred him, helping to unify his disparate genius. She was to become his stronghold and stability in an otherwise hostile, chaotic world. When, in times to come, her sexual attractions were eclipsed by passing infatuations, Shelley never failed to rely on, trust and admire her lucid judgement and breadth of understanding. When, in the future, he felt that her love and emotional support had been withdrawn from him, he became despairing and defeatist.

But these early days together were less complicated times when ill-fortune still lay in ambush. The final paragraph of Shelley's letter was elated with his sense of power through unity, and freedom through self-knowledge:

'How wonderfully I am changed! Not a disembodied spirit can have undergone a stranger revolution! I never knew until now that contentment was any thing but a word denoting an unmeaning abstraction. I never before felt the integrity of my nature, its various dependencies, & learned to consider myself an whole accurately united rather than an assemblage of inconsistent & discordant portions. Above all, most sensibly do I perceive the truth of my entire worthlessness but as depending on another. And I am deeply persuaded that thus ennobled, I shall become a more true & constant friend, a more useful lover of mankind, a more ardent asserter of truth & virtue – above all more consistent, more intelligible, more true....'⁸

The next day, a Saturday, a letter from Godwin arrived while Shelley and Peacock were out on further money matters. Mrs Godwin and he suggested that Jane return to them at Skinner Street. She was in part tempted to go; unhappy and emotionally disturbed, she was disenchanted with her indeterminate and vicarious existence. Nothing would make Mary happier than to be rid of the disruptive presence of her step-sister, but she could not express too much enthusiasm. Jane wanted to ask Shelley's advice before deciding. Mary walked out into the fields to meet him. He was late, it was growing cold and the light was fading; the longer she waited the more anxious she became. At last she discerned Shelley's slight figure walking rapidly out of the dusk with Peacock in tow. Jane told him about Godwin's proposal and he immediately said he did not think she should go. Mary was disappointed and deflated and wrote with hardly concealed irritation, 'Jane's letter to my Father. A refusal. Talk about going away, and, as usual, settle nothing.'⁹ She wondered if she would ever have Shelley to herself.

Shelley's financial negotiations were in deadlock; the situation was becoming more threatening daily. This stressful week exacerbated Mary's resentment of Jane's parasitic dependence on them. Jane sensed this too, and there followed arguments and grievances, both real and imagined. One of the most pressing debts was to Charters, a coachmaker, for the considerable sum of £50. The bailiffs had been trying to track down and seize Shelley, so far with little luck, but on the evening of Saturday, the twenty-second, the news that Mary had been fearfully expecting came via Fanny's loyal hand. The bailiffs had at last discovered their hide-out, having apparently extracted the address from Thomas Hookham. Meek, sweet Fanny had braved displeasure at Skinner Street to walk the two miles through the darkening streets of London up to Somers Town, and she stood nervously in the field beyond Church Terrace having asked a local boy to deliver her message. Mary read it quietly. Jane and Shelley, on learning from the boy that Fanny was still in the field, rushed out and Jane grabbed hold of her. This wild approach so alarmed the already quivering Fanny that she screamed and ran off. To find out more Jane and Shelley hurried to Skinner Street and skulked in the shadows outside the family's lighted window. They saw Charles, sent him a note, and eventually he came to speak with them. He denied all knowledge of the Hookham betrayal. All the time Mary was anxiously awaiting their return with more definite news. Charles's assurances seemed to have rung true, but they decided to try and see Fanny again the next day. Should Fanny's warning prove accurate, at least they had one day's grace for the morrow was a Sunday and the bailiffs' powers of arrest were legally waived for twenty-four hours from midnight on Saturday night.

That morning Mary was up at six and with Shelley and Jane she went to Skinner Street to discover more from Fanny. The moment the shutters opened she rang the bell and Fanny, whose domestic duties demanded she was up first, answered the door. She upheld her story and with a sinking heart Mary faced the fact that, until he could pay Charters' bill, Shelley would have to turn fugitive or end up in jail. By now she was hungry and they decided to call in on Peacock at Southampton Buildings in Chancery Lane and have something to eat there. Mary then returned to their lodgings with Jane, while Shelley and Peacock set out to confront Hookham. He was out; 'the sly little rascal got out of the Way',[10] wrote Jane, echoing Shelley's own angry disparagement.

When Shelley eventually returned Mary tried to get him to discuss how they were to raise the necessary £50. She was anxious and tired. Shelley was despondent about Hookham and despairing of ever extricating himself from the financial morass that threatened to engulf him. Jane was depressed and felt excluded and a financial burden. They all quarrelled. Mary was accusatory; nothing had been settled despite the weeks of visits to banks and lawyers and moneylenders. Shelley, the arch-peacemaker, calmed her down and dispelled Jane's fears. He would send an urgent letter via Jane to Harriet requesting money to help them out of their plight. Shelley had to be gone that night. By nine, Mary had kissed him and waved him into the dark, to begin an exhausting and precarious existence which Mary and he were to endure until their deliverance on 9 November.

It was to be a frightening and miserable fortnight for Mary. She had to continue living at Church Terrace with only Jane for company and protection. She made hurried and secret assignations with Shelley and would spend hours in the cold, waiting for him to turn up, fearing the worst, nearly fainting from hunger and emotional exhaustion. She had to deal with the bailiffs when they called, she had to sell what she could to raise enough money to feed herself and Jane. Some days they had nothing substantial to eat at all. And over all the hardship hung a pall of fear for Shelley's safety. However, there was always Sunday to look forward to when she could spend the night with him, the enforced separation and uncertainty of the future having concentrated wonderfully their love for each other. Their thoughts, letters and fleeting furtive meetings were suffused with passionate intensity. Their love letters during these feverish days were full of unfulfilled longing; Mary wanting to hold and comfort Shelley, he dependent on her emotionally, and full of sexual desire.

On the Monday, Mary received an early letter from Shelley directing her to their first meeting in a coffee house in Fleet Street. It was full of agitation and insecurity but optimistic too: 'I feel a solitariness & a desolation of heart where you have been accustomed to be. But my beloved this will not last. Prudence & self denial will discomfort our enemies. We must be circumspect & active.'[11] He ended it by urging her to be punctual and Mary set off from Church Terrace eager to see him. It was to prove an exhausting and frustrating day. She walked up and down Fleet Street, he did not come. She walked down to Peacock's lodgings to see if Shelley was there. He had been long gone. So she walked anxiously back to Fleet Street, paced about and finally gave up and returned to Peacock's. Very despondent, Mary decided to go back to Church Terrace. There, bailiffs had already called in the hope of surprising Shelley. Again in the afternoon Mary set off for Southampton Buildings and then on to the coffee house in Fleet Street, where her spirits revived at the sight of Shelley's wan but smiling face. He had some good news; having spent the morning at Ballechy's there was a chance of his obtaining some money from a benevolent client of his on very favourable terms. Perhaps the separation would not be protracted after all.

Mary had been deeply hurt and dismayed by the hard line her father had taken against them. His coldness and lack of concern for her when she most needed support, and even food to keep her from starving, had puzzled and discouraged her. She blamed it roundly on Mrs Godwin's influence, but knew at heart that he was less a slave to her than to the despicable world and its values. 'Why will not Godwin follow the obvious bent of his affections & be reconciled to us – not his prejudices, the world and *she* – do you not hate her my love

– all these forbid it ... dear good creature press me to you and hug your own Mary to your heart, perhaps she will one day have a father till then be everything to me love....'[12] Shelley, too, was disillusioned by the betrayal of one he had considered his spiritual father. 'My imagination is confounded by the uniform prospect of the perfidy & wickedness & hardheartedness of mankind. Mary most amply redeems their blackest crimes. But I confess to you that I have been shocked & staggered by Godwin's cold injustice .... in my absence from you oh light of my life my very spirit of hope I have at moments almost felt despair to think how cold & worldly Godwin has become.'[13]

Too quickly their reunion in the smoky, noisy coffee house was over and Mary walked back to Peacock's house and had something to eat there, the first meal since her scanty breakfast. She was so tired she could hardly stand and had to take a coach back to Church Terrace, an extravagance she could ill afford.

With Shelley out of the way, Mary was finding Jane more of a friend and support, which at least eased one of her domestic burdens. Jane had learnt from Fanny that her mother wanted her to go into a family either as a governess or a paying guest. She was contemplating accepting and was deep in gloom at the prospect.

In those hectic three months with Mary and Shelley, Jane had known more adventure and excitement, had glimpsed a span of ideas and opportunities the like of which she would never have encountered in any orthodox female role. However much she sometimes felt excluded from the mainstream of life and passion that Mary somehow had secured for herself, however uncertain she was of her own future, to relinquish this for the narrow predictability of some bourgeois family with marriage to some predictable and bourgeois man as the only, and dubious, liberation, was like turning her face from the sun. However, for the last week or so, that sun had been clouded and distant; life had been particularly difficult for Jane, she was even more unsettled than Mary who had Shelley as reason and reward for her sufferings. Enforced separation had meant Shelley's affections were acutely converged in an essential passion for Mary, and during this time Jane felt her presence was all the more subsidiary to the main drama.

Mary, too, had been dismayed to hear from Fanny that Charles Clairmont had known about Hookham's betrayal of them to the bailiffs but had misled them that anxious Saturday night. It deepened Mary's sense of their friendlessness and isolation.

Thursday, 27 October, brought a melancholy and confused letter from Fanny. She was caught between her loyalty and love for her father and her admiration and affection for Mary and Shelley. She, too, saw her predictable domestic seclusion as grey and featureless in comparison with the romantic love affair in which her younger sister was embroiled. She regretted the fact that Shelley was already husband and father and she probably shrank from their precarious way of life, but nevertheless Mary had found someone exceptional to love and be loved by and she saw little prospect of such a deliverance for herself. Mary spent the whole morning writing an explanatory, affectionate and reassuring letter in reply. She felt a protective and deep affection for Fanny, but with a natural cecity and self-centredness, borne of preoccupation with her own and Shelley's problems, Fanny was inevitably neglected. Years later, Mary was to realize just how tragically self-effacing Fanny could be, her sensibilities too delicate for the world. She had all of Mary's melancholy and emotionalism but none of her determined resilience.

Having written to Fanny, Mary set off for St Paul's with a hopeful heart, looking forward to seeing Shelley again. Their few stolen hours together tantalized and left them unfulfilled. Mary took her leave of him to spend yet another night alone. But before she went to bed a letter arrived hurriedly written by Shelley. Full of love and longing, on the verge of throwing caution to the winds just to spend the night with her, it was a loving declaration to sleep on: 'Oh my dearest love why are our pleasures so short & so uninterrupted [sic]? How long is this to last?... Oh! those redeeming eyes of Mary that they might beam upon me before I sleep! Praise my forbearance oh beloved one that I do not rashly fly to you – & at least secure a *moment's* bliss.... All that is exalted & buoyant in my nature urges me towards you – reproaches me with cold delay....' Then, impressed by Mary's letter to Fanny which he had read that afternoon, he ended with high praise, 'How hard & stubborn must be the spirit that does not confess you to be the subtlest & most exquisitely fashioned intelligence: that among women there is no equal mind to yours – and I possess this treasure. how beyond all estimate is my felicity.'[14] Denied her presence, he was all the more captivated by her uniqueness: the intellectual who could match his arguments, could grasp and distil his abstractions; the imaginative dreamer who recognized his wild fantasies; the pale beauty, the memories of whose passion taunted his fugitive days. To ease their deprivation and unite them in distance, Mary and Shelley assumed a ritual of making imaginary love to each other before going to sleep. He reminded her that he would be thinking of her, 'Adieu remember love at vespers – before sleep. I do not omit *my* prayers.'[15]

As the days passed, their meetings, unrelaxed and frequently interrupted, were miserably frustrating. Exhausted with the stress of his itinerant existence and financial straits, denied the counterpoise of Mary's strength and sanity, Shelley feared his creative powers were fading. 'Your thoughts alone can waken mine to energy. My mind without yours is dead & cold as the dark midnight river when the moon is down.'[16] The moon was to recur in his poetry as a symbol for Mary, waning to its saddest and most distant phase in his *Epipsychidion*, written six years later.

That same evening Mary received another letter, this time from Mrs Godwin. Whether it was bitterly accusatory or unctuous and conciliatory, it prompted an outburst from Mary: 'She is a woman I shudder to think of. My poor Father!'[17] All the suppressed anger and jealousy she had felt as a girl towards this crass interloper could be expressed with impunity now that Skinner Street had so coldly rejected her and Shelley.

The longed-for Saturday dawned. She had to wait until midnight before she could fearlessly take Shelley to bed. She met him in the morning; he was not well, the strain of the separation, the furtive fearful days, the dissipation of his creative energies and the feverish financial negotiations that continued daily, all took heavy toll of his precarious health and peace of mind. He was desperate for time with Mary to reorient and refresh his spirit. The night could not come fast enough. That evening Mary slept from nine until twelve to take the edge off her fatigue. Jane was up all evening pacing the floor, waiting for the sound of Shelley's eager footsteps up the stairs. Midnight struck. He came half an hour later and they went straight to bed. Jane was left to make her own way.

Sunday was 'a day devoted to Love in idleness',[18] as Mary confided to her journal. It was their one day for being lazy and lie-abed, indulgently talking of themselves rather than the daily intrusions of money and the world outside. Jane, who was excluded from their intimacy, found the love cloying and the pace slow: 'To sleep & talk – why this is merely vegetating.'[19] Too quickly the day was darkening into night. Shelley had said he could not bear to leave Mary again and they decided to go together into hiding for two more nights. Mary packed a few essentials and set off by coach under cover of dark to a sordid little inn called the Cross Keys in St John's Street. The people there were rude and uncouth and their room was dirty and bare, but at least Mary could be with Shelley for a little longer.

Remarkably, Mary managed to spend the morning studying Greek despite the squalor of the inn and the uncertainty and danger of their circumstances. On the Tuesday she was harassed by the inn's proprietors who wanted the bill paid. Nobody had any money and Mary and Shelley were starving hungry. The people at the inn refused to send up a bite to eat until they saw the glint of money. They tried Hookham for funds; Fanny and Charles and finally Peacock for food. At last, when Mary was nearly fainting away, Shelley rushed off to Peacock and returned with a bag of his mother's cakes. Hookham, too, sent money and the Cross Keys' bill was paid and the hostages could leave, Shelley to go to Peacock and Mary to Church Terrace once again.

After their three nights of illicit love, it was a wrench to be apart again. Mary got a letter from Shelley on the Wednesday warning her not to see him that day. Their landlady, Mrs Stewart, another creditor, was closing her net and he despaired of ever being free of the web of debts, that entrapped him:

'How lonely & desolate are these solitary nights! this wretched & comfortless waking. I cannot contemplate without a feeling that approaches to despair the continuance of this isolation.... Love me my dearest best Mary, love me in confidence & security: do not think of me as one in danger or even in sorrow – the remembrance & expectation of such sweet moments as we experienced last night consoles strengthens & redeems me from despondency. *There is eternity in these moments* – they contain the true elixir of immortal life.'[20]

Mary certainly needed the remembrance of those moments to redeem her spirits. The next day, Thursday, brought a painful disappointment, another stake marking her isolation. Her childhood friend, Isabel Baxter, to whom Mary had written an explanatory letter on her return to England, had, under the influence of her fiancé David Booth, severed their relationship. The rumour that Godwin had sold Mary and Jane to Shelley had been circulating among the London gossips during her elopement, and it had evidently got as far as Dundee: 'I should half suspect that there has been some communication between the Skinner St. folks and them',[21] remarked Mary cynically in a letter to Shelley. To her journal she confided, '... so all my hopes are over there. Ah, Isabel; I did not think you would act thus.'[22] To Shelley she allowed her bitter disappointment fuller expression:

> 'I am so out of spirits I feel so lonely ... dear Shelley you will say I was deceived I know I am not – I know her unexampled frankness and sweetness of character but what must that character be who resists opinions preach – oh dear what am I writing I am indeed disappointed – I did think Isabel perfectly unprejudiced – she adores the shade of my mother but then a married man it is impossible to knock into some people's heads that Harriet is selfish & unfeeling and that my father might be happy if he chose.'[23]

At twelve-thirty on Saturday night Shelley came home to Mary. He had at last reasonable hopes of settling his most pressing debts and was finalizing the terms of his £500 loan from Ballechy. However, until his creditors were paid off he still had to evade the bailiffs. By Tuesday, 8 November, the negotiations and settlements were completed, Shelley had even paid a debt of Godwin's which had been jeopardizing his freedom. They were free to live together again. The extremes of emotion endured during those two weeks had incised the period deep into Mary's memory. She resurrected it in almost exact detail in her autobiographical novel *Lodore*, published twenty-one years later. Mary packed up their books, her journal, her few clothes, and with Jane set off by coach to collect Shelley from Peacock's and move into new lodgings. They gratefully left the shabbiness of Somers Town and drove south through the city to the more salubrious district off the Blackfriars' Road. Number 2 Nelson Square was to be their home.

Money was still very tight and many of Shelley's days continued to be spent with lawyers and moneylenders unravelling the old debts and incurring new ones. Godwin was still coldly antagonistic, yet on hearing of Shelley's success with the loan from Ballechy he applied for financial help as his due. Shelley complied, practising the Utilitarian principles of *Political Justice* which he had embraced when he first met Godwin, when he had viewed him with the gloss of hero-worship. Despite his acceptance of these financial demands, Shelley became increasingly alienated and enraged by Godwin's personal failings: his arrogance, selfishness and hard-hearted worldliness.

Mary was still suffering at the hands of various members of her family. Charles Clairmont called often with desperate news of Skinner Street and demands for money. Jane was depressed and sullen, sulking until the patient peacemaker Shelley gave up an evening to talk her round. Her continual need for attention and cajolery irritated and oppressed Mary. Her father, too, had obdurately hardened his heart against her. On Sunday, the thirteenth, four days after their arrival at Nelson Square, Fanny reluctantly visited them with an important message for Jane. Fanny had been told by Godwin that if she so much as *saw* Mary, he would never speak to her again and, being excessively timid and easily terrorized, she complied and would only come to their lodgings if her sister removed herself. This much more spirited and wilful Wollstonecraft daughter admitted in her journal that she heard everything anyway. The story went that Mrs Godwin was dying and wanted to see Jane one last time. Jane had no appropriate clothes, so Fanny had to return to Skinner Street and bring her some to wear. Mary saw them off with relief and some curiosity as to what exactly was going on and what would come of it all. Shelley returned from Hookham's and 'disapproved'. But this did nothing to sour Mary's delight at Jane's departure. 'In the evening talk with my love about a great many things. We receive a letter from Jane saying she is very happy, and she does not know when she will return.'[24] She did of course return. Within four days her happiness at being back in the security of home, the centre of attention and affection, had given way to the longing for the stimulation and promise of excitement that seemed to incandesce from Nelson Square.

In the meantime, Mary's friendless and bookish life with Shelley was rippled by the re-emergence of Thomas Jefferson Hogg. Shelley had met him at Peacock's during his two weeks on the run. His old friend was now studying for the Law and he had been rather disconcerted by Hogg's increased vulgarity and worldliness; 'very witty ... but cold',[25] was Shelley's verdict to Mary, but Jane's journal disclosed the reason for Shelley's distaste: 'Hogg had been with him the Evening before & asked him after his *two wives*. He joked all the time & talked of the Pleasures of Hunting.'[26] On the evening of the Monday following Jane's departure, Hogg called at Nelson Square and met Mary for the first time. Shelley remained uncommitted: '... perhaps he still may be my friend, in spite of the radical differences of sympathy between us; he was pleased with Mary; this was the test by which I had previously determined to judge his character.'[27] It was in fact the beginning of an extraordinary and bizarre period in Mary's life.

7
A Runaway Dormouse

> 'On her hind legs the Dormouse stood
> In a wild & mingled mood
> Of Maieishness & Pecksietude.'
>
> Shelley's triplet describing Mary at this time and
> quoted in one of her letters to Hogg

At first Mary was not particularly impressed by Hogg. As his visits became more frequent, she engaged in cool intellectual rivalry with him, taking pleasure in confounding his arguments and sentencing them to death by *reductio ad absurdum*. During Hogg's first visits she wrote astringently of his fallible logic.

'Get into an argument about virtue, in which Hogg makes a sad bungle – quite muddled on the point, I perceive.'[1] 'In the evening Hogg comes. We have an argument about the Love of Wisdom, and Free Will and Necessity; he quite wrong, but quite puzzled; his arguments are very weak.'[2] His conservatism was equally contemptible; '... he is sadly perverted, and I begin to lose hopes; his opinion of honour and respect for established customs condemn him in the courts of philosophy.'[3] But within three weeks she was melting a little and liking him more: 'Talk about heaps of things, but do not argue tonight.'[4] His visits became daily occurrences; '... talk about a great number of things; he is more sincere this evening than I have seen him before. Odd dreams.'[5] Mention of their far-ranging discussions, and Mary's increased liking for this witty and urbane young man, became characteristic of the entries in her journal at this time. However, alongside the development of this new friendship ran the continuing strands of her life with Shelley. Mary's health deteriorated during the months of November and December, quite probably as a direct result of the stresses of the previous weeks and of general physical debility from her quite inadequate diet. She had not eaten sufficient quantity or quality of food for most of her early pregnancy when she was traipsing the Continent and then lurking penniless in Somers Town. Even though their finances were marginally easier, Mary was still following a haphazard vegetarianism. She was not a woman who bloomed naturally with robust good health during pregnancy. All five of her pregnancies were to be blighted by ill-health and low spirits; although all were concurrent with extremely difficult and at times tragic circumstances which exacted their own toll on her already vulnerable emotions.

Her poor health during this winter kept her indoors while Shelley daily went on his excursions 'to heaps of places'[6] around the town in the eager company of high-spirited Jane. Jane had returned to them, finally burning her bridges at Skinner Street. With this decision she began to adopt a more poetic name to match the emergence of a romantic heroine. Having been for sixteen years Jane and Mary Jane, after her mother, she tried variations of her middle name: Clara, Clary, Clare and finally Claire, by which she was known by all but her parents for the rest of her life.

It happened more frequently that Mary was feeling abandoned and neglected, left at home four months pregnant and feeling ill and down at heart. In the middle of this despondency and self-pity, she received a further blow to her own faltering sense of security and emotional status as Shelley's chosen one. 'A letter from Hookham, to say that Harriet has been brought to bed of a son and heir. Shelley writes a number of circular letters of this event, which ought to be ushered in with ringing of bells, etc for it is the son of his *wife*.'[7] Shelley's enthusiasm for the progeny of his deserted wife made her feel all the more emotionally bereft. That evening, when Hogg called by, he suddenly seemed to Mary to be almost attractive and she gratefully received his attentions and flattery as restoration in part of her self-esteem.

The financial depression at Skinner Street was becoming daily more acute and various envoys would arrive at Nelson Square to report the latest on Godwin's stricken circumstances and to importune Shelley for money. All this was wearying and depressing and Mary began to look forward to Hogg's visits as breezy, amusing, unburdensome interludes in otherwise lonely and solemn days: 'We talk about flowers and trees in the evening – a country conversation.'[8] Claire was still having fits of temperament which demanded Shelley's lengthy reassurances and Mary's 'all-powerful benevolence',[9] as

Shelley called it. At this time Mary was reporting a few odd dreams about Hogg. She was obviously enjoying his attentions and flirtatious company and Shelley was fully aware of the fact.

The year 1814 had been momentous for Mary and, as it slipped into a new year that was to prove even more eventful, the emotional balance at Nelson Square was gradually shifting. There was no doubt that at the heart of the quartet beat the love between the two principals, Mary and Shelley. However, from January through to April 1815 there was an attempt to extend and enhance that love by embracing Hogg and probably Claire, too, in an experimental, philosophical and sexually free community. Unlike Hogg's previously underhand approach to Harriet during Shelley's absence, this intimacy with Mary was fully approved, even encouraged, by Shelley. He believed, and had reasoned Mary into belief, that

> 'True love in this differs from gold and clay
> That to divide is not to take away'[10]

and should be honestly and reasonably shared at will. On 1 January he wrote to Hogg: 'Mary wished to speak with you alone, for which purpose I have gone out & removed Clare. If you should return before this evening & are at leisure I need not direct your steps.'[11] In his entry for that date in Mary's journal Shelley first used 'Maie' as one of the many pet names for Mary which, along with 'Pecksie' and 'Dormouse', were coined at this time of blurred identities.

Throughout the affair Mary was happy with the flirtation and affectionate talk but had to work at loving Hogg, and shrank from the sexual consummation that he desired and Shelley seemed so blatantly to encourage. All her letters were gently evasive on that point, pleading for more time to know him, for patience until her baby was born. Her first extant letter to him was sent on the same day as Shelley's:

> 'You love me, you say – I think I could return it with the passion you deserve – but you are very good to me and tell me that you are quite happy with the affection which from the bottom of my heart I feel for you – you are so generous, so disinterested, that no one can help loving you. But, you know Hogg, that we have known each other for so short a time, and I did not think about love, so that I think that *that* also will come in time & then we shall be happier.'[12]

She wrote again a few days later, 'Shelley and Jane are both gone out & from the number & distance of the places that they are going to I do not expect them till very late. Perhaps you can come and console a solitary lady in the meantime – but I do not wish to make you a truant so do not come against your conscience. You are so good & disinterested a creature that I love you more & more.'[13] Mary was eventually to dislike him for his very lack of disinterestedness, his self-centredness, his love of comfort and ease. Certainly with hindsight he would seem to have had a marked predilection for Shelley's women, eventually ending up in a permanent union with Jane Williams, the last of Shelley's inamoratas.

Hogg was a daily visitor to Nelson Square both while Shelley and Claire were out and in the evenings when the whole group assembled for philosophical discussions and readings aloud.

On Saturday, the seventh, Mary wrote another of her letters to Hogg, but was still subtly evasive about the sexual side of their relationship. There is no evidence that any emotion stronger than flirtatious affection motivated this affair with Hogg; there was certainly no trace of the passion and intensity of her letters to Shelley during their enforced separation. In this letter particularly she sounded as if she was putting on a brave face and doing her duty by radical sexuality:

> 'Dearest Hogg ... I sincerely believe that we shall all be so happy! My affection for you, although it is not now exactly as you would wish, will I think dayly become more so – then, what can you have to add to your happiness. I ask but for time, time which for other causes beside this – phisical causes – that must be given – Shelley will be subject to these also, & this, dear Hogg, will give time for that love to spring up which you deserve and will one day have.'[14]

Hogg duly visited her and they were both surprised to see reported in the papers the death of Shelley's old grandfather, Sir Bysshe. On hearing this Shelley was delighted; it would ease the worst of his straitened circumstances. Always tactless, even inflammatory in his approach to his family, he took Claire down to Field Place for the reading of the will. Mary was left in Hogg's care. Intriguingly, four and a half days of Mary's journal are lost for ever in the first of seven heavy-handed acts of censorship, probably by Mary herself, relevant to the period of her affair with Hogg.

The remaining pages began with the entry for Thursday, 12 January. A letter had arrived from Peacock who was incarcerated in debtors' prison for the sake of a sum of £40. Mary was amazed and mystified by the whole story. Peacock had run off with a woman whom he had believed to be an heiress. Unwisely anticipating the extent of her wealth he went on a spending spree and, on discovering she really was as impecunious as he, could not pay all his debts. Ironically, he had ended up in the exact situation from which he had so assiduously worked to keep Shelley. Mary wrote him a letter and enclosed £2. On the Friday, she was having breakfast when Shelley and Claire arrived back full of news of their abortive visit. Mary encapsulated it in her journal: 'The will has been opened, and Shelley is referred to Whitton [Sir Timothy's solicitor]. His father would not allow him to enter Field Place; he sits before the door, and reads *Comus*. Dr Blockstone comes out; tell him that his father is very angry with him. Sees my name in Milton.'[15]

The journal's pages covering the next two weeks were also excised, but during these lost days two letters were written, both on 24 January 1815, and both giving antithetical views of the Shelley character. A letter from Mary was one of them; a flirtatious but distanced note to Hogg firmly showing him where her real emotional and sexual allegiance lay:

> 'My own Alexy; I know how much & how tenderly you love me, and I rejoice to think that I am capable of constituting your happiness. We look forward to joy & light in the summer when the trees are green, when the suns brightly & joyfully when, dearest Hogg, I have my little baby, with what exquisite pleasure shall we pass the time ... but our still greater happiness will be in Shelley – I love him so tenderly & entirely, whose life hangs on the beam of his eye, and whose soul is entirely wrapped up in him – you who have so sincere a friendship for him to make him happy – no, we need not try to do that, for everything we do will make him that without exertion, but to see him so – to see his love, his tenderness – dear, dearest Alexy, these are joys that fill your heart almost to bursting and draw tears more delicious than the smiles of love from your eyes.'[16]

Hogg, as befitted his new romantic status in Shelley and Mary's community, had adopted the pseudonym of Alexy after the romantic hero in his novel, *Prince Alexy Haimatoff*. As he awaited Mary's consent to their sexual union or, as Shelley put it, 'your share of our common treasure',[17] he was probably less rapturous about Shelley's virtues. Harriet, who wrote on that same day to her old Irish friend, Mrs Nugent, was not as fortunate as Mary who, with Shelley as a lover, was holding another in abeyance. Harriet was alone, despairing and wounded by Shelley's very lack of love and tenderness:

'I am truly miserable, my dear friend. I really see no termination to my sorrows. As to Mr Shelley I know nothing of him. He never sends nor comes to see me. I am still at my father's, which is very wretched.... For myself happiness is fled. I live for others. At nineteen I could descend a willing victim to the tomb. How I wish these dear children had never been born. They stay my fleeting spirit, when it would be in another state. How many there are who shudder at death. I have been so near it that I feel no terrors. Mr Shelley has much to answer for. He has been the cause of great misery to me and mine. I shall never live with him again. 'Tis impossible. I have been so deceived. So cruelly treated, that I can never forget it. Oh no, with all the affections warm, a heart devoted to him, and then to be so cruelly blighted. Oh! Catherine, you do not know what it is to be left as I am, a prey to anguish, corroding sorrow, with a mind too sensitive to others' pain. But I will think no more. There is madness in thought. Could I look into futurity for a short time how gladly would I perceive the veil of mystery that wraps my fate. Is it wrong, do you think, to put an end to one's sorrow? I often think of it – all is so gloomy and desolate.'[18]

Harriet was in a tragic position, made worse by her own temperament. Since her marriage she had transferred much of her extreme dependence from her family to Shelley, and had added a child-like faith in his goodness and omnipotence. When abandoned by him, her trust betrayed, her misery and confusion were compounded by the fact that she could not retreat into being once again the pampered child of her family. She was now a mother herself and Shelley's desertion had thrust her painfully into adulthood, for which she was unwilling and cruelly unprepared. This poignant letter sadly presaged her eventual fate.

Mary's journal resumed in the middle of the entry for Saturday, 28 January, '... comes. He sleeps here. Clara and Shelley sit up until

2.'[19] Hogg was often spending the night with them at their new lodgings at 41 Hans Place. The social pairings continued; Shelley and Claire walking out into town, talking and Shelley explaining, while Mary worked and read at home, joined later by Hogg for discussion and sympathy. Evenings were communal and domestic; often Claire and Shelley would snooze or Shelley would read aloud from a current favourite; Lord Byron's poem, *Lara*, particularly delighted them. Life for Mary was still punctuated by dismal news from Skinner Street and by requests for Shelley's money to buoy their sinking finances.

On 8 February, Shelley and Claire found a new apartment in the late afternoon and that same day they all moved again to a different address at Hans Place. The following day's entry was partially destroyed by another mutilation of Mary's journal. It was a disconsolate day: 'Prate with Shelley all day. After dinner talk; put things away. Finish Gibbon's Letters; read his History. Shelley and Clara sleep, as usual. Hogg does not come till 10. Work and talk. Shelley writes letters. Go to bed. A mess....'[20] Whether that mess referred figuratively to their convoluted emotions or merely to the state of their new lodgings the day after they had moved in shall never be known. However, some entry between that Thursday and the following Monday was indiscreet enough to merit the removal of a page. The next weekend provoked the same brutal treatment, for a good many pages were ripped out, amongst them some lengthy entries.

However, the last and crucial piece of Shelley's entry for Wednesday, 22 February, remained intact. '[Mary] is in labour, and, after a few additional pains, she is delivered of a female child; five minutes afterwards Dr Clarke comes, all is well. Maie perfectly well and at ease. The child is not quite seven months; the child not expected to live. Shelley sits up with Maie; much agitated and exhausted. Hogg sleeps here.'[21]

Mary's premature labour was unexpected and its progress rapid. Shelley was probably with her as their baby was born, for the doctor had yet to arrive and Claire would not have been of much practical use. He showed great practicality and calm good sense when, years later in Italy, he sat Mary in an ice-bath to save her from bleeding to death after a miscarriage. He was quite capable of coping in crises, only to collapse as an aftermath. Mary weathered the birth far better than Shelley who was left wilting with nervous exhaustion. His illness and fatigue were to continue for a week in an expression of his anxiety about their tiny, fragile infant and his sense of losing something of his primacy in the household to the unexpected little being.

Mary's maternal feelings flowed protectively towards her delicate daughter lying in her arms, tenuously clinging to life. She lived through that day and night and the next day too. Mary's spirits rose, perhaps she would survive. Fanny was sent for and came immediately, delighted to see Mary, her own wealth of frustrated affections welling up at the sight of her sister contentedly suckling her baby. She was able to stay until the next day as Godwin and Mrs Godwin were away from Skinner Street for the night. Mrs Godwin had relented and sent some clothes for the baby, but there was still no word for Mary from her father. The next day her baby was still alive, looking stronger and feeding well. Mary and Shelley dared to hope that all would be well. Dr Clarke confirmed their optimism.

Mary and the baby continued to bloom while Shelley succumbed to illness. The two men in her life felt vaguely usurped and displaced. Shelley wrote in the journal on Saturday, 'The child very well; Maie very well also; drawing milk all day. Shelley is very unwell. In the evening Hogg comes; he is sleepy and goes away soon. Shelley is very unwell.'[22]

On the Sunday Mary was up and out of bed, following the commonsense approach of her mother and quite contrary to current custom, whereby a post-partum woman might languish in bed for up to a month. She returned to bed again at six in the evening, but stayed awake talking to Hogg until eleven and then, when Fanny arrived unexpectedly, remained talking until three-thirty in the morning. Shelley was still unwell. The next day Shelley and Claire went to buy a cradle for the baby. She had become a permanent fixture.

Mary and Shelley were pressurized into moving yet again, despite the prematurity of their baby. Their landlady was charging them an exorbitant rent and was making life unpleasant. The arrival of a baby on the scene made them all the more undesirable as tenants.

On 1 March the newspapers were full of Bonaparte's invasion of France on his defiant return from exile. And the next day Mary's household's move was on. Their new temporary roost was 13 Arabella Road in Pimlico, just next door to the King's Garden. Mary had three more days with her daughter. Her journal was spare: 'Read, talk, and nurse'[23] occurred in various combinations.

Then on Monday, 7 March, Mary awoke to find her baby dead

beside her. She seemed to have died from convulsions and Mary was horrified and full of grief at the sight of her pathetic little body. The entry in her journal was even more lean than usual: 'Find my baby dead. Send for Hogg. Talk. Miserable day.'[24] Mary's letter to Hogg begging him to come was full of pathos:

> 'My dearest Hogg my baby is dead – will you come to me as soon as you can – I wish to see you – It was perfectly well when I went to bed – I awoke in the night to give it suck it appeared to be *sleeping* so quietly that I would not wake it. It was dead then but we did not find *that* out till morning – from its appearance it evidently died of convulsions – Will you come – you are so calm a creature & Shelley is afraid of fever from the milk – for I am no longer a mother now.'[25]

Poor Mary, her baby daughter had released in her a new intensity of emotion and then suddenly that small life was taken cruelly from her. At this point, when she most needed Shelley, she could not rely on his whole-hearted support. They had become emotionally more distant during the last couple of months; the demands of Claire and Hogg were a distraction from their own relationship – contrary to Shelleyan ideals, they intruded rather than enhanced their love. Shelley, too, was often self-centred and tended to be a hypochondriac. Already suffering some illness, he was afraid of being contaminated by Mary's unsuckled milk. Hogg, attentive and pragmatic, seemed to Mary to be the only one who could help her, talk to her and soothe her pain and guilt.

The next morning Shelley and Claire went off again into town leaving Hogg with Mary. She wrote to Fanny, she talked, she read. She was low in spirit; not even Hogg could ease her despondency. Fanny did not come. Claire wrote the next day to her and there was still no sign of her. Mary had started some netting and was making a purse for Hogg. His law term holidays started on the tenth and from then he moved permanently into the family.

Mary was obviously happy to include Hogg in their domesticity but Claire's presence was beginning to become unbearable again. She felt she desperately wanted to be rid of her demanding presence. She wanted to have her beloved Shelley and her kindly flattering Hogg all to herself. The birth of her first baby had concentrated her emotions, surprising her with their fierce intensity. Her baby's death had deprived her of the natural object for these new and complex feelings. 'Still think about my little baby – 'tis hard, indeed, for a mother to lose a child',[26] she wrote miserably in her journal. She wanted to channel the flood of emotion back to Shelley. She was herself in need of love and wanted the luxury of one committed lover at least; she wanted peace, too, and these yearnings could only become reality with Claire gone, embarked on her own life.

But circumstances were against her and Shelley was not as adamant about the need for Claire's departure. 'Talk about Clara's going away; nothing settled; I fear it is hopeless. She will not go to Skinner Street; then our house is the only remaining place, I see plainly. What is to be done?'[27] Mary appreciated Claire's difficulties. In the eyes of the world she was a young woman whose virtue had been besmirched by her contact with Mary and Shelley. If she left their protection she could never really return to Skinner Street. On the other hand no profession was open to her, as a young woman of her social background, except that of being a governess or companion – both living deaths for a high-spirited girl whose sense of individuality and identity had been nurtured by her exposure to drily rational Godwinism, then forced by Shelley's passionate principles of responsible freedom. She was financially dependent and, without Shelley's patronage, she had nothing other than what she could earn.

Nevertheless, Mary's maternal passions and protectiveness had been awakened with her baby's birth; she wanted to hold to her heart those she loved, to shut the shutters and enclose her private world where Claire and her histrionics had little place. Her troubled mind took refuge in a series of vivid dreams. The only one she described in her journal was painful and pathetic. It occurred on the night of Sunday, 19 March: 'Dream that my little baby came to life again; that it had only been cold, and that we rubbed it before the fire and it lived.' She awoke not with relief that it was all a dream, but with recoil at the cold reality – her baby was not beside her, 'I think about the little thing all day. Not in good spirits.'[28]

The next night she dreamt about her baby again and a month later she recorded another 'very grim dream'.[29] Claire had meanwhile made an attempt at leaving and had advertised under the initials A.Z. for a situation as a companion. Nothing very promising came in reply to that. One letter Mary noted was signed 'Disconsolate Widow'.[30] It would have been a grim fate for Claire, and Mary, although longing to be rid of her, did not expect her to mortgage her freedom to that end.

During these few weeks Mary and the rest of the household indulged in a passing passion for chess. Most afternoons or evenings their books would lie discarded, their discussions petered out, temporarily superseded by the intellectual challenge of the game. Not once in all their encounters did Mary mention who won; obviously in true English spirit it was the playing of the game that really mattered.

Superficially, life continued unremarkably, yet three further mutilations of Mary's journal, destroying in all about twenty-one days of April and early May, give cause to wonder. The most extensive expurgation included Mary's account of a two-day holiday she and Shelley spent at the Windmill Inn, Salt Hill, near Windsor, in favourite Shelley country. On Monday, 24 April, they left London unexpectedly, possibly because the bailiffs were back on Shelley's tail as Mary mentioned in one of her subsequent letters, or possibly for personal reasons. Either way it was without Hogg's knowledge and Mary wrote a coquettish letter of apology and explanation. Hogg's brief flirtation with his romantic persona, Alexy, had been abandoned in favour of his more impressive middle name:

> 'Dear Jefferson, I am not hard hearted but Clary will explain to you how we were obliged to go away; you will perceive that it was indespensable. We shall return tomorrow night or the next morning, so dear Jefferson, do not think very hard of the poor Pecksie who would not for all the world make you uncomfortable for a moment if she could help it.... Dear Jefferson, love me all the time, as I did you. Affectionately yours The Pecksie dor to answer for.'[31]

However, Hogg was irritated by their desertion and the next day Mary was writing in high spirits and coy cajolery:

> '... when your letters arrived, Shelley's distitch was truly applicable.
>
> > On her hind paws the Dormouse stood
> > In a wild & mingled mood
> > Of Maieishness & Pecksietude
>
> ... I said that you would not be angry with a dormouse who had escaped from her London cage to green fields & acorns – dear Jefferson, I am sure that you are not so selfish (pardon the word) not

to be *very very* sorry.... Now think of me very kindly while I am away, & receive me kindly when I come back, or I will be no more
Your affectionate Dormouse.'[32]

These bouncy, lively letters were essentially distinct from those written to Hogg previously, full of evasion and restraint. These were spontaneous and familiar, dashed off to a friend with whom she felt relaxed and secure. A letter written by Shelley the following day gave a possible reason for this shift in Mary's attitude to Hogg:

'My dear friend
I shall be very happy to see you again, & to give you your share of our common treasure of which you have been cheated for several days. The Maie knows how highly you prize this exquisite possession, & takes occasion to quiz you in saying that it is necessary for [her] to be absent from London, from your sensibility to its value. Do not fear. We will not again be deprived of this participated pleasure.'[33]

Quite probably, sometime in the past weeks, since physically recovering from the birth of her daughter and emotionally from her death, Mary and Hogg had made love, the 'exquisite possession' had finally been shared.

This sharing, however brief, was not contrary to her true feelings, although on her side it probably owed more to affection and expediency than to passion. Despite her undoubted and primary love for Shelley, and within the circumstances of their life at that time and their experimental ideology, it was a natural and ingenuous progression. Hogg's attentions and affection helped restore Mary's spirits after the death of her baby. Shelley was too distracted by his complex financial dealings and ill-health, and dissipated by his emotional and probable sexual involvement with Claire to be able to give Mary the whole-hearted and exclusive support she needed. Hogg stayed indoors with her, read and talked to her, amused and beguiled her with his urbane wit and gossipy tales and anecdotes. His sexual attentions flattered her and made her feel desirable and womanly again. Her pregnancy and low health had deprived her of an essential vitality; the anguish of her baby's death had further sapped her sense of her own potency. Hogg, by liking her company, declaring his love for her and desiring her body rescued her from an emotional limbo.

Within this emotional and philosophical framework it was almost inevitable that they should share a sexual intimacy that was actively encouraged by Shelley. This would have explained Mary's good spirits for she was free from the pressures of Hogg's unfulfilled desire and free, too, of Shelley's experimental principles and intolerance of convention. She was also aware that at last she was casting off Claire's concentrated intimacy, for with the consummation of her affair with Hogg came the end of Shelley's attempt at setting up a community of friends; within weeks Claire was to leave, temporarily, and Hogg was once again to drift out of their orbit.

On the same day as Shelley wrote his note to Hogg, Mary also sent him two letters from Salt Hill, trying to coax him down to her Berkshire idyll: 'Jefferson, Jefferson, it is your duty not to keep any creature away from its home, so come; I shall expect you tonight, and if you do not come, I am off – not for London I promise you.'[34] She signed herself, with the whimsy that was characteristic of this interlude, 'A Runaway Dormouse'. The Runaway Dormouse was enjoying her country holiday, away from Claire's petulance and Skinner Street gloom. She was enjoying, too, having Shelley to herself, engaged in their customary talks while walking, exploring the wooded and hilly countryside which appealed so much to them both.

All too soon it was back to London again. Mary wrote to Hogg asking him not to go early to the law courts on the next day, Thursday, for they hoped to be back in town by nine: '... rise early to receive the Dormouse all fresh from grubbing under the oaks.'[35] The mutilation of Mary's journal has obliterated all mention not only of her visit to Salt Hill but of her return to Hogg and London, and the whole of the following week.

Mary had finally persuaded Shelley that Claire really had to go. Godwin was investigating Mrs Knapp in the hopes that she would take her, but when the lady refused Claire decided to go independently to Lynmouth in Devon. It is very likely that Shelley financed the venture. As departure day grew near, Mary, usually so circumspect and discreet in her journals, allowed her irritation to show. On Friday, 12 May, she wrote, 'Shelley and the lady walk out. After tea, talk; write Greek characters. Shelley and his friend have a last conversation.'[36] The next day Shelley walked Claire to the coach and Mary settled down to read Spenser's *Faerie Queene*. By late afternoon Shelley had not returned. Mary, suddenly cold, and filled with the fear that he had leapt on the coach with Claire, rushed out to meet him. There was still no sign of him and as it began to rain she returned home. At last he walked through the door at six-thirty, wet and tired out. Mary wrote with satisfaction, '... the business is finished ...'[37] 'The business' most probably referred to the whole emotional confusion of their sexual and social experiment; it also certainly referred to the unravelling of Claire from their lives. It was very possible that Shelley and Claire had been sexually involved in their short-lived agapemone. Certainly Claire, a year later, was to pursue and eventually seduce Byron with a brazenness and determination that suggested she had previously relinquished the psychological barrier of virginity. Byron too believed that Shelley and Claire had had a sexual relationship and implied in this letter to his friend Kinnaird, accepting responsibility for Claire's child, that it was previous to his affair with 'that odd-headed girl': '... is the brat *mine*? – I have reason to think so – for I know as much as one can know such a thing – that she had *not lived* with S[helley] during the time of our acquaintance – & that she had a good deal of that same with me ...'[38]

Optimistically Mary felt that Shelley's relationship with Claire and Claire's influence on her life would now become incidental. She accordingly closed her diary with the hope, 'I begin a new journal with our regeneration.'[39]

8
Birth of a Son

> 'Poor William! He was our darling and our pride!'
> *Frankenstein*, Mary Shelley

Mary's freedom of spirit coincided exactly with Shelley's attaining a measure of financial freedom. On the same day as Claire's departure, 13 May 1815, his lengthy negotiations had yielded a useful settlement: £4500 in a lump sum which was rapidly dispersed through personal debts, maintenance to Harriet, a provision for Mary to charge up to £300 whenever she chose, and a staggering £1000 to Godwin. Shelley was also assured an income of £1000 until his or his father's death. Having suffered cheerful penury during their honeymoon, and then on their return the alarms and threats of the bailiffs and prison, this reliable and adequate income meant that Mary and Shelley were free of their daily financial anxieties. Now that negotiations were complete, they could move out of London for the summer and satisfy their wanderlust and their love of the rural landscape.

To Mary, who had lived with poverty and thrift all her life, this alleviation of yet another burden made her feel all the more surely that her life with Shelley was really now beginning. They were starting anew with their family, for Mary conceived again in May. In a fortnight they had completed the disposal of Shelley's money, said their farewells to Hogg and Skinner Street and were off on their longed-for rustic retreat. It was June, bright summer, and they headed for the West Country. They toured the south coast of Devon and took lodgings in the pretty little harbour town of Torquay. Shelley was contemplating seclusion with Mary in the magnificent mountains of Merionethshire, but by the end of June he had received a letter from Peacock recommending a furnished house near Windsor.

It meant returning to that part of Berkshire which appealed so much to them both; it also meant they would be within easy reach of their few friends and of London. In the lazy warm days, it seemed to offer a more attractive summer retreat than the rugged isolation of wildest Wales.

On their way they probably crossed Devon to see Claire in Lynmouth, happily ensconced in her little cottage perched on a hill with a garden full of the heady scent of roses, jasmine and honeysuckle. She had written to Fanny, 'I am perfectly happy. After so much discontent, such violent scenes, such a turmoil of passion and hatred, you will hardly believe how enraptured I am with this dear little quiet spot.'[1] Meanwhile Fanny was slipping into chronic melancholy. She had probably suffered more than anyone from Godwin's prolonged financial crises. Fanny liked familiar company and yet both her sisters had fled Skinner Street to trace more exciting lives on distant horizons. She had neither the independence of Claire nor a lover, as had Mary, to offer her hope for the future. Claire, never one to be particularly subtle or sensitive, ended her letter with the hearty but helpful 'for heaven's sake be cheerful; "so young in life and so melancholy!"'[2]

From Lynmouth, they most likely travelled on up through Somerset to Bristol. From there Shelley went on to secure them a house while for some reason Mary stayed behind in lodgings in Clifton, an elegant new suburb of the city, full of crescents of white houses contouring the hills and looking out over the rugged cliffs of the Avon gorge. Shelley's house-hunting took much longer than Mary had anticipated. Left behind in Bristol, her loneliness turned to anxiety and mild panic as his vague letters and lack of progress seemed to augur the frustration of her hopes of setting up a permanent home with him. As the days passed a fear obsessed her: perhaps Shelley had recalled Claire to London and was whiling the time away with her, quietly replacing Mary in his heart. By now she knew without doubt that she was pregnant again and the shadow of Harriet stood behind her; Harriet had been abandoned for love of another woman, perhaps Shelley could as easily do the same to her. She wrote a letter to Shelley from Clifton on 27 July 1815 in which she could hardly contain her agitation: 'We ought not to be absent any longer indeed we ought not – I am not happy at it – when I retire to my room no Shelley – though I have heaps of things *very particular* to say – in fine either you must come back or I must come to you directly.... We have been now a long time separated and a house is not yet in sight.... I cannot bear to remain so long without you.'[3] Her feelings of unease and estrangement were heightened by Shelley's apparent neglect of the anniversary of their dramatic elopement on 28 July. It was a year since she had passionately committed herself to him and joined him in their headlong dash for Dover on that sweltering summer day. Within the last twelve months they had packed in so much living and loving and yet there she was, on the eve of their anniversary, languishing miserably in lodgings, pregnant for the second time and frequently frightened and near despair:

> 'Do not be angry dear love – your Pecksie is a good girl & is quite well now again – except a headache when she waits so anxiously for her loves letters – dearest best Shelley pray come to me – pray pray do not stay away from me – this is delightful weather and you better we might have a delightful excursion to Tintern Abbey – my dear dear Love – I most earnestly & with tearful eyes beg that I may come to you if you do not like to leave the searches after a house.'

She had added the tentative question, 'Pray is Clary with you? for I have enquired several times & no letters.'[4]

Although there was no evidence that Claire was up in London with Shelley, Mary, who was always so perceptive and often particularly well tuned to Shelley's thoughts, was possibly justified in fearing that he was keeping her at a distance that was more than spatial.

Perhaps the poignancy of her letter roused Shelley from his dreamy preoccupation, perhaps her fears were unfounded, but by the beginning of August he had leased a house on Bishopsgate Heath, bordering the expanses of Windsor Forest. It was small and square with two storeys and a veranda hung with creepers. Mary eagerly joined him and they settled in to a quietly productive routine of study, writing and walks through basking summer fields and the best of England's woodland. Shelley would work outside under the trees, taking inspiration from the elements. It was a tranquil and reflective time for him and with the approach of autumn came a gentle melancholy at the futility of human aspirations and the transience of life: '... who is there that will pursue phantoms, spend his choicest hours in hunting after dreams, and wake only to perceive his error and regret that death is so near?'[5] he wrote to Hogg at the end of August.

For Mary it was a perfect summer. She was living a peaceful, harmonious life, essentially private with only the very occasional visits from Peacock, Charles Clairmont or Hogg to disturb their sunny patch of the woods. On one such social event with Peacock and Charles, Shelley decided to plan a boat trip up the Thames to discover its source. It was September and the days were hot and dry. In high spirits Mary, with the three men, set off in a wherry to row to Lechlade or beyond. Peacock had insisted that for the sake of rowing efficiency Shelley had to abandon his vegetarian pap of tea, bread and cakes in favour of more muscular fare; three mutton chops, well peppered, was Peacock's prescription. The river meandered through slumbering meadows, edged with poplars and weeping willows, then on through the Goring Gap with the wooded slopes of the Berkshire downs rising sharply to the south-west and the swell of the Chilterns to the north. The weather was perfect high summer. They rowed leisurely by day and by night slept on the river banks under the stars. The trip became something special for every member of the crew. Mary noted everything with delight and her precise memory reworked the reality in her fiction. She always liked to write from life and her description of a Berkshire boat trip in a short story written years later has the stamp of this summer expedition:

'Our boat has floated long on the broad expanse; now let it approach the umbrageous bank. The green tresses of the graceful willow dip into the waters, which are checked by them into a ripple. The startled teal dart from their recess, skimming the waves with splashing wing. The stately swans float onward; while innumerable waterfowl cluster together out of the way of the oars. The twilight is blotted by no dark shades; it is one subdued, equal receding of the great tide of day .. We may disembark, and wander yet amid the glades, long before the thickening shadows speak of night.'[6]

They reached Oxford and spent one night there. Shelley showed Mary the Bodleian, the Clarendon Press and his college and rooms. It was his first return to the place since his life as a freshman there had been so dramatically curtailed. Mary was intrigued to see at last the stage on which her beloved heretic withstood the full wrath of Church and academe. They clambered back into their wherry and headed for Lechlade. The river wound its way through flat water-meadows in remote and uninhabited country. It became narrower and reedy, waterfowl and wild animals more numerous; they rowed on through the lush wooded banks around the village of Lechlade, but pressing on upstream, were thwarted by the tangle of weeds and lack of water. They returned to Lechlade and here in the still graveyard of the little fifteenth-century church, Shelley wrote his poem entitled *A Summer-Evening Church-Yard, Lechlade*. The trip had been a great success, he was in better health than he had been since Mary had first met him; he was fit with the rowing and ruddy from the sun. His melancholy and inertia had given way to a creative vitality that was to produce on his return his second long poem, *Alastor*, rich in river imagery.

Mary, too, had been restored to the blooming confident young woman of the previous summer. Hardly a cloud shadowed the sky; she loved Shelley and was secure in her relationship with him, financial problems no longer oppressed them and the baby within her, more carefully and tranquilly nurtured, would live to lay the ghost of her first born.

By 10 September Mary once again was settling into her rural routine of reading, writing and the diligent study of Latin under Shelley's taxing eye. Herself invigorated by the river expedition, it gladdened her heart to see Shelley so well and enthusiastically writing again; on sunny days he would work amid falling leaves under the spreading branches of the sovereign oaks on the fringe of Windsor Forest. Mary was committed and interested enough in her own projects happily to leave him to work for six hours at a stretch. Out of these months of quiet consolidation of her relationship with Shelley arose Mary's own sense of individuality and independence. When Hogg visited them in October he met a confident and enigmatic young woman. Reflective and emphatic, she was so different from the lonely, anxious and often unwell girl of Nelson Square. He was never to feel completely at ease with her again.

Shelley's poem, *Alastor*, was finished by the end of the year. It was full of river and forest imagery, a spirited allegory of self-discovery. '... didactic rather than narrative: it was the out-pouring of his own emotions, embodied in the purest form he could conceive, painted in the ideal hues which his brilliant imagination inspired, and softened by the recent anticipation of death',[7] was how Mary described it in her astute notes to the first collection of Shelley's poems. In this poem children creep into his imagery, here binding relationships with their insinuatively winning ways:

> 'the parasites,
> Starr'd with ten thousand blossoms, flow around
> The grey trunks, and, as gamesome infants' eyes
> With gentle meanings, and most innocent wiles,
> Fold their beams round the hearts of those that love,
> These twine their tendrils with the wedded boughs
> Uniting their close union'[8]

In fact their expected baby was very much in Mary's mind too. As November passed into December she was relieved to have reached her eight month of pregnancy without a recurrent premature labour. Every week that passed from then on meant her baby was growing bigger and stronger and more likely to survive at birth.

The first weeks of the new year of 1816 were animated by a continuous stream of letters between Godwin at Skinner Street, coldly demanding money and stiff with disapproval, and Shelley, concisely explanatory of his complex finances and coolly rebutting the worst of Godwin's insults.

'If you really think me vicious such haughtiness as I imputed to you is perhaps to be excused. But I who do not agree with you in that opinion, cannot be expected to endure it without remonstrance'[9] he reasonably wrote to Godwin in the middle of his patient exposition of financial details.

Mary was to be plagued by her father's complaining and demanding letters for the rest of her life with Shelley. In years to come, when she was struggling with her own grief, these letters distressed and distracted her so greatly that Shelley, in fear for her health and sanity, hid them from her sight. Mary was now heavily pregnant and apprehensive about the resilience of the small life within her. Her father's letters arrived at their home in Bishopsgate and his chilly self-centredness, his refusal to discuss anything other than money or see them in person, his rejection of his daughter and indifference to her health and happiness, all cut through Mary's contentment like a knife. Mary's novel, *Mathilda*, was based on the intense love of a daughter for her father, and her anguish at his death. Mary, too, had lost her beloved father, as if that familial part of him had died when she eloped. Even when Godwin embraced her and Shelley once again with hypocritical glee on the advent of their marriage, he had declined irrecoverably into a miserable, harsh and selfish old man. Yet, steadfastly, she was to support and love him for the rest of his life. With this epidemic of his letters invading their retreat from the world, Mary, as she grew near to becoming a parent herself, must have deeply regretted the degeneration of his relationship with her.

On 24 January, Mary went into a manageable and speedy labour. She gave birth to a son, at home. He was full-term and healthy and she was elated. With his strong pink body in her arms, the wound of her first baby's death was almost healed and her frustrated maternal love welled once again to encompass him. Despite her father's rejection, she and Shelley decided to name him William in memory of the man. Her journal for this time was lost and the only mention of William's birth was a low-key sentence in Shelley's letter to Godwin, written the following day, implicitly accusing him of indifference towards his one and only daughter: 'Fanny & Mrs Godwin will probably be glad to hear that Mary had safely recovered from a very favourable confinement, & that her child is well.'[10]

Mary and Shelley continued in a close, unruffled domesticity. Baby William was a wonder and delight to both of them. Mary was feeding him herself and relieved to see him grow stronger and more robust as they left cold winter behind. In her garden the spring bulbs were gleaming in the pale sunshine and their neighbour, the great forest, was stirring into life. But beyond this the world was less serene. Godwin's hectoring letters steadily persisted through February and March, worrying Shelley and spoiling Mary's tranquillity. Their mention of exile to escape the censure and contempt of family and society failed to fill Godwin with remorse; rather did he panic at the prospect of losing this source of revenue. Shelley's irritation and disillusionment with the increasingly blatant self-interest of this man, once his philosopher-hero and spiritual father, burst through his usually restrained replies. In a letter quivering with hurt and long-suppressed fury, he wrote on 6 March:

'In my judgement neither I, nor your daughter, nor her offspring, ought to receive the treatment which we encounter on every side. It has perpetually appeared to me to have been your especial duty to see that, so far as mankind value your good opinion, we were justly dealt by, and that a young family, innocent and benevolent and united, should not be confounded with prostitutes and seducers.... Do not talk of *forgiveness* again to me, for my blood boils in my veins, and my gall rises against all that bears human form, when I think of what I, their benefactor and ardent lover, have endured of enmity and contempt from you and all mankind.'[11]

It was written while Shelley was in London on business and away from Mary's mitigation. She would have told him that it would only do harm, for nothing could now permeate her father's withering self-righteousness. In fact it drove a bulldozer through the breach already separating them, and never again were they able to bridge that chasm. The continued harassment from Godwin, the sense of being misunderstood and mistreated by society, enhanced by the hostile, ignorant and largely indifferent reception to the publication of two slim volumes of Shelley's poems – a collection of his early works including an expurgated *Queen Mab*, and *Alastor* – all hastened the exile that both Mary and Shelley had resisted.

Their projected Continental escape was of deep interest to Claire, who had entered their lives again. At the beginning of the year she had had enough of rural delights and uneventful solitude and had returned to London, all the while financed by Shelley. She put into action an extraordinary and bold plan creaking with naïve machinations. There was very little orthodox employment for a young woman such as her. She was nearly eighteen and would have liked to go on the stage, but above all longed to do as her clever step-sister had done and capture herself a poet. Her romanticism, the heady influence of Shelley and Mary's affair, the promise of personal freedom and divine purpose in the elevated role of poet's confidante, inspiration and friend, all determined her to set her sights on the most glamorous poet in the land, Lord George Byron. With youthful arrogance and admirable persistence, she succeeded in becoming briefly his mistress, fleetingly his inspiration, but neither confidante nor friend. This brief liaison was to be the cause of the greatest tragedy in Claire's life, a source of corrosive, accumulative bitterness.

At the beginning of 1816, Byron was caught in a vulnerable, disillusioned and indecisive period of his life. In January his marriage had been declared a fiasco with his permanent separation from his wife and daughter. He had had to contend with a measure of innuendo, censure and thrilled prurience over his relationship with his half-sister Augusta. Although Byron still had friends it was a sterile and depressing time for him. Then into his life came an effusive girl, writing two letters under different pseudonyms, begging for an audience.

'If a woman, whose reputation has yet remained unstained, if without either guardian or husband to control she should throw herself upon your mercy, if with a beating heart she should confess the love she has borne you many years, if she should secure to you secresy and safety, if she should return your kindness with fond affection and unbounded devotion, could you betray her, or would you be silent as the grave?'[12] He was momentarily interested; she might divert him for a time from the boredom of his present limbo.

She contrived to spend a night with him, despite her protestations: 'I have no passions; I had ten times rather be your male companion than your mistress.'[13] But this way she was sealing his membership of the Shelleyan community of enlightened spirits. Perhaps she hoped, too, that by bringing such a prize to Shelley's circle she was ensuring and improving her status in the group. To this end, Mary was brought by Claire to see her trophy and be seen by him. Drawing a formidable picture of Mary, she wrote this unwittingly funny and breathless note:

> 'Mary has promised to accompany me tonight. Will you be so good as to prepare your servants for the visit, for she is accustomed to be surrounded by her own coterie who treat her with the greatest politeness. I say this because on Monday evening I waited nearly a quarter of an hour in your hall, which though *I* may overlook the disagreeableness, *she* is not in love and would not. I have informed her of your name. So you need not appear in a mask; she is very curious to see you. She has not the slightest suspicion of our connection. For pity's sake breathe not a word. Do not mention my name. Talk only on general subjects....'[14]

Part of the grand plan was that Byron and Shelley should be great friends and Mary should become Byron's lover. Mary did not in fact collaborate on this point, but became his friend and was to find him disturbingly attractive, 'dear, capricious, fascinating Albé',[15] although at the same time she was repulsed by his excesses and weaknesses, so antithetical to Shelley's own severe idealism.

In any event Mary was immediately impressed, even beguiled.

Claire wrote to Byron after the meeting, 'Mary is delighted with you as I knew she would be; she entreats me in private to obtain your address abroad that we may, if possible, have again the pleasure of seeing you. She perpetually exclaims: "How mild he is! How gentle! How different from what I expected." '[16] Claire believed that Mary was still in the dark about the real nature of the liaison, that her and Byron's circumspect talk 'on general subjects' had laid the intended false trail. By April Claire had conceived, although she was not to know for sure until Byron had lumbered out of England in his monstrous coach, heading for Switzerland. She lost no time in pressing Shelley into taking her with them and in directing his thoughts to Geneva, in pursuit of the noble poet. No doubt Mary was not averse to seeing Byron again and, with that in prospect, Claire's living en famille once again seemed more bearable.

It was early summer and Mary and Shelley were ready to leave England for Geneva. There was no tie of family or friendship to keep them. By 3 May 1816, they, with baby William and an excited Claire, had set off to make their modest way to Switzerland, retracing in part the steps of their honeymoon expedition, this time in slightly greater comfort. They were gone 'perhaps forever',[17] although Shelley intended to return within a fortnight to finish some business and collect Hogg to take him back to their sequestered community in the Alps. Throughout Mary and Shelley's years abroad there was to be little embracing of the natives or their ways. The people of the various countries in which they lived or travelled were largely incidental, only impinging on the Shelleys' insular Englishness when they were particularly barbaric, picturesque or scholarly. Although in the years to come Mary was to reminisce longingly about her glorious Italian interlude, it was the spirit of place, rather than the people, that she missed. The sensuousness of the landscape, the climate, the redolence of the air, the Mediterranean light, all added impulse to their own inspiration and to the interaction of imported English friends who joined them in their introspective circle. Byron alone fraternized with the local community and his open house and cheerful profligacy raised a few expatriate eyebrows and fed the scandalmongers at home.

9
Frankenstein and the Villa Diodati

'How I, then a young girl, came to think of and to dilate upon so very hideous an idea?:
Introduction to *Frankenstein*, Mary Shelley

Mary and Shelley's journey took ten days in all. Everything had been uneventful until they approached the phalanges of the Jura. Their carriage trundled up the Alpine foothills in a fury of wind and rain, 'by the light of a stormy moon'.[1] The next day they continued their sluggish ascent through characteristic Alpine spectaculars. Between the eternal mountains and the mist-filled chasms lay expanses of dark impenetrable forest, crowding to the edges of their serpentine road. All had become familiar images. Although it was May, spring was unusually late, so they were told by locals, as they plunged into an obliterating snowstorm.

For the last haul up into Geneva, Shelley had to bribe village officials to be able to use the safer route via Nion. In order to survive on even this road they had to hire four horses and ten men to force the carriage through the snowdrifts and prevent it from slipping off the precipitous road to crash into any of numerous ravines below. These last few onerous miles were through a silent desert of snow and monster pines, along an invisible road delineated merely by the morse of marker poles.

Mary, and the rest of her party, were subdued neither by their precarious state nor by the relentless snow 'pelting against the window of our carriage',[2] as they travelled on into an early twilight. '... never was scene more awfully desolate',[3] exclaimed Mary, and her retentive memory stowed away the dramatic images to be reclaimed later and worked with affecting power into *Frankenstein*.

They booked into the Hôtel d'Angleterre in Secheron on the outskirts of Geneva. Once again Mary was entranced with the landscape, her senses intoxicated by this basin in the Alps, all lake, mountain and sky. The wild flowers, the warmth and the smell of the place, were more vivid than in memory or imagination. Sometimes her reserve gave way to the highest spirits which would burst through in an access of giddiness and wild jubilation. Her fate and Shelley's were intimately entangled with boats and water. This time that combination filled her with glee: 'We have hired a boat, and every evening, at about six o'clock, we sail on the lake, which is delightful, whether we glide over a glassy surface or are speeded along by a strong wind. The waves of this lake never afflict me with the sickness that deprives me of all enjoyment in a sea-voyage; on the contrary, the tossing of our boat raises my spirits and enspires me with unusual hilarity.'[4]

Her studying was not neglected. At midday when it was too hot to go out she sat in the hotel and read Latin and Italian. With Shelley more committed to her than ever, with their little baby son already weaving his wiles around both of them, with freedom from the cares of Skinner Street and with her growing maturity and greater self-confidence, 'this delightful spot during this divine weather' was the magic spell that released her creative powers. 'I feel as happy as a new-fledged bird, and hardly care what twig I fly to, so that I may try my new-found wings.'[5] While Mary was pointing out the rabbits in the garden to little William and watching the lizards basking on a wall in the sun, Shelley was less enthusiastic in a homesick letter to Peacock: 'Our Poets & our Philosophers our mountains our lakes, the rural lanes & fields which are ours so especially, are ties which unless I become utterly senseless can never be broken asunder. These & the memory of them ... will make the name of England, my country dear to me forever.'[6]

Meanwhile an agitated Claire was awaiting the arrival of Byron whose progress had been more stately and ponderous; several times his gigantic coach had had to be rescued from the Flemish mud. She now knew that she was probably pregnant, and wrote him bright little notes addressed to *postes restantes* along the way. His increasing indifference goaded her to further outbursts of passion and pique; she had little idea of the man she purported to love and even less idea of the gulf that separated them. In letters to his half-sister Augusta and to his friend Douglas Kinnaird, Byron protested that she had made all the running and had given him little alternative. 'I never loved nor pretended to love her, but a man is a man, and if a girl of eighteen comes prancing to you at all hours, there is but one way. ...'[7]

He finally arrived with his grand entourage on 23 May and signed his name with a flourish in the hotel visitors' book, putting his age at 100. According to William Polidori, his young Italian doctor, Byron first met Shelley, and made a reacquaintance with Mary and Claire, as he was climbing out of a boat on the shore of the lake. Byron was shy and Shelley a little over-awed, yet they managed to make an appointment to dine together in the evening, minus the ladies. It was the beginning of a singular friendship for both. It was never a completely relaxed relationship but it was extraordinarily creative and dynamic. They were intellectually matched and temperamentally antipodean. Byron was worldly, red-blooded and extravagant; taking an objectively humorous and sceptical view of life, he was undoubtedly a natural winner at the game. Whereas Shelley, intensely idealistic, philanthropic and impressionable, was essentially humourless, subjective and passive, a victim of fate. Mary, who was a keen and astute spectator of Shelley and Byron's dialogues, characterized and contrasted them both in *The Last Man*:

> 'No two persons could be more opposite than Adrian [Shelley] and he. With all the incongruities of his character, Raymond [Byron] was emphatically a man of the world. His passions were violent, as these often obtained the mastery over him, he could not always square his conduct to the obvious line of self-interest, self-gratification at least was the paramount object with him. He looked on the structure of society as but a part of the machinery which supported the web on which his life was traced. The earth was spread out as an highway for him; the heavens built up as a canopy for him.
>
> 'Adrian felt that he made a part of a great whole. He owned affinity not only with mankind, but all nature was akin to him; the mountain and sky were his friends; the winds of heaven and the offspring of earth his playmates; while he the focus only of this mighty mirror, felt his life mingle with the universe of existence. His soul was sympathy and dedicated to the worship of beauty and excellence.'[8]

Despite their differences, they intrigued each other: Shelley by his scholarliness, his passionate revolutionary principles, his frankness and simplicity; Byron by his machismo, his expansiveness and a laconic eloquence rooted in earthy realism.

Mary herself was diffident in Byron's presence. She was a little overwhelmed by the largeness of his personality and by the physical magnetism of the man. His lame foot, a mysterious defect in an otherwise strong athletic body, supreme at most sports, made his physical presence all the more poignant. His bold, bad reputation added its own peculiar spice. But above all, his greatness as a poet, his apparent ease of composition, ensured him Mary's unbounding admiration – Shelley's too, although at times it was clouded with frustration and envy. This professional admiration was to survive the fluctuations of their affections for him. Mary sensed that Byron was uneasy in her company. Certainly she was an extraordinary young woman whose very resistance to categorization perplexed most of her male acquaintances. She was unlike the women Byron had known; she was as far from the social butterfly or the sweet, adoring little woman as she was from the forthright and intellectual feminist of her mother's sorority. What most disconcerted her friends and yet unfailingly attracted and impressed Shelley was her powerful and discerning intellect, her unerring intuition, incongruously set within a demure figure and girlish mien.

Mary was keen to rent a home of their own and escape the society and curiosity of hotel life. Byron, too, had decided to set up house for the summer and both households found two adjacent properties on the opposite shore of Lake Geneva. Mary and Shelley and baby William and Claire moved on 1 June, and Byron followed ten days later. Their cottage was called Maison Chapuis and nestled amongst trees and vineyards on the bank of the lake, with a small, private harbour sheltering their boat below. Up through the vineyards behind their house, the Alps towering in the distance, was the Villa Diodati, an altogether grander establishment where Milton had once stayed. It was an ideal domicile for Byron. A narrow track ran between the two houses, and at least once a day an eagerly loping Shelley, a hopeful Claire and a thoughtful Mary would climb up through the vines to share breakfast or pass the evening hours in philosophizing and literary discussion.

The boat and their water trips were as always an important part of Mary and Shelley's life and in this swift summer Claire, Byron and Polidori were included on their expeditions. The good-natured boatload would row on the lake most evenings and then return to Mary and Shelley's little house for tea. One such moonlit episode was related by Mary to Tom Moore for his *Life of Byron*:

> 'The waters were high and inspiring, – we were all animated by our contest with the elements. "I will sing you an Albanian song," cried Lord Byron; "now, be sentimental and give me all your attention." It was a strange, wild howl that he gave forth; but such as, he declared, was an exact imitation of the savage Albanian mode – laughing, the while, at our disappointment, who had expected a wild Eastern melody.'[9]

Albé, Mary and Shelley's nickname for Byron, may well have originated with this memorable night, as a shortened form of 'Albaneser', or it may, less romantically, have sprung from the sound of his initials, L.B.

Mary, along with Shelley, was flattered and delighted by Byron's friendship. They had so few friends in England and those they had, namely Peacock and Hogg, were not particularly interesting. Yet here in exile with them was the most fascinating literary character in Europe. Despite his vast circles of influence, he was as ostracized, as unorthodox in behaviour, and as misunderstood as they were.

Spring had been late in coming and the summer was wet and stormy. When the rain prevented their evening's boating, Mary, Shelley and Claire would pick their way through the muddy vineyard to the imposing Villa Diodati sitting squarely in the evening light. In the long, shadowy drawing-room Shelley and Byron would sit talking in the candle-light with Polidori's interjections adding to and distracting their far-flung discussions. Claire would position herself carefully to be sure to catch Byron's eye and Mary, partially withdrawn from the pale circle of light, would listen and watch and wonder on all that was said. Beyond the windows stretched the darkening sky with the flickers of light from the distant shore and the shouts of the boatmen and snatches of song floating up on the breeze. By day the view was breathtaking: the polished curve of the lake with its bold, dark shores was enclosed within ranks of make-believe mountains. It was an Alpine perfection but it was never to capture Mary's heart so fully as would the voluptuous landscapes of Tuscany.

Part of the conversation on these nights was concerned chillingly with ghosts. Some volumes of German horror stories, translated into French, had been found and their relating enthralled the candle-lit gathering. On one particular night, possibly 14 June, having discussed such mundane creepies as the *History of the Inconstant Lover*, whose brides turned into wraiths in his arms as punishment for his unfaithfulness, Byron exclaimed, 'We will each write a ghost story', and then turning to Mary he said, 'You and I will publish ours together.'[10] There was general enthusiasm. Polidori outlined some tale about a skull-headed lady who peeped through keyholes, but it was immediately derided. Shelley thought his might be based on his early experiences. Byron's was to be about a vampire; in outline Mary thought it 'very dramatic & striking'.[11] Only Claire and Mary were unable to think of a theme.

Mary was not to be beaten; the search for the idea for a ghost story so good that it proved her ability in the eyes of two such lustrous poets occupied her thoughts for the rest of the night. She would not be satisfied with the pale mediocrity of those in the German book. She determined that hers 'would speak to the mysterious fears of our nature and awaken thrilling horror – one to make the reader dread to look around, to curdle the blood, and quicken the beatings of the heart'.[12]

That night Mary, Shelley and Claire slept at the Diodati, and on coming down to breakfast Mary was asked by Polidori and Byron if she had found her ghost story. She spent much of the day at her house in thought. The weather was particularly wet. Later, Mary went to visit Byron and as she was toiling up the muddy slope to the Diodati she saw Polidori and Byron standing on the balcony watching her progress. Suddenly, goaded by Byron, Polidori jumped from the parapet to offer his arm to Mary, but slipped in the wet and badly sprained an ankle. Byron came to the aid of the ludicrous gallant and carried him indoors. Poor Polidori was infatuated with Mary. He could be arrogant and foolish and was generally the butt of the party. She had startled him one evening by her dramatic recital of Coleridge's poem, *Fire, Famine, and Slaughter*, an emotive denunciation of Pitt. She liked to practise her Italian with him and impressed him with her sedulity and formidable intelligence. Mary was fully aware, however, of Polidori's attachment to her and a few nights later as he lay with his leg up on the sofa feeling sorry for himself, she sweetly put him in his place; 'Mrs S called me her brother (younger)',[13] he noted ruefully in his diary. The parenthesis revealed her condescension, for she was merely eighteen to Polidori's twenty years.

That evening as the damp night drew in, Mary, having fed William and put him to bed, returned to Diodati with Shelley and Claire. She had acquired a Swiss maid, Elise, who would care for her baby should he awake in their little house below. The candles were lit and the talk began to flow. Mary was silent and attentive as usual: '... incapacity and timidity always prevented my mingling in the nightly conversations of Diodati, they were as it were, entirely tête-à-tête between my Shelley and Albé.'[14]

The projected ghost stories were still in everyone's minds when Shelley and Byron began to speculate on the principle of life and whether that vital spark could ever be isolated and used to reanimate or even animate things at will. Shelley's hero, the poetic scientist Doctor Erasmus Darwin, was mentioned, for he had reputedly managed to galvanize a piece of vermicelli in a glass case so that it appeared to have life.

In a logical progression their discussion turned to whether a corpse could be brought back to life; whether, more gruesomely, a creature could be manufactured of separate parts and then animated.

It was well past midnight before the party split up and Mary went to bed. Beyond sleep yet not fully awake, her mind, freed by her body's torpor, was turbulent with vivid images. In her own words she told of the birth of her story:

'My imagination, unbidden, possessed and guided me, gifting the successive images that arose in my mind with a vividness far beyond the usual bounds of reveries. I saw – with shut eyes, but acute mental vision – I saw the pale student of unhallowed arts kneeling beside the thing he had put together. I saw the hideous phantasm of a man stretched out, and then, on the working of some powerful engine, show signs of life, and stir with an uneasy, half-vital motion. Frightful must it be; for supremely frightful would be the effect of any human endeavour to mock the stupendous mechanism of the Creator of the world. His success would terrify the artist; he would rush away from his odious handiwork, horror-stricken. He would hope that, left to itself, the slight spark of life which he had communicated would fade; that this thing which had received such imperfect animation would subside into dead matter, and he might sleep in the belief that the silence of the grave would quench forever the transient existence of the hideous corpse which he had looked upon as the cradle of life. He sleeps; but he is awakened; he opens his eyes; behold, the horrid thing stands at his bedside, opening his curtains and looking on him with yellow, watery, but speculative eyes.

'I opened mine in terror. The idea so possessed my mind that a thrill of fear ran through me, and I wished to exchange the ghastly image of my fancy for the realities around. I see them still: the very room, the dark parquet, the closed shutters with the moonlight struggling through, and the sense I had that the glassy lake and white high Alps were beyond. I could not so easily get rid of my hideous phantom; still it haunted me. I must try to think of something else. I recurred to my ghost story – my tiresome, unlucky ghost story! Oh! If I could only contrive one which would frighten my reader as I myself had been frightened that night!

'Swift as light and cheering was the idea that broke in upon me. "I have found it! What terrified me will terrify others; and I need only describe the spectre which had haunted my midnight pillow."'[15]

The next morning, with memory of her receding nightmare still vivid, Mary announced that she had thought of a story. She started it as soon as William had been fed and dressed and breakfast had been cleared away.

At the head of a sheet of clean white paper Mary wrote, 'It was on a dreary night of November that I beheld the accomplishment of my toils',[16] and on that June day in 1816 *Frankenstein* was born. It was to prove a prodigy, a marvellous, flawed but awesome creation: a monster popular hit that spanned time and place to become a part of modern mythology. As with most folklore, time has obscured its origins and author, and the two protagonists with distance have become one. The name 'Frankenstein', now, almost invariably denotes the monster he created, a transference not so very far removed from Mary's original intent.

The flesh and bones of *Frankenstein* sprang from Mary's own circumstances, her experiences and personality, her scholarship and philosophy, her early nineteenth-century background. There have been lengthy discussions as to the sources of this work.[17] We have her word that the immediate impulse came from Shelley and Byron's discussions at Diodati and her subsequent waking dream.

The successful birth and survival of her darling William, followed by this trip to Geneva, had freed her spirit from the oppression of her family and of the tragedy of her first baby's death. Her creative energies, impelled by the dramatic scenery, the peace and security of her relationship with Shelley and the uniquely stimulating company of Lord Byron, were ready for the concentration and challenge of a work such as this. She loved to write directly from experience and this *tour de force* grew on a web of recalled images of landscapes she had known in Scotland, Geneva, the Alps. There were dramatic echoes of Coleridge's *Ancient Mariner*, always a favourite since she was a little girl at Skinner Street. Milton's *Paradise Lost* had a more substantial role. Mary extracted Adam's declamation against God and placed it on the frontispiece of the first edition of *Frankenstein*:

> 'Did I request thee, Maker, from my clay
> To mould me man? Did I solicit thee
> From darkness to promote me?'

Miltonic imagery and themes abound. There is even a strong case for postulating that, inspired by *Paradise Lost*, Mary made her monster a disadvantaged Adam, who through hatred and rejection became reluctantly aligned with the devil, with Frankenstein as his bungling God.

Mary was also steeped in Godwinism, an influence that spread through childhood, reaching the most affecting proportions in Godwin's novel of grim pursuit and gross social injustice, *Caleb Williams*. This she read for at least the third time in the year of Frankenstein's genesis. In it the pursuer and pursued, Falkland and Caleb Williams, are as Frankenstein and his monster, inseparable but antagonistic parts of the whole.

Shelley's philosophy and personality were threaded even more significantly into the story. He was firstly of the greatest practical use for he urged and encouraged Mary to persevere and enlarge upon what she initially conceived as a short story. He interfered very little if at all with the unfolding of the plot but throughout, most markedly in the intellectual aspirations of Victor Frankenstein, the Shelleyan ideal burns with an unmistakable brightness. Like Shelley, Frankenstein was enthralled by the spirit of scientific enterprise: 'It was the secrets of heaven and earth that I desired to learn; and whether it was the outward substance of things or the inner spirit of nature and the mysterious soul of man that occupied me, still my enquiries were directed to the metaphysical, or in its highest sense, the physical secrets of the world.'[18] This curiosity and inevitable meddling was to be Frankenstein's tragedy.

Shelley's youthful speculations and compositions were much concerned with occultism and death. In *Alastor*, which was his most mature poem to date, and was keenly studied and admired by Mary, Shelley spoke for the yet unborn Frankenstein:

> 'I have made my bed
> In charnels and on coffins, where black death
> Keeps record of the trophies won from thee,
> Hoping to still these obstinate questionings
> Of thee and thine, by forcing some lone ghost,
> Thy messenger, to render up the tale
> Of what we are.'

He continued with an even gloomier precursor of Frankenstein's fatal obsession:

> 'In lone and silent hours,
> When night makes a weird sound of its own stillness,
> Like an inspired and desperate alchymist
> Staking his very life on some dark hope,
> Have I mixed awful talk and asky looks....'[19]

Shelley's personality and life were distinctly fugitive. In his youth he had been pursued by real and imaginary aggressors; as a young man, until his death, he was restlessly, endlessly on the move, rather from something unsatisfactory than towards some promise of fulfilment. Shelley, like both Frankenstein and his monster, was outside society. Feared, ostracized, misunderstood, he was as solitary as Frankenstein became and as socially outcast as his monster.

Not only did Mary's novel spring personally from her own knowledge, experiences and ideas but it was also a product of its social and historical background. Mary had been growing up during one of the most dynamic periods of modern European history. The end of the eighteenth and early nineteenth centuries was a time of dramatic political and social revolution. The principles and successes of the French Revolution had inspired radicals everywhere with a tremendous zeal for debate, for agitation towards a new order of things, for freedom and opportunity for change. The traditional God-centred universe was being challenged by the rapid advances in physical, chemical and biological science. The world appeared to be less simple and less immutable than orthodox religion would allow. With the discrediting of God, man's stature grew: why should he not be capable, in theory, of Creation too? *Frankenstein* was Mary's awful warning to such presumption. However much she might experiment with Shelley's anarchism and atheism, she was innately conservative, and romantic about religion, believing in a comfortable, anthropomorphic God and life after death.

The concurrent industrial revolution, rapidly changing the lives of Englishmen and the priorities and wealth of the nation, was by then, to the discerning few, beginning to raise the spectre of a mechanistic monster, crushing the life from the people. Literature at the time was extraordinarily flourishing. No other period could boast so many literary giants; in England alone there were Wordsworth, Coleridge, Southey, Byron, Keats, Scott, Blake. These writers and their fellows were all involved in politics in its widest sense; the effects of the dual revolution and their general unease about some of the consequences, were expressed in passionate, extreme 'natural' and metaphysical terms which characterized the Romantic movement. In England this was too informal and diffuse to be truly labelled a movement. However, there was a shared and deep antagonism towards the materialism, the rise of the bourgeoisie, the exile from 'natural', primitive values and individual, spontaneous expression – all blamed largely on modern industrialized society.

Yet despite the richness of Mary's sources for her novel, despite its obvious affinity with the historical context of its generation, its power and permanence belong in her timeless and universal themes. The retribution inherent in challenging or parodying Nature, the innate human need for love and society, the perversity of human ambition and the evils of personal rejection and social ostracism – 'I was benevolent and good; misery made me a fiend. Make me happy, and I shall again be virtuous',[20] the monster laments – all live beyond literary fashion.

The coexistence and interdependence of good and evil and the ambiguity of each was exemplified in the indissoluble bond between

Frankenstein and his monster. The dark shadow in everyone was something of which Mary was acutely aware, burdened as she was with her own black dog of melancholy and living with a man who seemed at times to be a genius of goodness and yet, through her life with him, was to attract such evil to them both. With remarkable subtlety and insight, Mary ended her story leaving this struggle and pursuit unresolved. Frankenstein lay dead from frozen exhaustion and despair and the monster, crouched on an ice floe, was 'borne away by the waves and lost in darkness and distance'[21] on his way to the North Pole to fulfil his promise of self-immolation.

Mary was always the most affected by her writings, chock-full as they were with characters and incidents taken from her own life and surprising with uncanny intuition and prophecy. In *Frankenstein* the murders by the monster of Frankenstein's baby brother William, his friend Clerval, his bride Elizabeth, proved to be an ominous and dreadful prescience of the tragedies that were to overtake Mary and Shelley.

However, her story also became a lasting popular success eventually diffusing into myth, for Mary had found an idea that really 'would speak to the mysterious fears of our nature and awaken thrilling horror'.[22] The horror resided largely in the humanity and pathos of her monster forced through the ignorance and prejudice and fear of others from natural benevolence to reluctant malignancy. He was no mere cipher for evil. He had potential, affection, human emotions and needs, but these were blighted and perverted by the clumsy imperfection of his presumptuous creation. Frankenstein, being only human, had failed him and made him physically not a man but a monster-man. Mary scored a second triumph: her monster was not a figment of imagination, an insubstantial ghost or ghoul like those which ineffectually haunted the pages of the Gothic novels of the time. Mary's monster, although unnamed, was real, was possible, manufactured and animated according to purely scientific (although unspecific) principles. She did not have to rely on supernatural forces, magic or suspension of belief. Although Mary was vague about Frankenstein's means of imparting the vital spark to the spare-part carcass lying inert in his laboratory, this detracted not one bit from the power of her story.

To her early nineteenth-century public, Frankenstein's monster was scientifically more feasible than he is today. The Age of Science had begun: Erasmus Darwin was its prophet, the Romantics, and especially Shelley, its poets. Darwin's theories of evolution as a self-propelled and perpetual process obviated the necessity of divine interference. With God's demise the way was free for Man, with science as his tool, to intercept and harness Nature. Frankenstein's monster was then both literally and figuratively a real and appalling possibility. Shelley in the first line of his anonymous and tempering preface to the book's first edition laid the tenability of this frightful idea at his hero's feet: 'The event on which this fiction is founded has been supposed, by Dr Darwin and some of the physiological writers of Germany, as not of impossible occurrence.'[23]

As Mary began writing what she thought would be merely a good short story, chilling enough to amuse and hopefully impress Byron and Shelley on one of the rainy evenings to come, she was unaware of the perturbation it was to cause on its eventual publication, with ramifications rippling outwards through theatre, the cinema and on into folklore. Sitting in the warmth of that June day she applied herself with characteristic diligence to her project. The originality and creativity that Shelley insisted she possessed was now to be put to the test. She had always been so covert and diffident about her writings, eloping two years before with her box of secret works and keepsakes to show shyly to Shelley. Now she was writing for a small but illustrious audience. She wanted to fulfil Shelley's faith in her powers and do herself justice in front of Lord Byron; to create something that would draw her from the shadows of the Diodati drawing-room and establish her in her own right as a woman of some talent and ingenuity.

Ghosts and horror were still the preoccupation of the evening discussions at Byron's villa. By 18 June everyone had begun their stories and interest and enthusiasm ran high. By twelve o'clock that night, Polidori reported that they 'really began to talk ghostly'.[24] Byron recited from memory some of Coleridge's poem, *Christabel*, in suitably chilling tones. The witch, a deadly serpent, had taken the form of a beautiful princess and sought shelter in Christabel's father's castle. She was assigned to Christabel's room and as she undressed before the entranced girl she revealed her ghastly serpentine body and evil intent. Byron emphasized the lines:

> 'Then drawing in her breath aloud,
> Like one that shuddered, she unbound

> The cincture from beneath her breast:
> Her silken robe and inner vest
> Dropped to her feet, and full in view
> Behold! her bosom and half her side
> Hideous, deformed and pale of hue
> A sight to dream of, not to tell!
> And she is to sleep by Christabel!'

Everyone in the dimly-lit drawing-room was silent and a little shivery, for the hour was late and the air from the lake was damp and still, and imagination was in riot. Shelley's dramatically got the better of him and 'suddenly shrieking and putting his hands to his head, ran out of the room with a candle'.[25] Despite his still painful ankle, Polidori hobbled out to minister to him, throwing cold water in his face and giving him ether to revive him. Mary had run to Shelley's side and he explained that he was looking at her as Byron recited the poem and suddenly saw her naked with eyes instead of nipples. The hallucination had terrified him. Still vulnerable and upset, Shelley confided to Polidori the particular injustices in his past which still rankled deeply: Hogg's attempted seduction of Harriet, Godwin's incessant demands for money, and the various physical intimidations from schooldays onwards, particularly during his politically active period with Harriet.

With Shelley exhausted and the others highly wrought, the party broke up. The boating on the lake and communal evenings at Diodati continued until the twenty-third, a Sunday, when Byron and Shelley set off on an expedition to sail round the lake. Despite erratic weather conditions, including a sudden storm which threatened their lives, the eight days that they were gone were of the greatest pleasure and inspiration to both. It was this sentimental journey revisiting the lakeside settings for Rousseau's *La Nouvelle Héloïse*, which Shelley read and delighted in for most of the trip, that inclined the poets' minds away from dark, close evenings and unhealthy spectres and out into the summer air with ideal imaginings.

Meanwhile Mary was persevering with her story. Polidori, rather at a loose end having been left behind ostensibly because of his sprained ankle, but more probably because Byron found him a bore, spent as much time as he could with Mary at Maison Chapuis. Busy as she was with her chuckling baby William, and enthusiastic about finishing her story before Shelley's return, the constant presence of the garrulous and temperamental young doctor often tried her patience severely.

Claire, too, was demanding and tiresome. She was restless and not particularly happy. She had managed to renew her affair with Byron but it was all very desultory and one-sided. In her realistic moments she knew that her pregnancy made her future all the more insecure and unpromising, but she clung to her romantic hope that the fact and sight of his child would smite Byron with something of the love and gratitude that had been so painfully lacking. Claire had managed to conceal her pregnancy from Mary, although that deception could not last much longer. With those large, contemplative eyes and acute perception, she had guessed inevitably the nature of Claire's involvement with Lord Byron. So Mary became the calmly industrious focus for Claire's moods and tantrums and Polidori's dogged attentions.

Shelley and Byron returned on 1 July, healthily ruddy from the wind and sun and full of enthusiastic tales and descriptions of the sights. Mary was alarmed at Shelley's relation of the freak tempest that almost scuppered the boat and drowned him: '... the wind gradually increased in violence, until it blew tremendously; and ... produced waves of a frightful height, and covered the whole surface with a chaos of foam ... the boat was on the point of being driven under water by the hurricane ... one wave fell in, and then another. My companion [Byron] an excellent swimmer, took off his coat, I did the same, and we sat with our arms crossed; every instant expecting to be swamped.' Once again Shelley's beloved water had threatened his life. Again he regarded the prospect with philosophical resignation: 'My feelings would have been less painful had I been alone; but I knew that my companion would have attempted to save me, and I was overcome with humiliation, when I thought that his life might have been risked to preserve mine.'[26]

Mary was far more suspicious of this rapacious element; the sea prostrated her with sickness; even the serener waters of the lake, so dark and inscrutable, seemed to be merely awaiting an opportunity for treachery. Mary was instinctively fearful of what might be the fatal outcome of Shelley's fascinated surrender to the sea. Two of her novels, written before her forebodings were realized at Lerici, cast the sea as appallingly indifferent and predatory. In *Mathilda*, her beloved father, an impassioned Shelley figure, committed suicide by throwing himself into the tempestuous sea, and in *Valperga*, Euthanasia, the heroine, was a Mary/Shelley amalgamation, was lost in a freak storm on her way to Sicily. The description of this as seen from shore was strangely similar to the reports from land of the squall that embroiled the *Ariel* with Shelley and Williams on board, two years after the book was written. Mary's grim suspicion of the sea was fixed even then: 'She was never heard of more; even her name perished. She slept in the oozy cavern of ocean; the seaweed was tangled in her shining hair; and the spirits of the deep wondered that earth had ever trusted so lovely a creature to the barren bosom of the sea, which, as an evil step-mother deceives and betrays all committed to her care.'[27]

Mary showed Shelley her work so far on *Frankenstein* and he was delighted with her progress. The subject was of such magnitude that he suggested that she expand it into a full-length novel. Shelley's critical enthusiasm spurred her modest expectations for the story and encouraged her in dilating it to something far more ambitious, affecting and uncomfortable. She was to write years later in her journal, 'I was nursed and fed with a love of glory. To be something great and good was the precept given me by my Father: Shelley reiterated it.'[28] But during that summer at Diodati, Mary's thoughts were more on testing her own talents and proving herself worthy of Shelley and Godwin than on gaining glory beyond her immediate circle. She could not foresee then and would never know the full impact that *Frankenstein* would make on the world.

The ghost stories had been dropped by all but Mary. The boating on the lake and visits to the Villa Diodati continued but the harmony and inspiration of the inclement June days were seeping away, leaving an unease between the households. Claire was largely to blame. Her dark, hurt eyes and dogged adoration goaded Byron to exasperated anger. She faithfully copied out the third canto of his *Childe Harold* during the first week of July and embarked on *The Prisoner of Chillon*, but her constant presence and desperate eagerness to please resulted in his demanding that Shelley restrain her from coming to the Diodati again.

Luckily Mary and Shelley were planning a trip to Chamonix and Mont Blanc and would be able to remove the unhappy Claire from the immediate vicinity of her irascible lover. Most likely it was such examples as this of his temperamental self-centredness which prompted Shelley's perplexed verdict, 'Lord Byron is an exceedingly interesting person, and as such is it not to be regretted that he is a slave to the vilest and most vulgar prejudices, and as mad as the winds.'[29]

Mary had also been discussing with Shelley the possibility of their returning to England with their beloved son, their maid, Elise, and an adopted kitten, to settle permanently near Windsor Forest or at least along the Thames. They remembered with nostalgia the serene and solitary summer they spent together in Bishopsgate and Shelley wrote to Peacock, in a spontaneous wave of patriotic reminiscence, to ask him to find them an appropriate house, 'a fixed, settled, eternal home'.[30]

Mary was happy and content, healed by William's birth and growing charms, purposeful now that her story was daily gaining life and strength, and fulfilled in the familiar intimacy and security of her life with Shelley. On Sunday, 21 July, she and Shelley, taking Claire but reluctantly leaving William behind with their maid, set off for Chamonix. Mary always found travelling uncomfortable but was spurred on by her enthusiasm for the melodramatic Alpine scenery that crowded around them. Her third journal began with her vivid descriptions of this tour. Their route via Bonneville delighted her with its variety. There a wide, fertile valley, fenced in with mountains, was sharply constricted into a chasm with room only for the rushing river and their precarious sliver of a road. Near Maglands they stopped and gazed at two fine waterfalls that cascaded from such heights that they seemed to turn to mist in flight. And all about them was the chiaroscuro of the encroaching forests, the sun highlighting the poplar and the chestnut amongst the darkness of the pines.

At Chamonix they set off on mules for the Chamonix valley, climbing higher into the Alps and through even more spectacular scenery. Glaciers spread their icy fingers down from the mountains, reaching almost to the road along which their mules plodded. Then suddenly the air was full of a rumble and in front of her eyes Mary saw the smoke of a glacier as it crashed down the opposite mountain, instantaneously disrupting a river's course and demolishing most of the road.

On the Thursday, Mary set out with Shelley and Claire and a party of fellow sightseers and guides to see the famous Mer de Glace, a valley choked with a turbulent river of ice. They picnicked on the grassy bank, breathing the chill air and surveying the scene. 'This is the most desolate place in the world; iced mountains surround it; no sign of vegetation appears except on the place from which we view the scene',[31] Mary wrote in her journal. She was to take Frankenstein on the same pilgrimage to the valley of Chamonix, dramatizing the very details she and Shelley had remarked upon. As a fitting climax to the journey she staged Frankenstein's bitter confrontation with his monster, after the murder of little William, on the awesome and desolate Mer de Glace. Mary had continued writing *Frankenstein* at spare moments throughout the expedition and the fiction was blended closely with the fact. As Mary, Shelley and Claire sat eating their meal, Mary's imagination probably already envisaged the dark and towering silhouette of a man 'advancing towards me with superhuman speed. He bounded over the crevices in the ice, among which I had walked with caution; his stature, also, as he approached, seemed to exceed that of man....'[32]

The little party of tourists returned to the town of Chamonix. Mary was exhausted, 'but pleased and astonished by the world of ice that was opened to our view'.[33] The weather had been variable and, as the next day dawned full of rain, they decided to return home. Mary was now longing to see William, 'my pretty babe'.[34] Shelley had written to Byron and asked after his little son too. By Saturday evening, 27 July, they were home and had him in their arms.

The next day was the second anniversary of Mary and Shelley's elopement. Mary was much happier than she had been that year ago when she had languished in Clifton desperately insecure and lonely, separated from her unpredictable lover.

Her work on *Frankenstein* and her reading continued. Shelley still went up to the Diodati but Mary and Claire more frequently stayed behind at Chapuis. On 2 August Mary went with Shelley into the town to buy him a telescope for his birthday two days later. Shelley and Claire had probably determined by now that they had to discuss her and her baby's future with Byron. That evening was a likely date, for Claire and Shelley went up to the villa and Mary stayed behind 'for Lord Byron did not seem to wish it'.[35] In a letter Claire wrote to Trelawny years later, she explained that Byron accepted responsibility for the child and yielded to her protestations that it should live with one or other of its parents by agreeing to shelter it under his own roof until it was at least seven years old. Claire was to be called its aunt and could thus be involved without arousing suspicions.

On their return Mary would have been told of Byron's reaction and had the evening's plans related to her. Having given birth to two children and known the inextricable bonds of mother love, she must have been dubious of Claire's delighted resolve that her baby would grow up under the auspices of Byron, but separated from herself. The next day they discussed their communal plans – foremost was the need to return to England.

On 4 August, Shelley's twenty-fourth birthday, Mary and he went on a birthday boat trip. When they were off-shore, scudding with the breeze behind them into a solitary stretch of the lake, Mary read aloud to him from Virgil. That evening they were out in the boat again attempting to set off one of Shelley's favoured fire balloons, but the wind was up and they rowed back to the more sheltered shore to set it free there. It caught fire and blazed in mid-air.

On the following Friday Mary received a long and miserable letter from Fanny. She immediately replied, guiltily aware of how Fanny's oppression and distress so cruelly contrasted with her own freedom. Mary felt a sharp sorrow at her neglect of her sister. She had been too engrossed in her own good fortune in having an exceptional man to love, in her healthy, happy baby, in her story that was working well, in the exciting company of Byron – all this amongst a sublimity of mountain landscape, that she fed from and daily gazed upon. She went to town to buy Fanny a Swiss watch, a small piece of Swiss genius to brighten her life a little and make some amends.

On 14 August, Matthew Gregory (Monk) Lewis arrived at the Diodati for a visit. The weather was still unpredictable and unsummery, wet days confining everyone indoors to read and write and talk. Shelley spent most of the evenings in Byron's drawing-room with him and Lewis and occasionally Polidori. To Shelley's disappointment, both Byron and Lewis insisted on the illogic that a belief in ghosts was dependent on a belief in God. The candle-lit room was once again filled with ghostly talk. Mary was not there to hear 'Monk' Lewis's grim but predictable tales, although Shelley related them to her and wrote them in her journal. Both Mary and Shelley knew that her idea was far more effective than these insubstantial horrors. Mary showed Shelley the extent of her story so far and discussed its merits with him.

He was enthusiastic and keen that she persevere. She and Shelley had decided to leave at the end of the month and in the remaining ten days Mary continued industriously reading and writing. She seldom went to Diodati but Byron came down more often to see them at Maison Chapuis.

On the twenty-eighth, Polidori and Lord Byron came to say goodbye. Mary was surrounded by the chaos of packing, but they all had time for one last evening's boating trip together. The next day at nine in the morning Mary with Shelley, William, Claire and Elise, departed, bundled into a laboriously slow coach with all their books and belongings and Shelley in charge of Byron's precious third canto of *Childe Harold*. The return journey was unremarkable except for their tours of the palaces of Fontainebleau and Versailles. Shelley thought them magnificent but his republican principles found them over-rich and cloying, 'something effeminate and royal.... The vacant rooms of this Palace imaged well the hollow show of monarchy.'[36]

10
Two Suicides

'Her voice did quiver as we parted,
Yet knew I not that heart was broken
From which it came, and I departed
Heeding not the words then spoken.
        Misery – O Misery
This world is all too wide for thee'

              Shelley's verse on Fanny Godwin

By 5 September, the travel-worn party had arrived at Le Havre. They had to wait two days for the wind to change and when their captain eventually decided to sail it was still blowing slightly contrary. Mary was once again suffering the day and night ordeal of terrible seasickness. Having arrived at Portsmouth and finally been cleared by customs, Mary, William, Claire and Elise set off on a coach to Bath while Shelley made for London for business and to deliver *Childe Harold* to Byron's publishers, John Murray.

Mary and Claire set out immediately to look for lodgings and eventually settled on rooms at 5 Abbey Church Yard. Despite all the disruption and unsettlement, Mary continued with little hiatus in her study and writing. On about 15 September, Shelley moved down to Marlow to stay with Peacock and look for a permanent house there for Mary and their family. On the following Thursday, Mary left Willy with Claire and went to Marlow to stay with Shelley and Peacock for a week. She went on long, rambling walks with Shelley through lovely autumn countryside. On one such expedition they walked to the ruined Medmenham Abbey, scene of the notorious Hell-Fire Club.

Mary and Shelley travelled back to Bath together, full of plans for the future. They greeted William, related the news to Claire and Mary got back to work. The days passed peacefully and productively: reading, work for Mary, playing with their baby, long walks and optimistic plans for their future home 'in some lone place'[1] with garden, woods and river to secure them.

Shelley and Mary had slipped into an easy domestic contentment that was to be tragically elusive in the months and years to come. Godwin's financial problems, with Fanny shouldering the weight of importuning Shelley's help, had not yet reached grave proportions. Mary was happy and light-hearted, amusing Shelley with her mythology; 'Mary put her head through the door and said, "Come and look; here's a cat eating roses; she'll turn into a woman; when beasts eat these roses they turn into men and women" ',[2] he wrote in her journal.

Then amid these peaceful autumn days the first of two tragedies coldly intruded. On 9 October, Mary received 'a very alarming letter' from Fanny written at Bristol. Shelley set off immediately and Mary and Claire sat up until two in the morning fearing the worst. Shelley returned but with little further information. Mary spent the rest of the night full of foreboding and dread. The following day he returned to Bristol and discovered that Fanny had proceeded to Swansea. The day after that he set off from Bath yet again and travelled to Swansea, returning on 12 October with the dreadful news that Fanny had killed herself with an overdose of laudanum. There was nothing to identify her to the authorities but her stockings were marked with a G and her stays were her mother's, characterized by those simple initials, M.W. On her wrist was the little gold watch sent by Mary from Geneva. By her side was her suicide note:

'I have long determined that the best thing I could do was to put an end to the existence of a being whose birth was unfortunate, and whose life has only been a series of pain to those persons who have hurt their health in endeavouring to promote her welfare. Perhaps to hear of my death will give you pain, but you will soon have the blessing of forgetting that such a creature ever existed as ...'[3]

She had torn her name from the end to protect her family from calumny in a last characteristic subjugation of her own needs for the good of others. This pathetic act and the despairing abnegation of her letter smote Mary with grief and guilt. Shelley's health was immediately and injuriously affected. Claire, who by her own admission had never cared particularly deeply for Fanny, was afflicted by the general gloom in the household. By now she was six months pregnant and had reasons enough of her own for despondency.

Godwin's reaction was callously realistic; afraid of public opinion he urged Mary and Shelley neither to identify Fanny nor to attend her funeral. In his first letter to Mary since she left his house he set out his wishes and their justification:

> 'I did indeed expect it. I cannot but thank you for your strong expression of sympathy. I do not see however that that sympathy can be of any service to me; but it is best. My advice and earnest prayer is that you would avoid anything that leads to publicity. Go not to Swansea; disturb not the silent dead; do nothing to destroy the obscurity she so much desired that now rests upon the event. It was, as I said, her last wish ... we are at this moment in doubt whether, during the first shock, we shall say she is gone to Ireland to her aunt, a thing that has been in contemplation. Do not take from us the power to exercise our own discretion ... what I have most of all in horror is the public papers, and I thank you for your caution, as it might act on this.'[4]

So, under pressure from Godwin, the facts of Fanny's death were suppressed. It passed unmourned, unmarked, by all but her immediate family; to the world it was as if Fanny Godwin, in having lived twenty-two years, had never indeed existed. The reasons for her suicide are equally obscure. Mrs Godwin propagated the story that all the Godwin girls were in love with Shelley and he was guilty of their various ruin. It was more likely that Fanny had only recently learned the full story of her birth from her aunts. Already subject to accesses of Wollstonecraft melancholy and despair, she had been living a loveless and unpromising life, her days full of toil and responsibility and her nights lonely and filled with regrets. In her letters to Mary and her affection for baby Will she implied a reluctant resignation to spinsterhood and the role of dutiful and caring daughter. To an intensely emotional and vulnerable girl the realization that Godwin was not her true father, that motherless and abandoned by her father she had no blood ties within Godwin's family, could have been enough to precipitate her customary depression about her life into a determination to end it.

It was left to Mary and Shelley to immortalize in a small way her loving, undemanding self. Of Mary's characterization of her in her novels, Fanny Derham, in *Lodore*, is perhaps the most poignant: 'One who feels so deeply for others, and yet is so stern a censor over herself – at once so sensitive and so conscientious – so single-minded and upright, and yet open as day to charity and affection, cannot hope to pass from youth to age unharmed....'[5] She lives more lastingly, however, in Shelley's tribute to her:

> 'Her voice did quiver as we parted,
> Yet knew I not that heart was broken
> From which it came, and I departed
> Heeding not the words then spoken.
>   Misery – O Misery
> This world is all too wide for thee.'[6]

Mary knew that Fanny's despair and death were a result more of her unhappiness in an unfulfilled and purposeless domesticity at Skinner Street than of unrequited passion for Shelley, for she wrote to him at the end of the year when their house in Marlow was being negotiated: 'Poor dear Fanny if she had lived until this moment she would have been saved for my house would then have been a proper asylum for her.'[7] And how much happier the next few years might have been for Mary if it had been Fanny and not Claire who shared her domestic life with Shelley.

Their daily life at Bath continued superficially much the same. Mary had drawing lessons with Mr West on Mondays and Thursdays. Their intensive reading programme progressed, Mary and Shelley often studying the same works, although Shelley eschewed most of the contemporary novels which were Mary's light relief from such stately fare as Clarendon's *History of the Civil War*. In the evenings Shelley read aloud to Mary from *Don Quixote* following that with *Gulliver's Travels* and *Paradise Lost*, all good dramatic stuff. Nevertheless, Fanny's death had fractured the circle of serenity and optimism for the future in which Mary had sought to charm her life with Shelley and little Willy. There was a growing realization of their vulnerability, an uneasy expectation of the next blow. Mary was subdued and melancholy. She had lost her trust in fate, she had seen too much of the sad side of life to ever recapture that exuberant sense of omnipotence that had amazed Shelley as she lay in his arms on their first and perilous Channel crossing, seeming 'insensible to all future evils'.[8] Claire, too, was low in spirits. Her pregnancy was well advanced and she had to contemplate childbirth without the security and propriety of marriage or the support of someone wholly committed to her. Her future either with or without her child promised to be financially and socially difficult. Fanny's death had made her and Mary peculiarly aware of the frailty of life; Claire was about to risk hers to bring another into the world and Mary, with memories of the sudden loss of her first baby, hugged William to her. Frankenstein's lament at the inopportunity of death might well have been part of her own thoughts that winter: 'Death snatches away many blooming children, the only hopes of their doting parents; how many brides and youthful lovers have been one day in the bloom of health and hope, and the next a prey for worms and the decay of the tomb!'[9]

In the beginning of December Shelley had set off to stay with Peacock at Marlow in a further attempt to find a home for himself and Mary. Mary sent him a loving letter urging him, 'Do not be long away! take care of yourself, & take a house.... Ah – were you indeed a winged Elf and could soar over mountains & seas and could pounce on the little spot – A house with a lawn a river or lake – noble trees & divine mountains that should be our little mousehole to retire to. But never mind this – give me a garden & *absentia Clariae* and I will thank my love for many favours.'[10]

The need for *absentia Clariae* to make her happiness complete spoke of the tensions and disruptions of Claire's influence whenever she was particularly unhappy or insecure. As she approached her last month of pregnancy, anxious for the future and rejected by Byron, her moodiness and temperamental outbursts were understandable but difficult for Mary to bear. Her private times with Shelley and their babe were precious and too often distracted by the demands of her self-centred step-sister.

Fanny's death had sharpened Mary's appreciation of her loved ones and she wanted to pull them closer and secure them. William was all the more poignantly delightful: 'The blue eyes of your sweet boy are staring at me while I write this he is a dear boy and you love him tenderly', she wrote to Shelley. William was nearly a year old and Mary was beginning to feel emotionally ready for another baby. 'Tell me shall you be happy to have another little squaller?'[11] She was not yet pregnant but was teasing Shelley, testing his reaction.

Shelley had been on a visit to Leigh Hunt, poet and journalist, at his family house in Hampstead. There he met Keats for the first time and impressed Hunt who promised him a review of *Alastor* in the *Examiner*, the radical paper of which he was editor. With this good news, and feeling confident and high on admiration and generous hospitality, Shelley returned to Bath and Mary. The next day, 15

December, brought news that compounded Mary and Shelley's individual burdens of guilt. Thomas Hookham wrote to tell them of Harriet Shelley's suicide. Her body had been dragged from the Serpentine on 10 December. She was far advanced in pregnancy. These brief circumstances of her death were horrifying and Mary walked with Shelley in an attempt to soothe him, agreeing with his denials of personal guilt and his justifications for deserting her. They discussed what had to be done, for Shelley wanted to claim his children, Ianthe and Charles, and had to move decisively and immediately.

After lunch he set off for London to see his solicitors. Shelley had told Longdill that he intended to marry Mary and this he was assured would clinch in his favour the custody of his and Harriet's children. Agitated and emotionally overwrought, Shelley's letter to Mary written on the following day showed him to be full of love for her and dependent on her serene strength and realistic support, full of hopes that together they could win the children from the Westbrooks and give them a home. 'My only hope my darling love, this will be one among the innumerable benefits which you will have bestowed upon me, & which will still be inferior in value to that greatest of benefits – yourself – it is thro' you that I can entertain without despair the recollection of the horrors of unutterable villainy that lead to this dark dreadful death.'[12] This dark, dreadful death Shelley laid hysterically at Eliza Westbrook's door, with a melodramatic tale of how Harriet had been driven from her father's house, thereby forced into prostitution, living with a groom who impregnated and then deserted her, leaving suicide as her only choice. All this was apparently machinated by Eliza in order that she should inherit old Mr Westbrook's fortune. In fact Harriet had left her children with her family in Chapel Street on 9 November and had taken rooms in Chelsea, possibly to have her baby away from her family. It was from here that she went to the Serpentine and in the grim chill of December drowned herself.

The reason for Shelley's vituperative attack on Eliza became clearer in the rest of his letter to Mary: "Everyone does *me* full justice; – bears testimony to the uprightness & liberality of my conduct to her'.[13] Poor Shelley protested too much; he was Mary's Frankenstein, declaiming his utter innocence and freedom from culpability. Mary knew Shelley's doubts and was quick to reply with a loving and reassuring letter, although she, too, was agitated and discomposed. She reiterated and emphasized her love of Ianthe and Charles, whom she had never seen and Shelley hardly knew, stressing how keen she was to care for them, 'these darling treasures that are yours'. Rather than lodge them in the interim with Hunt and his brood, as Shelley projected, Mary with a spontaneous and good-hearted concern wrote, 'My heart says bring them instantly here.' The only note of uncertainly was in her reference to the familial demotion of her own William, tactlessly banged home by the irritated Claire: 'There will be a sweet brother and sister for my William who will lose his pre-eminence as eldest and be helped third at table – as his Aunt Clare is continually reminding him.'[14]

Although joining in Shelley's enthusiasm for the idea of sheltering and loving these two unfortunate little children, Mary must have wondered a little at Shelley's previous detachment and lack of interest in their everyday welfare. Perhaps this determined activity was a means of making amends for the neglect and abandonment that had preluded Harriet's miserable end.

Mary and Shelley's marriage appeared to be an imperative in his fight for the children. Godwin had softened remarkably on hearing of Harriet's death and was applying pressure on both his daughter and Shelley to formalize their union. For Mary the prospect of marriage to the man she loved and whose children she had borne can only have been a happy one. She had purposely outlawed herself from society and from an orthodox life by her headlong commitment to Shelley in those heated days in the summer of 1814. Now, unexpectedly, she was to be elevated in the eyes of the world from Shelley's mistress to his wife, thereby legitimizing her children, establishing their place in the Shelley line and giving her the name she was to love and value, Mary Shelley. Years later in some banter with Trelawny about her marrying again, she wrote emphatically, 'Never, – neither you nor anybody else. Mary Shelley shall be written on my tomb, – and why? I cannot tell, except it is so pretty a name that though I were to preach to myself for years, I never should have the heart to get rid of it.'[15]

Shelley, too, loving Mary, enjoying life with her and William, relying on her for anchorage and understanding, and intrigued and inspired by her intellectual powers, was quite willing to smooth life a little for themselves and their children and to make the woman who had suffered to be with him happy.

At the end of December Mary joined Shelley in London, visiting both Skinner Street and the Hunts' home. On the twenty-ninth, the eve of their marriage, they had supper with the Godwins. It was the first time in two years that Mary had eaten at her old home and the overwhelming associations with Fanny made it hard to keep the melancholy from impinging on their celebrations. Godwin was ingratiatingly civil, showing 'the most polished and cautious attentions to me and Mary',[16] as Shelley remarked in a letter to Claire.

The following day, a Monday, the marriage 'so magical in its effects'[17] of Shelley and Mary took place in St Mildred's church, Bread Street. Both were little deceived by Godwin's hypocritical *volte face* but it made things easier to be on more favourable terms with him, for Mary, despite all his neglect and selfishness, still loved her father dearly. The Godwins had not the slightest inkling of Claire's plight and by Wednesday Mary and Shelley turned back to Bath to be with her as the time for her confinement approached.

On 12 January, Claire gave birth to a little girl and decided to call her Alba, as a form of Albé, their private nickname for Byron. Claire had a good labour and her baby was beautiful. Mary's maternal affections, already over-active, embraced this little girl whose unusual liveliness and brightness she immediately noticed. She wrote to Lord Byron the following day and calmly informed him of the safe delivery, sending Claire's love and proudly signing herself Mary W. Shelley.

Shelley had had to return to London on 6 January to untangle the mass of evidence he had to put before the courts in his bid to win Ianthe and Charles from the Westbrooks. Despite his very real support from Leigh Hunt and his renewed communications with Godwin, it was Mary whom he needed most when agitated and threatened. He wrote a heartfelt letter to her, positive and hopeful of the outcome, but emotionally desolate: 'How painful in these difficult & in one sense tremendous circumstances it is to me to be deprived of the counsel of your judgement & the consolation of your dear presence.'[18] Perhaps Shelley, too, was gaining some emotional security in knowing that Mary, 'my own darling Pecksie', was now his wife.

Mary was almost invariably discreet in her early journals. Her marriage was merely marked by, 'A marriage takes place on the 30th December 1816',[19] and Claire's childbearing was nonchalantly accounted for as 'Four days of idleness'.[20]

Little William's first birthday, 24 January, was the day that the Chancery suit for custody began. Mary hoped this coincidence boded well. 'How many changes have occurred during this little year; may the ensuing one be more peaceful, and my William's star be a fortunate one to rule the decision of this day. Alas! I fear it will be put off, and the influence of the star pass away.'[21] The influence of William's star did pass away. The case struggled on for weeks. Two days later Mary left Bath for London and alternated between Skinner Street and the Hunts' home at Hampstead. She stayed up in town with Shelley for over a month to see him through the worst of the case. It was a busy, varied and stimulating period for Mary, enjoying the unaccustomed society of the literary set who gathered at Hunt's informal and hospitable home. Hazlitt stayed one night until three in the morning arguing with Shelley about monarchy and republicanism. They enjoyed rambles on the Heath with Keats. Mary was missing William, 'Blue Eyes', who had been left with Elise, Claire and Alba, but the Hunts were very kind to her, taking her to the opera to see Mozart's *Marriage of Figaro*, including her and Shelley in the casual suppers and musical evenings.

It was a time, too, for Mary to renew and restore her fractured relationship with her father. He was benign and more inclined to be emotionally generous than he had been for years. However, Mrs Godwin and Mary never having managed to forge a relationship in the past, had resigned themselves to mutual antipathy.

During February Mary would have realized that she was pregnant again. Her diary began to record days when she was 'not well'; pregnancy never really agreed with her.

Mary and Shelley were delighted to see their William again after eight weeks without him. He had travelled up with Claire, Elise and Alba and was taken the next day to be introduced to his Godwin grandparents. He was talking and almost walking, a real 'blue-eyed boy'.[22] At the end of February, their literary life in London was relinquished for the rural delights of Marlow. Claire and Alba stayed behind with the hospitable Hunts while Shelley and Mary, with their son and maid Elise, moved down to Peacock's house to wait for their furniture, for they could not move into Albion House, their new home that Shelley had leased, for a fortnight.

Mary was delighted with the appearance and situation of the house, full of hopes for the future: '... flowers – trees & shady banks – ought we not to be happy',[23] she wrote to the Hunts, brimming with enthusiasm for these new friends, for real friends had proved a rare commodity in her life. Even faithful Peacock and his mother she found tiresome and uninspiring.

The weather was warm and the lovely countryside was beginning to green with the spring. But beyond these everyday pleasures Mary was suspended in a strange melancholy, impressed with a sense of impotence in the face of destiny. She wrote to Hunt, 'A year ago, I remember my private hours were all made bitter by reflection on the certainty of death – and now the flight of time has the same power over me. Everything passes and one is hardly conscious of enjoying the present before it becomes the past.'[24]

Although still only nineteen, having lived so vividly during the last eventful year and a half, Mary was covetous of the fleeting days and regretful of the transience of experience. She wrote in a similar vein to Shelley three months later, 'Why is not life a continued moment where hours and days are not counted – but as it is a succession of events happen – the moment of enjoyment lives only in memory and when we die where are we?'[25]

Mary knew that only in her writing could she arrest the evanescence of experience and preserve something of her fleeting life beyond individual memory and even death. On 18 March they claimed Albion House as their home. As soon as she and Shelley had moved their possessions, their books and their dependants, had sited the statues they had ordered and issued invitations to the Hunts and Godwins, Mary settled herself in their pride, the library-room, and finished her first draft of *Frankenstein* in a burst of sustained effort.

Mary had also been writing twittery, solicitous letters to Leigh and Marianne Hunt. She was obviously fond of them and valued their new friendship but was unsure of her approach and how to express her affection. She was one moment coy and teasing and the next withdrawn and apologetic. She was never readily at ease with people, her warm heart was frequently aroused but her shyness and self-consciousness hindered and distorted the natural expression of her feelings, making her appear aloof and cold or alarmingly intense. On odd occasions she would swing to the other extreme in a fit of high spirits which were just as misleading. Mary was persistent in her invitations to the Hunts: 'Come then, dear, good creatures, let us enjoy with you the Beauty of the Marlow sun and pleasant walks that will give you all health spirits & industry.'[26] In fact when the Hunts did come on Sunday, 6 April, the weather had changed and it was chilly and miserable. Marianne was not well, but a major point of their visit was to return Alba. Claire had moved into Albion House a week previously but, as Godwin was expected for four days, Alba had been left behind with the accommodating Hunts, camouflaged amongst their numerous children.

Albion House was a perfect home for the summer, with its large cool rooms a refuge from the sun-baked gardens, but in winter the coolness turned to damp and the shade to oppressive gloom. It stood on the main road from London to Henley, the lovely lazy Thames was only a short walk away and the expanse of secluded gardens behind was in peaceful contrast to the business of the road. They had space enough for their servants, a cook and a maid, Claire and Alba and Elise and for the occasional visitors. Shelley had already secured a boat for himself and, as the weather improved, expeditions on the river to Medmenham and Maidenhead and into Bisham Woods were organized.

They were idyllic summer days. Shelley was in good health and wildly buoyant spirits, gambolling with the children, talking and reading with Mary, or cajoling Claire out of her dejection at Byron's indifference. Mary was working hard again. She revised *Frankenstein* solidly for a week and then carefully copied out with a quill the full 80,000 words. Throughout this month's labour Mary still found time to play in the garden with Willy and to go boating on the Thames with him and Shelley. William had captured Shelley's heart as surely as he had his mother's. He was by now a proficient walker and it amused Shelley to watch his small sturdy form waddling in keen exploration of the garden. He wrote to Hogg with paternal pride, 'My quadruped has been metamorphosed since you were last here, into a featherless biped; he lives, & inhabits his father's house but he has ceased to creep. He walks with great alacrity.'[27] His metaphor from *Alastor* likening parasites on trees to:

> 'Gamesome infants' eyes,
> With gentle meanings, and most innocent wiles,
> Fold their beams round the hearts of those that love,
> These twine their tendrils with the wedded boughs
> Uniting their close union;'

had come home.

However, the fate of his other two children was in the balance and there was little promise that the outcome would be a happy one. On 17 March Chancery had declared Shelley ineligible to bring up his own children. This was a blow which made Shelley fear that William, too, might be snatched from his side.

In the cool evenings, everyone would congregate and Shelley, most nights, read aloud from Spenser's *Faerie Queene*. Summer had already arrived when, on 14 May, Mary could finally write '*Finis*'[28] in her journal. Without losing any time she and Shelley set off a week later for London to try and get her book published. John Murray, Byron's publisher, was number one on the list. They stayed at the Godwins' and Mary spent a long weekend with Shelley before he returned to William and home. They went to the opera to see Mozart's *Don Giovanni*, they went to an exhibition of Canova's sculptures and Turner's landscapes, they dined with Hogg and debated with Hazlitt. On the Monday, Mary saw Shelley off on the coach for Marlow. That afternoon she walked to Somers Town to sit at her mother's grave, a pilgrimage she had neglected for a long time. On her return she heard that John Murray had liked *Frankenstein* but she did not hold much hope of this 'courtly' publisher's acceptance.

Mary missed Shelley and William and the familiarity of their home. Sitting alone at Skinner Street, still full of poignant memories of Fanny, she read the third canto of *Childe Harold* and her despondency deepened. Her heart was heavy with nostalgia for the associations of the first time that Shelley had read it to her at Maison Chapuis. She felt also a yearning for Byron's inspiring company, his friendship, his intellectual energy. But there was a feeling, too, of the ultimate futility of those hopes and pleasures. 'We may see him again, and again enjoy his society; but the time will also arrive when that which is now an anticipation will be only in the memory. Death will at length come, and in the last moment all will be a dream.'[29]

Mary assuaged some of her depression with a shopping spree for essentials for the growing household in her charge. The Hunt family was still with them at Marlow having rather out-stayed their welcome. Mary returned home on Saturday, 31 May, to find that Shelley and Marianne Hunt were unwell. She and Marianne were both pregnant and Mary advised Mrs Hunt to abandon her stays in the interests of herself and her baby.

It was little wonder that Mary herself was not particularly well during June. The strain of the constant presence of the Hunts and their numerous and boisterous children was beginning to tell on both her and Shelley. Mary's doubts about John Murray's acceptance of her book were well founded for on the eighteenth her manuscript arrived at Marlow, rejected. It was to be rejected by Charles Ollier, too, before it found a publisher in Lackington Allen & Company in Finsbury Square. Shelley negotiated an extremely favourable contract whereby half the profits went to Mary. By the end of June the Hunt parents and their son Thornton had finally departed, but leaving the younger children for another fortnight in the charge of a Miss Kent.

During July the summery days were forgotten as a spell of wet and cloudy weather settled over them. It enervated and irritated the household. Mary was by now nearly eight months pregnant and, unable to go for long walks to escape the household, was depressed by this inactivity and discomfort. However, she extolled in a letter to Marianne Hunt the virtues of cold baths to which she subjected herself, doubtless for the benefit of both body and spirit.

Hogg spent a few days with them at the end of July but stayed at Peacock's house for Mary was finding him disagreeable and vulgar, wondering what ever had attracted her to him. In her diary she dismissed him characteristically: 'Hogg returns to London, talking of ducks and women.'[30] Mary was busy making preparations for the birth of her baby. She wanted a nurse to be vetted by Mrs Hunt and sent from London, for she had little confidence in one chosen from the poverty-stricken population of Marlow.

Amid this activity they received news of the placement of Ianthe and Charles Shelley. The master of the court had approved an elderly reverend gentleman in Warwick, a friend of the Westbrooks and a stranger to Shelley. In indignation Shelley, with his solicitor Longdill's direction, wrote a letter of appeal and after a further report and yet another year, Shelley's second choice (Longdill – his first choice – having been rejected) was agreed to. Dr and Mrs Hume became the little Shelleys' foster-parents in a case that seemed less concerned with the unfortunate children's welfare than with the thwarting or promoting of the interests of the two protagonists.

On 4 August 1817, Shelley celebrated his twenty-fifth birthday. He was nearing the end of his poem *Laon and Cythna* which was to be revised and retitled *The Revolt of Islam*. He had composed much of it floating alone in his boat gazing up at the interlaced branches of the trees or striding through the fern-filled beech woods and on over the green hills of Buckinghamshire.

Mary was writing too. This time she was transcribing from her journals and letters the account of her honeymoon with Shelley which was to be published as *History of a Six Weeks' Tour*. She turned twenty on 30 August. Two days later she went into labour and gave birth to a baby daughter, Clara. This new baby slipped into the household inconspicuously. William was too interested in private conversations and joint expeditions with Alba to be at all concerned. Mary's reading continued unabated, although it consisted more of novels than weighty tomes, as one concession to her condition. Mr Baxter, Isabel's father, had come for a few days' visit on the day before Clara's birth and was so seduced by the charm and intelligence of the Shelleys, so admiring of *Queen Mab*, that he resolved there and then to urge Isabel to resume her friendship with Mary otherwise, he insisted, his daughter would be the loser.

But Clara's birth was the precursor for Mary of a wretched autumn. The riot of hormones produced in pregnancy and particularly post-natally can distemper the most serene and sunny of natures. With Mary's dark stream of melancholy this post-natal vulnerability was the flood that burst the banks of her despair. As always there were other contributing factors that exacerbated her problems. As the September mists rolled up from the river, Shelley's health declined, so much so that he believed he was a dying man. Claire, too, was low-spirited but demanding and disruptive. Alba's presence was causing much speculation locally as to her parentage: in this unorthodox *ménage à trois* at Albion House Shelley seemed the obvious father. This embarrassed and hurt Mary particularly. There were discussions about when and how the little girl should be despatched to Byron, presently in Venice. To add to it all, and partially as a result of it all, Mary was having difficulty suckling Clara properly; she feared she did not have enough milk, yet trying to fill the little thing up on cow's milk merely upset her digestion. This complication made Mary withdraw into anxiety which grew into a poignant fear of losing this tiny daughter as she had cruelly lost her first. She felt that she was losing her beloved William too: 'I have had some pain in perceiving or imagining that Willy has almost forgotten me – and seems to like Elise better.'[31] The vicious circle of depression, ill-health, anxiety and loneliness was closing about her. Albion House was still full of the voices and bulky presences of a stream of visitors with their own needs and demands. The Hunts descended once again for a stay of nearly a week. Mr Baxter returned. Peacock would drop in for tea and stay and stay. But the most difficult thing of all to bear was Shelley's prolonged absence in London which lasted, apart from the occasional weekend, from the end of September through to the beginning of November. All Mary's trials at Marlow became magnified and distorted by her loneliness, her lack of support and her real anxiety at losing her day-to-day contact with Shelley.

He had left for London on 23 September with his newly-finished poem and in the company of Claire. Claire returned three days later but Shelley stayed on: seeing his doctor, Sir William Laurence, about his recurring pulmonary disorders (for a long time he thought he was consumptive), correcting the proofs of *Frankenstein*, organizing the publication of his own poem and trying to order his eternal financial entanglements.

Mary's one consolation was the simple and beautiful poem Shelley had written 'To Mary', a dedication to his *Laon and Cythna*:

> 'So now my summer task is ended, Mary,
>   And I return to thee, mine own heart's home;
> As to his Queen some victor Knight of Faery,
>   Earning bright spoils for her enchanted dome....'

It is straightforwardly autobiographical, a statement of Shelley's abiding love for her, 'thou child of love and light', and an acknowledgement of the courage and devotion that made her join him in obloquy, of his gratitude for her strength, serenity and loving auspices:

VII

> 'Thou Friend, whose presence on my wintry heart
>   Fell, like bright Spring upon some herbless plain;
> How beautiful and calm and free thou wert
>   In thy young wisdom, when the mortal chain
>   Of Custom thou didst burst and rend in twain,
> And walked as free as light the clouds among,
>   Which many an envious slave then breathed in vain
> From his dim dungeon, and my spirit sprung
> To meet thee from the woes which had begirt it long!

VIII

No more alone through the world's wilderness,
   Although I trod the paths of high intent,
I journeyed now: no more companionless,
   Where solitude is like despair, I went.—
   There is the wisdom of a stern content
When Poverty can blight the just and good,
   When Infamy dares mock the innocent,
And cherished friends turn with the multitude
To trample: this was ours, and we unshaken stood!

IX

Now has descended a serener hour,
   And with inconstant fortune, friends return;
Though suffering leaves the knowledge and the power
   Which says: — Let scorn be not repaid with scorn.
   And from thy side two gentle babes are born
To fill our home with smiles, and thus are we
   Most fortunate beneath life's beaming morn;
And these delights, and thou, have been to me
The parents of the Song I consecrate to thee.'

These shared injustices and misfortunes, their fragile moments of good fortune, had strengthened and extended that summer passion into an involved and substantial web of tenderness and dependence, of love and admiration. In this subdued love poem, Shelley expressed the power, reality and substance of their relationship with a subtlety that is more telling than any high-flown and extravagant eulogy:

XI

'And what art thou? I know, but dare not speak:
   Time may interpret to his silent years.
Yet in the paleness of thy thoughtful cheek,
   And in the light thine ample forehead wears,
   And in thy sweetest smiles, and in thy tears,
And in thy gentle speech, a prophecy
   Is whispered, to subdue my fondest fears:
And through thine eyes, even in thy soul I see
A lamp of vestal fire burning internally.

XII

> They say that thou wert lovely from thy birth,
>   Of glorious parents, thou aspiring Child.
> I wonder not – for One then left this earth
>   Whose life was like a setting planet mild,
>   Which clothed thee in the radiance undefiled
> Of its departing glory; still her fame
>   Shines on thee, through the tempest dark and wild
>   Which shake these latter days; and thou canst claim
> The shelter from thy Sire, of an immortal name.'

Mary's intellectual heritage from the celebrated Wollstonecraft/Godwin connection was always a source of pride and pleasure for both Shelley and herself. Shelley ended with hope:

> '– thou and I,
> Sweet friend! can look from our tranquillity
> Like lamps into the world's tempestuous night, –
>   Two tranquil stars, while clouds are passing by
>   Which wrap them from the foundering seaman's sight,
> That burn from year to year with unextinguished light.'

Shelley's celestial imagery pointing his and Mary's constancy and luminescence was to be proved with the years to be obliquely prophetic.

Mary must have been touched and gratified by this public declaration of her permanence and place in Shelley's life. She had been angry and hurt by the rumour that she and Claire had been sold by Godwin. She had been undermined and irritated by Claire's insidious presence and persistent claims on Shelley. Characteristically hypersensitive, she had always been aware that friends thought Shelley too volatile, too prodigal to be constant in love, half expecting him to abandon her in a whirlwind of passion as once he had abandoned Harriet. Harriet's miserable death was already a weight on Mary's conscience.

Shelley had decided while in London that they would have to leave dark and gloomy Albion House for the sake of his health. He wrote asking Mary to choose between Italy and the English seaside. Mary was loath to return to a nomadic, unsettled way of life but, if moving would restore Shelley to well-being and if their finances could stand it, she favoured Italy. Expeditions abroad, although she found the travelling physically wearing, always roused and acuminated her creative powers. Above all, Italy's delights included the undoubted attraction of Lord Byron.

Shelley was pressing Mary to come with their domestic entourage to London and from there he would direct the selling of the house lease. But Mary was alarmed by the lack of money and exasperated by Shelley's falsely optimistic view of their complex financial juggling.

Mary's letters to Shelley during this time alternated anxious protestations of love with pleadings in desperation for his presence, concern for his health with wifely nagging and domestic commissions. Incarcerated in the autumnal damps and gloom of Albion House, Mary was oppressed with her own apparent powerlessness in directing their lives. She was plagued by petty domestic irritations and despondent at having no writing project to consume her frustrated energies:

'Your letter received per parcel tonight was very unsatisfactory. You decide nothing and tell me *nothing* . . . my love I most earnestly entreat you to come – I do not understand what you are doing or how things are going on – Pray come – . . . Little Alba's affairs weigh heavily on my mind – I am not at peace untill she is on her way to Italy – Yet you say nothing of all this – in fact your letter tells me nothing.

'I wish to hear extremely the account of your money at the bankers.

'I earnestly hope that you have written C. C.

'I shall be truly miserable if you do not come Saturday – I think then I must come up myself yet cow's milk does not agree with the child & to bring her lodgeings in town is an expence & discomfort I cannot think of

'Oh my love pray pray do come – everything will go wrong if you do not –

'How wretched this unsettled state of affairs makes me – how I wish we had not come to Marlow – I daresay after all you will not come – if so God knows what I shall do but you will surely you will if it is only to hinder my being unhappy.'[32]

This was written on Thursday, 2 October. Shelley responded to her distressed call and travelled down on the London coach on the Friday evening to discuss their immediate plans, quell her fears and revive her spirit. That done he was back in town again on Saturday.

Mary's fleeting quietude ebbed away as October swept on in a flurry of dead leaves. She would daily leave the cold of Albion House and its gardens to find the wan but surprisingly warm sun shining in the street outside. But she had no local friends in Marlow; she found 'country friends are not very agreeable'[33] and these country people were equally unsympathetic to the strange and wild-looking Mr Shelley, his pale, solemn wife with the searching eyes and the whole domestic mélange in which they lived.

At this time Mary was being pestered by one of Shelley's creditors who was threatening his arrest. She was in despair about Godwin's financial state and hated having to keep from him their proposed quitting of England. Just twenty, she was feeling keenly the various burdens of responsibility that had accumulated in the last four years. Her little children, and indirectly Claire and Alba, relied absolutely on her. Her father roused in her a strong filial duty but bound up with intense love, guilt and pain. She felt responsible, too, for their own money and few possessions; she could be practical and had a large household to support. But most of all she was responsible for Shelley, her lover, her genius, the father of her children and brother of her soul. During this autumn he was not only frequently ill and in pain, but was also depressed and emotionally detached from her, something she sensed sharply, exaggerated all the more by his absence.

Mary's grim autumn eased gradually into a more hopeful and happy winter. By November they had decided to sell the house, *Frankenstein* was being printed and Shelley, always remarkably shrewd about the processes of publishing, was urging Lackingtons to advertise it well, all the while keeping a very close eye on the proofs and the printing schedule. They spent their precious days together in their traditional pursuits: writing, reading and walking, translating Spinoza and playing with the children. Having decided to abandon the house, its dark dankness seemed to them all the more abhorrent. The books in the library were musty and mildewed and both Shelley and William were susceptible to the cold and damp. Shelley grew paler and was beset with a cough; William's fine fair skin was chapped and raw from the cold.

Mary, with a less burdened heart, rewarded herself with a break from Marlow monotony and solitude. She spent ten days in London with Shelley during early November, socializing, catching up on literary personalities and gossip, seeing her father and the Hunts. The society of interesting, provocative and talented people was always of great importance to Mary. She had grown up largely in the centre of London's literary life, the moon to her father's sun, basking in his reputation, listening shyly and unobtrusively to the tantalizing discussions and dissertations that buzzed above her young head. Mary's imagination was rooted in experience, her constructions began with people; emotions, motives, aspirations and personal interaction intrigued her. The company of sympathetic friends was her elixir.

In the middle of Mary's London holiday Mr Baxter introduced Mr Booth, Isabel's husband, in an attempt to prove to his self-righteous son-in-law that Mary and Shelley were neither libertines nor defiantly pernicious. Sadly for Mary, this exercise did not impress the recalcitrant Scot; two weeks later she was writing to Mr Baxter, 'Isabell promised to write to me some time ago and not having performed this promise I am afraid that she is ill will you let me know about this.'[34]

She saw a good deal of the Hunts and of her father. The evening before Mary and Shelley returned to Marlow, Hunt brought Keats to their lodgings but the young poet remained unseduced by Shelley's charisma and wary of his aristocratic eccentricities.

The next day, 19 November, they took the coach to Marlow and slipped back into their routine of work, walk and talk. Mary was cheered by a spell of unseasonably warm weather which drew the damp from the house and coaxed the garden's primroses into premature and fragile bloom. But then Shelley's health and spirits slipped away with the sun and, as the wintry weather closed in, he became subject to wild extremes of emotion and activity. Periods of intense sensory excitement were countered by a deadly torpor. The hallucinatory nature of the one and the irritable lethargy and empty hours of the other were intensified, if not produced, by his liberal dosings of laudanum. It was a depressing time for them both and their retreat to the balmy climes of Italy became pressing. If only they could sell Albion House.

However, the publication of Godwin's novel, *Mandeville*, had sent a ripple to temporarily disperse the gloom. It arrived on publication day, 18 September, and Mary pounced on it and read it straight through. It was powerful, ponderous and full of doom and Mary was engrossed. Her admiration for and pride in her father was reinforced by this convoluted fiction and she handed it over to Shelley who read it as rapidly. His circumspectly glowing critique of the book, written informally to Godwin, so pleased the old egoist that he had it published in the *Morning Chronicle*.

At the end of December Mary and Shelley received a strange letter from William Baxter explaining that he wished to curtail their friendship on account of the disparity in rank, fortune and aspirations between the Shelleys and himself and his daughters. Between the lines Mary recognized the broad hand of the dour Mr Booth. But she felt that Isabel Booth's friendship was worth fighting for. Shelley wrote by return of post a characteristically clever yet subtle letter revealing the sophistry of Mr Baxter's explanations of his 'determination to deprive Mary of the intercourse of her friend'. Shelley continued, '[I] most highly respect the motives, as I know they must exist in your mind, for this proceeding. May I ask *precisely what* those motives are?'[35] Mary was more directly appealing in her postscript: 'I wish I had you by the fire here in my little study.... I could quickly convince you that your girls are not below me in station, and that in fact I am the fittest companion for them in the world; but I postpone the argument until I see you, for I know (pardon me) that *viva voce* is all in all with you.'[36] It was the rejection and misjudgement of friends which hurt her most and gradually cauterized her spontaneous affections.

The year 1817 trickled out on a low note.

At the end of the next month Mary's forbearance was rewarded by the surprise sale of Albion House. Peacock came to supper and there was general rejoicing. At last the Italian plan could be put into operation. The predictability of her Marlow routine gave way to bustling activity. Mary began packing their books, clearing the shelves in the musty library, dusting off the winter's mildew. Shelley went up to London to finalize his negotiations for loans and chivvy his and Mary's publishers. On Tuesday, 10 February, Mary's tasks were complete and she and the children joined Shelley and Claire in London. She was to spend a marvellous, sociable month with Shelley visiting the opera, for Mozart's *Don Giovanni* and *Figaro*, and the British Museum to see the Elgin marbles. Their evenings at the Hunts were enlivened by the local luminati, Vincent Novello, Keats, Mary Lamb, and often ended with songs and music. Shelley enjoyed himself enormously, shrieking with delight at the machinations and fantasies of the pantomime and transported by the drama of the opera. It was a carefree whirl of a month, one that Mary remembered with pleasure for the rest of her life.

One task remained to be done: two days before their departure William and Clara and Alba were christened at St Giles-in-the-Fields. At Byron's request Alba's name was formalized to Clara Allegra. This spiritual insurance for the three beloved children, unwittingly doomed by their Italian exile, heartened Mary. Despite her upbringing and Shelley's fundamental apostasy, she wanted to believe in a God and certainly in a life after death. 'I trust in a hereafter – I have ever done so. I know that that shall be mine....'[37]

On the next day, Tuesday, 10 March, Mary and Shelley made their farewells. Leigh and Marianne Hunt stayed the whole day, helping with packing the last bits and books, delaying their final good-byes. As it was, Shelley had fallen asleep on the sofa and, not wishing to wake him, the Hunts embraced Mary and quietly left. Mary Lamb called by; Godwin came in the evening, rather sheepishly, hoping to make some amends, for his increasing demands for money during the previous weeks had estranged his son-in-law. Mary still felt remorse at abandoning her father to his financial problems and advancing age with neither herself nor Fanny to supplement Mrs Godwin's inadequate care.

The next day the household was up at dawn, the children were dressed, nightclothes packed, and five adults – Mary, Shelley, Claire, their Swiss maid Elise and a Marlow girl Milly Shields – carrying the luggage and the three sleepy children, quietly left their lodgings in Great Russell Street. Mary had embarked on a journey that was to become an exile, essentially romantic, but fractured and finally broken by an accumulation of terrible tragedy.

11
Italian Exile

> 'What is there in our nature that is forever urging us towards pain and misery?'
>
> *The Last Man*, Mary Shelley

Their journey south was leisurely, stopping at Dartford for breakfast, travelling through pretty Kentish country and arriving at Dover in the evening. The next day was windy and the waves were running high. Although there had been some doubt as to whether they should sail, the wind was behind them and blew them roughly but briskly into Calais. It was the third time Mary had arrived by boat at Calais and the familiarity and nostalgic promise of the place made her bright with anticipation. With Europe before her and Italy, that 'Paradise of Exiles', beckoning, there was little room for suspicion of the future and dread of the unknown.

Allegra and William, sick and sleepy during the voyage, had recovered their spirits. Their childish enthusiasm fed Mary's own excitement. Mary never had much time for the French or their 'dismal' countryside and with her eyes on the Alps and Italy basking beyond she dismissed it: 'There is a disconsolate air of discomfort in France that is quite wretched.'[1] However, they did stay three days in Lyons before embarking on their Alpine crossing on 25 March. Their carriage trundled through foothills laced with luxuriant vines and inlaid with white châteaux and neat cottages reflecting the sun.

At Pont Beauvoisin, on the border between France and the Sardinian empire, Mary and Shelley's books were impounded and sent to a censorial priest in the next town. There the works of such reprobates as Rousseau and Voltaire would be consigned to the flames.

As they climbed higher into the mountains, snowdrifts encroached on their road. Mary, Claire and Shelley sang all the way. The going was at times alarming and precarious. Mary wrote in her journal, 'The scene is far more desolate, and there is something dreadful in going on the edge of an overhanging precipice.'[2] They had to cross from this precipice to another with only a rickety suspension bridge, 'the Devil's Bridge', to keep them from the gorge below.

After Sousa they arrived at Turin. Ever keen on culture, Mary with Shelley and Claire went off to the opera but could neither interpret the name nor follow the story. Even the music was obscured by the voluble audience and only the two lead singers managed infrequently to surface above the society gossip. Three days later, on 4 April, Mary and her family arrived in Milan. Optimistically they went to the opera there. The decorations and sets were magnificent but the work was inaudible above the feasting, card-playing and carousing in the audience. However, the ballet *Vigano's Othello*, more a tragic pantomime by Mary's definition, impressed all three by its living sculpture and studied gestures. Here the music was audible and enjoyed.

Having settled the children and Claire and the maids, Elise and Milly, into the hotel, Mary and Shelley set off for Lake Como to find a house there for the summer. Always happy by water and remembering their extraordinary summer on Lake Geneva, Mary and Shelley were bound to be won by this dark ribbon of water unfurled between mountains and fragrant woods. They toured the available houses and Mary was seduced by a decaying palace, Villa Pliniana, boasting a spring in its courtyard described by Pliny. Terraced and colonnaded, set in a landscape of immense waterfalls, bigger mountains and a spectacular and verdant water-front, it was a house to which they could proudly invite the noble Lord Byron.

While Mary and Shelley were at Lake Como a strange incident occurred, recorded by neither of them but related to Claire on their return to Milan. Apparently Shelley wandered off to a solitary spot in order to discharge his pistol which he had kept loaded during their journey from England. He was followed by two policemen who thought he was acting suspiciously and possibly about to take his own life. Shelley was escorted to the prefect's office and politely told the pistol would be confiscated until Mary had testified that Shelley was not suicidal. Mary was well aware of Shelley's tenuous hold on life; at times his negligence could have been interpreted as a death wish, and this episode unnerved her. There was no mention of it in her journal or chatty letters to the Hunts as an illustration, along with the operatic fiascos, of the peculiar vagaries of the Latin race.

Back safely in Milan, Mary's days of reading, walking and study were enlivened with some horse riding along the Corso. Shelley and Claire were writing to Byron about his arrangements for the reception of little Allegra. He seemed at first obdurate, set against Claire's access to himself and more seriously to their child. Claire was down-hearted but blindly believed that Allegra would lead a privileged life as Lord Byron's daughter and that this beautiful and beloved little girl of hers would blind the errant Albé to her and help resurrect the small flame of their distant and fleeting encounter. Shelley, more practically, wrote reasonable, appealing letters, firmly allying himseof on Byron's side but arguing for more generosity and understanding of the plight of a foolish girl.

'Improbable and monstrous'[3] tales about Byron's conduct in Venice had travelled to Milan, and Mary and Shelley were regaled by their hero's legendary excesses; 'Albé! Albé everywhere!'[4] wrote Mary with intrigued amusement. Shelley was concerned at sending Allegra into Byron's dubious care but Claire was obstinate too; she was going to go through with this self-sacrifice for the sake of her child.

So, on 28 April, the fifteen-month-old toddler was relinquished by her mother and sent with Elise as surrogate on a journey to her illustrious and undomesticated father. For Claire the agonizing decision to part with her 'itty Ba'[5] was a calculated risk; she hoped that both she and Allegra would gain in the end. But Claire calculated on false premises and it was a decision that she was rapidly to regret, for the ensuing tragedy extended bitter and remorseful strains down the length of her long life. Shelley was sad to see Allegra go and anxious about her future, for he, too, loved and delighted in her. But his immediate problem was Claire's restless despair. Mary, although relieved to be free of the idle curiosity and innuendo about Shelley's relationship with Claire and Allegra, missed the little girl who had become an affectionate and lively member of her family and William's playmate. Feeling concerned about her future, Mary instinctively feared for her happiness and welfare.

On 1 May, their books and belongings were packed and the two Shelley children and Milly piled into a coach with Mary, Shelley and

Claire. They took a week to journey down through fertile plains and over the Apennines to Pisa. Despite its leaning tower, which she climbed, Mary was disgusted and depressed by the chain-gangs of wretched prisoners working in the streets, manacled together and guarded by armed ruffians. They hastily quitted the town and travelled to Leghorn on the Tuscan coast, 'a stupid town'.[6]

Here Mary lost no time in making the acquaintance of Maria and John Gisborne and thus began a friendship, with Maria especially, that was to afford Mary great pleasure and consolation in the years to come. At first this interesting and remarkable woman struck Mary as 'reserved, yet with easy manners'.[7] The reserve was to melt, for every day during the following month Mary met her to walk and talk. She fascinated Mary with her perceptive and first-hand observations about Mary Wollstonecraft and Godwin in the early days. To be able to talk at length with someone who had known and loved the woman, not merely the Wollstonecraft legend, was for Mary the best kind of luxury. With it came priceless information for a daughter who idolized an inevitably romantic and hazy view of her mother, and felt irrevocably bound to her difficult and self-centred genius of a father.

During this month at Leghorn, Mary set to work on her Italian, reading Italian plays and studying her grammar. Shelley spent two days at Bagni di Lucca, a fashionable spa nestling amongst the foothills of the Apennines. He procured a compact, newly-painted house, the Casa Bertini, perched on a hill and surrounded by chestnut woods and mountains.

On Thursday, 28 May, Shelley was back in Leghorn with the good news of his find. Within a fortnight they had packed yet again and trundled north towards the mountains to settle into their new home. They discovered later, to Shelley's pique, that the place in summer was overrun with fellow countrymen. Mary, too, for all her love of society, was irritated by finding herself amongst an invasion of conspicuously English tourists:

'We see none but English, we hear nothing but English spoken. The walks are filled with English nursery maids, a kind of animal I by no means like, & dashing staring Englishwomen, who surprise the Italians who always are carried about in Sedan Chairs, by riding on horseback – For us we generally walk except last Tuesday, when

Shelley and I took a long ride to *il prato fiorito*, a flowery meadow on the top of one of the neighbouring Apennines.'[8]

Thus she wrote indignantly to Maria Gisborne.

Nevertheless Mary was delighted with the house. It was secluded, set at the end of a track that wound up from the town and petered out in the wooded hills beyond the house. They had a small garden hedged with generations of unpruned laurel. It was private and peaceful, 'we hear no sound except the rushing of the river in the valley below',[9] and the immediate landscape was full of mystery and promise. 'We are surrounded by mountains covered with thick chestnut woods – they are peaked and picturesque and sometimes you see peeping above them the bare summit of a distant Apennine.... The walks in the woods are delightful; for I like nothing so much as to be surrounded by the foliage of trees only peeping now and then through the leafy screen on the scene about me....'[10] Mary was also freed of much of her domestic duties. They had hired Paolo Foggi, a hardworking but amoral Italian who cooked and generally ran the household, and a local woman who came daily to clean and do the washing. At noon Shelley would retreat to a series of waterfalls and pools cascading down a rock in the depths of the woods. Here he would sit naked in the sun, reading Herodotus, and then plunge into the large pool at the base of the fall. After splashing about he would clamber like a pale sprite up through the spray. Despite the magnificent scenery, despite the climate that was restoring his health, Shelley was homesick for the softer landscapes of England. He wrote to Peacock: 'I have seen nothing so beautiful as Virginia Water in its kind. And my thoughts forever cling to Windsor Forest, and the copses of Marlow, like the clouds which hang upon the woods of the mountains, low trailing, and though they pass away, leave their best view when they themselves have faded.'[11]

Meanwhile Mary had been excited and nervous as reports of the critical reaction to *Frankenstein* filtered through via the letters of Godwin and Peacock. It had been published in March; her monstrous baby was exposed to public gaze. Mary was gratified to hear that it created a great deal of serious interest and merited generous space in the important reviews. These were generally favourable and complimentary, taking it for granted that *Frankenstein* was a man's creation, written by one of Godwin's disciples, possibly even Shelley himself.

The eventual discovery that the author of such a terrific saga was a woman, in fact little more than a girl, caused much consternation and sheer amazement. It was unseemly, unladylike for a woman to think of, let alone express, such impious and monstrous ideas. If these pillars of the literary establishment overlooked the impropriety, they were wont to exclaim, as did *Blackwoods*, 'For a man it was excellent, but for a woman it was wonderful.'[12]

The *Quarterly Review* was the first off the mark and the most outraged. As the work of a man, *Frankenstein* was 'a tissue of horrible and disgusting absurdities'. Then followed some doubts as to the author's sanity, with the whole of the Godwin school under fire: 'Mr Godwin is the patriarch of a literary family, whose chief skill is in delineating the wanderings of the intellect, and which strangely delights in the most afflicting and humiliating of human miseries. His disciples are a kind of *out-pensioners of Bedlam* and, like "Mad Bess" or "Mad Tom" are occasionally visited with paroxysms of genius and fits of expression, which make sober-minded people wonder and shudder.'[13] Mary, after years of Godwin and Shelley's influence, should have ignored the opinion of such a sober-minded journal: it probably encouraged many of the new reading public to buy and borrow the book. Nevertheless she waited in some trepidation for the other verdicts. She need not have worried. The *Edinburgh Review* was shocked by its impiety but greatly impressed by its grip and power; the effective juxtaposition of 'harsh and savage delineation of passion' with 'the gentler features of domestic and simple feelings' was masterly:

> 'There never was a wilder story imagined; yet like most of the fictions of this age, it has an air of reality attached to it, by being connected with the favourite projects and passions of the times. The real events of the world have, in a day, too, been of so wondrous and gigantic a kind, – the shiftings of the scenes in our stupendous drama have been so rapid and various, that Shakespeare himself, in his wildest flights, has been completely distanced by the eccentricities of actual existence....'[14]

The eccentricities of existence have long since outdistanced all Mary's metaphorical monsters of mechanism and materialism – undoubtedly there have been Victor Frankensteins too; only his monster, her conglomerate man, remains secured in fiction.

All reviews agreed on the power and accuracy of language but

Blackwoods, most probably written by Sir Walter Scott, an avowed admirer of the work, was generously enthusiastic in its praise: 'The author seems to us to disclose uncommon powers of poetic imagination ... the work impresses us with a high idea of the author's original genius and happy power of expression ... if Gray's definition of Paradise, to lie on a couch, namely, and read new novels, come anything near truth, no small praise is due to him, who, like the author of Frankenstein, has enlarged this sphere of this fascinating enjoyment.' That must have delighted Mary; it was high praise indeed from such a master storyteller.

Shelley's long poem, *The Revolt of Islam*, also published in 1818, fell largely on stony ground. Byron's status as a poet was soaring on the blazing trail of *Childe Harold*. Shelley had hoped to gain a measure of popularity with this work. If he was not ignored by the critics he was subjected to virulent personal attacks on his way of life and morality. The public, except for a small underground following, were largely indifferent. To Peacock he wrote, '... my own book of course acquires little attention.'[15] He wrote to be heard, he wrote to be understood; this silence was a source of anguish to him, it quickened and confirmed his exile. Trelawny expressed Shelley's ultimate creative frustration, '... his works fell still-born from the Press.'[16] Yet Shelley begrudged Mary not one scintilla of critical acclaim.

July passed peacefully. Their only attempt at socializing was an occasional visit to the Sunday balls at the casino where the waltz and other seductive dances were danced. Neither Mary nor Claire joined in; 'I do not know whether they refrain from philosophy or protestantism',[17] Shelley wrote to Peacock. He had no such scruples and danced with the local girls. He found the waltz disconcertingly sensual but the woman were plain and stupid, so he assured Peacock half-seriously, that there was little danger of his senses being roused, except perhaps in the dark. By day Mary and Shelley would ride on horseback along the criss-cross paths through the woods to local beauty spots, startling the natives in their sedans. Claire was a typically wild and nervous rider and frequently fell off, often hurting herself quite badly. She had never given up her hope or intention of seeing Allegra again, and when on 14 and 16 August two urgent letters arrived from Elise in Venice, confused and disquieting in their news, Claire determined to go immediately to see her child and ensure her welfare. It was a long, exhausting journey of well over 200 miles and Claire could not be expected to travel it alone. Strategy and duplicity were necessary in order to stand any chance of seeing Allegra: undoubtedly Shelley had to go with her. They left the next day, Monday, 17 August, for Florence, the first stop on their journey. Both Shelley and Mary felt it would prove to be a wild goose chase but in order to satisfy Claire it had to be done.

Meanwhile Mary was left in their house which now seemed very empty. Only her William and baby Clara and Milly Shields remained. Paolo Foggi had gone with Shelley and Claire to Florence but was to return to help her out at Casa Bertini. Mary wrote that day to Maria Gisborne, 'come and cheer my solitude';[18] it was a plea which the Gisbornes could not ignore. In a week they arrived and immediately joined Mary in reading Tasso and Shelley's own remarkable and subtle translation of Plato's *Symposium*. She had received a long animated letter from Shelley; Claire and he were obviously enjoying their adventure away from the domestic retreat of Casa Bertini. Having described their breakfast of 'figs very fine, & peaches unfortunately gathered before they were ripe whose smell was like what one fancies of the wakening of Paradise flowers', he enquired about Mary's state of mind. 'Well my dearest Mary are you very lonely? Tell me truth my sweetest, do you ever cry?'[19] Then with admonitions to keep up her spirits he suggested how nice it would be if she could put her time to good use and create another masterpiece in his absence, as she had *Frankenstein* in awaiting his own and Byron's return at Geneva.

The next letter that arrived, on 28 August, was even more demanding: Mary was to pack, scoop up her two children and within two days, with Paolo's help, embark on five days of gruelling travel. Her presence was needed to authenticate Shelley's assurance to Byron that Claire was safely out of his way, staying with Mary and the children at Padua. Claire was in fact breathing Byron's air, waiting for news in the company of the Hoppners, the British consul and his wife. Unknown to Byron, Shelley and Claire had already seen Allegra, for Elise and the little girl, now paler and subdued, were temporarily in the care of the charming Hoppners.

Albé was in an unexpectedly good mood, delighted to see Shelley and sympathetic about Claire's desire for some time with Allegra, as long as he did not have to suffer her presence. Having heard that Mary and the children were lodged with Claire at Padua, in a generous impulse, Byron offered Shelley his summer villa Casa Capuccini at Este in the Eugean Hills. Here Allegra would be allowed to join her mother and long-lost friends for a summer holiday.

From Claire and Shelley's viewpoint it was imperative that Mary should go post-haste to Este. The journey, which they had found strenuous and debilitating, would be even more difficult for Mary, struggling across Italy with two small children in the intense August heat. But these considerations were of little import in the face of Claire's immediate happiness and Shelley's threatened integrity.

However, there was one consideration of which Shelley and Claire were unaware but which made Mary even more reluctant to travel: baby Clara, not yet one year old, had been ill, possibly from a combination of the heat and teething. She was very young, not particularly robust and delicate-skinned; the perils of an Italian summer, the fevers, the food, the water, the heat, were all concentrated by travel. Mary consulted with the Gisbornes. Clara seemed better and William was well. She could hardly refuse Shelley and let down both him and Claire, possibly alienating Byron and destroying Claire's chances of ever seeing Allegra again.

Mary began to arrange for her trip. Maria Gisborne said she would travel with her to Lucca to help with the children. On 30 August it was Mary's twenty-first birthday and she spent it packing. The next day she left the cool seclusion of Casa Bertini and set off for Florence. It was a sweltering day and the going was slow. Mrs Gisborne disembarked at Lucca, and Mary, very sad to see her go, faced the rest of her journey up the Arno Valley to Florence, through the Etruscan Apennines and across the plain of the River Po.

On the way poor little Clara, already weak, succumbed to an attack of dysentery and when Mary finally arrived exhausted in Este, the baby was 'dangerously ill'.[20] To add to Mary's burden, she found Shelley extremely anxious at her delay in arriving and ill from 'taking poison in Italian cakes'.[21]

The cool airy house eased Mary's fatigue and Clara slowly regained a little colour and strength. Nevertheless, even a week later, Mary was writing anxiously to Maria Gisborne: 'She is still in a frightful state of weakness and fever and is reduced to be so thin in this short time that you would hardly know her again.'[22] Mary was far more anxious about Clara's state than was Shelley. He recovered from his stomach upset and was working hard on *Prometheus Unbound*. However, the house was a consolation. Mary loved the light, spacious rooms and spreading gardens, bountiful with laden vines and fruit trees. Beyond the garden was a ruined Gothic castle, made all the more melodramatic by the owls and bats which inhabited it. The castle had once sheltered the Medicis before they made Florence their own.

Claire was also unwell and Shelley took her to the doctor at Padua on Tuesday, 22 September. They intended to ask his advice on Clara who was still very thin and weak but they missed their appointment and made another for the Thursday. Shelley, who had been keen to set out for Venice and Byron's intoxicating company but had stayed reluctantly and anxiously on account of Clara's health, now decided to take the opportunity. He travelled on from Padua and Claire returned to Mary with his letter: 'Am I not like a wild swan to be gone so suddenly?'[23] He was not only wild but self-centred and demanding too. Mary and the ailing Clara were to go with Claire to Padua on the Thursday, meet Shelley there and travel on to Venice. But Claire's appointment with the doctor was at eight-thirty in the morning; 'You must therefore arrange matters so that you should come to the Stella d'Oro [in Padua] a little before that hour – a thing only to be accomplished by setting out at $\frac{1}{2}$ past 3 in the morning.'[24]

Mary was once again forced to gather up her children regardless of their health and chase through Italy at the convenience of Shelley and Claire. However, Shelley's extreme thoughtlessness was largely prompted by his all-engrossing enthusiasm for Byron's company. He had gone in trepidation to Venice and had been delighted by the welcome Byron had given him. He was flattered by the friendliness and intimacy of his conversation. Shelley recognized in Byron a great poet whose work was growing in maturity and depth. But he was both fascinated and repulsed by Byron's extravagance and profligate way of life. Venice, too, distressed him with the obscene juxtaposition of its physical beauty with the degradation and misery of its populace. As he had been before and would be again, Shelley was insulated within his own uneasy compulsion, where there was little room for the mundanities of domestic life: Mary's anxieties and Clara's troublesome malaise.

Mary, like many of his acquaintances, found he could be an irresistible force. Quieting her fears and wrapping Clara against the cool pre-dawn air, she set off on the first stage of a nightmare journey.

By the time Mary arrived at Padua, Clara was rapidly declining.

Shelley met them and rather than see the doctor there, who had failed to impress him, they hurried on to Venice. Mary grew increasingly fearful as they rattled and bumped through the heat of the day. The small, shrunken daughter in her arms was failing visibly, her eyes occasionally rolling back into her head. The journey seemed an interminable agony 'when life and death hung upon our speedy arrival at Venice.'[25] At last, at five in the evening, they were on the outskirts of Venice. Some twenty-five years later, when Mary returned to the city in her middle age, the passions of that terrible journey repossessed her as if the long years were merely hours. She recalled the 'dread to see her child even at that instant expire'[26] and on approaching Venice, her horror and confusion as her fraught senses were assaulted 'by a storm of *gondolieri*; their vociferations were something indescribable; so loud, so vehement, so reiterated; till we had chosen our boat, and then all subsided into instant calm'.[27]

In the gondola Clara suffered a convulsive fit. They arrived at the inn and Shelley left immediately to try and contact Byron's physician, Dr Aglietti. Mary was left in the hall, holding the fragile body of her child, watching her life flutter away. Sitting there alone in a strange, dirty and inhospitable inn, hundreds of miles from home, with her second daughter dying in her arms, Mary was overwhelmed by the horror of it all. Shelley returned to find her 'in the most dreadful distress'.[28] Having failed to contact Dr Aglietti, another doctor arrived but by now there was no hope. Helplessly Mary held her, and Shelley watched appalled as in less than an hour their little daughter was dead.

Mercifully the Hoppners came immediately and rescued the stricken Shelleys. Mary was desolate; she knew deep down that Clara need not have died and that knowledge, intensifying her grief, withered a part of her heart. Shelley's explanation to Peacock that 'she died of a disorder peculiar to the climate',[29] was not the whole truth and Mary was unable to pretend it was. In blaming Shelley, she withdrew into a black despair which gripped her spirit. She managed to avert a complete breakdown by restraining her guilt, resentment and grief. She resolutely continued with the practicalities of everyday life, reading, working, sightseeing, caring for William, but her emotional intimacy and with it her physical passion for Shelley were quenched at source.

Shelley had always pursued his own enthusiasms and obsessions but equally he had always relied on Mary's tacit support and collaboration. Now he was hurt and bewildered by her spiritual withdrawal. He felt lost without the 'sister of my soul'.

Nothing of Mary's suffering was recorded in her journal. She admitted to none of the bad dreams and miserable days that followed the death of her first baby. The Hoppners were very good to her, taking her and Shelley under their wing. Mrs Hoppner was, according to Shelley, 'so good so beautiful so angelically mild that were she wise too, she would be quite a Mary'.[30] Probably with characteristic kindness and lack of wisdom she did not encourage Mary to express her grief, such things being best overcome and forgotten. Instead sightseeing trips were arranged to the Doge's Palace, and the art exhibition at the Academy. She was taken shopping and introduced to friends, all of which she stoically endured.

Byron came to alleviate some of the gloom. He was in such sparkling form, he seemed so much happier, that he could afford to be generous and solicitous. He gave Mary his poem *Mazeppa* to transcribe in her careful hand. The next day she and Shelley returned to Este and she set about her task diligently. It was a labour of love and helped to revive her intellectual enthusiasms.

On Mary's return to Este, Claire and the children were not at the villa but in Padua. She longed to see and hold her William again to reassure herself; her precious children now seemed to be so tragically mortal. The following day, 30 September, they returned. William's delicate skin was rosy and his whole being burst with health and good spirits.

Mary's reading and study continued as earnestly as ever. Her Italian was much improved and she applied herself to a life of Tasso, in the original Italian. They walked in the evenings. Shelley had taken to reading aloud again while Mary and Claire delighted in the view before them, accentuated by the Gothic ruin at the bottom of their garden complete with hooting owls and swooping bats.

This ordered calm was, however, fractured by their fear of losing William too. In the week after Mary and Shelley's return to Este, he had become ill and with the horrors of Clara's decline so fresh in their minds they decided to take him to Venice to put him under the care of Byron's physician.

On 11 October, an anxious Mary, with William cradled in her lap, set off with Shelley and Elise. It was a much more leisurely journey than Mary's previous flight to Venice; they spent the night at Padua and arrived in Venice at two in the afternoon. William was duly examined, treated and recovered, but Mary and Shelley stayed on until 31 October. They dined at the hospitable Hoppners' every night whence Shelley would hurry to spend the rest of the evening with Byron. Mary was less lucky; she was escorted to the theatre in the company of the Hoppners and their friend Chevalier Mengaldo to see a comedy 'stupid beyond measure' and was taken again the next night to the same farce 'with the same party'.[31] Poor Mary; Mrs Hoppner was charming and kind but could be foolish and was far from being stimulating company. Mr Hoppner had been dismissed rather precipitately by both Mary and Shelley as a dreadful bore, as was the chevalier, an Italian noble with a weakness for his own protracted anecdotes about predictable ghosts and his Napoleonic campaigns in Russia.

All this time Mary kept her grief to herself, only expressing something of her despair in a letter to her father. The help she got from him was typically dictatorial but cruelly unloving and inappropriate:

'I sincerely sympathise with you in the affliction which forms the subject of your letter, and which I may consider as the first severe trial of your constancy and the firmness of your temper that has occurred to you in the course of your life. You should, however, recollect that it is only persons of a very ordinary sort, and of a pusillanimous disposition, that sink long under a calamity of this nature. I assure you such a recollection will be of great use to you. We seldom indulge long in depression and mourning, except when we think secretly that there is something very refined in it, and that it does us honour.'[32]

The old man had forgotten the emotions awakened by Mary Wollstonecraft, her life with him, her love and her death. With his heavy-handed authority and misguided logic he failed Mary when she needed him most. He helped suppress and contort her grief by his disdain for her weakness and self-indulgence in expressing it. Having severed associations with her when she eloped with Shelley, he now abandoned her emotionally. Never before had she felt her motherless state so keenly; as never before she was alone and isolated from those she loved.

A few days before they were due to leave, Shelley returned to Este to collect Allegra from Claire and entrust her again to the Hoppners and Byron's charge. She was nearly two, a special sister to their William, all the more so since Clara's death. Mary and Shelley had become particularly uneasy about leaving the little girl in Venice. Not only was she being prised once again from Claire's side, from a life of simple and loving domesticity, but the environment and influences to which she would be subjected were unpredictable and insecure, with neither a mother-figure nor indeed any permanent love relationship on which to pin her existence. Shelley's evenings spent with Byron in Venice had given him a distressing insight into the extravagances and follies of the lord's life there. Like the polarities of Venice itself, Byron's greatness and beauty as a poet, and his attractiveness as a man were to Shelley disturbingly entangled with his connivance and participation in corruption and depravity. In a letter to Peacock written in December Shelley's passion fired his words:

'The fact is, that first, the Italian women are perhaps the most contemptible of all who exist under the moon; the most ignorant the most disgusting, the most bigoted, the most filthy.... Well L[ord] B[yron] is familiar with the lowest sort of these women, the people his gondolieri pick up in the streets. He allows fathers & mothers to bargain with him for their daughters, & though this is common enough in Italy, yet for an Englishman to encourage such sickening vice is a melancholy thing. He associates with wretches who seem almost to have lost the gait & phisiognomy of man, & who do not scruple to avow practices which are not only not named but I believe seldom even conceived in England. He says he disapproves, but he endures. He is not yet an Italian & is heartily & deeply discontented with himself, & contemplating in the distorted mirror of his own thoughts, the nature & destiny of man, what can he behold but objects of contempt & despair.... You may think how unwillingly I have left my little favourite Alba in a situation where she might fall again under his authority.'[33]

But back she went. Shelley, without Mary's realistic and wholehearted support, was incapable of contradicting that authority. He valued a father's natural rights having been deprived of his own two eldest children, and he valued the friendship of a genius spirit, poet and itinerant exile like himself.

On the last day of October, Mary and Shelley with a blooming

William left Venice for Este. Here they tarried only long enough to pack their belongings and organize their journey south through Rome to Naples. The first stage of their route was extremely difficult and the weather inclement. The rutted roads deteriorated further with the rain and at times they had to resort to oxen to drag their laden carriage on its tedious progress south. At one of the many farms they passed, the sight of sixty-three magnificent white and honey-coloured oxen, tethered and contented in the yard, delighted the whole Shelley family. They stayed two days en route at Bologna where Mary in her low and depressed state was particularly moved by the religious paintings of Correggio, Raphael and Guido.

On 11 November Mary and Shelley resumed their travelling schedule. Although tiring, travel stimulated and distracted many from her emotional turmoil. They trundled on south through the 'pretty English country'[34] around Faenza and Cesena. They travelled on dule. Although tiring, travel stimulated and distracted Mary from ascent through the Apennines. The inns deteriorated with the increasing altitude and Mary slept fully clothed as some protection from the filthy beds and their predatory inhabitants. They were fitful and miserable nights providing little respite from the exhausting days. Paolo was allowed to drive their coach in an economy measure that Mary heartily regretted as they endured the rough and perilous ride. However, some of the scenery was reward enough. Spoleto, embedded at the heart of the spiny range of mountains, made Shelley gasp, '... the most romantic city I ever saw.'[35] Mary was more particular and less effusive. She wrote in her journal, '... we visit a magnificent aqueduct, built, they say, by the Romans, and repaired by the Goths; it is thrown across a deep narrow valley.'[36] The joy and enthusiasm of her early travelogues was distinctly missing from her journal's entries during this trek south. She saw only the shadows not the sun, felt only the exhaustion and little of the inspiration in discovering new and dramatic landscapes.

The next day, 18 November, the grand waterfall at Terni in its roaring splendour pierced her dulled senses and prodded a spark of her old imagination: '... the thunder, the abyss, the spray, the graceful dash of water lost in the mist below – it put me in mind of Sappho leaping from a rock, and her form vanishing as in the shape of a swan in the distance.'[37] The half hour that she and Shelley spent gazing at the spectacular fall momentarily lifted her spirits out of their own abyss and she looked up at the stars: 'As we return home, we behold Venus, brighter, and nearly as large, as the moon in her first quarter.'[38]

Within two days the weary travellers were approaching Rome. Overhead an immense hawk wheeled and hovered, a presage of the tragedies to come. Mary, in an hypersensitive and morbid state of mind, was disquieted by the uncanny shadow of that bird of prey, warning and waiting. She gathered William to her as they passed on to the city to be diverted by the ancient glories of Rome.

Mary and Shelley embarked on a strenuous week of sightseeing: 'visit the Capitol, the Coliseum, the Forum, the Pantheon, St Peter's, etc' all in one day, capped by the opera in the evening – 'the worst I ever saw'.[39] The full impact of these classical monuments was diminished by the crews of shackled prisoners working on propping the Colosseum and excavating the Forum.

The road from Rome to Naples was notorious for its footpads and thuggery but the locals were keen to reassure the young Shelley party that it was safe and had been free of any robbery for the previous eight months. Although a gross exaggeration, Shelley naïvely believed the prognosis and on 27 November he went on alone to Naples to secure lodgings there. He himself was not robbed but was appalled to see a young man murdered on the road before his eyes. Mary and Claire packed and set off with William and the maids the following day. Her glutted diet of Roman antiquities had rekindled something of her ardour for travel and for seeing the sights. The four days' journey from Rome to Naples, exhausting as it was, elicited enthusiastic and detailed descriptions in her journal. Their carriage bounced and rolled down the coastal road, shaded by sentinel trees and sandwiched between the hills on their left and the coastal plain then the sea to their right. Mary was enchanted by the classical associations of the bay of Gaeta, its natural beauties sanctified by the presence of Cicero's villa and tomb.

On 1 December as they drove into Naples at dusk Mary, quite pale with exhaustion, could see the flames of Vesuvius incandescent against the night sky. Shelley had found cheap lodgings at 250 Riviera di Chiaia, overlooking the Royal Gardens and the blue waters of the bay beyond but she was so torpid with fatigue that she hardly noticed the view.

However, within four days she was recovered enough to go on an expedition with Shelley to investigate the bay. They took a boat at dawn and in the fairest weather spent the whole day on a crystal sea exploring the bay of Baiae and its promontories. This idyllic day was recalled exactly, even to the date, in the beginning of her other major work, *The Last Man*, published in 1826:

> 'I visited Naples in the year 1818. On the 8th December of that year, my companion and I crossed the bay, to visit the antiquities which are scattered on the shore of Baiae. The translucent and shining waters of the calm sea covered fragments of old Roman villas, which were interlaced by sea-weed, and received diamond tints from the chequering of the sun-beams.... Though it was winter, the atmosphere seemed more appropriate to early spring; and its genial warmth contributed to inspire those sensations of placid delight which are the portion of every traveller, as he lingers, loath to quit the tranquil bays and radiant promontories of Baiae.'[40]

Mary continued her explanation with the fiction of how she and her companion discovered in the forgotten gloom of Sybil's cave a pile of leaves and bark inscribed with the fragmented legend, in various obscure languages, relating the desolate story of the Last Man.

It was the luminescence of the water in the bay that wove enchantment that day at Baiae. The moment Mary and Shelley forsook it for the land to explore the picturesque ruins and countryside, which had seemed so magical as they floated off-shore, the spell was broken and the lambency was found to be mere illusion. They turned back to their boat full of disappointment. 'The colours of the water & the air breathe over all things here a radiance of their own beauty',[41] Shelley wrote to Peacock.

On tranquil expeditions such as this, which fed Mary and Shelley's mutual passion for classical antiquities, for discovery and for landscape, Mary once again felt for him that old intimacy and comradeship. Her sorrow and depression were overpowered by the flamboyant natural beauty, the soft scents and sights and noises that crowded her senses. Shelley, too, was coaxed into an ecstatic appreciation which lifted his thoughts beyond the vagaries of his health.

Just over a week later, on 16 December, Mary went with Shelley and Claire on a further expedition, this time to Vesuvius. It was another long day with Mary and Shelley making the first part of the ascent on mules. Claire was carried ceremoniously in a chair-like

William Godwin by
James Northcote, 1802

Mary Wollstonecraft
by John Opie,
probably painted
in 1797

This portrait by S. J. Stump, painted in 1831, is thought to be most probably of Mary Shelley. Certainly the description of Mary at this time by a contemporary, Eliza Rennie, closely corresponds with the lady in this picture. 'I have never seen a portrait that at all did her justice. If not a beauty, she was a most *lovable*-looking woman; with a skin exquisitely fair, and expressive gray eyes; features delicate, yet of that style and proportion which have won the term of 'aristocratic'; hair of a light but bright brown, most silky in texture and luxuriant in profusion, which hung in long drooping ringlets over her colourless cheek, and gathered in a cluster behind, fell wavingly over her shoulders; a large, open forehead; white and well-moulded arms and hands. She was a degree under the middle height, and rather inclining to *embonpoint*.'

Shelley by Amelia Curran, painted in 1819 at Rome

ABOVE Mary Shelley at the age of 44, painted by Rothwell in 1841

RIGHT Sir Percy Florence Shelley, from a photograph taken about 1880

William Shelley by Amelia Curran, painted in May 1819 when he was 3 years old. He died one month later.

Claire Clairmont by
Amelia Curran,
painted in 1819 when
she was 21

Jane Williams by
George Clint

Byron in 1813, by Richard Westall

Trelawny by Joseph Severn, 1838

The Casa Magni, Lerici

Field Place in 1812

contraption by four wild-looking men and was understandably rather nervous of the whole venture. As Mary's mule picked its way amongst the billows of petrified lava she was reminded of the Mer de Glace at Chamonix, where her monster's dramatic confrontation with Frankenstein was set against the surrealism of that turbulent sea frozen in suspended motion.

Frankenstein's thoughts as he surveyed the smoky glacier were hers too as she gazed on Vesuvius: 'These sublime and magnificent scenes afforded me the greatest consolation that I was capable of receiving. They elevated me from all littleness of feeling, and although they did not remove my grief, they subdued and tranquillised it.'[42]

They had to make their way by foot up the final ascent between the steaming, crackling streams of molten lava. Mary was less impressed by Vesuvius than by the Mer de Glace, but as evening darkened the sky she was entertained and a little alarmed by the firework display. The lava streams glowed red; the rocks spewed out by the choleric old volcano were now white with heat and trailing smoky tails through the darkness. Exhausted by the day's exertion and excitement, they began their descent. It was spoilt by Shelley's sudden affliction with intense pain in his side. Claire, too, had a perilous and contentious descent with her outlandish Italian bearers.

In Naples Mary and Shelley lived an insular life. Friendless and contemptuous of the locals, they continued their classical studies; Shelley was writing *Prometheus Unbound* and Mary duly transcribed it. In retrospect, in her notes to Shelley's poems, she deeply regretted the 'utter solitude' of their Neapolitan winter, 'for then, at least with those who have been exposed to adversity, the mind broods over its sorrows too intently; while the society of the enlightened, the witty, and the wise, enables us to forget ourselves by making us the sharers of the thoughts of others, which is the portion of the philosophy of happiness'.[43] They were keen tourists, however, revelling in the ancient ruins and voluptuous countryside which temporarily anaesthetized Mary's grief with its grandeur.

Just before Christmas, on 22 December, Mary and Shelley made an expedition to Pompeii. They were amazed to see so much of the marble temples, the houses and city streets intact and to feel the spirit of the place still active. Shelley was most moved by the harmony of the city and its surrounding landscape, where each was intrinsically part of, and a setting for, the other. It was an out-of-doors city with its theatres and temples open to the sky, where its people could see the sea and the lush hills and towering grumbling Vesuvius beyond. With this panorama to gaze upon and wonder at Mary and Shelley sat and ate their picnic lunch of oranges, figs and bread.

But these few happy days were infrequent diversions in an otherwise bleak and low-spirited winter. Shelley was not very well for much of the time and, to add to his misery, was subjected by his Italian doctor to a particularly painful and ineffectual cure. The poetry he was writing then has a distinctive strain of melancholy, even despair. He was still suffering grief and remorse for Clara's death and, while delighting in the sensuous countryside and liberal scatterings of antique ruins, he was offended and distempered by the vulgarity, immorality and barbarism of the Italians themselves. It was true that he was frequently in pain. He was sometimes intensely homesick, hurt and resentful at his enforced exile from a country he loved, effected by the antagonism of the establishment, culminating in the Chancery case, and confirmed by the continuing indifference of the public. But above all he was bewildered and stricken by Mary's withdrawal from him in spirit, emotionally and sexually. He had always needed a strong emotional bond with his women. Mary had from the beginning shared his thoughts and his feelings, each had immediate knowledge of the other. Mary, as his mother, his sister, was security, serenity and wisdom. Mary, as his lover, renewed his life and gave him power. But this power source, this flow of confidence and energy was blocked by the wall of grief that immured her. Sadly, Mary was constitutionally subject to melancholy and had always found it difficult to dispel her negative moods, her depressions, self-pity and fatalism. Shelley kept from Mary the poems he wrote at this time, amongst them *Misery* and *Stanzas written in Dejection, near Naples*:

> 'Alas! I have nor hope nor health,
>   Nor peace within nor calm around,
> Nor that content surpassing wealth
>   The sage in meditation found,
>   And walked with inward glory crowned –
> Nor fame, nor power, nor love, nor leisure.
>   Others I see whom these surround –
> Smiling they live, and call life pleasure; –
> To me that cup has been dealt in another measure.'[44]

When she found them after his death Mary was impressed with a terrible guilt. The 'unspeakable regret and gnawing remorse' at her short-sighted lack of sympathy and of selflessness haunted Mary for the rest of her life: '... had one been more alive to the nature of his feelings and more attentive to soothe them, such would not have existed – and yet enjoying, as he appeared to do, every sight or influence of earth or sky, it was difficult to imagine that any melancholy he showed was aught but the effect of the constant pain to which he was a martyr.'[45] Her retrospective sense of having failed Shelley at some of the crisis points in their life together, barbed her saddest memories and prevented their timely quiescence.

To her diary Mary turned a closed face. Christmas came and went uneventfully with probably a small celebration for the sake of William, who was nearly three and the only remaining child in the party. But there was trouble already brewing.

Two days later another much more mysterious and equally ill-fated child officially joined in name the ranks of the depleted Shelley family. Elena Adelaide Shelley, 'my Neapolitan charge' as Shelley called her, was registered by him on 27 February 1819, her day of baptism, as having been born to him and to Mary on 27 December 1818. These are two of the scanty facts in an episode that has since spawned endless theories and speculation. Little else is undisputed except the following skeleton of events: that Shelley, Mary and Claire, William and Milly Shields, left Naples on 28 February, the day after Elena's baptism and registration: that Elise had married Paolo Foggi in late January and both had left the Shelleys' employment: that the baby remained, probably with Elise who eventually deposited her with foster-parents, in Naples; that Shelley paid some sort of maintenance until poor little Elena Shelley sickened and died in Naples on 9 June 1820; and that on her death certificate her age was given as fifteen months and twelve days, counted not from her alleged birth date but from her registration and baptism. Mary and Shelley were then in the Bagni di Pisa and three days later, on the twelfth, they received Paolo's first attempt at blackmail. This was immediately put in the hands of an eminent Italian lawyer.

The most revealing and extraordinary exchange of letters, however, took place in September 1820. Byron in Ravenna had written to R. B. Belgrave Hoppner, the British consul in Venice, regretting that he should have relinquished his good opinion of Shelley and probing for more information: 'You seem lately to have got some notion against him.' His ending his letter with 'I think Madame Clare is a damned bitch. What think you?'[46] was enough to prompt Hoppner's eager reply tinged with moral justification, '... on Allegra's account it is necessary that you should know.'[47]

It seemed that Elise had left Paolo and had returned to her old job as a maid to an English lady traveller. A month or so after the death of Elena she had dropped in to see the Hoppners with whom she had stayed with Allegra during their Venetian summer. To them she related a wild and highly-coloured account of how the baby born in Naples had been Claire and Shelley's. How, after an attempted abortion, the birth had been kept from Mary. Accordingly the child was deposited at birth in an orphanage. There was added incidental drama with stories of Claire's hatred for Mary and Shelley's indifference and cruelty towards her.

Byron's laconic reply, a good three weeks later, was extraordinary and his ready acceptance, even reinforcement, of this story has been a problem for his apologists ever since. 'The Shiloh [Shelley] story is true no doubt, though Elise is but a sort of *Queen's evidence*. You remember how eager she was to return to them, and then she goes away and abuses them. Of the facts, however, there can be little doubt; it is just like them.'[48] Certainly it was impossible that Elena could be Mary and Shelley's child. Mary, always so indisposed when pregnant, could not have been expecting a baby and enjoying all their strenuous sightseeing; she would have had to go up Vesuvius on a mule in her ninth month. Neither would she or Shelley ever relinquish a baby of theirs to the unsupervised care of others. But if Mary was not the mother, who was?

Claire and Shelley have been considered as possible parents for Elena. In some ways Byron was right, parts of the story were typical of them, but the gist was grimly inapposite. Claire had been living for three and a half years with Mary and Shelley in a familiarity that was often uneasy and at times, or at one time, included sexual intimacy with Shelley. Relations between Mary and Shelley, particularly since the death of Clara, had been strained and unhappy but there was nothing to suggest in letters or journals that Claire assumed ascendancy in Shelley's affections at that time. Despite the few coincidences of Claire's illnesses corresponding roughly with Elise's story of her pregnancy and confinement, Elena Shelley was almost certainly not the child of Claire and Shelley.

Claire discovered a wealth of maternal emotion with Allegra's birth which was cruelly denied expression by the cession of her daughter to Byron. As a thwarted mother, she would never give up another baby daughter, especially one by Shelley. She would never relinquish her at birth and abandon her to an uncertain and unpromising fate in the care of Neapolitan foster-parents. Claire's diaries of the time between her departure from Naples and Elena's death in 1820 contain neither a backward glance nor any hiatus or change of tone in the busy entries at the time, and after, the news of the baby's death reached the Shelleys. The seal on this refutation comes from Mary. In August 1821 Shelley, having been told by Byron of Elise's malicious tale, urged Mary to write to the Hoppners and forcefully correct their misapprehensions. Mary, who by now knew the facts of the story although not necessarily every ramification, wrote a magnificently impassioned and loyal letter, ending with an oath which asserts beyond doubt that Claire and Shelley had no child in Naples: '... by all that I hold sacred upon heaven and earth by a vow which I should die to write if I affirmed a falsehood – I swear by the life of my child [her fourth and last surviving] by my blessed and beloved child, that I know these accusations to be false.'[49]

Shelley was far more emotionally involved in Elena's fate. His general depression during the winter of 1818 could be easily blamed on the possible complexity of his domestic situation at that time. Certainly Elena's death affected him deeply. He wrote to the Gisbornes in despair: 'My Neapolitan charge is dead. It seems as if the destruction that is consuming me were as an atmosphere which wrapped and infected everything connected with me.'[50] Shelley had great sympathy with children and took his responsibilities towards them seriously, apart from his uncharacteristic neglect of his first children while Harriet was alive. It is possible that Shelley had meant to adopt Elena in an attempt to bring Mary back from the grief-encircled desert she had inhabited since Clara's death. In the past Shelley and Mary had been very casual about adoption; during their honeymoon they had, on a whim, decided they wanted to take a young girl, Marguerite Pascal, with them. This time Shelley may well have registered this baby as his and Mary's daughter to by-pass any awkward legalities. They may then have decided against the adoption and left the baby with its parents. The small sums of money Shelley paid Elena's parents/foster-parents could easily be explained in the light of his understandable concern and readily-assumed responsibility. Having taken Elena into his sphere of influence in this way, his despair at her death, having already lost his own second beloved child, was tragically justified. Certainly his real anger and disgust at Elise's story, as related to him by Byron, was centred on the accusation that he should abandon a child, especially his own, an 'unutterable'[51] crime. However, given that Shelley had innocently attempted to adopt Elena and then generously acted as a form of guardian to her, there seems very little reason for Paolo's blackmail attempts which upset the Shelleys badly enough for them to employ a top Italian lawyer, and yet still be plagued by the threats for over a year. Possibly Paolo knew something that Shelley did not want to become public knowledge.

Elise was the one other woman in the Shelley party who could have been the mother of Elena. She was much more than a maid, an unusual and intelligent woman whom Mary valued. Separated from her husband, she already had a daughter of her own who was looked after by her family. She was in her late twenties and hardly an innocent abroad. According to Mary, Elise was definitely pregnant in December:

> 'You well know that she formed an attachment with Paolo when we proceeded to Rome and at Naples their marriage was talked of. We all tried to dissuade her; we knew Paolo to be a rascal, and we thought so well of her that we believed him to be unworthy of her. An accident led me to the knowledge that without marrying they had formed a connection; she was ill, we sent for a doctor who said there was danger of a miscarriage. I would not turn the girl on the world without in some degree binding her to this man. We had them married at Sir W. A'Court's – she left us; turned Catholic at Rome, married him, and then went to Florence.'[52]

If Mary's facts were correct about discovering Elise's pregnancy with her threatened miscarriage it meant effectively that the baby could not have been Paolo's. Mary, usually so precise in her information, wrote that 'she formed an attachment with Paolo when we proceeded to Rome'. The Shelley entourage started out on the first leg of their trek south on 5 November; even given that Elise conceived almost immediately after that date, by December her condition would hardly be certain and such an unestablished pregnancy would never merit diagnosis by a doctor of that day of 'in danger of miscarriage', rather would it be a late period. However, if Elena was Elise's baby and if she was born on 27 December, Elise's bleeding in early December similarly would hardly be classified as a miscarriage, rather as the beginnings of slightly premature labour.

It is quite likely therefore that the baby, if it was Elise's, was not born on 27 December but much nearer the date of her baptism and registration on 27 February, the date from which her age is recorded on her death certificate. If this is so, Elise's threatened miscarriage falls at about the six-and-a-half-month mark and merits the doctor being called, the diagnosis, and the measure of alarm. It is also quite possible that her pregnancy up until then could have been kept from Mary, who on discovering it dispensed with principle and expedited the marriage she had opposed, to protect Elise and legitimize her child.

Of course for this later birth date, there is a correspondingly later date of conception, spanning April and May 1818. Elise was in the Shelley party until 28 April, travelling across Europe to Italy, cramped in a carriage with fractious children, fatigued adults, all sleeping in dingy and often disgusting inns, sometimes not daring to undress. She and Shelley could have had a fleeting sexual encounter but circumstances were far from propitious and Shelley, full of principles and positive with the promise of a new lease of life in Italy, was unlikely to find room enough for dalliance. But perhaps he did. Nevertheless Elise left with Allegra on the twenty-eighth to travel to Byron at Venice and there she lived until the end of August.

Given the later birth date, Byron could just as easily have been the father of Elise's baby. He was leading a particularly dissolute and sexually promiscuous life at that time. Wild rumours of his profligacy were gleefully circulated: rumours which distressed the Shelleys, about to send Allegra with Elise into his lascivious circle, rumours in fact which reached Byron's two friends Hobhouse and Kinnaird in London and which Byron, far from rebutting, boldly reinforced:

'... which "piece" does he mean? Since last year. I have run the gauntlet. Is it the Tarriscelli – the Da Mosto – the Spinola – the Lotti – the Mizzato – the Eleanora – the Carlotta – the Giulietta – the Aloisi – the Gambieri – the Eleanora da Bezzi (who was the

King of Naples' Gioachino's mistress – at least one of them) – the Theresina of Mazzurati – the Glettenheim and her sister – the Luigia and her mother – the Fornaretta – the Santa – the Caligari – the Portiera Vedova – the Bolognese figurante – the Tintora and her sister – cum multis aliis. Some of them are countesses and some of them cobbler's wives, some noble, some middling, some low, and all whores. . . . I have had them all and thrice as many to boot since 1817.'[53]

And Elise, living under his roof and at the Hoppners looking after his child, was quite probably one of that number. It was almost inevitable that the personable and love-starved Elise would find Byron as irresistible as did the rest of the female population of Venice. After Elise had left their employ, Mary was to write to Marianne Hunt, who had known and valued Elise when the Shelleys lived in Marlow, 'Venice quite spoiled her [Elise] and she appears in the high road to be as Italian as any of them.'[54] To be as Italian as the rest of them meant in Mary and Shelley's stern tones to be completely lacking in moral fibre; the women were promiscuous and the men dishonest. In Mary's eyes Venice had obviously corrupted Elise and led to her decline. This odd little comment gains full weight and meaning in the light of a Byronic seduction in Venice, leaving Elise pregnant and with a reawakened sexual appetite which resulted in her affair with the unsuitable Paolo Foggi.

If Byron was, or thought it possible that he was, the father of Elise's baby it would neatly explain the two anomalies of his behaviour during the whole incident. His almost eager acceptance of Hoppner's vituperative account of Elise's story has never been explained away. But if this story deflected censure from him, all the better, for Shelley had ruined his reputation long ago; he was more of a social outcast than Byron who valued his status and the approval of his peers. Shelley had outrageous political views and was wild and a little mad; an accusation like this would make little difference to him or the world. Given Shelley's peculiar domestic situation it seemed a plausible enough tale.

The second anomaly concerned Mary's passionate and convincing refutation of Elise's story that was addressed to Mrs Hoppner, but sent to Shelley to copy out and pass on to Byron who had promised to deliver it to the Hoppners. Mary's spirited and impressive letter never reached its destination. It was found with its seal broken in Lord

Byron's belongings after his death. If Byron had been somehow involved with Elise and her baby, it was more convenient to leave the Hoppners their misapprehensions, unchallenged by Mary's passionate rebuttal.

However, given that Byron was quite likely to have had an affair with Elise during that hot Venetian summer, and given that he was quite possibly the father of her child born in January/February the following year, three further questions arise: why should Shelley register the baby in his name as a child of his and Mary's; why should Paolo's threats of blackmail be taken seriously and cause such consternation; and why should Elise, just after Elena's death, tell the Hoppners a lurid story about her being Claire and Shelley's child?

So much of the case is obscure and after concerted efforts by Shelley researchers it seems likely to remain so. Perhaps there had been some attempt at a sexual relationship between Elise and Shelley before she went to Venice, perhaps Shelley knew or suspected that Byron, too, was involved. Either way, Elise's baby was someone special, someone to whom he owed a little care and responsibility. With an illustrious and genius Byron, or with he himself, for a father, Shelley could hardly abandon the child to Paolo, whom he despised, and brand her with the name Foggi. Father or no, Byron's name could not be entered, so it remained for Shelley and Mary to become Elena Shelley's official parents. Perhaps in his utopian way, he hoped to be able to embrace the baby into his family when Mary was happier and the wounds had begun to heal. All this was reason enough for blackmail. Possibly Foggi approached Byron, too, although he was much grander, more powerful and physically aggressive, and altogether more dangerous opponent than the altruistic and eccentric Shelley.

Elise's story, coming just after the death of her child, may well have been the result of her grief and remorse and an uneasy guilt at leaving her little girl with foster-parents. The Hoppners had been good to her during her time with Allegra in Venice and possibly, in wanting to relieve herself of some of the burden, she chose to tell them the story of Elena's birth, transferred to Claire and Shelley and embellished with crude exaggerations in a misguided attempt to make it more valid. Perhaps she regretted it immediately after the telling; certainly she wrote to Mary a year later asking for money 'with great professions of love',[55] which Mary took as sincere. Mary never believed Elise to be part of Paolo's blackmail plan. In fact Mary's letter to the Hoppners, when she was in possession of the salient facts about Elena, bore remarkably little malice towards Elise, only censuring her for her 'infamous tale'. Perhaps Elena Shelley was another baby Byron after all. However, regardless of whether Elena was Byron's, Shelley's or Elise's child, or that of some poor Neapolitan woman, the little girl's life and death became a further tragedy for which Mary and Shelley paid dearly.

12
My Lost William

> 'The treasures of my youth lie buried here ...'
> On entering Rome, *Rambles in Germany and Italy*,
> Mary Shelley

On the last day of February 1819 Mary and Shelley together with William, Claire and Milly Shields left Naples for Rome. Mary was only just pregnant. The stirring of spring through the beautiful countryside, 'the divinest in the world',[1] found an echo in her own instinctive knowledge of the new life within her. Mary's barren winter of despair was beginning to retreat.

Their journey was leisurely; a full day was spent at Gaeta, playing chess on the terrace of the inn, 'and strolling about the woods and by the sea-shore'.[2] With great anticipation they approached Rome again, this time from the south where there was no hawk to mark their coming.

Mary was due a few months' respite from tragedy. The treasures of Rome and its spanning history were balm to her unquiet mind; 'it has such an effect on me that my past life before I saw it appears a blank & now I begin to live'.[3] She and Shelley and Claire saturated themselves with art and culture. Mary was taking drawing lessons, Claire singing and Shelley was writing poetry.

The city was 'stuffed with the loveliest statues in the world'[4] and Mary, often with little William's hand in hers, would make pilgrimages to her favourite views. William at three and a quarter was a dearly beloved son, a lodestar to her life. He was by now more adept at both Italian and English and Mary and Shelley would delight in his bilingual chatter. He was frequently called by his pet names of 'Willman' and 'Willmouse' and his happy character and ingenuousness brightened their days. On a solemn occasion at the Vatican when they saw the frail old Pope, Pius VII, 'upon the brink of the Grave', so Claire thought, William in a loud voice lamented the 'man *sotto*'.[5]

The ruins of classical Rome were everywhere, scattered massive and immovable over the fertile plains that lay as the setting to the city. The ruined colonnades and ancient temples bulkily thrust their clean proportions, holding at bay the modern Rome. And everywhere these massively severe lines were softened by springing moss and wild flowers, waving on tops of pillars and tumbling down marble walls. Mary would walk out with Shelley in the evening between the ruins, with grass so close-textured and fine sprung like the best English lawn beneath their feet. They exclaimed at the fragrance of the wild flowers, and the trees and shrubs of the countryside beyond wafted on the evening air a voluptuous mixture, almost too heady for their uncloyed English senses.

They had moved into lodgings in the Palazzo Verespi at number 300 Corso, a narrow but extremely fashionable and entertaining street where the local nobility and courtesans would parade. After their isolation and friendlessness at Naples, Mary was happy to make a few new acquaintances. Signora Marianna Dionigi, an extensively educated, talented and interesting woman in her early sixties, lived just a few doors down the street from the Shelleys at 310 Corso. She was a celebrated artist, writer and archaeologist and held civilized literary evenings and musical soirées which the Shelleys and Claire regularly attended. Mary described her concisely and cuttingly as 'very old, very miserly & very mean',[6] but she had been generous in extending her hospitality to the young English tourists who had become her neighbours.

Probably at one such evening Mary met Signor Delicati, an artist who drew her portrait and called frequently at the Shelleys' lodgings until eclipsed by the rapid rise in favour of Miss Amelia Curran. She was the artist daughter of the eloquent Irish patriot, John Philpot Curran, and was an unusual and talented woman, full of wit and grace. Mary, Shelley, Claire and William all sat for their portraits. Claire did not like hers, probably feeling it did not flatter her enough. Both Mary and Amelia Curran were disappointed in Shelley's, although it is now the most famous, and William's was no more than a sketch. Mary met Miss Curran nearly every day either to sit in her study while she painted or to walk with her to points of interest in the city. Their friendship so grew that on 7 May, within ten days of meeting, Mary and Shelley moved from the bustling Corso to 65 Via Sistina, right next door to Miss Curran. Mary was to remember her with great affection for the rest of her life, grateful for her hospitality and for what was to be the priceless record of the faces and expressions of the two beings she loved most in the world, Shelley and William.

Although on her own admission Rome had given life back to her, Mary was still subject to her black moods of despair: 'God knows why but I have suffered more from them ten times over than I ever did before I came to Italy evil thoughts will hang about me',[7] she wrote in a letter to Leigh Hunt. Mary was always extremely sensitive to the people and places around her, always receptive to atmosphere and aura. Perhaps largely due to this increased awareness, she was sometimes alarmed by a premonitory sense of doom. Given this and the memory of Clara's wretched death in Venice, it was hardly surprising that, although delighting in and loving Italy, she should be dogged by anxiety and despair. Despite the pleasures of Rome, by the end of April Mary's presentiments began to surface uneasily. She was writing to her old friend and comforter, Maria Gisborne, fearing that the Roman air was responsible for the degeneration in Shelley and William's health. She planned, during the first week of May, to move back south again to the bay of Naples for the summer. This early retreat from Rome was delayed; perhaps the attractions of Miss Curran's company or the excitement of the city quashed her fears. If Mary had acted on that first instinct of flight, one of the greatest tragedies in her life could possibly have been averted.

As it was, William succumbed to a nasty attack of worms on 25 May which persisted for three days. By the thirtieth he appeared to be recovering his strength. He was now under the care of a Dr Bell, an eminent English physician, who called daily. He advised Mary against the heat of Naples, which she had hoped would help Shelley's health, and they were now turning their eyes to the Bagni di Lucca, Lucca or Pisa. Mary and Shelley's exile in Italy was complicated and burdened by the knowledge that the heat that seemed so beneficial to Shelley's health jeopardized and indirectly destroyed their children.

Poor little William had not fully recovered when on 2 June he was prostrated by a serious attack, possibly of dysentery, accompanied by convulsions, so reminiscent of Clara's nightmare death. Dr Bell called three times and Mary, Shelley and Claire took turns in seeing little

Willmouse through the night. During the ebb hours of that dreadful first vigil Mary's conviction of being persecuted by fate chased out all hope. However, the little boy survived the dangers of the night and appeared to rally. Mary was able to dash off a postscript to Maria Gisborne that was eloquent of her own and Shelley's anguish: William is in the greatest danger – we do not quite despair yet we have the least possible reason to hope – Yesterday he was in the convulsions of death and he was saved from them – Yet we dare not must not hope – I will write as soon as any change takes place – The misery of these hours is beyond calculation – The hopes of my life are bound up in him....'[8]

Mary gave up keeping her diary on 4 June for the days had lost hope and meaning. She and Shelley stayed by William's bed day and night; '... he watched 60 miserable – deathlyke hours without closing his eyes',[9] she wrote in blank despair to Marianne Hunt. They watched helplessly as the life they had so cherished slipped inexorably away. Mary was rigid with horror and disbelief that she was losing her third and last child this way. But more than that, she was losing William, a very special individual and a powerful symbol: his life made sense of the privations of their exile, for their flight from England was in part propelled by an illogical fear that the Lord Chancellor could deprive Shelley of William, just as he had his two eldest, Charles and Ianthe; his life in part compensated for the deaths of his two sisters; while William lived he was proof of Mary's successful mothering and provided necessary expression for her maternal passions; in surviving, in being such a lovely child, in giving Mary so much pleasure, William kept at bay the ever-present fear that her griefs were reparation for the wrong done to Harriet and that she and Shelley would be haunted by misfortune until fate had redressed the balance.

In *The Last Man*, written six years later and full of autobiographical detail, Mary described exactly the agony of watching her child die:

'We watched at his bedside, and when the access of fever was on him, we neither spoke nor looked at each other, marking only his obstructed breath and the mortal glow that tinged his sunken cheek, the heavy death that weighed on his eyelids. It is a trite evasion to say, that words could not express our long drawn agony; yet how can words image sensations, whose tormenting keenness throw us back, as it were, on the deep roots and hidden foundations of our nature, which shake our being with earthquake-throe....'[10]

Claire's journal, too, faded out at 2 June. On 7 June, the day William died, she simply wrote 'at noon-day'.[11] William had lived a mere three and a half years.

Both Mary and Shelley were stricken with grief. It was a death blow to Mary that destroyed a part of her spirit. The intensity of emotion burnt out her heart and she never again recovered the full range of her affections. Still only twenty-one, Mary had lived through enough tragedy to last a lifetime. She was marked for life. She could never love a child of hers again with the depth and spontaneity of affection in which William had basked. By now she knew she was definitely pregnant and her unborn baby was beginning to make his presence felt. This promise of life, however, was not a consolation but rather a reinforcement of her despair at the transience and futility of life, the agony of mother love. This baby became merely a symbol of another frustrated life, a further blighted hope, a painfully direct route to sear her vulnerable heart.

Shelley, too, was desolate. He had now been cruelly deprived of his fifth and favourite child. 'His heart, attuned to every kindly affection, was full of burning love for his offspring',[12] Mary wrote later in her notes for his poems of 1819. Amongst them were these few lines *To William* written in June just after his burial in the lovely Protestant Cemetery that had enchanted Mary and Shelley on their first visit to Rome in November:

I

'My lost William, thou in whom
  Some bright spirit lived, and did
That decaying robe consume
  Which its lustre faintly hid, –
Here its ashes find a tomb,
  But beneath this pyramid
Thou art not – if a thing divine
Like thee can die, thy funeral shrine
Is thy mother's grief and mine.

II

> Where art thou, my gentle child?
>   Let me think thy spirit feeds,
> With its life intense and mild,
>   The love of living leaves and weeds
> Among these tombs and ruins wild; –
>   Let me think that through low seeds
> Of sweet flowers and sunny grass
> Into their hues and scents may pass
> A portion.'[13]

And another poignant fragment:

> 'Thy little footsteps on the sands
>   Of a remote and lonely shore;
> The twinkling of thine infant hands,
>   Where now the worm will feed no more;
> Thy mingled look of love and glee
> When we returned to gaze on thee.'

Both unfinished, almost as if Shelley was too distressed to continue, these poems simply and pathetically express the loving and losing of a child. William's death confirmed Shelley's grim conviction that the Fates were ranged against him and that everything he loved was thereby tainted and ultimately doomed.

Mary and Shelley wanted to quit Rome as quickly as they could. They packed up their books and belongings; their grief was made all the more unbearable by the gathering of William's clothes, his little worn shoes and his favourite toys, all so alive with memories that Mary expected him to come running into the room and replace her memories with warm reality. But those small shoes would never again enclose the fat little feet of her son; the swiftness of his decline from health had left Mary unbelieving, feeling cheated by his death. To her old friend Marianne Hunt she expressed something of her outraged grief:

> 'William was so good so beautiful so entirely attached to me – To the last moment almost he was in such abounding health & spirits – and his malady appeared of so slight a nature – and as arising simply from worms inspired no fear of danger that the blow was

as sudden as it was terrible – Did you ever know a child with a fine colour – wonderful spirits – breeding worms (and these of the most innocent kind) that would kill him in a fortnight.'[14]

The depleted and now childless Shelley party made its dejected way north to Leghorn. It was a miserable journey and neither Mary nor Shelley were in any state to take interest in the countryside, let alone make notes and write descriptions. Claire, however, continued her diary and it is she who noted that they arrived at Leghorn after seven days' lethargic travel, and spent a further week there with Mary deriving some motherly comfort from the generous-hearted Maria Gisborne.

They then moved into a light, airy house, the Villa Valsovano, near the sea between Leghorn and Monte Nero. With William's death Italy had shown its hostile face. Once again Mary and Shelley longed for England: for the security, the familiarity, the temperance and peace of the Thames Valley with its rolling fields, its bright, broad river and the green light of its beech woods.

Shelley began slowly to recover his spirits, he was reading again and writing *The Cenci* in a little glassed-in study perched on top of the villa with an expansive view of the fertile land below, the sea to the west and the blue Apennines smudging the opposite horizon. Twenty years later Mary still recalled vividly the sights and sounds that characterized that summer. The peasants working in their fields below the villa would sing their peculiar traditional songs that in the shimmering heat haze seemed to suspend time. When dusk eventually seeped in 'the water-wheel creaked as the process of irrigation went on, and the fire-flies flashed from among the myrtle hedges'.[15] Mary would walk with Shelley in the cool evenings while the cicadas rattled in the perfumed brush. Together they discussed his dramatic tragedy, *The Cenci*, the only poem he shared with Mary during its creation. It was a work she greatly admired and viewed as an exciting extension of his powers.

Her love of storms, nurtured by the spectacular displays on Lake Geneva, was again excited by the dramatic storms that rolled in from the sea: 'Sometimes the dark lurid clouds dipped towards the waves, and became waterspouts, that churned up the waters beneath as they were chased onwards and scattered by the tempest',[16] she recalled vividly in her notes to Shelley's poems.

Yet all this help from the elements, the love and care that Shelley gently offered, Maria Gisborne's kind and consoling presence, the shared work and discussions, all failed to disperse the despair and anguish that shackled Mary's spirit. A shared grief that could have strengthened the bonds between them became in Mary an exclusive despair that immured her and estranged Shelley. The one being on whom he could rely in a hostile world had withdrawn her support; she had retreated from him and from life and Shelley could neither reach her nor ease her pain. He felt powerless to bring her back into the world. Two fragments of poetry written at this time poignantly expressed the barrenness of life without her:

> 'My dearest Mary, wherefore hast thou gone,
> And left me in this dreary world alone?
> Thy form is here indeed – a lovely one –
> But thou art fled, gone down the dreary road,
> That leads to Sorrow's most obscure abode;
> Thou sittest on the heart of pale despair,
>   Where
> For thine own sake I cannot follow thee.
>
> The world is dreary,
> And I am weary
> Of wandering on without thee, Mary;
> A joy was erewhile
> In thy voice and thy smile,
> And 'tis gone, when I should be gone too, Mary.'

In effect Mary's protracted depression was beyond her will; William's death, following in the wake of the tragedies and difficulties of her life over the previous five years, precipitated her into a nervous and emotional breakdown which time and tranquillity and care alone could mend. She had to work through her grief and pain, in her own time, but felt continually guilty at her lingering despondency and morbid preoccupation with the tragedy. She wrote apologizing to Amelia Curran for her 'stupid letter': 'I no sooner take up my pen than my thoughts run away with me & I cannot guide it except about *one* subject & that I must avoid....'[17] Although she denied herself the necessity of expressing her grief fully, albeit tediously and, to her and her father's mind, self-indulgently, she allowed that pen to run freely in private. She formalized her depressions, guilt and despair in a novella called at first *The Fields of Fancy* and eventually *Mathilda*. This was to be her therapy: 'when I wrote Matilda, miserable as I was, the inspiration was sufficient to quell my wretchedness temporarily',[18] and the birth of her baby in November was to complete the healing as nearly as possible.

She resumed her journal again on 4 August, Shelley's birthday: 'We have now lived five years together; and if all the events of the five years were blotted out, I might be happy; but to have won and then cruelly to have lost, the associations of four years, is not an accident to which the human mind can bend without much suffering.'[19]

Written during August, Mary made Mathilda a motherless girl (her mother an idealized Mary Wollstonecraft) brought up by a stern aunt in Scotland, while her ideal father, grief-stricken at the death of his wife, is travelling abroad. When she is sixteen he returns and she is passionately reunited with this wonderful man. All her frustrated emotions are lavished on him but gradually she discovers his passion for her is more than paternal; he sees her as an extension, a replacement of her dead mother, and they are both horrified and burdened by guilt at this realization. Having left her a long letter of explanation he steals off into the night and there follows Mathilda's desperate pursuit eventually leading her to the sea. Full of dreadful forebodings, Mathilda finds her drowned father's body in an isolated cliff-top cottage. In grief she runs from life and lives in isolation in Scotland, brooding on her state until Woodville, a wholly selfless and self-sacrificing poet, invades her solitude. Although she falls in love with him, she selfishly continues to nurture her grief, demanding his consolation but giving little in return. She never reveals the source of her misery and obstinately insists that life holds nothing for her. When Woodville is called away to see his sick mother, Mathilda, through self-neglect, succumbs to consumption and picturesquely declines in health and dies. It is while she is awaiting death that she writes out her story for him as explanation of her grieving and peevish behaviour.

The work is an extraordinary and tragic record of Mary's feelings during the previous months: her sense of estrangement from the world and those she loved, her loneliness, her despair at having at last found love and then having to suffer its tragic souring. Always sharply self-critical and realistic, the story reveals a harsh judgement on her own self-centred, unreasonable preoccupation with her grief. There is clear realization, too, that Shelley, held at arm's length and ineffectual in alleviating her pain, was at this time unfailingly generous and selfless in his treatment of her.

There are so many interesting elaborations that illuminate something of Mary's crisis at this time. Throughout Mathilda's discussions with Woodville there is a strong sense of her disbelief in his love, her captiousness, hysteria and suspicion.

The climax of the story is the revulsion from sexual desire. Considering the extreme circumstances and emotions that inspired its creation, considering its therapy as an expression of Mary's guilt, her grief and recriminations, considering, too, her remorse after Shelley's death for her apparent coldness, it is perfectly reasonable to interpret this powerful repulsion from sexuality in *Mathilda* as a mirror of Mary's own withdrawal from and sexual rejection of Shelley. Having suffered the deaths of her three children, her sexual relationship with him no longer seemed a creative and fulfilling extension of their love. Instead it had become a travesty of life, a lure and a prelude to death and despair.

In the story it is her father who incestuously desires Mathilda, but the father in many ways resembles the forceful side of Shelley, and his death by drowning and Mathilda's nightmare pursuit in search of news of him find a parallel in Shelley's own death, a prognostication that Mary recognized in retrospect: 'Mathilda fortells even many small circumstances most truly – and the whole of it is a monument of what now is',[20] she wrote bleakly to Maria Gisborne the year after Shelley's death.

Mary had denied herself for so long the easy intellectual and emotional intimacy she had enjoyed with Shelley. She had also a clear realization of how difficult she was to love, over-emotional yet unresponsive, 'hardened to stone by the Medusa head of Misery'.[21] She feared that she was unwittingly destroying the very relationship that mattered most to her.

The story gives a strong sense of the vitality of Shelley and their relationship when he and Mary first met ('he opened up the world to me') and a regret at the shadows they had both become through grief and experience. Woodville is loving, philosophizing, ineffectual, lacking the passion and dynamism that might have stormed Mathilda's, and Mary's, prison which enchained both in self-loathing and misery. 'I had always been of an affectionate and forbearing disposition, but since those days of joy alas! I was much changed. I had become arrogant, peevish, and above all suspicous.'[22]

Of course Mary also explored her intense relationship with her father. Passionate and idealizing, she loved the obdurate, selfish old man until he died. But his abandonment of her when she eloped with Shelley, his lack of support and understanding and love during the crises of the deaths of Clara and William distressed and disillusioned her and dispirited their relationship.

So cruelly insensitive and self-centred were Godwin's letters to Mary after William's death that Shelley had to intervene. He wrote angrily to Peacock:

'Poor Mary's spirits continue dreadfully depressed. And I cannot expose her to Godwin in this state. I wrote to this hard-hearted person, "the first letter I had written for a year", on account of the terrible state of her mind, and to entreat him to try and soothe her in his next letter. The *very* next letter, received yesterday, and addressed to her, called her husband (me) "a disgraceful and flagrant person" tried to persuade her that I was under great engagements to give him *more* money (after having given him 4,700 pounds), and urged her if she ever wished a connection to continue between him and her to force me to get money for him. – He cannot persuade her that I am what I am not, nor place a shade of enmity between her and me – but he heaps on her misery, still misery.'[23]

Shelley had finished his dramatic tragedy, *The Cenci*, and had sent it to Covent Garden in the hopes of having it performed. Shelley's authorship was a closely-guarded secret in the conviction that his name would destroy its chances.

Mary's pregnancy progressed easily. She and Shelley had decided to move to Florence in time for the birth of their baby, her '*new work*, now in the press'[24] was their private joke. In Florence they had booked an eminent Scottish physician, not trusting the natives in that quarter, to preside at her confinement.

Mary's twenty-second birthday passed by with the melancholy reflection that 'when I was 21 – I repined that time should fly so quickly and that I should grow older so quickly – this birthday – now I am 22 ... I only repined that I was not older – in fact I ought to have died on the 7th of June last....'[25] She was aware how much her lamentations sounded like morbid self-pity but still in a state of breakdown she was unable either to contain or to overcome her depression; 'why do I write about this – why because I can write of nothing else & that is why I write so seldom'.[26]

They left their little villa with a view on 30 September and travelled to Pisa on the first stage of their journey inland to Florence. There they saw Mrs Mason, formerly Lady Montcashell, a high-spirited, forceful woman who as a girl was taught and inspired by Mary Wollstonecraft, as it turned out much to her parents' dismay. On 2 October they arrived at Florence and settled into lodgings at Palazzo Marini, 4395 Via Valfonda, which Shelley had secured the previous week.

Mary's baby was expected at the end of the month and as October became November the waiting grew tedious. She was fair-copying Shelley's poem *Peter Bell the Third*, written in a week at Florence, and reading Madame de Sévigné's *Letters*. Perhaps as she awaited the first signs of labour she feared that this child inside her swollen body was a monster, gestated in such trauma and suffering. Would she fail her monster as Frankenstein failed his?

She would never have to face that judgement for on 12 November, after an extraordinarily easy labour of two hours, a small, pink and pretty boy slipped into the world. Her journal was as laconic as ever: 'I have little to say, except that on the morning of Friday, November 12th, little Percy Florence was born.'[27]

It marked the end of '5 hateful months';[28] Mary was human again, her letters, no longer miserable and introspective, were jaunty, even jokey. Shelley was immensely relieved to have something of the old Mary back with him: 'Poor Mary begins (for the first time) to look a little consoled. For we have spent as you may imagine a miserable five months,'[29] he confided to Leigh Hunt.

Percy, although small at birth, liked his food and suckled well. He grew rapidly and Mary's forebodings diminished. Her submerged affections were beginning to rise. She could no longer be so engrossed in her own agonies as she looked down on her sleeping baby, 'with all his heart in his shut eyes'.[30] Here was a being more vulnerable, more demanding than she could ever rightly be, and in loving him she had to look outwards a little and forget herself. It was Percy's birth which brought Mary back to life, although she was to find that life's temper and tribulations were still set to confound her way. With the dispersal of one anxiety another had surfaced to discomfort them.

Godwin had been taken to court to get a ruling to force him to pay his back rent on Skinner Street, a property he had thought was rent-free. On 9 November, Mary and Shelley received a letter from him with the news that judgement had gone against him. Godwin, as always, was in desperate financial plight and looked to Shelley to provide the £1500. Her father's precarious position and the prospect of Shelley risking his health, and as they thought his freedom, to return to England filled Mary with dismay: 'I see nothing but despair. His journey, to say the least, is next door to death for him',[31] she wrote to Maria Gisborne. This deterioration in Godwin's affairs, although Shelley did not in fact have to make the journey to England, marked the beginning of his renewed harassment of Shelley, often via Mary, for money. This was to destroy what little peace of mind and contentment Mary managed to achieve. Shelley duly suffered through her distress, angry and dismayed that her father, who professed to love her, could be so selfish and cruel. They were not to be free of these demands until Shelley's own death sealed off the money supply.

However, their solitary existence was briefly enlivened by the arrival, just before Percy's birth, of Sophia Stacey, the pretty young ward of a distant relation of Shelley's. She proved an appealing distraction for Shelley from his physical sufferings and she repaid Mary's and his hospitality with undisguised admiration. In her diary she described with some awe, their quiet and bookish ways: 'He is always reading, and at night has a little table with pen and ink, she [Mary] the same.'[32] It was a tenor of self-contained study, which was hardly ruffled by Mary's confinement and re-established motherhood.

🌿 13 🌿
Rumours and Blackmail

'To love is to exist.... If grief kills us not, we kill it....'

Fortunes of Perkin Warbeck, Mary Shelley

The autumn winds, immortalized for ever by Shelley's *Ode to the West Wind*, written in that fruitful Florentine autumn of 1819, grew colder and blew snowy weather down from the mountains. According to Claire's music master, it was the harshest winter for seventy years. Apart from the aggravation of the rheumatic pain in Shelley's side, the cold winter was a welcome chance for Mary to re-establish her close family life. She was contented and occupied with baby Percy and Shelley preferred to stay in with her, too, in the evenings, reading aloud, gossiping and working alongside her as she wrote letters or translated Spinoza.

Once again they were about to take flight and Shelley's health was one of the prime determinants as to where in Italy they would alight. The current medical opinion was that either extremes of temperature exacerbated his condition and therefore most favourable would be the temperate climate of Tuscany, 'The Paradise of Exiles – the retreat of Pariahs'.[1]

Within these directives Pisa seemed a good choice with its aristocratic buildings in warm, worn stone curving along the banks of the River Arno. And of course, set amongst the mellowed palaces and squares, was the attraction of the Masons, made all the more intriguing for Mary by Mrs Mason's memories and lively anecdotes of Mary Wollstonecraft as governess, inspiration and friend.

They packed up once again and on 25 January, the day before leaving, they had Percy Florence baptized, named after his father and his birthplace. Shelley had decided to make the trip to Empoli by boat down the Arno. There was a bitter wind blowing that chilled them through, increasing Mary's discomfort and anxiety for Shelley and her precious baby. A carriage from there then rattled and bumped them all the way to Pisa.

Having spent the night in lodgings, Mary and Shelley wasted no time in calling upon the Masons at Casa Silva. Mrs Mason was in fact the common-law wife of George William Tighe, known as Mr Mason but invariably called 'Tatty' by Mary and Shelley. They had two daughters: Laurette, ten and a half, and Nerina, who was four and a half. Claire, during her stay in Pisa, was to act as a sort of older sister to these girls and in turn Mrs Mason took a motherly interest in Claire's personality and prospects. Mary was relieved to have Claire's thoughts and energies distracted from the painful contemplation of her lost Allegra, the despicable Albé and her periodic competitiveness with and envy of herself.

Mrs Mason was a keen admirer of the revolutionary spirit and had been in her youth an active member of the United Irish Movement. At the turn of the century she had written some pamphlets espousing the cause and on one of their frequent visits to Casa Silva, Mary and Shelley read these and discussed the Irish problem into the night.

Mary was missing Maria Gisborne and wrote frequently urging them to come to Pisa. She was still suffering from cowardice and dependence of spirit, which she recognized in retrospect five years later: 'The memories of careless, fearless youth can never be renewed. What a blessing fearlessness is. Since William's death, I have lost that feeling which was before my attribute – since then I walked on shifting sands[2] . . .' Since William's death she had looked all the more to Maria for motherly consolation and would have liked nothing better than to have her stay with them, leaving her husband and son, Henry, to go alone to England to settle the boy's inheritance: 'If I could get a *pretty boat* & come down in 2 hours I would come but a carriage & a child are discords – But you will come surely.'[3] Come they did for a few days, but Maria Gisborne was fixed in her intention of returning to England. Among other more mundane commissions, Mary had given the Gisbornes a draft of her story *Mathilda* to show to Godwin and get his advice on publishing. The Gisbornes were very impressed by the work, and recorded in Maria's journal in Mr Gisborne's hand was the simple conviction, 'I am well persuaded that the author will one day become the admiration of the world.'[4]

Mary and Shelley, without baby Percy, had travelled to Leghorn to make their fond farewells to the Gisbornes. On their return Mary was unsettled and depressed. Maria Gisborne was a warm, intelligent woman with whom she felt securely at ease. She had been a good friend to Godwin and Mary Wollstonecraft, and Mary could go to her for comfort and advice about her father, his disastrous circumstances and his persistent demands on Shelley. She was loving and sensible and the only one of the Shelleys' friends who really understood and appreciated Mary's difficult personality, full of complexity and conflict. She saw beyond the intellectual intensity, the shy aloofness and the periods of remote melancholy. Maria recognized the vulnerable, deeply emotional woman that Mary rarely exhibited to others: longing for the close domesticity she had never had as a child, yet loving the intellectual stimulus of travel and, nurtured in unorthodoxy, unable to live within the restrictions of a fully conventional life.

Mary loved passionately and steadfastly. Yet one of the abiding sorrows of her life was that this love was too often an underground river of which only she was intensely aware. If only she had allowed it to surface when it was most needed, a spontaneous and unequivocal spring to reassure and revive those she loved. Despite this constraint and despite the misunderstandings and mistreatments by her family and friends, Mary was to continue to love and serve and sacrifice herself for them right to the end. She was to prove herself generous and strong, yet all the while longing to escape into weakness and dependence. All her life she was to be desperate for love, for friends who were like-minded spirits, but she was sadly unsuccessful in making and keeping relationships. Her very need for friends and her emotional intensity and possessiveness frightened many away. Her personality and talents, too, were unusual and disconcerting. Other young women of her age had little in common with the solemn, intellectual daughter of Godwin, author of the increasingly famous *Frankenstein* and wife of the eccentric polemicist and poet-in-exile. Men, too, were often disturbed by that clear, cool gaze which seemed to slice through artifice and affectation to the shrinking soul within. She was incapable of easy flattery and coquetry, although she would banter and tease those she liked and admired. Only men, like Byron, who were confident and secure could cope with and like her, untroubled by the implicit challenge of an intellectual and successful young woman.

But Maria Gisborne was old enough to be Mary's mother. She, too, was obstinate and strong-minded and was to repay Mary's love and constancy in full measure. Maria having gone to England, Mary was not certain that she would return. She felt nostalgia, too, for her own country and the friends whom she would love to see again. She and Shelley were still not reconciled to the Italians and tended to choose their friends and acquaintances mainly from the straggling but distinctive coteries of British-abroad. On the day following the Gisbornes' departure, 30 April, a letter from one of that number arrived relaying the news of the most illustrious of exiles.

Byron had written to Mr Hoppner a week earlier of Allegra's good health and in contrast the Shelleys' misfortunes with their own children: 'Had they *reared* one?' was his cruel and rhetorical question. He felt justified in refusing Claire's request in a recent letter to have Allegra back if only for a short stay: '... the Child shall not quit me again to perish of Starvation, and green fruit, or be taught to believe that there is no Deity.'[5] This sentiment had been relayed in garbled form by Mrs Hoppner and Mary felt keenly the insensitive criticism of her quality and care as a mother. She already suffered ineradicable remorse that their nomadic way of life was largely to blame for all three tragic deaths. Byron and the Hoppners' lack of loyalty and understanding increased her feelings of being once again friendless and isolated in a hostile land. Byron's obstinacy over Allegra also distressed her. While she was a baby Mary had cared for her like one of her own; she was a precious connection with her lost William, once his playmate, his sister, the bluff little 'commodore'. Claire, too, was upset and unsettled by what she interpreted as Byron's brutality. She and Shelley had been going to travel to Ravenna in May to collect Allegra if Byron had permitted it, but a forceful letter, severely critical of Claire, put an end to that immediate plan. Shelley wrote back to Byron gently chiding him for his insensitivity and intolerance of Claire: 'I do not say – I do not think – that your resolutions are unwise; only express them mildly – and pray don't *quote me*.'[6]

Mary was once again finding Claire's presence and demands particularly irritating and distracting. Both she and Shelley longed for a peaceful house. But Claire's unpredictable temper, her self-centred emotionalism, was roused by her frustrated contention with Byron over Allegra. She was justifiably unhappy but petulant and accusatory towards Mary and Shelley. Shelley was wont to excuse her extremes of behaviour as being merely a result of her immaturity and unfortunately powerless position in the dispute. But Mary, on whom fell always the brunt of domestic strife, found it much more difficult to be continually understanding. She was herself very worried over her father's imminent financial collapse; his letters to her spared nothing and never failed to play on her susceptibilities and anxieties for him.

Claire's absence from her house for a whole day on 8 June was therefore hailed as a welcome relief from one of the irritants in her life. It was to be but a day's respite for a more serious disruption in the form of Paolo Foggi's first blackmail attempt arrived four days later. It was obviously something to do with the Shelleys' connection with Elena Adelaide Shelley. The little girl, according to her death certificate, had died on 9 June and this had no doubt inspired the blackmail. But at the time Mary and Shelley received the threat, they were yet to learn of Elena's fate. By 30 June, Shelley was only aware that she was very ill and he gloomily expected her to die.

Although Paolo's allegations were strenuously denied and dismissed out of hand, his threat alarmed Mary and Shelley enough for them to abandon their plans of migrating to Lucca in favour of seeing their lawyer, del Rosso, at Leghorn. They were already aware of animosity amongst some of the English community. Shelley, always prepared for persecution, already in exile and suffering isolation from society, understandably exaggerated in his own mind and perhaps also in Mary's the degree of antagonism nurtured in England against him. Inevitably they felt exposed and vulnerable to any further scandal. They had suffered enough social ostracism since their elopement to boldly ignore the tatty blackmail of an acknowledged scoundrel like Paolo. There was a flurry of packing and hurried arrangements. Mary was under very great stress. She was already extremely anxious for her father in his financial death throes and this sordid incident shocked and pressurized her further.

Shelley had persuaded the Gisborne servants to open up the Casa Ricci for them to use during their sojourn at Leghorn. Both felt rather sheepish at having set up in residence without asking Maria's permission, but immediacy and expedience were the foremost considerations.

Inevitably all the turmoil and upset affected Mary's milk and, still breast feeding, she suffered the acute agony of seeing her baby Percy afflicted with raging diarrhoea, in much the same way that little Clara had succumbed in Venice. Immediately Dr Palloni was summoned to do what he could. Saturday, 17 June, was a miserable day for all, full of regrets, recriminations and renewed fears. The doctor called again the next day but rubicund Percy had rallied and was getting better, 'he is the merriest babe in the world'.[7] Mary's relief welled disproportionately; she felt as if the Angel of Death had passed over and for once had let her be. That day she wrote a vivacious, happy letter to the Gisbornes but this elevation of spirit was to be sadly short-lived.

Godwin's problems, always weighing on her mind, were forcibly rammed home. It appeared he was about to be evicted from his house, unable as he was to pay his rent arrears. Mary was in despair and suggested to the Gisbornes that they lend Godwin £400 and that Shelley should assume full responsibility for the loan. The Gisbornes did not in fact comply. Mary's nerves and temper were strained and irritable with worry and the whole household suffered. Shelley wrote plaintively to the Gisbornes: 'Domestic peace I might have – I may have – if I see you, I shall have – but have not, for Mary suffers dreadfully from the state of Godwin's circumstances.'[8]

Claire was petulant and bad-tempered, rebellious towards Byron and unhappy about Allegra. Her miseries accumulated when she was parted from the diversions of Mrs Mason's gossipy company and the recreation of her daughters. She escaped boredom and discontent with mild hypochondria and cynicism, which irritated Mary increasingly and brought the highly volatile household to flashpoint. In her diary for 4 July Claire wrote:

> 'Heigh-ho the Clare & the Maie
> Find something to fight about every day.'[9]

The removal of Claire from the tense household would considerably diminish the stress on Mary. In the past when relationships between the two step-sisters had become unbearably strained Mary always had been thwarted by Claire's reluctance to leave the freedom and security of life with them and the undoubted attractions of Shelley, and by Shelley's own uneasiness at parting with and excluding Claire. Whereas before, Mary had never been able to demand uncompromisingly that Claire make a life for herself, for fear of alienating both her and Shelley, here the redoubtable Mrs Mason stepped in, sensibly assessing the situation and pushing for the only solution.

Unfortunately an attempt at finding Claire a position in Paris was abandoned for political reasons: 'the French are become surly having lost their politeness, and hating the English in an incredible manner',[10] as Mary reported to Maria Gisborne. But Mrs Mason was not to be deterred; for the sake of Claire's maturity and the sake of Mary and Shelley's marriage and peace of mind she had to go. It was in October that Claire finally left the Shelleys, already having spent some time during the summer with the Mason family at Pisa.

Meanwhile Leghorn bored Mary. Rome, despite its unhappy associations, was where she would like to be. The bustle, the antiquities, the history, she remembered all with nostalgia, isolated as she was in genteel, anglicized Leghorn. Mary was working very hard at the time. She was 'deep in Greek';[11] 'I pass [sic] five lines or more every day – reading them over again and again, so that now I may boast that I know perfectly sixty lines of Homer's Odyssey',[12] and she desperately needed Jones's *Greek Grammar* which was ordered via Peacock. She was also beginning to give form to her second novel, after a lengthy and irregular gestation. She called it *Valperga: or the Life and Adventures of Castruccio, Prince of Lucca* and had kept the idea in mind since 1817 in the hazy, child-centred summer at Marlow. In Naples in 1818 she revived the idea with study 'raked out of fifty old books'[13] and further thought. By autumn 1820 she was ready to begin committing it to paper. Shelley expected it to be excellent and successful: '... if what is wholly original will succeed, I shall not be disappointed.'[14]

Mary was troubled by the lack of communication from Maria Gisborne. By mid-July, almost three months since Maria's departure, she was still waiting for a first letter, keen as she was to hear all the news and recent history of London friends, current opinions and passing fashions. Above all, Mary waited impatiently to hear Maria's verdict on Godwin and his predicament. This silence in fact marked the beginning of a period of coolness and estrangement between the Gisbornes and the Shelleys. Godwin's vehemence against Shelley, malicious rumour-mongering at dinner parties and soirées may have given the Gisbornes a different emphasis on situations formerly accepted at face value: Claire's relationship with Shelley, the Neapolitan baby, Shelley's dealings with Godwin. Whatever caused the withdrawal of Gisborne affection and enthusiasm, it was to cause Mary great pain. Nevertheless, during the summer she discounted her fears of the Gisbornes' faithlessness and continued to write animated letters to Maria implicitly wooing her back from 'smokey London' to 'bella Italia'[15] where 'the vines are weighed down by their clusters, and the trees loaded with figs. Come and eat! Will you?'[16]

During July news of the Carbonari's activities around Naples reached Leghorn and Mary and Shelley were delighted and excited by the reported revolt there which had forced Ferdinand IV to grant the people a constitution. Mary wrote to Maria Gisborne: 'Thirty years ago was the era for Republics, and they all fell. This is the era for *constitutions* ... what a glorious thing it will be if Lombardy regains its freedom – and Tuscany – all is so mild there that it will be the last, and yet in the end I hope the people here will raise their fallen souls and bodies and become something better than they are.'[17]

During the summer Mary and Shelley's thoughts turned to England. Not only were Godwin's finances teetering on the catastrophic and the Gisbornes there enjoying their friends, hearing the news, sharing the discourse Mary and Shelley so missed, but there was disturbing news of John Keats, who was on the last long haul to death. He had been ordered to winter in Italy and Shelley wrote immediately offering their hospitality in a generous but patronizing letter. Keats gracefully declined. His powers as a poet, his seemingly inevitable death curtailing in youth the exploration and maturation of his genius, reminded Mary forcibly of Shelley's own fragile mortality.

There was less depressing news from England too. A royal scandal was rocking the isle. The Regent, having become King George IV, had attempted to divorce his poor wife, Caroline, by accusing her of adultery amongst other things. She had the whole-hearted support of the populace and this great surge of sympathy was partly responsible for the abandonment by Parliament of the Bill of Pains and Penalties against her. Mary and Shelley were as interested as were their countrymen. Mary was impassioned and sympathetic: 'I have great pity for this woman ... whose greatest fault is to enjoy herself amongst her servants instead of staying alone by herself, when entirely abandoned by the slavish grandees of England.'[18] Shelley was more intrigued: 'I wonder what in the world the Queen has done. I should not wonder, after the whispers I have heard, to find ... that she imitated Pasiphäe, and that the Committee should recommend to Parliament a bill to exclude all Minotaurs from the succession.'[19]

The Shelleys' stay in the Gisborne's house at Leghorn had been merely a temporary expedience to deal with Paolo's blackmail attempt and decide on their winter migration. They wished to avoid any town with accretions of ex-patriot English. Not only could they be snobbish about the English abroad, but they feared further ostracism as a result of Paolo's mischief. Mary longed for the mountains but the climate, too, had to palliate Shelley's physical afflictions. They decided on the Bagni di Pisa called locally San Giuliano. It was a small, untroubled village of mellowed stone buildings clustered about four miles from Pisa itself, 'under the shadow of mountains & with delightful scenery within a walk'.[20] On 28 July, Shelley went to the Masons at Pisa to look for suitable accommodation for his family. He returned on the first day of August, having acquired spacious lodgings at the Bagni, and full of the news that, like Naples, Sicily too had revolted and was free, but at the reported cost of many lives.

Immediately Mary started packing and they left Casa Ricci and Leghorn on 4 August. The next day they were installed in their spacious, airy lodgings at Casa Prinni, at the Bagni. Mary was delighted with the house and its situation; she had a garden for Percy Florence and the beauties of the Tuscan countryside spread before her while she worked. Mary was beginning to trust in her son's robust constitution and glowing good health. With tentative confidence the spectre of a jinx upon her children faded from her conscience. She could begin to believe that at least this child had a future and would survive. But the shock and grief over the deaths of Clara and William, the fear when Percy was born that she would love him, nurture him, give herself and her hopes to him, only to have him cruelly snatched away, all conspired to constrain her emotional involvement with her baby. Afraid that something malignant in the Shelley fortunes or the Italian air was cankering and destroying everything she loved, she could never offer baby Percy the intensity of emotion and carefree intimacy that had distinguished William's infancy.

Even then in Bagni di Pisa as Percy approached his first birthday, Mary realized that he was more than likely to reach his second, third and fourth. She loved him dearly and was a good, warm mother, who did everything in her power to make him happy, but the spontaneity of maternal passion had been restrained for ever by William's death. However, with Percy happily playing by her side, with Shelley spiritually renewed and free from pain, with the hills to walk in and the warm sun on her back, Mary at last began to feel contentment seep into her bones. To complete her happiness she longed for that perennial *absentia Clariae* but did not expect Mrs Mason to conjure the magic to effect it.

On the evening of Friday, 11 August, Mary, Shelley and Claire set off on horseback for Lucca. The air was balmy and the land through which they rode lay in long shadows from the setting sun. On the Saturday morning Shelley made his promised pilgrimage up the Monte San Pellegrino by foot and alone. This expedition delighted and inspired him to write, in the days following his return, *The Witch of Atlas*, a fantasy clothing the flight of his imagination in glittering imagery. Although Mary admired its 'brilliant congregation of ideas'[21] she regretted his 'discarding human interest and passion',[22] the very qualities she believed would win Shelley some part of the public recognition and acclaim that were his due and for which he longed. Shelley was writing 'because his mind overflowed, without the hope of being appreciated',[23] writing in a vacuum and sending his creations out into a void where only his few friends seemed to note the passing of another poem.

While Shelley climbed the Monte, Mary spent an equally happy and productive day at Lucca where she and Claire rode round the walls of the town. They climbed to the top of the ancient tower on the Guinigi Palace, overgrown with wild flowers, and surveyed the spreading plain of Lucca beyond, the lush banks of the River Serchio and to the west a dark wood in which lay ruins of a castle reputedly built by Castruccio. In this romantic landscape Mary decided to set her novel of Castruccio, *Valperga*. They visited, too, the church of San Franceno and wondered at Castruccio's tombstone sunk into the wall with the dramatic legend, 'I lived, I sinned, I suffered.... Attend and be mindful that you too are soon to die.'[24]

Her imagination stirring with ideas and steeped in the spirit of the place, Mary rode back with Claire to the Bagni di Pisa and turned once again to her books and her notes. Shelley returned on the Sunday, tired out and in need of rest but with the conception of his poem pulsing in his brain. They were happy, harmonious days. Before setting out on his expedition, Shelley had drafted a forceful letter to Godwin expressing sentiments that were long overdue, thus unburdening much of his justifiable anger and resentment of his father-in-law's increasingly unconscionable behaviour. Since the fright Shelley and Mary had had in June when a letter from Godwin plus Paolo's blackmail had so upset Mary, and through her their baby Percy, she had agreed that Shelley could intercept any letter from Godwin which could in any way threaten her peace of mind and the health of their baby. He had done this with a letter written on 21 July, pressing for a further £500.

Shelley's letter in reply was boldly eloquent, fair and impassioned and it infuriated Godwin: 'I have given you within a few years the amount of a considerable fortune, & have destituted myself, for the purpose of realising it of nearly four times the amount. Except for the *goodwill* which this transaction seems to have produced between you & me, this money, for any *advantage* that it ever conferred on you, might as well have been thrown into the sea.' In this draft Shelley showed that he was painfully aware of his own creditors, some of whom were no doubt in just as straitened circumstances as was Godwin. He was powerful and forthright, and courageous, too, in suspending temporarily Godwin's communication with his daughter:

> 'Mary is now giving suck to her infant, in whose life, after the frightful events of the last two years, her own seems wholly to be bound up. Your letters from their style & spirit (such is your erroneous notion of taste) never failed to produce an appalling affect on her frame.... Mary at my request authorised me to intercept such letters or information as I might judge likely to disturb her mind. That discretion I have exercised with the letter to which this is a reply. ... She has not, nor ought she to have the disposal of money, if she had poor thing, she would give it all to you.'[25]

Shelley's masterful action against her father's baleful influence helped win for Mary a happy and peaceful autumn during which she re-established something of the old spark and easy intimacy of their early life together. With the temporary evasion of the familiar and various demands of both Godwin and Claire, Mary's spirits revived. She learnt once more to live not in remorse for what had passed or in fear of what was to be but with quiet pleasure in her everyday existence with Percy Florence and Shelley.

During much of September Claire was at Leghorn for the sake of her health. Shelley had accompanied her there on 31 August, the day after Mary's twenty-third birthday, and reported to Mary the rife and excited rumours that the Carbonari at Naples had kidnapped the royal family there and threatened to execute them all should the Austrian troops be sent in to quell their revolt. There were rumours, too, that the mob had risen in Paris and with the rumour came a prickle of unease that the whole of Europe was on the brink of revolution.

On Shelley's return without Claire, the peaceful routine of work, reading, walking and riding in the surrounding hills returned for Mary and Shelley. Relaxing in the Baths gave some relief to Shelley's nephritic pains in his side. The whiff of revolution on the air made him restless for action, involvement, for travel; but with peace at home, with Mary once again relaxing into loving him, with the warm days preserving him in health, he was content enough.

At the beginning of October, Mary at last began to write the novel she had carried in her head for so long. With her creative energies roused and with the relief of Claire's absence, Mary's new-found happiness and serenity began to creep into her journal. For so long this faithfully kept diary had recorded the passing of the days with terse entries such as 'Read Greek; walk; write'[26] and 'Walk up a mountain with Shelley. Read Villani, and Greek'.[27] Now she felt once again the pleasure in observation and the wish to describe her impressions, as she had in her adolescent travels with Shelley. On 18 October her journal expanded into:

'Rain till 1 o-clock. At sunset the arch of cloud over the west clears away; a few black islands float in the serene; the moon rises; the clouds spot the sky; but the depth of heaven is clear. The nights are uncommonly warm. Write. Shelley reads "Hyperion" aloud. Read Greek.

> My thoughts rise and fade in solitude;
> The verse that would invest them melts away
> Like moonlight in the heaven of spreading day.
> How beautiful they were, how firm they stood,
> Flecking the starry sky like woven pearl!'[28]

It seemed to Mary that autumn, the season of her birth, effused a benign grace, assuming guardianship of herself and her loved ones. In a life surprised by tragedy and the vagaries of fortune, she had learned to mistrust spring, the season spoiled for her by the deaths of her first baby and William, by Claire's affair with Byron and Paolo's blackmail attempt. She was ashamed of the superstition, but in autumn she felt the heavens were at last in sympathy with herself, her life and desires.

This autumn of 1820 supported her prejudice as she sat in the slanting sun, writing her novel with blond, round Percy crawling at her feet and Shelley, ruddy from the summer's sun, sprawled out reading Keats' poetry. Mary's vivid memory was to carry the sensations of this rare tranquillity with her into a far from tranquil future. She wrote in her journal on 9 October 1827 in Italian:

> 'How well do I remember seven years ago, in this same season, the thoughts, the feelings of my heart. Then I began *Valperga*. Then alone with my beloved I was happy. Then the clouds were driven by the furious wind before the moon, – magnificent clouds, which grand and white seemed as stable as the mountains, and under the tyranny of the wind appeared more fragile than a veil of finest silk. Came then the rain, despoiling the trees. Autumn, you were beautiful then.'[29]

The rains did come and torrents would rush down the mountains behind the Bagni di Pisa and threaten the little town with flooding.

Mrs Mason's exertions, on behalf of Claire's permanent extraction from the Shelley household and inception as an independent young woman making her way in the world, were completed on 20 October. Mary and Shelley had ridden to Pisa to see Claire and say their farewells. From there Shelley accompanied her to Florence to the house of Dr Bojti and his family, in which Claire was to reside as a sort of paying guest, making her way in society and possibly preparing herself for an eventual post as governess.

Neither Claire nor Shelley were very happy with the arrangement although both, having been propelled into action by Mrs Mason, saw the necessity in part. For Mary it seemed as if it would be autumn for ever.

However, her happiness was shadowed with a disappointment she had been dreading yet half-expecting. The Gisbornes, having decided to settle in England, were on their way back to Leghorn to sort out their affairs. At the end of September Mary had written twice urging them to drop by at Casa Prinni, even to stay a few days to recover from their journey. Yet there was neither word nor sight of their old friends. News reached Mary that the Gisbornes had in fact arrived at Leghorn on 5 October and it had to be faced that they had pointedly neglected to see the Shelleys whose house lay directly on their route home. Mary was hurt and puzzled. Eventually she travelled over to Leghorn herself on the fifteenth and had a cool and evasive meeting with Mrs Gisborne who, by way of explanation, said she had already written 'a foolish letter'. Mary read it on her return and immediately replied; '... since you did not explain away any part of it, of course you meant it should remain in full force. – A good dose on my return.' This response to Maria Gisborne's letter was emphatic and full of fight:

> 'A Veil is now taken off from what was mysterious yesterday, and I now understand your refusal to visit us, and Henry's curious and, at last, almost rude reply to my invitation – I see that the ban of the Empire is gone out against us, and they who put it on must take it off.... But what terms need be made with Pariahs. And such, thank God a thousand and a million times, we are; long – very long may we so continue. – When you said that that filthy woman [Mrs Godwin] said she would not visit Hunt, how I gloried in our infamy. Now is the time! join them or us – the gulph is deep, the plank is going to be removed – set your foot on it if you will, and you will not lose the sincere affection of one who loved you tenderly.'[30]

It was a letter full of confidence and impelled by righteous indignation. However, Mary grieved that Maria Gisborne should have given credence to Mrs Godwin's prejudices and the malicious rumours that enlivened society dinner tables and bored salons. Shelley decided to deliver the letter himself. Nevertheless despite this combined *tour de force* Mrs Gisborne did not completely cross that gulf and restore their precious close relationship until the Gisbornes' return to England at the end of July 1821.

Mary and Shelley's disappointment and dismay at their old friends' apostasy was made all the more bitter by their feelings of being unjustly exiled and abused by their countrymen, and their consequent over-reliance on the support of the few friends who had stood by them. Shelley's outburst to Claire expressed something of the power of their feelings: 'The Gisbornes are people totally without faith. – I think they are altogether the most filthy and odious animals with which I ever came in contact. – They do not visit Mary as they promised and indeed if they did, I certainly should not stay in the house to receive them I have already planned a retreat to Mrs Mason's.'[31]

Meanwhile the rainy season at Bagni di Pisa had begun. Mary, waiting for Shelley's return from Florence, watched the rain sweep over the Pisan plain. At last she saw him come, not alone as she had hoped but with another figure in tow.

Thomas Medwin, Shelley's cousin, had at long last come south for the winter and, quite by chance, Shelley had met him in Florence and brought him home. Medwin was younger than Shelley, had been at school with him and then a lieutenant in the Indian army. At first Shelley was entertained by his store of anecdotes of life in the army but, when these ran out and his tedious literary pretensions replaced them, Shelley withdrew into his study to work. Mary, who had never been particularly susceptible to Medwin's bravado in the first place, was left to take the brunt of his persistent demands for attention and admiration.

However, just after his arrival at Bagni di Pisa, other more momentous events claimed her attention. The continuous rain of the previous days filled the River Serchio and the Baths to overflowing. At the bottom of Mary's little garden the canal that joined the Serchio with the Arno coursed, brimming with the floodwater. Then, on 25 October, rain through the night brought another surge of water down the mountains, bursting the Serchio's banks and flooding the surrounding plain. Mary and Shelley watched the black waters fill the square of the Baths in front of their house. Their canal behind surged up and over their garden and the murky waters, assaulting their house to the front and rear, forced open the doors and met in the hall to rise to an awesome six feet.

Mary was quite unalarmed. It said much for her newly-regained strength and peace of mind that she could enjoy it all: 'It was a picturesque sight at night, to see the peasants driving the cattle from the plains below, to the hills above the baths. A fire was kept up to guide them across the ford; and the forms of the men and the animals showed in dark relief against the red glare of the flame, which was reflected again in the waters that filled the square.'[32]

The time had come to move house and they decided to go the four miles to Pisa, 'this quiet, half-unpeopled town'.

14
Pisan Acquaintances

> 'And Mary saw my soul,
> And laughed, and said, "Disquiet yourself not;
> 'Tis nothing but a little downy owl."'
>
> *Do You Not Hear The Aziola Cry?* Shelley

By the end of October, Mary, Shelley and Percy, with Medwin, had moved into Casa Galetti in Pisa. The weather continued changeable: warm and sunny one day with heavy rain the next. Mary, uprooted from her happy associations at Bagni di Pisa, was repelled by the local Pisans, 'Crawling and crab-like through their sopping streets.'[1] She had a lingering inflammation of the eye which prevented her working and did not improve her temper.

Claire had not been very happy in Florence with the Bojti family, neither had she been very well. Shelley urged her to return to them at Pisa before committing herself to another three months. She came and arrived at Mary's new lodgings on the Lung' Arno on 21 November. Mary drew the sign of the sun, her symbol for Claire, against the day in her journal.

Medwin described her then at the age of twenty-two: 'She might have been mistaken for an Italian, for she was a *brunette* with very dark hair and eyes.... She was engaging and pleasing, and possessed an *esprit de société* rare among our countrywomen.'[2] Medwin, having been at the receiving end of Mary's coolness, may well have been comparing Claire favourably to her daunting step-sister. Mary's looks were certainly in direct contrast: contemplative and restrained, delicately fair where Claire's were distinct and dramatic. Mary's intellect shone from her serene grey eyes under that remarkable expanse of pale forehead. As she grew older her fine bones supported her good looks, and age and experience softened their imperiousness.

On 24 November Mary and Shelley met Francesco Pacchiani, *il diavolo*, a sometime professor at the university of Pisa. He was a social entrepreneur whom everyone knew but for whom nobody cared – introducing people, entertaining them, an opportunist always with an eye for the main chance. He could be brilliant and witty and at first he fascinated Mary with his ideas and his luxuriant and poetic use of the Italian language, which she had long been studying.

He was responsible for the sudden influx of friends and acquaintances into the Shelleys' quiet lives. Within three days of their first meeting with Pacchiani, Mary had been introduced to Tommaso Sgricci, the famous *improvisatore* who could act out a full two-and-a-half-hour tragedy in the Greek manner on a subject suggested by the audience. Mary and Shelley were greatly impressed and their admiration for him, unlike that for Pacchiani, did not diminish; 'a man of great talent, very well up in Greek and of an incomparable poetic mind'.[3] He was a snob and an hysteric, and as Byron with wonderfully characteristic irony pointed out: 'He is also a celebrated Sodomite, a character by no means so respected in Italy as it should be; but they laugh instead of burning, and the women talk of it as a pity in a man of talent, but with greater tolerance than could be expected, and only express their hopes that he may yet be converted to adultery.'[4] Despite these small disappointments he was amazingly popular and entertaining.

Less remarkable was an Irish poet, John Taaffe. His poetic pretensions irritated Shelley, who was nevertheless impressed enough by his commentary on the *Divine Comedy* to help get it published.

There were two further acquaintances who were to play more than a fleeting part in both Mary and Shelley's lives. Prince Alexander Mavrocordato, a brilliant young Greek prince some thirty years old who had fled to exile in Pisa, was introduced to Mary and within days was giving her Greek lessons in return for English. He was short and striking with a very large head and great flashing eyes. Physically in absolute contrast to Shelley, he nevertheless had a remarkably incisive intellect. He was a man of action who was to play a most important part in the Greek War of Independence and ended up a noble and capable Governor-General of Western Greece. Mary wrote to Maria Gisborne: 'Do you not envy my luck, that, having begun Greek, an amiable, young agreeable, and learned Greek Prince comes every morning to give me a lesson of an hour and a-half?'[5] Mary had her new enthusiasm and Shelley, too, was to meet his.

At the end of November Pacchiani had taken Mary and Claire to the convent of St Anna to introduce them to Emilia Viviani, a beautiful young woman of about nineteen, who had been deposited in the convent by her jealous mother. She had been there for about three years and was unable to leave until a marriage had been arranged for her. Mary was horrified at such barbaric treatment, although it was common enough then for young unmarried Italian girls. Mary described her to Hunt as 'romantic and pathetic ... very beautiful, very talented, who writes Italian with an elegance and delicacy equal to the foremost authors of the best Italian epoch. She is, however, most unhappy.'[6] Mary and Claire visited her regularly to read to her and to walk with her. Inevitably Shelley met her too and, to a young and clever beauty shut away from the world, this fascinating, fair Englishman with his poetry and susceptibilities was a much more thrilling diversion than his serious wife and girlish sister-in-law.

Shelley could not fail to be enchanted. Medwin's description explained the force of her appeal:

'Her profuse black hair, tied in the most simple knot, after the manner of a Greek Muse in the Florence gallery, displayed to its full height her brow, fair as that of the marble of which I speak. She was also of about the same height as the antique. – Her features possessed a rare faultlessness and an almost Grecian contour, the nose and forehead making a straight line, – a style of face so rare that I remember Bartolini's telling Byron that he had scarcely an instance of such in the numerous casts of busts which his studio contained. Her eyes had the sleepy voluptuousness, if not the colour of Beatrice Cenci's. They had indeed no definite colour, changing with the changing feeling, to dark or light, as the soul animated them. Her cheek was pale, too, as marble, owing to her confinement and want of air, or perhaps "to thought".'[7]

No wonder she seemed to Shelley to be his ideal woman, his ideal of love incarnate, a novel and fascinating sister to his soul. He immortalized her in *Epipsychidion*:

'I knew it was the Vision veiled from me
So many years – that it was Emily.'[8]

Her attraction was made all the more irresistible by the pathos of her situation. She was captive, her freedom abused by parental and religious oppression, the two forces of evil bound to spur Shelley's impulse to save and succour. She was also romantic and eloquent. Her letters to Shelley cleverly played her part to the full:

'My dear Friend and Brother,
I write to you by moonlight. I can't resolve to take another light than this. It would be like doing an injury to this clear and splendid Daughter of Heaven. What sweetness is mine, looking at it! What an inexpressible enchantment! But you know it too, and you understand it as well as I, because you are like me ... I felt surprised finding myself so absorbed in reverie that I did not know any more where I was, shuddering and frightened before the gloomy walls of my prison and the malefic ghosts which surrounded me everywhere ...'[9]

and then sweetly enquiring of Shelley about Mary's neglect:

'Mary does not write to me. Is it possible that she loves me less than the others do: I should be very much pained by that. I wish to flatter myself that it is only her son and her occupations which cause this. Is not this the case?'[10]

Mary in fact was being wise and restrained. She knew Shelley well enough by now to realize that Emilia did not constitute any real threat. She continued kindly to visit her and bring her books. Claire had returned to Florence and Mary's letters, full of news of acquaintances, mentioned calmly that Emilia 'was in much better spirits when I did see her than I had found her for a long time before'.[11] To Hunt, she allowed herself a little more asperity: 'It is grievous to see this beautiful girl wearing out the best years of her life in an odious convent where both mind and body are sick from want of the appropriate exercise of each....'[12]

In many ways it was Shelley's circumstances, too, which made him long for the idealized escape with Emilia:

'Emily,
A ship is floating in the harbour now,
A wind is hovering o'er the mountain's brow;
There is a path on the sea's azure floor,
No keel has ever ploughed that path before;
The halcyons brood around the foamless isles;

> The treacherous Ocean has forsworn its wiles;
> The merry mariners are bold and free:
> Say, my heart's sister, wilt thou sail with me?'[13]

Shelley's restlessness and dissatisfaction with life had been a long time growing. That winter he was dogged by pain, illness and a deadly torpor. Yet he was uneasily aware that he was in the prime of life and, although not robust physically, his mental faculties were keen and vigorous. He sensed the quiver of revolution in the air, he longed for adventure and activity: 'I wish I had something better to do than furnish this jingling food for the hunger of oblivion, called *verse*: but I have not.'[14] Numerous pockets of resistance all over Europe were in revolt against repression and misrule. Medwin had filled his imagination with stories of the Indian Interior and fired him with enthusiasm for a scheme to sail to Greece, Syria and Egypt, a plan he dared not express to Mary for fear of unsettling her and of accepting its impracticalities in the face of his own responsibilities.

Shelley felt himself to have been marking time for too long. His poetry was largely ignored or abused: 'I can compare my experience in this respect to nothing but a series of wet blankets.' He was politically inactive, in exile, denied the mainstream of intellectual activity and removed from the conflict between the oppressed and their oppressors. 'I have great designs, and feeble hopes of ever accomplishing them', he wrote despondently to Peacock. 'I read books, and, though I am ignorant enough, they seem to teach me nothing.'[15] He felt insulated from the real experiences of life. Domestic pleasures and academic pursuits no longer seemed enough. He was missing Claire's stimulating presence and fluctuating friendship. The lack of a second woman in his life and his general discontent with himself made him ripe for this passionate interlude with Emilia. She was a way of escaping from himself.

Mary in the real world was as imperfect as that world and knew she had to bide her time. Shelley loved her and was far too perceptive to pursue his illusion for long. Rapid and dazzling as had been Emilia's ascendancy, so would be her decline. Nevertheless, Mary's pride was hurt and her feelings deeply wounded by *Epipsychidion*. The moon had always influenced and entranced her. It was a constant, predictable companion, 'so often friendly to me'.[16] It was always to be Shelley's symbol for her, luminous, reflective, mysterious, but in this poem he pointed to the moon and Mary's passivity and lack of incandescence. This characterization was all the more painful because she knew it to be largely true of the undemonstrative side of her character. But it did not mean she did not feel and love and suffer:

> 'The cold chaste Moon, the Queen of Heaven's bright isles,
> Who makes all beautiful on which she smiles,
> That wandering shrine of soft yet icy flame
> Which ever is transformed, yet still the same,
> And warms not but illumines.'[17]

Mary was distracted and consoled by the attentions of Prince Mavrocordato. Not only did he enliven her assiduous Greek studies, but he made the language leap from the page and live. His conversation was fascinating, his looks strange and magnetic, and to study with him and to indulge in mild flirtation helped Mary through an otherwise disconsolate time. His attentions and Mary's eager acceptance of them irritated Shelley, so used to sharing his own affections but discomposed at having to share hers.

Already by the middle of February 1821, Shelley realized the transience of his passion for Emilia and the illusion of escape she offered. In sending *Epipsychidion* to his printer, he included an advertisement crediting the poem to a fictional poet who 'died at Florence, as he was preparing for a voyage to one of the wildest of the Sporades'[18] as a protection against its autobiographical revelations. He wrote sadly to Ollier, '... in a certain sense, it is a production of a portion of me already dead; and in this sense the advertisement is no fiction.'[19]

Mary and Shelley continued to see Emilia and report on her to Claire but it was a year before either felt ready to mention the affair openly to friends. Mary's sarcasm slipped through her restraint:

> 'Emilia married Biondi – we hear that she leads him & his mother (to use a vulgarism) *a devil of a life* – The conclusion of our friendship *a la Italiana* puts me in mind of a nursery rhyme which runs thus –
>
>> As I was going down Cranbourne Lane,
>> Cranbourne Lane was dirty,
>> And there I met a pretty maid,
>> Who dropt to me a curtsey;

I gave her cakes, I gave her wine,
I gave her sugar candy,
But O! the little naughty girl!
She asked me for some brandy.

'Now turn Cranbourne Lane into Pisan acquaintances, which I'm sure are dirty enough, and brandy into that wherewithall to buy brandy (& that no small sum *però*) & you have the whole story of Shelley's Italian platonics.'[20]

Shelley was saddened and philosophical. In a letter to John Gisborne in the summer of 1822 he wrote, 'The "Epipsychidion" I cannot look at; the person whom it celebrates was a cloud instead of a Juno.... I think one is always in love with something or other; the error, and I confess it is not easy for spirits cased in flesh and blood to avoid it, consists in seeking in a mortal image the likeness of what is perhaps eternal.'[21]

New acquaintances still continued to home in on Mary and Shelley in Pisa. Thomas Medwin's friends, Edward Ellerker Williams and his common-law wife, Jane, had been entertained since the previous summer by Medwin's tales of Shelley. They finally arrived in Pisa on 16 January to meet this phenomenon for themselves.

Both Mary and Shelley were immediately attracted to Edward. Mary reported her first impressions to Claire, still not very happily attempting to make her way in Florence: 'Ned seems the picture of good humor and obligingness, he is lively.... He seems to make all he sees subjects of surprize & pleasure';[22] he also had a soft, melodious speaking voice unlike Jane's 'low monotonous' tones. Mary and Shelley liked her well enough but felt her to be shallow and uninspired. It was only later that for both the Shelleys she was to become in different ways an object of love. 'Jane is certainly very pretty but she wants animation and sense; her conversation is *nothing particular* ... but she appears good tempered and tolerant',[23] was Mary's dismissive verdict.

The Williams certainly relieved Mary of some of the burden of Medwin's company. His interruptions of her study, his mundanities and self-esteem had driven her to dub him 'commonplace personified'.[24] Her friendship with the Williamses grew gradually and securely. During February she walked out with them almost every day. Jane already had one child and was expecting her second within a month, and Mary was sympathetic and supportive.

Shelley, having recovered from Emilia and the pains and stresses of the winter, was in good health and full of plans. Spring had blown in early and the days were breezily warm, full of sun and cloud with the occasional sirocco-borne storms. At the beginning of March, Mary and Shelley moved to the Casa Aulla, still in the Lung' Arno. For Mary the days were full and serene. The unpredictable weather invigorated her senses and perceptions, 'every moment of the day is divided, felt and counted'. With characteristic truth and gravity she pointed out that 'one is not gay – at least I am not – but peaceful and at peace with all the world'.[25]

Mary's Greek lessons with Mavrocordato continued daily. On 1 April he came bounding in to see her, 'never did man appear so happy', to exclaim – Greece had declared its freedom. Mary was almost as overjoyed as the prince. She wrote a happy, effusive letter to Claire to impart the news. A Greek general, Ipselanti, had with 10,000 men marched into Wallachia and declared his country's freedom. Mavrocordato intended to join the struggle against the Turks. 'He sacrifices family – fortune – everything to the hope of freeing his country. Such men are repaid – such succeed',[26] Mary declared admiringly. Mavrocordato's life as the revolutionary hero highlighted for Shelley the lack of physical challenge and tangible achievement in his own.

Their odder Pisan acquaintances had fallen away. Pacchiani was now regarded by Mary with marked distaste. However the Williamses' friendship had begun its ascendancy. Edward Williams was a generous, good-hearted, outdoor man and gave Shelley the sort of bluff easy-going male companionship he had never really experienced before. Feeling his health return and his spirits rise with the spring, Shelley together with Williams and the Gisbornes' son, Henry Reveley, went to Leghorn to buy a small, crude boat to sail up and down the Arno. Boats and water belonged as surely to his life as did his books and pen, but unfortunately this one was flat-bottomed and unstable, fitted by Henry Reveley with a makeshift rudder and sail. On its maiden voyage back to Pisa, Williams accidentally capsized it and landed all three men in the deep, cold water of the Arno. Reveley had to save Shelley who was no swimmer. On grasping him around the shoulders and telling him to remain calm Reveley was deeply impressed by Shelley's passivity and apparent fearlessness. This became amazement when Shelley answered his anxious enquiry as to how he was: 'All right, never more comfortable in my life; do what you will with me.'[27] However, the cold and the shock was too much for him and on reaching the shore, Shelley fell in a dead faint. They had to spend the night in a local farmhouse and the next day Henry Reveley took the boat back to Leghorn for repairs and further modification. Shelley's ducking only served to increase his fervour for such boating expeditions and he waited impatiently for the return of his flat-bottomed vessel. Perhaps he had found his own peculiar challenge, his answer to the Mavrocordatos and their revolutions; he, too, was both in concert and in conflict, but with the elementals of water, sky and wind. Being quite unable to swim and having little intention of learning, he, too, was staking his life in the struggle.

A letter from Horace Smith brought Mary and Shelley an unexpected shock. Horace Smith was a good friend in London who personally, every quarter, collected Shelley's money and sent it to him at Pisa. Mr Smith wrote indignantly that he had been informed that no more money was to be forthcoming and that a suit had been instituted against him in Chancery by Dr Hume, Charles Shelley's guardian, for a year's unpaid allowance.

The precariousness of their life in Italy was brought sharply home: that their life-line could be cut without warning by the connivance of solicitors or the whim of Sir Timothy Shelley. Mr Mason's advice was sought, a short-term loan acquired and Horace Smith's 'warlike operations'[28] in London on behalf of his exiled friends assuaged their initial panic.

With summer in the air, Mary wrote to Maria Gisborne: 'You see the fine weather is come, doubly fine if it brings friendship with it. So we may expect you. I have only time to say this word and to enquire concerning the convalescence of the boat; when it is quite well let us know, since Shelley wishes to convey the delicate young lady here himself.'[29] Mary's plea did in fact bring the Gisbornes on a visit. They stayed for four days and returned to Leghorn on the last day of April with Shelley and Williams who were keen to collect their boat from Henry Reveley. This visit restored some of the old cordiality between Mary and Maria, although Shelley remained, in his own words, 'gentle, but cold'.[30]

Mary had Claire to worry about too. She had been very upset to hear that Byron had put Allegra into the convent at Bagnacavallo. She wanted the little girl to have an English education and was dismayed at her being brought up a Roman Catholic and an Italian. She wrote to the Shelleys begging their help in prising her child from the convent and restoring her to her own safe-keeping. Mary, on 11 May, the day she received Claire's distressed letter, wrote back at length. She was conciliatory and sympathetic, agreeing that Allegra would be best out of Byron's control but arguing that this would stand some chance of success if Claire bided her time a while and restrained any impulse to further exasperate the lordly poet.

Mary and Shelley had decided to try and recapture the serenity and peace of the previous autumn and on 8 May had moved for the summer back to the Bagni di Pisa. It was as solitary and as peaceful as they remembered, much to Shelley's relief. He was still subject to days of pain which intensified his dislike of society. Their house looked towards the mountains where Mary and Shelley had wandered and explored.

Edward and Jane Williams had moved to the Villa Marchese Poschi in Pugnano some four miles away but accessible by the canal. The boat here became the greatest pleasure to both Mary and Shelley. Apart from Shelley's expeditions alone or with Williams, Mary, Percy and Shelley would often shuttle to and fro by boat between their own house and the Williamses' at Pugnano. In later years she remembered the journey well; their boat sailing the swollen stream, parting the reeds, sliding under the overhanging trees where senses were lulled by the play of light and shade, the slap of the water and the fragrant banks with their colonies of wildlife and flowers. Mary's memory for sounds was always acute, and certain cadences, tones and voices never failed to evoke in her memories of their circumstances and scenery. 'By day, multitudes of ephemera darted to and fro on the surface; at night, the fire-flies came out among the shrubs on the banks; the cicale, at noon-day, kept up their hum, the aziola cooed in the quiet evening,'[31] she recalled eighteen years later in her notes to Shelley's poems of the time.

That early summer was a perfect idyll, a surprise paradise of a few week' interlude in an everyday life of alarms, illness, anguish and disconsolation. Soothed into thinking this peace might last, Mary and Shelley began to feel attached to that part of Tuscany, began to dream of putting down roots, perhaps taking a farm in the hills, 'surrounded by chestnut and pine woods and overlooking a wide extent of country'.[32] Their desultory conversations in the serene and solitary evenings were captured in a poem Shelley wrote then:

> ' "Do you not hear the Aziola cry?
>   Methinks she must be nigh,"
>   Said Mary, as we sate
> In dusk, ere stars were lit, or candles brought;
>   And I, who thought
> This Aziola was some tedious woman,
>   Asked, "Who is Aziola?" How elate
> I felt to know that it was nothing human,
>   No mockery of myself to fear or hate:
>   And Mary saw my soul,
> And laughed, and said, "Disquiet yourself not;
>   'Tis nothing but a little downy owl." '

Mary's relationship with Shelley had clearly a basic strength and sympathetic knowledge. Perceptive, intuitive and generous as she was, having grown up with him and shared such extremes of joy and tragedy, Mary understood him well. Only when sinking in the mire of her own despair, did she fail to recognize his pain, or in half-recognizing it fail to reach out to him despite her grief. The boating trips and walks to the Williamses' for supper continued. Mary had been working hard and consistently at *Valperga* and hoped to finish the rough draft in July. She read it piecemeal to Shelley as she finished each section and his enthusiasm spurred her on. 'It has indeed been a child of mighty slow growth, since I first thought of it in our library at Marlow',[33] she wrote to Maria Gisborne.

She was also sitting for Edward Williams who, a proficient amateur artist, was executing a miniature portrait of her as her birthday present for Shelley. The Gisbornes were due to leave Italy in August and Mary was very keen that they come to stay before departing for good. She looked forward to reading to Maria the first volume of *Valperga* as her first critic other than Shelley.

John Taaffe, the Irish poet they had met in Pisa, called on them quite frequently during July. A gift of some guinea-pigs for Percy came with a note to Mary, 'O, that I were one of these Guinea pigs that I might see you this morning!', which caused Mary and Shelley the greatest amusement.

Prince Mavrocordato continued to call occasionally but he was very busy with his arrangements for sailing to Greece. Mary was sad to lose his sparkling company, although Shelley was secretly relieved when on 28 June he was already cast off for the Ionian Sea.

Claire, still in an emotional state about Allegra, making wild plans and nursing bitter resentments against Byron, had quarrelled with Mary and was refusing to write to her. Mary had always felt most fond and sympathetic towards Claire when they were apart; she understood her turmoil of regret and frustrated maternal affections, but she also intended to hold tight to the hard-won freedom from her fractious presence. Shelley interceded between them, writing to Claire: 'I am trying to persuade Mary to ask your pardon – I hope that I shall succeed – in the meantime, as you were in the wrong you had better not ask hers, for that is unnecessary, but write to her – if you had been in the right you would have done so....'[34]

From the middle of June to the beginning of November Claire was on holiday from Florence with the Masons at Pisa, at Leghorn for the sea-bathing and then eventually for a few weeks with the Williamses at Pugnano. She did not stay with the Shelleys at all, although both Shelley and Mary spent days with her.

At the end of July the Gisbornes stayed another four days with Mary and Shelley; they had at last allowed their affection for the young couple to overrule the case made in London against them through exaggeration, rumour and falsehood. Mary embraced them and parted from them with love. Shelley accompanied them on their way as far as Florence, where he hoped to find a house for Horace Smith, who was coming to Italy. On his return on 2 August he found a letter from Byron informing him of his move to Ravenna and Allegra's vicinity and inviting him for a visit.

Shelley leapt to comply and the next day, 3 August, he set off for Ravenna despite missing his twenty-ninth birthday and Mary's special present for him the following day. He stopped off on the way to see Claire at Leghorn. Mary serenely spent Shelley's birthday sitting for Williams, who was finishing his portrait of her. Anniversaries were for Mary a time of assessment and hopes: 'Seven years are now gone; what changes! what a life! We now appear tranquil; yet who knows what wind – but I will not prognosticate evil; we have had enough of it. When Shelley came to Italy, I said all is well if it were permanent; it was more passing than an Italian twilight.

I now say the same. May it be a Polar day; yet that, too, has an end.'[35]

Shelley had arrived at Ravenna to a lordly welcome and to the immediate intelligence that Elise had related to the Hoppners her infamous tale of Claire and Shelley's cruel treatment of their putative infant and of Mary. It was to deny the story that Mary wrote her impassioned and powerful letter to Mrs Hoppner, that apparently never got beyond Byron's perusal. It upset and unsettled Mary that ugly rumour was once again rearing its head and this time amongst such influential compatriots as the Hoppners and Lord Byron.

Shelley's letters from Ravenna, apart from the first one stingingly indignant that Elise should accuse him of cruelty to any child, let alone his own, were full of news and enthusiasm for Byron. Shelley was relieved to see his dissolute Venetian ways pared down to 'strict adultery'[36] with the enduring Countess Guiccioli, but nevertheless he felt something of a provincial, a country cousin, in the face of Lord Byron's extravagant style and bizarrerie. He ended his long, informative letter to Mary of 8–10 August with an observation that would have made her smile. 'Here are two monkeys, five cats, eight dogs & ten horses – all of whom (except the horses) walk about the house like the masters of it. *Tieta* the Venetian is here, & operates as my valet: a fine fellow with a prodigious black beard, who has stabbed two or three people & is the most goodnatured looking fellow I ever saw.'[37] By the next day when he wrote to Peacock the menagerie had grown to include 'an eagle, a crow and a falcon.... I have just met on the grand staircase five peacocks, two guinea hens, and an Egyptian crane. I wonder who all these animals were before they were changed into these shapes.'[38] Although both Mary and Shelley disapproved of Albé in his absence, with no more than the most fleeting contact the old Byron magic began to work on them again.

Shelley, however, was never fully at ease with him; he was overwhelmed and diminished by Byron's undeniable poetic genius and his lordly magnetic presence. Shelley felt trapped in an unequal contest and tried to retreat from the competition by swearing he would never write again:'If I cannot be something, I had rather be nothing.'[39] To Mary he admitted the strain in his relations with the lord; 'The demon of mistrust & of pride lurks between two persons in our situation poisoning the freedom of their intercourse.'[40]

Nevertheless, he was full of enthusiasm for Byron's projected move to Pisa, even more for the stimulation of his company than for the hopes that Allegra would be removed from Bagnacavallo and be nearer at hand. Mary heard all this news philosophically; she had even been urged to find and immediately rent an unfurnished Pisan palace suitable for Byron's occupation. She carried on peacefully with her fair copy of *Valperga*, seeing the Williamses, walking and playing with Percy. In Shelley's absence she and the Williamses went over to Claire at Leghorn on 17 August to bring her back to Pisa for a ten-day stay. Again Claire probably stayed with the Williamses but Mary walked over at six every morning to breakfast with them all.

She had sent Shelley's birthday present, her miniature by Williams, to him at Ravenna but he had been far too busy keeping up with Byron's exhausting way of life and intellectual muscle-flexing to have much time to appreciate it.

By 22 August Shelley was back with Mary at the Bagni di Pisa, but now their tranquil stream of life there was disturbed by ever-widening ripples. Shelley was immediately off to Pisa to secure a residence for Byron. He ended up with the Palace Lanfranchi, the grandest establishment in the Lung' Arno. He was writing, too, to Leigh Hunt, urging him to come with his family and help Byron and himself set up a periodical to be published from Pisa. During this time Shelley was painfully lacking in confidence in his own talents and abilities, declaring to Leigh Hunt, 'I am, and I desire to be, nothing.'[41] He hid his private and rankling disappointment at his lack of public appreciation and acclaim. Only Mary knew how much this increasingly dispirited him.

The Countess Guiccioli had arrived in Pisa before Byron, and Mary visited her often and enjoyed her company, describing her to Maria Gisborne as 'a nice pretty girl without pretensions, good hearted and amiable'.[42] Mary looked all the more favourably on La Guiccioli's family's revolutionary connections with the Carbonari.

On 25 September Mary and Shelley removed their modest household to Pisa, to the top floor of the Tre Palazzi di Chiesa. The Williamses moved too, renting a lower flat. Mary was delighted with their lodgings. They were sunny and airy and the windows were soon filled with a profusion of plants, framing an expansive view that stretched to the sea. Being at the top of the Palazzi they were in an oasis of quiet, hardly penetrated by the bustle of the street below. Mary had a small pride in the fact that she had managed to furnish the place herself with money saved over the previous two years. It was the first time that they had their own furniture in lodgings – a good measure of their increasingly settled state.

On 1 November Byron arrived in style with a wagon-train of books, clothes, furniture, his zoo and his servants. He had decided to leave Allegra in her convent and poor Claire was banished back to Florence with strict instructions not to embarrass Byron and certainly not to antagonize him with her presence.

With the Williamses' removal to Pisa, with Horace Smith on his way and Hunt's promise to finally make the trip, Shelley was beginning to collect his colony of like-minded spirits. 'So Pisa, you see, has become a little nest of singing birds',[43] Mary wrote to her old friend Maria.

Valperga, or as it was still called *Castruccio, Prince of Lucca*, had been offered to Shelley's printer, Ollier, in July. At the end of September there was still no move by Ollier to accept or reject it. Mary had fair-copied it and almost finished correcting it. She intended to give all the proceeds of the book to help ease Godwin's predicament. Ollier's procrastinations so frustrated her that in spring 1821 she sent the manuscript to Godwin and asked him to sell it as best he could. More delays and a free-handed editing job by Godwin further postponed publication. Only in spring 1823, after the tumult and trauma of the intervening two years, did it finally reach its public.

Shelley, Godwin and the reviewers considered *Valperga* a noble successor to *Frankenstein*. Its inevitable prolixity and at times surprising lack of integration has put off modern readers, but Mary's concept was ambitious and her characters, particularly her heroines, Beatrice and Euthanasia, vividly portrayed. The novel traced the life of Castruccio, a fourteenth-century prince of Lucca, but in doing so examined grand political issues and moral dilemmas. Mary, having grown up in the aftermath of the French Revolution and Napoleon's ascendancy as a demi-god, was at the time of writing *Valperga* surrounded and enthralled by the political upheavals in Europe. Not surprisingly this work dealt forcibly with the destructiveness of personal political ambition and the nullity of the Napoleonic hero striving for military success and political bravado at the expense of the real values of the heart.

There were broad yet striking similarities with Frankenstein who, in the pursuit of knowledge and a fatal determination to fathom the secrets of life, neglected Elizabeth, the woman he loved, with ghastly consequences. Castruccio chose personal ambition and power rather than love and domestic happiness. His greed for eminence and influence so isolated and imprisoned him that in the end what had become the monster of his own ambition drew him inexorably towards destruction.

15
Presentiments of Evil

'My bliss was more rapid than the progress of a sunbeam on a mountain, which discloses its glades & woods, and then leaves it dark and blank; to my happiness followed madness and agony, closed by despair.'

Mathilda, Mary Shelley

Winter was late in coming but when it came it was with a vengeance. December was stormy with high winds and suddenly cold nights. Mary, gazing out on the windswept countryside, was most anxious about the Hunts and their six children, who as far as she knew were out there tossed on the hostile sea. In fact the Hunts had been delayed at Dartmouth due to a relapse in Marianne's health and did not arrive in Italy until the summer. But both Mary and Shelley were agitated at the lack of news, expecting them any week.

Mary was very busy and enjoying the first real chance she had had to indulge in social activity with friends. She would give small supper parties amongst the plants that made the flat their first real home. When happy with friends she was bright and shining, animated with the spirit of friendship and the pleasure of feeling appreciated and loved. She would go riding with the Countess Guiccioli, walking and dining with the Williamses and reading to Jane. Thomas Medwin had returned and John Taaffe was still a frequent visitor. She seldom made a social call on Byron; he was a man who much preferred the company and conversation of men.

Shelley, however, was both unwell and in low spirits. Although he was gathering his friends around him he was often agitated and irritated by company, feeling unable to cope with any more than one or two at a time. He was still very despondent and deprecatory about his poetry, and Byron's presence pointed for him his very lack of achievement. News of successes in Greece and of Mavrocordato's valour there encouraged his uneasy feelings of impotence.

An opportunity for Shelley to engage in a blow for freedom arose on 12 December. Pisa was astir with the rumour that a man was to be burnt alive at Lucca for stealing the wafer box from a church. Mary and Shelley were horrified, and Shelley immediately suggested to Lord Byron that both of them and a party of English should enter the town and, with force if need be, free the man. Byron deflected Shelley's more extreme plan but intended to use his influence to intercede. In the meantime Taaffe, who had gone to Lucca to gather more news, returned to report that it was a false alarm; the man, a priest, had fled to Florence and the Grand Duke of Tuscany had granted him asylum there.

The Williamses were increasingly good friends to Mary and Shelley, both of whom were finding Jane sweet and complacent, and blessed with a lovely singing voice. Within this band of Pisan acquaintances and friends Mary was learning greater independence from Shelley and his philosophies and ideas. She was developing friendships for herself and pursuing her own studies; Greek, although hard work, was a constant delight and tranquillized her spirits. Her curiosity also drew her to attend a few of the church services held on the ground floor of the building where they lived, despite the fact that by doing so, in the face of Shelley's notorious atheism, she created something of a stir.

The predictable rounds of friends and activities were spiced by the arrival, on 14 January 1822, of Edward John Trelawny. The swaggering entrance of this swashbuckling adventurer meant that all the players in the ensuing tragedy had assembled on stage, as if in response to some irresistible dramatic convention. Trelawny was nearly thirty when he burst into the Pisan circle, the embodiment of the Romantic hero. Byron recognized him immediately as 'the personification of my Corsair' and found him greatly amusing.

He was the younger son of an old Cornish family, ill-educated but bold, expressive and perceptive, a man ruled, often misruled, by his heart; as much a romancer as a Romantic. He was dazzled by the company of the two poets whose presence had attracted him to Pisa. Byron disconcerted Trelawny; not only intellectually but physically he was a challenge to him, deflating him with his sophistication and cynicism and matching his sporting prowess, lame leg and all. Shelley was Trelawny's favourite; physically delicate he roused in him a protectiveness where there was little competitiveness and less aggression.

Kindly, serious and eccentric, Shelley entranced him with the vitality of his language and imagination.

Mary was always discerning in her assessment of herself and others and, having met Trelawny once, relayed her impressions to Mrs Gisborne:

'Trelawney – a kind of half Arab Englishman – whose life has been as changeful as that of Anastatius & who recounts the adventures of his youth as eloquently and well as the imagined Greek – he is clever – for his moral qualities I am yet in the dark – he is a strange web which I am endeavouring to unravel – I would fain learn if generosity is united to impetuousness – nobility of spirit to his assumption of singularity & independence – he is six feet high – raven black hair which curls thickly & shortly like a Moors – dark grey – expressive eyes overhanging brows upturned lips & a smile which expresses good nature & kind-heartedness – his shoulders are high like an Orientalist – his voice is monotonous yet emphatic & his language as he relates the events of his life energetic & simple – whether the tale be one of blood & horror or of irresistible comedy His company is delightful for he excites me to think and if any evil shade the intercourse that time will unveil – the sun will rise or night darken all.[1]

This outlandish stranger who sparked her imagination and enlivened 'the everyday sleepiness of human intercourse'[2] was a welcome addition to the coterie of talented expatriate British. Trelawny's first impressions of Mary were less penetrating; he noted her fairness of skin and light hair and 'the most striking feature in her face . . . her calm grey eyes'.[3] He was impressed by her wit and the colour and accuracy of her language in conversation and, although not reaching the heights of Shelley's eloquence, it was in marked contrast to 'the scanty vocabulary used by ladies in society, in which a score of poor hackneyed phrases sufficed to express all that is felt or considered proper to feel'.[4] Mary, looking back a year later on her early friendship with Trelawny and those few happy days, recalled, 'You found me, so full of spirits and life that methinks when you first saw me you must have thought me even a little wild. . . .'[5]

Shelley's love of water and of boats was further encouraged by the presence of Trelawny with his exotic tales of seafaring adventures.

The idea of spending the summer near the sea had been in his and Mary's mind all winter and as spring approached his spirits and enthusiasm lifted. On 7 February he and Williams set off for the bay of Spezia, some fifty miles away, to look for houses for the Pisan colony. Originally it was proposed that Byron and his countess and her brother, Count Gamba, Jane and Edward Williams, Trelawny and Mary, Shelley and Percy, were together to migrate north to this savage, beautiful and isolated bay. But on Shelley's return it was obvious that there were not enough houses available. After two house-hunting expeditions only one appropriate house was found and that, Mary and he decided, had to be shared by them with the Williamses.

Mary was enjoying the first days of spring: '... the sky clear – the sun hot – the hedges budding – we sitting here without a fire & the windows open – I begin to long for the sparkling waves the olive covered hills & vine shaded pergolas of Spezia ... if April prove fine we shall fly with the swallows.'[6] She and Jane Williams would go on country walks together and 'talk morality and pluck violets by the way'.[7] But it was spring, and Mary had learnt to mistrust the season. To her journal she confided uncharacteristically her fears of the transience of human experience and the fickleness of fortune.

Mary's mentality was an extraordinary mix where acute perceptions were combined with an awareness and intuition that at times became prescience. These sensibilities were given grit by her vigorous and unsentimental intellect and her distinctive imagination, an essentially private side of her life which probably only Shelley recognized or understood. It was the force within her triumphant fictions of *Frankenstein* and *The Last Man*. Yet casual acquaintances were always surprised that such a serene and modest young woman was the creator of such frightful fantasy. Mary herself was regretful at the misleading impressions she gave, even to friends. Certainly she felt her letters were pedestrian and her journals, after Shelley's death, woebegone, both lacking the vital spark of her inner world of inspiration. Mary, years later wrote in her journal:

> 'It has struck me what a very imperfect picture (only *no one* will ever see it) these querulous pages afford of *me*. This arises from their being the record of my feelings, and not of my imagination ... my imagination, ... my treasure ... my Kubla Khan, my pleasure grounds ... occasionally pushed aside by misery but at the first

opportunity her beaming face peeped in and the weight of deadly woe was lightened.'[8]

Trelawny, with his buccaneering looks and cult of individualism, inspirited her imagination, too often constrained by the rigours of study. His flesh-and-blood adventures, be they fact or fiction, were a surprising change from the intellectual voyages she had shared with Shelley. She was to make him the hero in a later novel, *Falkner*, and he was to prove himself a generous friend and eventually harsh critic. Ten years later Mary was moved to remark with cool and devastating accuracy, 'He is a strange yet wonderful being – endured with genius – great force of character and power of feeling – but destroyed by *being nothing* – destroyed by envy and internal dissatisfaction.'[9]

Yet in the early part of their relationship Trelawny brought to Mary's philosophy a broader view. With his untutored vitality, his experiential approach to life, he diverted her a little from her emotional intensity and the strictures of academic study. Her journal showed a burst of spontaneity and a more relaxed tolerance of imperfection: '... let me, in my fellow creature, love that what is, – and not fix my affection on a fair form endued with imaginary attributes; where goodness, kindness and talent are, let me love and admire them at their just rate, neither adorning, or diminishing....'[10] It could have been an equally appropriate creed for Shelley too.

Claire's agitation and sense of foreboding had increased with Byron's removal to Pisa. The thought of her pathetic little daughter abandoned in her convent with neither parent at hand caused her extreme distress. She decided she had to leave Italy and wrote to Byron asking for one last meeting with her child: 'I can no longer resist the internal inexplicable feeling which haunts me that I shall never see her any more.'[11] She wrote a miserable letter on the same lines to Mary at Pisa on 19 February. All Mary's old jealousy and distrust of her step-sister were put aside in the face of Claire's anguish: 'Come here directly ... I think in every way it would make you happier to come here, – and when here, other views may arise, – at least discuss your plans in the midst of your friends before you go.'[12] Mary sent a servant to collect her and Claire was with them the following day. For four days she talked with Mary, Shelley, Mrs Mason and the Williamses and returned to Florence reconciled to carrying on as before and biding her time. She had met Trelawny for the first time and it was the beginning of a life-long relationship, full of affection and strife.

On 24 March Mary's prognostication of the ill-fortunes of spring seemed to her to be borne out by an affray that, although speedily resolved, alarmed everyone concerned at the time. Byron, Shelley, Trelawny, Captain Hay, Count Gamba, and Taaffe were returning on horseback to Pisa. Mary and the Countess Guiccioli were travelling in a carriage behind. An Italian soldier galloped through the English company and jostled Taaffe. He immediately interpreted it as insolence and encouraged Byron and Shelley and all to pursue the man. Argument and curses gave way to skirmishing when the soldier reached the security of the city gate and the support of the guards. He drew his sabre and knocked Shelley from his horse, cut Captain Hay across the face and generally frightened everyone, not least the two ladies in the carriage. As the soldier made his get-away, one of Byron's servants, thinking his master had been wounded, went for him with a pitchfork, seriously wounding him.

The dishevelled English party decamped to Mary and Shelley's lodging where Jane and Edward Williams were awaiting their promised supper. 'Lord B. came in, the Countess fainting on his arm, S. sick from the blow, Lord B. and the young Count foaming with rage. Mrs S. looking philosophically upon this interesting scene, and Jane and I wondering what the devil was to come next',[13] was how Williams related it in his diary.

While the soldier's life was in danger, anti-English feeling welled up among the local populace. Even Jane Williams's music master and Shelley's celebrated physician, Vacca, suddenly turned antagonistic. The police intervened and interviewed witnesses, questioning Mary and the Countess for five hours. They arrested two servants, both quite innocent. Rumours were rife and feelings ran high. Trelawny and Williams felt it best to arm themselves when out in the streets. But, as the soldier recovered, the alarm and excitement diminished, until within a week it was all over – so much so that Mary, with her characteristic pessimism or indeed accurate prescience, wondered whether the 'King of Gods and men will not consider it a sufficiently heavy visitation',[14] and make up the balance with a further blast from fate.

Once again Mary's forebodings were tragically fulfilled. Claire had arrived on 15 April with an invitation to spend the summer between the Shelley's and the Williamses at Spezia while Lord Byron was secure at Leghorn. She went off with the Williamses to help look for a house. In her absence Byron and the Shelleys received the dreadful news that little Allegra had been taken ill with the typhus that was raging in the environs of the convent at Bagnacavallo and had died there amongst the nuns. She was just five years old. Mary was deeply upset; Italy had claimed yet another beloved child. She felt overwhelming sympathy for Claire's loss and memories of her own tragic history as a mother came flooding back. Once again she felt the precariousness of Percy Florence's small life.

Shelley's distress was mixed with apprehension as to Claire's reaction to the news. He feared she would attack Byron in her grief. Byron himself was miserably regretful at the whole sad episode. Shelley decided he would have to remove Claire from Byron's immediate vicinity and on her return with the Williamses from house-hunting he bundled Mary and Percy off to take the reluctant Claire back to Spezia. Trelawny went with them on the journey. All their furniture and belongings, with equal precipitation, were packed up and sent by boat. The Williamses were induced to follow as rapidly.

After a trying journey they arrived at Spezia on 27 April. Mary had been told by Shelley to rent the Casa Magni, just outside Lerici. It was the only available house and the one they were to have to share with the Williamses and their two children. Mary was just pregnant and had not been well. Already in a sensitive state, heightened by the miserable knowledge she had to keep from Claire, the bay of Spezia's savage beauty and remoteness affected her deeply. The bay was a great loop of rock and sea, almost land-locked by the jutting promontories saddled with the small towns of Porto Venere to the west and Lerici to the east. There were no roads, only a rugged footpath along the cliff to Lerici. The precipitous rocks jutted down into the tideless sea where neither sand nor shingle blurred their collision. Here the Casa Magni clung to the cliff just above the waterline.

On Mary's arrival an April storm was blowing. The turbulent sea beat and foamed against the rocks below the house. Although Shelley had since arrived within days Mary was bedevilled by increasing alarm and an inexplicable sense of doom. Everyone was disturbed. They felt isolated from civilization and set adrift on the ocean: 'The howling wind swept round our exposed house, and the sea roared unintermittently, so that we almost fancied ourselves on board ship.'[15]

Mary found the local peasants repugnant and forbidding. 'The natives were wilder than the place. Our near neighbours, of Sant' Arenzo were more like savages than any people I ever before saw. Many a night they passed on the beach, singing or rather howling, the women dancing about among the waves that broke at their feet, the men leaning against the rocks and joining in their loud wild chorus',[16] she recalled in her notes to Shelley's poems. It was an appropriately dramatic stage to contain the gathering forces of tragedy.

Claire was restless and wanted to return to Florence. Mary and Shelley realized they had to break the news of Allegra's death to her, but were dreading doing so. On 2 May Claire sensed that something was wrong and the terrible news was shared. She was wildly despairing. She slipped a vilifying letter to Byron through the Shelleys' defence. She begged Shelley to write to the poet and demand Allegra's portrait and a lock of her hair. She was obsessed with seeing her little daughter for the last time, but after pressure from Mary and Shelley relinquished that idea. Everyone suffered for her and through her. The household was unsettled and emotionally fraught. While walking in the moonlight with Williams, Shelley was transfixed by what he saw as a naked child with its hands clasped, rising up out of the sea.

Claire's recovery was more rapid and complete than Mary had hoped, 'although, of course, until she forms new ties; she will always grieve yet she is now tranquil – more tranquil than when prophesying her disaster'.[17]

There was also a growing unrest and sense of stressful expectation as the arrival of Shelley and Williams' new boat was daily more overdue. Every eye looked out to sea, straining to catch a glimpse of sail in the distance, against the dazzle of sunlight on the water. At last on 12 May, with cloudy, thundery weather lying heavily over the bay, the speck of a strange sail was spotted rounding Porto Venere. Everyone came running, the 'perfect plaything for the summer'[18] had arrived.

The only blot on this beautiful boat and on their pleasure in it was the name *Don Juan* which Byron had insisted be painted on the mainsail, much to the Shelleys and Williamses' disgust. Three weeks of scrubbing was to no avail except to further besmirch the pristine cloth:

'For days and nights, full twenty-one, did Shelley and Edward ponder on her anabaptism and the washing out the primeval stain. Turpentine, spirits of wine, buccata, all were tried, and it became dappled and no more. At length the piece has been taken out and reefs put, so that the sail does not look worse. I do not know what Lord Byron will say, but Lord and Poet as he is, he could not be allowed to make a coal barge of our boat.'[19]

The enchantment with Byron was over.

Claire had left Casa Magni on 21 May to spend a few days with Mrs Mason at Pisa on her way to Florence, but still planned to spend the summer with the Shelleys and returned on 7 June. Mary's pregnancy was taking a worse toll than ever on her health. As Shelley described to Claire, she was suffering 'terribly from langour and hysterical affections'.[20] Her hysterical affections were largely an instinctive revulsion from the house, the place, the people of the bay and a pervading sense of approaching doom. Shelley, who had never been fitter and happier, was fully occupied with the boat, sharing with Williams a boyish escapism, spending days sailing her, fiddling about with the rigging, living the life of a Sunday sailor where every day was a pleasure day. He could not understand Mary's brooding fears and prejudices. He came out of the sun which he loved and under which he flourished, away from the laughter of the Williamses and into the obscurity of Mary's depressed and melancholic state. He became more enamoured of Jane Williams. Her placidness, sweetness and her lilting singing voice outweighed her 'lack of literary refinement'[21] and superficiality. He envied Edward Williams his tranquil domestic life and felt cheated and burdened by Mary's lack of happy participation and her hostility to the place. He felt he had at last found somewhere on earth to be happy. But Mary was a barrier to that; 'my only regret is that the summer must ever pass, or that Mary has not the same predilection for this place that I have, which would induce me never to shift my quarters',[22] he informed Horace Smith.

Mary herself felt at odds with the simple-hearted Williamses. Sharing a house with them was made all the more difficult by Jane's excessive domesticity which conflicted with Mary's haphazard approach to practicalities. Jane was flattered by Shelley's verses and attention and, as only to be expected, played on her sweet temper and her compliant undemanding femininity, losing no opportunity of singing and playing the guitar Shelley had given her. Williams was a bluff man's man who had little time for the vagaries of female emotions. All he understood was that Mary's moods and miseries were making life difficult for his friend.

Pregnant and unwell, over-sensitive to the savagery of the scenery, unhappy at the isolation, sensing an hostility in the house, burdened with a presentiment of evil too often proved true in the past and reinforced with memories of Claire's premonitions and Allegra's death; all these conspired to make Mary joyless, fearful and melancholic. She could not partake in the general enjoyment and so distanced herself from the activities, her companions, and from Shelley. It was little wonder that Shelley found her depressing to come home to. He once again felt alienated and alienating. 'I only feel the want of those who can feel, and understand me. Whether from proximity and the continuity of domestic intercourse, Mary does not',[23] he wrote damningly to John Gisborne.

In fact Mary felt too much. It was the relation, after his death, by the Williamses and Hunt of these occasional expressions of resentment and examples of the dissonance in her relationship with Shelley, of her failing him, which seared her with bitter remorse, spreading suffering through the years. But Mary's remorse was largely unjustified. She was a writer too, her temperament was neither domestic nor placid. She was not the mother-figure that so many great artists need, running the practicalities of her husband's life, her own needs sublimated through service, her fulfilment gained in buffering genius from the cold, harsh world. Perhaps it would have made Shelley's life easier if she had been. But Shelley had chosen her largely for her intellectual parity; he still enjoyed the fertility of her own ideas and imagination. For the stimulation of her company he had had to pay, at times quite highly, through her emotionalism, and self-centred griefs.

But Mary, too, in delighting in the intellectual highs of sharing her life with a genius, accepted, not always gratefully, the debits of his preoccupations, idealizations and susceptibility to women. The union of two such people with singular talents and fine sensibilities, whose lives were stalked by personal tragedy and persistent tribulation, could never be easy. It was Mary's ill-fortune that Shelley's untimely death should occur during a crisis period for her, whereby, intensely miserable and making him suffer too, her consequent remorse and guilt, denied forgiveness, were frozen for ever.

Mary sought to explain to Maria Gisborne her constitutional recoil from Lerici, the agitation, the unformed fears and extreme emotional discomfort which made it such agony for her to remain there:

'My nerves were wound up to the utmost irritation, and the sense of misfortune hung over my spirits. No words can tell you how I hated our house & the country about it. Shelley reproached me for this – his health was good & the place was quite after his own heart – What could I answer – that the people were wild & hateful, that though the country was beautiful yet I liked a more *countryfied* place, that there was great difficulty in living – that all our Tuscans would leave us, & that the very jargon of these *Genovese* was disgusting – This was all I had to say but no words could describe my feelings – the beauty of the woods made me weep & shudder – so vehement was my feeling of dislike that I used to rejoice when the winds & waves permitted me to go out in the boat so that I was not obliged to take my usual walk among tree shaded paths, allies of vine festooned trees – all that before I doated on – & that now weighed on me. My only moments of peace were on board that unhappy boat, when lying down with my head on his knee I shut my eyes & felt the wind & our swift motion alone.'[24]

As if that was not enough, Mary also had to cope with her own deep anxiety and sympathy for her father who had finally lost his lawsuit and was out of a home. He had written self-pitying, implicitly reproachful letters to her which had been mercifully intercepted by an ever-vigilant Shelley.

June was blazing. The land was parched with the effects of a prolonged drought and the uncouth villagers had resorted to primitive processions of religious relics through the streets with much wailing and noisy incantation. The stress under which she was living proved too much for her. On 9 June, Mary started to bleed with a threatened miscarriage. There was no doctor within miles. Shelley and Williams were out in the boat all day. Luckily Claire had arrived the previous day and she and Jane Williams got Mary to bed and looked after her as best they could. By evening the bleeding had stopped and she looked much better.

However, she did not recover and, after a week of ill-health, Mary lost her baby in a massive haemorrhage that started at eight o'clock on Sunday morning and continued unabated for seven hours.

Between fainting fits she was plied with brandy, vinegar and eau-de-Cologne. Everyone was filled with dread that she was dying. A doctor had been sent for but took hours to reach the remote Casa Magni. Meanwhile Shelley, characteristically bold and decisive in emergencies, demanded buckets of ice from the village and, despite Claire and Jane's demurs, sat Mary in an ice-bath. This uncomfortable but effective treatment checked the flow of blood and when the doctor eventually arrived he congratulated Shelley on his timely action.

Years later, looking back on this alarming episode, Mary remembered her own 'tranquillity of soul' in the face of death.

> 'My feeling ... was, I go to no new creation, I enter under no new laws. The God that made this beautiful world (and I was then at Lerici, surrounded by the most beautiful manifestation of the visible creation) made that into which I go; as there is beauty and love here, such is there, and I felt as if my spirit would when it left my frame be received and sustained by a beneficient and gentle Power. I had no fear, rather, though I had no active wish, but a passive satisfaction in death.'[25]

Neither Godwin's arid rationalism nor Shelley's fervent atheism could erase Mary's fundamental belief in God, beneficent power, and life after death. This was just one of many instances when she retained her idiosyncrasies and individualism in the face of the powerful ideologies of both a loved father and her beloved Shelley.

Mary's convalescence was prolonged. She was confined to her bed. Around her an infectious hysteria had taken hold of the household. Shelley had been frightened by Mary's illness; if Mary had died, she believed, he would never have recovered from the sense of his 'eternal misfortune',[26] his deathly touch that blasted everything he loved. A week after Mary's miscarriage, when she was still bedridden, she was awoken in the middle of the night by Shelley's piercing scream. He burst into her room. Mary tried to waken him but his continued screams terrified her so much that she leapt out of bed. She weakly staggered to the Williamses' bedroom door where she collapsed, managing through will and fear to scramble up again. Shelley had meanwhile been woken by Mary's exit and related what he called a waking vision but what Mary thought was more a nightmare. He had seen Edward and Jane come into his room 'in the most horrible condition, their bodies lacerated – their bones starting through their skin, the faces pale yet stained with blood.... Edward said – Get up, Shelley, the sea is flooding the house & it is all coming down.'[27] Then his vision of the sea rushing into the house was replaced by the ghastly sight of himself strangling Mary. It was this which had caused him to rush screaming to her room. The knowledge went deep that the prerequisites of his good health and life itself, had in part sacrificed the lives of little Clara and beloved William, finally almost destroying Mary too.

Shelley admitted to having experienced recently other visions of which that was the most violent. Mary was troubled by this recurrence but, knowing how imaginative Shelley could be, how tenuously anchored in reality, particularly when under stress, she did not think much further about it. The fact that Jane Williams, usually so phlegmatic and, as Mary aptly remarked, 'though a woman of sensibility, has not much imagination & is not in the slightest degree nervous – neither in dreams or otherwise',[28] had also been infected with such hallucinations was far more remarkable. On one occasion Jane had seen Shelley pass along the terrace twice, going in the same direction – a near impossibility without recrossing the window had Shelley been in the house. But as it was he had been out in the bay sailing his boat.

The epidemic of visions and hallucinations during these few weeks surrounding Mary's miscarriage was a clear expression of the emotional tension in the household. Possibly also it was a response to what Mary had so vividly sensed and feared about the place: its barbaric beauty and exclusion from civilized life, the intrinsic antipathy of the place, even its endemic evil.

16
Lost in Darkness

> 'He was soon borne away by the waves and lost in darkness and distance.'
>
> The last line of *Frankenstein*, Mary Shelley

Mary had heard that the Hunts had sailed from Genoa. She was still very weak and unwell and installed on the sofa to convalesce when Shelley decided to set off to meet them at Leghorn. Mary was inexplicably panic-stricken at Shelley's departure. She called him back two or three times and begged him not to go. He, full of enthusiasm for the journey, for seeing Hunt again after all the years and experiences that had separated them, could not understand her tedious hysterics and firmly took his leave of her. Years later she still remembered vividly the sensations of that day: 'a vague expectation of evil shook me to agony'[1] and she cried bitterly at his departure. But strangely she did not fear for Shelley's safety. His own and Williams's confidence in the sea and their mastery of it had so grown in their happy summer of boating and seafaring that Mary, too, feeling as she did at that time more secure on water away from the hostility of the land, had been lulled from her usual mistrust of the sea. Her premonitions of ill turned rather on the life of her son, Percy Florence.

The first of July dawned a clear, hot day with a brisk wind blowing favourably. The little boat with Shelley, Williams and Captain Roberts, the man who had built it, set out for Leghorn on the longest journey they had yet attempted. With him Shelley carried a sealed letter from Mary to Hunt which in its uncharacteristic lack of restraint and coherence painfully illustrated Mary's torment and her hysterical fear that if Hunt brought his family to settle in Lerici for the rest of the summer she could never escape the place:

'My dear Friend –

I know that S has some idea of persuading you to come here. I am too ill to write the reasonings only let me entreat you let no persuasions induce you to come. Selfish feelings you may be sure do not dictate – but it w[oul]d be complete madness to come –

'I wish I c[oul]d write more – I wish I were with you – I wish I c[oul]d break my chain & leave this dungeon – adieu – I shall [hear] about you & Marianne's health from S   Your fr[iend]
M'[2]

Her sense of foreboding increased as she waited for Shelley's return. She felt impotent, caught up in the inexorable workings of a fate which, she had long suspected, was generated through Shelley; the price all who were part of him had to pay for his genius. Already the tragedy had begun. Mary recognized the relentless progression of the drama, 'accompanied by circumstances so strange so inexplicable, so full of terrific interest (words are weak when one speaks of events so near the heart) that you would deem me very superstitious if I were only to narrate simple & incontestable facts to you . .'[3] and passively endured the trauma she knew must come. She wrote a distressed letter to Shelley: ' "... the feeling that some misfortune would happen," I said "haunted me" ... did not my William die? & did I hold my Percy by a firmer tenure?',[4] but still she did not conceive that anything could happen to Shelley. Both she and Jane Williams received letters from Shelley relating his safe arrival and the confusion that reigned at Pisa. Byron, who had promised to participate and totally finance the setting up of the *Liberal*, the sole reason for Leigh Hunt and his family's difficult expedition to Italy, had decided capriciously to leave Tuscany and follow the Gambas to America or Switzerland, or Genoa or perhaps even Lucca.

Shelley was fully occupied in settling the exhausted and despondent Hunts into the ground floor of Byron's house and persuading Byron to stay. He ended his last letter to Mary, 'How are you my best Mary? Write especially how is your health & how your spirits are, & whether you are not more reconciled to staying at Lerici at least during the summer.'[5] His letter to Jane closed more romantically, 'Adieu, my dearest friend – I only write these lines for the pleasure of tracing what will meet your eyes. – Mary will tell you all the news.'[6] Shelley had been bursting with good health and high spirits while at Pisa, looking dashingly sunburnt with his weather-bleached hair and vivid blue eyes. It was a tragedy in itself that Mary's last contacts with him were so distracted and distressing.

The women at Casa Magni could only wait now for their men's return. A week had passed and Monday, the eighth, was stormy. Mary did not think for a moment that Shelley would attempt to sail in such conditions. In fact at Leghorn all was fine but unsettled when Shelley and Williams, with their sailor-boy Charles Vivian, set out on their journey home. The experienced local sailors had more respect for the fickleness of conditions at sea.

Trelawny and Captain Roberts waved them off in the heavy heat of the afternoon. Roberts anxiously continued to watch them until their sails were lost in the haze of heat and distance. By early afternoon a tremendous thunderstorm was accumulating, rolling in from the darkening horizon.

Mary, alone in her bed, was woken by it and the thunder, the hammering rain and the roar of the sea reminded her chillingly of the hostile world outside. The Tuesday passed without word or sign, then on Wednesday a felucca from Leghorn arrived and the sailors confirmed that Shelley and Williams had sailed on the Monday. Mary and Jane refused to believe it, immunized against the possibility of the men's deaths by the unreality of the place and the enormity of such an idea. Mary described it: '. . . a sort of spell surrounded us, and each day, as the voyagers did not return, we grew restless and disquieted, and yet, strange to say, we were not fearful of the most apparent danger.'[7]

Friday was letter day for them and at noon Mary tore open Hunt's note addressed to Shelley. ' "Pray write to tell us how you got home, for they say you had bad weather after you sailed Monday and we are anxious" – the paper fell from me – I trembled all over – Jane read it – "then it is all over!" she said. "No, my dear Jane" I cried "it is not all over, but this suspense is dreadful come with me, we will go to Leghorn, we will post to be swift & learn our fate!" '[8] Mary had awoken from the dream into a nightmare.

Mary with Jane in tow set off on her nightmare journey to Lerici and from there to Pisa, distraught, asking everyone for any news of any boat. She had still not fully recovered from her miscarriage but force of will, despair and a wavering hope drove her on. 'It must have been fearful to see us – two poor, wild, aghast creatures driving –

(like Matilda) towards the *sea* to learn if we were to be forever doomed to misery.'[9]

At Pisa a carriage took them exhausted to Byron's house. Mary's fair skin was drained of colour and life and she blurted out to the Countess Guiccioli, 'Where is he – Sapate alcuna cosa di Shelley.'[10] Neither she nor Byron had any more information to add to Hunt's brief letter. It was then midnight and Mary insisted they had to go to Leghorn to find Trelawny or Captain Roberts. The women lived on manufactured hope.

After a few hours of fitful rest at a Leghorn inn, at the first hint of dawn they toured the other inns and tracked down Captain Roberts, 'with a face which seemed to tell us that the worst was true'.[11] However, having heard from him how he had watched the boat disappear into the haze of an approaching storm, Mary still clung desperately to a figment of hope – the boat had been swept off course, to Corsica or beyond. Roberts could only agree that was a possibility and his concurrence restored Mary's spirits. Roberts took her to Trelawny's lodgings and they decided to send a messenger to go to each tower along the coast and report any rumours or sightings. She and Jane felt they had to return to Lerici immediately and Trelawny elected to accompany them.

As they were approaching Via Reggio they decided to ride down to the town and ask for news. A small dinghy, similar in description to the one Shelley kept on his boat, and a water flask had been found floating in the sea. Momentarily desolated by the weight of this implication, Mary, to preserve herself and Jane who was now visibly wilting, rationalized it; such things could well have been cast off in a storm. But the days of exhaustion and irresistible despair were beginning to tell.

That night, nearing Lerici, they forded the River Magra; it was a terrible homecoming: 'I felt the water splash about our wheels – I was suffocated – I gasped for breath – I thought I should have gone into convulsions, & I struggled violently that Jane might not perceive it – looking down the river I saw the two great lights burning at the *foce* – A voice from within me seemed to cry aloud that is his grave.'[12] Mary went back through the wildly dancing peasants on the beach, back to the dark house with an anxious Claire and the children subdued, sensing that something terrible had happened. There was no news. The sea kept up its ceaseless boom. With Mary's acute susceptibility to sound, the eternal dirge of the greedy sea, echoed in turn by the peasants' primitive and eerie chant below the house, imprisoned her within a wall of sound which pointed to the unendurable truth – that Shelley was dead. 'To tell you all the agony we endured during those 12 days would be to make you conceive a universe of pain – each moment intolerable & giving place to one still worse.'[13]

Trelawny was of the greatest support, open-hearted with his affections and tireless and generous with his time and energy. He did all he could to comfort the three women whose lives were so entangled with the lives of those lost men. He left Casa Magni on 18 July to go to Leghorn in the hope of gleaning some news, and towards the evening of the following day, Mary was beginning to hope again.

Then: 'About 7 o'clock P.M. he did return – all was over – all was quiet now, they had been found washed on shore – well all this was to be endured.'[14]

17
A Funeral Pyre

> 'Yet my hope was corruption and dust and all to which death brings us....'
>
> *Mathilda*, Mary Shelley

The next morning Mary, Claire and Jane packed up all their portable belongings and with the children left immediately for Pisa. With Shelley and Williams dead there was nothing to keep them at Casa Magni, indeed nothing could now induce Mary to stay.

United in grief, the three women decided to set up home temporarily together with a kitty for housekeeping and everyday expenses. All were now impecunious and alone, facing an uncertain future secured only by marriage or the limited prospects of working for a living. Claire was eventually to turn to governessing, one of the few occupations open to women of her background, Jane to another common-law husband and Mary, declaring immediately, 'I would not change my situation as His widow with that of the most prosperous woman in the world',[1] was to battle to keep herself and her son Percy with a variety of editing and writing jobs and a further four novels.

With the news of Shelley's death and the dreadful realization that she would never again see that familiar face, living now on nothing but her memories, she wrote to Amelia Curran requesting her portrait of Shelley, painted while they were all together in Rome in 1819. Although she had not thought it a particularly good likeness when it was done, she now longed to see it. After spasmodic correspondence between herself and Amelia, through complicated arrangements for collection and delivery and increasing impatience and despair, Mary eventually received it three years later at the end of 1825.

To surmount each day demanded an effort of will. She had survived a nightmare to face an inescapably grim reality. 'I never look first upon the morning-light but with my fingers pressed tight on my bursting heart, and my soul deluged with the interminable flood of hopeless misery.'[2] Mary was bleak and despairing about the barren years that stretched ahead:

> 'I am now on the eve of completing my five & twentieth year – how drearily young for one so lost as I! How young in years for one lives ages each day in sorrow – think you that these moments are counted in my life as in other people's? – oh no! The day before the sea closed over mine own Shelley he said to Marianne – "if I die tomorrow I have lived to be older than my father, I am ninety years of age." Thus also may I say – The eight years I passed with him were spun out beyond the usual length of a man's life – and what I have suffered since will write years on my brow & intrench them in my heart.'[3]

She confided much of her anguish in long letters to Maria Gisborne. With her friends, with Byron and the Hunts she restrained her feelings. Only when alone did the turmoil of remorse and pain overwhelm her. Only with Trelawny would she allow herself the necessary luxury of endless talk about Shelley; reminiscences, regrets, adulation and love for the man with whom she had spent her life. Trelawny with his romanticism, his attachment to Shelley, his generosity, was happy to talk and listen and, in easing some of his own feelings, slip a little of the weight of grief from Mary's slight frame.

On the night Trelawny brought the fateful news, he immediately burst out with a spontaneous eulogy to Shelley, his simple, forceful language inspired with emotion. This act was one of many at that time for which Mary was lastingly and deeply grateful. He assumed responsibility for the disposal of Shelley and Williams's remains and worked tirelessly for permission to carry out the incineration himself and for the widows to dispose of the ashes as they wished.

The Italian authorities were so alarmed at any possibility of disease that the bodies had been buried in the sand in quicklime. Trelawny, having won his concessions from the Health Office, had an iron furnace made at Leghorn and, in wishing to perform for Shelley a simple funeral rite resembling those of the funeral pyres of his beloved Greeks, he bought frankincense and salt for the flames and wine and oil to pour over the body.

Byron and Hunt wished to be present and on 16 August the men gathered on the wild and lovely shore about a mile from Via Reggio, with dragoons and officials from the Health Office. Shelley's shallow grave in the sand was marked by three bleached sticks and the soldiers silently started digging to recover his body. The fire was kindled and the heat was intense as Shelley's remains were committed to the flames. Byron had wanted to save his skull which was a beautiful shape, fine and small, but Trelawny, remembering having seen Byron use one as a drinking-cup, was determined 'Shelley's should not be so profaned'.[4]

As the flames leapt and seethed and the furnace turned white hot, Trelawny was amazed to see Shelley's heart unusually large and intact. He thrust his hand into the fire to grasp it from the flames.

When the fire had burnt low, they cooled the furnace in the sea and Trelawny collected the human ashes and placed them in a box. The soldiers and the friends departed. Such a simple and appropriate ceremony performed by Shelley's friends in love and honour was a great service to Mary who feared that officialdom would prevail and Shelley's remains be despatched by uncaring strangers. It was Trelawny's efforts which secured her that peace of mind. She intended Shelley's ashes to be buried beside their son William's in the Protestant Cemetery at Rome. And on 21 January 1823, after negotiations and difficulties, many of which were resolved by Severn, Keats's old friend, the modest box of ashes was buried there, although sadly William's grave was never located.

'Shelley! my own beloved! You rest beneath the blue sky of Rome; in that, at least, I am satisfied.'[5]

Mary longed to be able to be weak and dependent, to escape from the present through death or fantasies of death. But she was a fighter, albeit an unwilling one. Something of her precious Shelley remained in fair, blue-eyed Percy Florence, and his future and happiness were now her responsibility alone. There was Jane, for whom Mary felt great sympathy and affection in their mutual distress. Jane was prostrated by the tragedy and barely managing to care for herself or her children; Mary forgot her own heartbreak to support and comfort her.

Claire was now quite alone with no ties to keep her in Italy. She planned to join her brother Charles Clairmont in Vienna but, as with Mary and Jane, lack of money was to be a sore problem. Mary was always generous with what money she had and promised Claire help with the expenses of the journey from her own depleted purse, although they hoped that Byron with his capricious generosity, and in the sway of remorse, would take some responsibility for the mother of his dead child. That hope was to prove vain.

Mary, with her usual lack of self-delusion, courageously accepted that her illness, her dreadful despondency and consequent emotional withdrawal from Shelley during the desperate weeks at Lerici clouded his last days. In a long autobiographical poem, *The Choice*, which she wrote after Shelley's death she faced squarely that cruel sting:

> 'Now fierce remorse and unreplying death
> Waken a chord within my heart, whose breath,
> Thrilling and keen, in accents audible
> A tale of unrequited love doth tell.
> It was not anger, – while thy earthly dress
> Encompassed still thy soul's rare loveliness,
> All anger was atoned by many a kind
> Caress or tear, that spoke the softened mind. –
> It speaks of cold neglect, averted eyes,
> That blindly crushed thy souls fond sacrifice: –
> My heart was all thine own, – but yet a shell
> Closed in its core, which seemed impenetrable,
> Till sharp-toothed misery tore the husk in twain,
> Which gaping lies, nor may unite again.'[6]

Her suffering and regrets were further embittered by Hunt's coldness to her. She had long considered him and Marianne to be faithful and close friends and when she most needed warmth and small acts of caring, she was offered an icy shoulder and ill-disguised reproach. Hunt was responding, he felt justifiably, to the little information about Mary's frame of mind that Shelley had confided to him during the few days at Pisa. Jane Williams had added her bit too, relating incidents when 'the intercourse between Shelley & Mary was not as happy as it should have been'.[7] Hunt further distressed Mary by refusing at first to give her Shelley's heart that he had secured from Trelawny at the funeral. In his letter of refusal he implied that she did not deserve the treasure and that his rights as a loving friend were greater than hers as a failed wife.

This tittle-tattle and sanctimony from those she considered friends left Mary all the more isolated and alone. Her natural emotions of remorse and self-denigration were distorted and driven deeper by their very lack of compassion.

Partly because she could not exorcize such intractable griefs, she could not turn from the past and allay Shelley's ghost. She wished to do for him in death what she felt she and the world had failed to do in life. She resolved to study and write, care for their son, and collect and present to a more sympathetic public Shelley's prose and poetical works, winning for him something of the just appraisal and acclaim of which he had felt cheated during his life by critical prejudice and public cecity. In her moments of optimism and power she felt she would embark on a life of Shelley: 'Thy name is added to the list which makes the earth bold in her age and proud of what has been.'[8] With that she hoped to replace the world's demon with her view of a loving, gentle genius. However, she knew that this was an idealization, that it would compromise her honesty, her unerring perception and astute apprehension of the failings and foibles in his nature, and in hers. Her loyalty to Shelley in death, her understandable sanctification of his memory, could not allow the whole truth to be told, yet her own intellectual integrity would not allow otherwise. This would explain one of the reasons why she never really accomplished anything of this projected biography. Just as the world was not ready to appreciate and forgive the Caliban in her Ariel she was unwilling to reveal it.

Shelley's uniqueness, his extraordinary character and genius made it particularly difficult for Mary to bury him. Her youth had been a lifetime, inextricably bound with his. She was convinced that 'Adonais is not Keats's it is his own elegy'.[9] In poring over the poem, reading it time and time again, she felt Shelley was speaking to her of his death and her grief:

'I would give
All that I am to be as thou now art!
But I am chained to Time, and cannot thence depart!'[10]

was her cry.

With neither a mother nor a close friend with whom to indulge in spontaneous and uninhibited grief, Mary's necessary anguish had to be constricted and formalized into the written word, becoming painful, self-pitying letters to Maria Gisborne and despairing entries in her journal, once so laconic and discreet.

This was a cruel state; in her everyday communications she kept her passions in strict control: 'Those about me have no idea of what I suffer; for I talk, aye & smile as usual – & none are sufficiently interested in me to observe that though my lips smile, my eyes are blank.'[11] Yet in releasing the part of her suffering that could be put to paper she was aware of how obsessed and self-pitying she sounded, how her attempts at easing her pain became an ossified monument to what would seem, with distance and detachment, a selfish and morbid indulgence.

Mary, too, felt guilty for burdening her friend with her despair. She wrote to Maria Gisborne, 'Pardon, dear friend, this selfishness. There are moments when the heart must *sfogare* or be suffocated; & such a moment is this – when quite alone, my babe sleeping, my dear Jane having just left me....'[12] Without someone present and loving to restore her sense of self-esteem, Mary, dispirited and humbled, assumed even the hair-shirt of *Epipsychidion*, Shelley's poem which had hurt her so with its characterization of her as 'the cold chaste Moon'. Not only in the privacy of her journal did she write, 'Moonshine may be united to her planet and wander no more, a sad reflection of all she loved on earth',[13] but even to Byron she admitted, 'There might be [have been] something sunny about me then, now I am truly *cold moonshine*.'[14] Yet despite this humility, filled with regrets as she was, she never allowed it to obscure or degrade what she knew to have been a dynamic and loving relationship. The strength of her relationship with Shelley was extraordinary, considering their youth when they met and the trials, the tragedies and illness which, throughout their life together, worried at their heels like wolves. Mary and Shelley were both highly individual, talented and temperamentally volatile; in different ways the genius in each of them inevitably set them apart from the world, and even from one another. Each found it difficult to live contentedly in orthodox domesticity yet both keenly needed intimacy, encouragement and companionship. Mary knew that few people could have given her such quality of love and inspiration. But Shelley had failed her too. The noble spirit could be an inexorable force determined on self-gratification. She was justified in believing that her contribution to Shelley's life was as valuable and only as temporarily flawed. She had been so often the eye in his storm, his one constant friend, intellectually his match, perceptive and wise. With reason she knew it had worked.

But she had to live and practicalities had to be faced. Mary would have stayed in Italy if she could, but fear for the life of baby Percy, her last surviving hope, meant that before the next summer she would have to return to England. In Italy she could live frugally and well and Byron, as Shelley's executor, had agreed to try and negotiate, via Whitton, with Sir Timothy Shelley for a fixed allowance.

Jane Williams was returning to England to seek help from her own and Edward's relations. Claire was off to Vienna and Mary, dreading loneliness and abandonment, was grateful to accept the offer of living with the Hunt family and nursing the ailing Marianne through her next confinement. She was always made use of by her friends and on 11 September she and Percy, with Jane and her children for company, left Pisa for Genoa with the brief to find a house for herself and the Hunts as well as a suitably palatial dwelling for Byron and La Guiccioli. She managed to rent the Casa Negroto, a large house just outside Genoa in the village of Albaro. She had also secured an even larger mansion, the Casa Saluzzo, a ride away, for Byron and his entourage. Mary hoped to pass here a peaceful winter copying Shelley's manuscripts, doing her own writing, going for invigorating walks and helping to educate the older Hunt children.

She had not written to her father. He had heard of Shelley's death via Leigh Hunt and then had read Mary's very long and detailed letter of 15 August to Mrs Gisborne. He was puzzled and hurt by her silence and wrote her a selfish, predictably unsympathetic and strangely self-satisfied letter implying that now she, too, was suffering: 'surrounded with adversity and with difficulty' she would better understand his problems and he could at last confide them to her fully. It was little wonder that Mary was in no hurry to return to England.

Byron arrived in Genoa on 5 October. He was thoroughly fed up with the Hunt children. 'They are dirtier and more mischievous than Yahoos',[15] he complained in his letter to Mary on his arrival. Hunt and he had very little in common and, although he recognized Hunt's virtues, he was bored by the man and irritated by his lack of dynamism. The journal, the *Liberal*, on which they were meant to collaborate, had become a disappointment and an embarrassment. Byron no longer wished to be identified with it but realized he had little choice but to go on financing it until Hunt returned to England, a possibility he wished would be speedily realized. It had been a great mistake ever to share his house with them and one which Byron vigorously regretted.

Mary could not afford to be so choosy. Marianne and Hunt and their assorted Yahoos arrived and Mary's quiet solitude was invaded by the clatter of six pairs of children's feet, their shouts and arguments and general undisciplined boisterousness. The Hunts were long-suffering parents who believed that their children should not be corrected until they were at an age to be reasoned with. In practice, this free-ranging horde wore their sick mother's nerves to a frazzle and sorely distracted their already anxious father. Marianne was ailing, pregnant and ill-organized. Mary was not naturally domesticated. The children could do as they pleased and the house quickly deteriorated into shabbiness and squalor.

Mary managed to do some work in her room. She gratefully accepted from Byron the task of transcribing his tenth canto of *Don Juan*. Unfortunately, in uniting herself with the Hunts, Mary had separated herself from Byron. The irritated condescension with which he regarded Leigh Hunt had a tendency to tar Mary too. Certainly Byron did not enjoy visiting the house. In contrast to his and Teresa Guiccoli's kind attentions at Pisa, Mary now saw Byron once or twice a month. But, when she did spend time with him and when he was approachable and relaxed, he held her in thrall with his magic.

On 19 October she spent two hours in his company and returned to the Casa Negroto feeling turbulent and disturbed. 'Albé, by his mere presence and voice, has the power of exciting such deep and shifting emotions within me. For my feelings have no analogy either with my opinion of him or the subject of his conversation.'[16] Mary's responses to Byron had always been ambiguous; she recoiled from his fickleness and profligacy, she regretted his egoism, his petulance, arrogance and ambition, she was cowed by his worldliness and cynicism; but his vigorous physical presence, his wit and vitality, the very force of the man seduced her with an uneasy fascination. Byron stalked through her fiction in various guises, as Castruccio in *Valperga*, Lord Lodore in *Lodore*, and most convincingly as Raymond in *The Last Man*. Mary wrote this soon after hearing of Byron's death and her bold characterization owed most to her memories of Byron during the happy summer at Villa Diodati. Her description of Raymond nevertheless explained the qualities that so attracted her to Byron then and continued to delight her on their infrequent meetings: '... with, hilarity, and deep observation were mingled in his talk, rendering every sentence that he uttered as a flash of light. He soon conquered my latent distaste; I endeavoured ... to keep in mind every thing I had heard to his disadvantage. But all appeared so ingenuous, and all was so fascinating, that I forgot everything except the pleasure his society afforded me.'[17]

Another shrewder comment revealed a further facet to Byron's character that appealed particularly to the widowed Mary: '... full of contradictions, unbending yet haughty, gentle yet fierce, tender and again neglectful, he by some strange art found easy entrance to the admiration and affection of women; now caressing and now tyrannising over them according to his mood, but in every change a despot.'[18]

In the winter after Shelley's death Mary was feeling desperately lonely and unloved, lowered with responsibility and the insecurity of her future. She would have liked an irresistible Byronic force to divest her of responsibility and the burdens of choice. Then she would be loved and dominated, a dependent and suppliant being. After years of familial responsibility and sustained effort in surmounting the peculiar tragedies of her life, the longing for such an escape disturbed her daily round.

But Mary had not been disturbed solely by the equivocal nature of her feelings for Byron. She was always highly sensitive to sound, aware particularly intensely of voices. The distinctive timbre and cadence of Byron's voice, to her ear, could only be complemented by the lighter, higher tones of Shelley's. 'When Albé speaks and Shelley does not answer, it is as thunder without rain – the fall of the sun without heat or light – as any familiar object might be, shorn of its best attributes; and I listen with an unspeakable melancholy that yet is not all pain.'[19]

The turbulence of Mary's feelings that October evening were soon to be matched by the weather. A freak thunderstorm broke over Genoa at the end of October. So violent and torrential was the rain that the town was flooded, houses and walls swept away, a child drowned, half the countryside awash. Both the Casa Negroto and Casa Saluzzo, Byron's house, were safe on the tops of their respective hills, but so unexpected and devastating was the storm that the locals thought it an act of God. Mary, surveying the scene from above the floodline, philosophically remarked that Genoa's poky, enclosed streets could have done with a few less walls.

The days were getting colder and a chill wind buffeted the house on the hill. Mary had never liked Genoa and, sitting in her cold, draughty room trying to copy out Shelley's manuscripts, she now hated it. The new stove that local workmen had spent a disruptive month installing in her room smoked too profusely to use and the cold would force her downstairs to the only other fireplace in the house, in the Hunts' family sitting-room. The unruly younger children, who teased Percy for speaking only Italian, Hunt's continuing coldness towards her – 'Hunt does not like me: it is both our faults, I do not blame him but so it is'[20] – and poor, harassed Marianne's low health and spirits, spoiled what little repose Mary might have achieved, and destroyed any chances of study. Alone in her room, she took her irritation out on the useless stove by kicking it heartily.

With Trelawny's departure from Genoa for Leghorn on 20 December Mary felt lost in her desert existence. Letters were mirages of friendship but they came so seldom and brought so little consolation that she feared she was truly forgotten. Letters were life-lines, not only because they brought affection and news from friends, but they were also the only means of communication on essential negotiations with Whitton and Sir Timothy Shelley, on her book *Valperga*, on requests for copies of Shelley's letters and other manuscripts, on small but important commissions like the pansy and a shell from the Shelley arms that Mary wanted embroidered on velvet. The frustrations of having to rely so heavily on others to act for her and never hearing their progress increased the nervous tension she already suffered. Even Maria Gisborne often neglected to write, pleading 'an almost insurmountable difficulty in expressing my ideas'.[21] Mary in desperation suggested:

'I wish you would enter into an *unbreakable* engagement to me to write to me once a month. Your letter may be the work of several hours scattered over the month; but put a long letter into the post for me the first day of every month. I want some object, some motive, great or small – I should look forward to your letter as a certain thing, & it would be something to expect ... it would be a great solace to me indeed it would.'[22]

She never got that promise and letters were still as rare and as longed for as water in the desert.

Mary had been waiting long to hear the outcome of Byron's negotiations with Sir Timothy; her financial future was so insecure that in her depressions she feared that she and Percy would starve. She was finding it very difficult to write but managed a short story set in medieval Italy called 'A Tale of the Passions' for the second number of the *Liberal*, published on 1 January 1823. She was paid £33 which delighted her for it meant that for the time being she did not have to accept any financial aid from Byron, and could even send some money to Claire who was seriously ill in Vienna.

Mary was learning that the only way of suppressing her bitter memories was to opiate her grief with study. It was an effort to maintain her concentration against the persistence of memory and self-pity but when intellect prevailed she was rewarded: 'I have felt myself exalted with the idea of occupation, improvement, knowledge, and peace . . . study has become to me more necessary than the air I breathe',[23] she wrote in her journal.

This tremulous peace was shattered on 24 February by Sir Timothy's long-awaited reply to Byron's letter about Mary's allowance. The old man wrote that Mary's conduct had been despicable, that she had alienated Shelley from his family and only if Percy Florence was relinquished and placed under the care of a guardian approved by himself would he then consider providing the child with adequate though limited maintenance. It cut Mary to the quick. She was particularly hurt by the implications that she would part with Percy for any reason and that her own and Shelley's son, once wrested from his sole surviving parent, was not good enough to be brought up in the Shelley home but instead would be farmed out to some stranger as a commercial proposition. Haunted by the myth of her cold nature she wrote to Byron in reply, 'I am said to have a cold heart – there are feelings however so strongly implanted in my nature that to root them out life will go with it.'[24]

Not only was she hurt, she was frightened, suddenly weak and vulnerable. Byron said he thought she should comply and that shocked and disconcerted her. Instantly the fears that winged Shelley's flight from England infected Mary with the dread that somehow the authorities could deprive her of her precious child. In a state of agitation, deprived of support and protection, unable to make decisions but adamant that she and her boy stayed together, she wrote to Hogg for counsel. 'If I go to England will they not try to force him from me? It would require force indeed, I would die in the struggle....'[25]

Mary often saw Shelley in her dreams and in her journal she asked him to come to her that night as consolation for the troubled day.

She sent a copy of Sir Timothy's letter to her father so that he might judge if there was any hope of softening the old Shelley's heart. Mary was resigned to returning to England, for Percy's health and for the slight chance that having the boy on English soil might tip the balance of family suspicion in their grandson's favour. It was worth the sacrifice of Italy. And it was a sacrifice indeed: 'I love Italy – its sky canopies the tombs of my lost treasures – its sun – its vegetation – the solitude I can here enjoy – the easy life one can lead – my habits now of five years growth – all & everything endears Italy to me beyond expression. The thought of leaving it fills me with painful tumults – tears come into my eyes.'[26] The most memorable times of her life had been lived there. In leaving Italy Mary knew she would be breaking the continuum of past and present, losing the *genius loci* that in the scent of the breeze, the angle of the sun, inspirited her memories and made sense of her life. She would stay to see Marianne Hunt through the birth of her baby in June and then she would gather her son and her few belongings and make the break.

Byron had once again rallied and offered help. Mary reluctantly accepted the offer of the costs of her journey. Trelawny had written to say he had moved Shelley's ashes to a less populated spot in the cemetery, beside the Pyramid of Cestius, and had personally planted cyprus and laurel and added to his gravestone the lines from Shakespeare which had delighted Shelley in life:

> 'Nothing of his that doth fade
> But doth suffer a sea-change
> Into something rich and strange.'

This care gratified Mary immensely. She was amused and touched by the other reason for Trelawny's industry. He had marked his plot to the left of Shelley: 'I have likewise dug my grave – so that when I die, there is only to lift up the coverlet, and roll me into it – you may lay on the other side, or I will share my narrow bed with you, if you like. It is a lovely spot.'[27] Mary had added the aside to Maria

Gisborne, '(T–y you know, one of the best and most generous of creatures, is eccentric in his way).'[28]

Trelawny on hearing Mary was to leave Italy wrote urging her to stay, offering to share gladly with her his meagre income. But Mary had to go and Trelawny and Byron were dreaming of Greece and the War of Independence there.

Marianne's baby, Vincent, was duly born on 9 June and much to Hunt and Mary's relief she was well and recovered without the traumatic relapse that the doctors had threatened. Mary approached Byron to say she was ready to go. The capricious lord first stalled about the promised money and then, when reminded by Hunt that he owed Mary £1000 on a wager Shelley had won, turned petulant and decided he had not liked either Shelley or Mary anyway. Mary's pride would not allow her to accept money offered in such bad grace and she had to write to Trelawny for help. Again she was saved by his generosity. He left for Greece with Byron and Teresa Guiccioli's brother, Count Gamba, on 17 July. 'They sailed together; Lord Byron with £10,000, Trelawny with £50.'[29]

Mary had lost the presence of Trelawny as a dear friend but she had gained Leigh Hunt. He had slowly recognized Mary's profound grief and silent suffering, he had seen her selflessness, always willing to help, interceding with Byron on his behalf, supporting Marianne and caring for the children. Percy was attached to his new-found family. He hoped that now there was a new baby he and Mary could have the old one, Sylvan, a particular friend of his.

Now with Hunt so changed and her presence so valued, it was doubly difficult to turn her back and go. Already the July heat was shimmering out over the valley and on the twenty-fifth she and Percy climbed into the *vetturino* on the start of their journey. Hunt and Thornton, his son, travelled the first twenty miles with her in an affectionate gesture to ease the wrench of departure.

Mary's overwrought emotions were agitated but strangely elated by the motion of travel and the thrill of once again passing through foreign scenery and strange towns. Her first letter to the Hunts revealed in its fragmented, breathless confusion the turmoil of her thoughts and her active affections:

'Dearest Friends – Very Patient and Patient Very – How do you do – I am very well – I think so – I think percy is very well my boy is a good boy – I think so – you will receive this letter from your affectionate Mary Wollstonecraft Shelley I hope – I love you – I think I do – I love Henry Sylvan and Mary Florimel Leigh Hunt I hope – and so kiss her, one of you, if she be good – and Thornton also to whom I shall write soon – and Baby Nuovo – and the rest in a lump, scape grace Johnny, giggling swinny and Percy the Martyr.'[30]

It also revealed a common feature of the loving letters written to the Hunts during her journey. She never failed to send messages to the children, always treating them individually and with affection. Children of large families so often suffer through being addressed as a unit and Mary, with her sweetness and unusual awareness, gave each child its due attention. Her message to Thornton in the same letter was a cry from the heart, 'Thorny – you have not been cross yet – Oh my dear Thorny ... do not let your impatient nature ever overcome you – or you may suffer as I have done – which God forbid! – be true to yourself....'[31]

The scenery around Susa was full of memories of her first flight to Italy with Shelley. The countryside was so beautiful that Mary succumbed to romantic reverie, with herself and Percy and the Hunt family living in idyllic rural retreat.

Loving letters continued to wing from her pen to the Hunts, about to move to Florence. The protracted journey was beginning to take its toll on Mary's health. She arrived at Paris feverish and weak. There she met Horace Smith and spent three pleasant days with him and his ailing wife at Versailles. She caught up on what news he had of England: gossip about Hazlitt and his new-found propensity for young women; news of the Lambs' visit to Paris the previous year and poor Miss Lamb 'taken ill in her usual way'[32], Wordsworth's ageing and Horace Smith's rejuvenescence.

There she met James and Louisa Kenney. He was a successful dramatist and producer and she was Thomas Holcroft's widow. With Holcroft having been a friend of Godwin's there was much to tell of the spirits and circumstances of Mary's father and step-mother, now living in the Strand. Mrs Kenney was full of consternation at the thought of Mary sharing a roof, even temporarily, with the woman who had declared her to be 'the greatest enemy she has in the world'.[33]

Mary realized that her sunny Italian exile away from the world was ebbing and that the tide of London life and its social pressures was beginning to trickle in. She heard some unexpected and encouraging news from both Horace Smith and the Kenneys. *Frankenstein* had been staged and the awesome appearance of the monster was fairly packing them in in the cheaper seats. When Mary parted from the Kenneys on 19 August, Mrs Kenney, who had known Mary Wollstonecraft, took Mary aside to tell her how like her mother in manner she had become: '... this is the most flattering thing anyone could say to me,'[34] she wrote to the Hunts. These last few days had seen her first social contact since Shelley's death and, in bravely and determinedly keeping herself from melancholy, she was rewarded with the sense that she had pleased them and lived up to the memories of her mother and 'mine own Shelley'.

18
The Lonely Survivor

> 'I am a cloud from which the light of sunset has passed....'
>
> Mary Shelley's journal

On 25 August Mary finally arrived in England. How different were her circumstances from those of the rebellious girl five and a half years previously. Then she had been surrounded by a family: Shelley, William and baby Clara, Claire and Allegra and two servants, Elise and Milly Shields. Now all had gone; all three precious children had died under that Italian heaven and finally Shelley, too, had fulfilled his prognostication and died young. Mary with her foreign son, with the few remaining coins of Trelawny's money in her pocket, returned, 'the last relic of a beloved race, my companions extinct before me'.[1]

But she was determined to do as Hunt had advised and work at keeping up her spirits. Her father and step-brother, William Godwin, were at the wharf to meet her. Percy, with his high excitement at the voyage and his babbling Italian, was a surprise to his grandfather. Mrs Godwin made her welcome, finding little to hate in this slight, pale and restrained young woman.

Mary was reunited with Jane Williams – she feeling a rush of affection and memories, but Jane less effusive and altogether cooler. However, she agreed to go with Mary and her father and William Godwin to the dramatization of *Frankenstein* at the English Opera House. It amused Mary tremendously. It was ham-fisted and not very faithful to her story but it was rather thrilling to see an audience held spellbound by her creation. She wrote with surprised delight to Hunt: 'But lo and behold! I found myself famous – Frankenstein had prodigious success as a drama and was about to be repeated for the twenty-third night....'[2] Godwin had arranged for a reprint of her book to coincide with the play's run, quite possibly having already made use of the royalties earned so far, while Mary was away in Italy.

Her reunion with the Gisbornes the following day, on her birthday, 30 August, filled her with a melancholy and a nostalgia for Italy which swamped her attempts at buoying her spirits. The weather, too, conspired against her. As she picked her way home through the muddy puddles she could not allow herself to think, 'for I am a ruin where owls and bats live only and I lost my last *singing bird* when I left Albaro'.[3]

Another old friend, for whose friendship she had for years so longed, proved sad and disappointing. Isabel Booth, the beloved Isabel Baxter of her girlish Dundee days, was ill and deranged and Mary was only sustained through the painful interview by gratitude for Isabel's obvious affection and her own memories of happier days long gone.

In early September she moved into lodgings in Brunswick Square. Despite her welcome from the Godwins, she had never been an easy, accommodating daughter and now, a woman individualized by time and experience, she was incapable of trying. But already Godwin had attempted to shackle her with filial duty, making her projected return to Italy 'an affair of life and death'.[4]

Mary was far more generous to her friends in Italy than any had ever been to her; she wrote the Hunts long and frequent letters, full of news about mutual friends, the latest publications, literary gossip. She also interceded between Hunt and his brother over money and the *Examiner* and executed any commissions, reporting on progress: all the practical help she had longed for when she was far away.

Hunt's great friend Vincent Novello and his family became firm favourites of Mary's. Love and appreciation of music had been her and Hunt's common ground and here in London in the home of the good-hearted Novellos every visit ended up an extended musical soirée, much to Mary's delight: '... as I listen to music (especially instrumental) new ideas rise & develop themselves, with greater energy & truth than at any other time.'[5] During such positive and inspired moments her thoughts turned to her next novel, 'wild & imaginative & I think more in my way'.[6] This was to be *The Last Man*.

In society she persisted in keeping her troubles to herself. She appeared serene and capable, clever and cultured, always interested in everything and generous with help and affection. Only when associations proved too painful, as when meeting Hogg again and hearing his familiar voice, did she escape the pain with the same wild high spirits that used to erupt in her girlhood.

She saw Jane Williams often. Lacking her usual judgment and perception she had idealized her 'sister-in-sorrow' into some pure and celestial being whose heart had stopped with Edward's and whose pleasures lay in memory alone. In fact, Jane was an ordinary, kindly but superficial woman who needed the love and support of a man and realistically encouraged the dogged attentions of Hogg. Mary could talk of Shelley only to Jane and her greatest relief and pleasure was in reminiscing about the happier Italian days.

Mary's first few months in England were full and busy. There was work, collecting and collating copies of Shelley's unpublished poems for a volume which sold well until she had to recall the remaining copies on orders of Sir Timothy, and meeting acquaintances who considered her an interesting, enigmatic young woman; as the author of *Frankenstein* and Shelley's widow her pale good looks were enhanced with the sheen of celebrity and scandal. Henry Crabb Robinson, diarist, journalist and frequenter of literary circles, met Mary again soon after her return: 'She is unaltered, yet I did not know her at first; she looks elegant and sickly and young. One would not suppose she was the author [of Frankenstein],'[7] he confided to his diary.

But as the novelty and excitement subsided, routine and lack of money began to dictate her way of life. She could not afford to reciprocate her new friends' hospitality with dinners and opera tickets, yet she longed most of all for human companionship and for love. Alone with Percy in her small lodgings, living through a dismal English winter, she felt isolated from everything that had once inspired her. 'My imagination is dead, my genius lost, my energies sleep',[8] she cried to Shelley in her journal. Her inability to set her imagination free, her disconsolation with study, the failure of her literary powers while struggling to write *The Last Man* made her despair that her spirit was dying, starved of Italy and of love.

She reached the nadir of despair the evening before she heard of Byron's death in Greece at Missolonghi, a month previously. Her prescience of that news seemed to explain to her the exaggerated depression of her spirits. Her journal for 15 May recorded the affection and nostalgia that she felt for 'the dear, capricious, fascinating Albé …

that resplendent spirit whose departure leaves the dull earth dark as midnight'.[9] It was not only the poet's physical magnetism and literary prowess that had long attracted and unsettled Mary. More significantly she had felt a basic sympathy with Byron's relaxed conservatism that she had never felt for Shelley's brand of fervid and principled radicalism. Intellectually Mary supported the main liberal tenets of freedom of expression and equality of opportunity to which Shelley had been committed, and was to do so for the rest of her life, but emotionally, constitutionally, she valued social order and security and was impressed by social status. Like Byron she believed in God, although her intelligence meant she dismissed the cant and prejudice of much of religion. With Byron's death Mary felt overwhelmed by the sense of her tragic uniqueness; she alone survived from those golden days at Diodati. At twenty-six she felt as an old woman; no longer at home in life, her generation gone to the grave.

But summer was near and with Byron's death the past relinquished a little of its hold on Mary's spirit. Jane Williams had moved to Mortimer Terrace in rural Kentish Town for the sake of her health and Mary was to move at the end of June to 5 Bartholomew Place to be near her. After a happy day with Jane, walking through early summer fields and under spreading English trees, Mary felt her creative powers stirring at last. Her imagination, her 'Kubla Khan',[10] the special faculty in her life, had come to her rescue. She was off and away from the commonplace, the loneliness and poverty; she was writing again: '... the eclipse of winter is passing from my mind. I shall again feel the enthusiastic glow of conversation. Again, as I pour forth my soul upon paper, I feel the winged ideas arise, and enjoy the delight of expressing them.'[11]

Yet still she felt that lack of commitment to life and the future. At the end of a happy day with her own moon 'hung out in heaven'[12] she would still send her customary prayer, 'from the depth of my soul I make it – May I die young!'[13]

Friends were few and always important to Mary. Living close to her beloved Jane she saw her nearly every day, which was a pleasure which relieved her solitude. She realized with sadness that the intensity of love she felt for her was largely unrequited. All the passion, that she longed to be able to sink into an ideal relationship with another Shelley, she centred on Jane who was irritated and fettered by the force of Mary's feeling and by her implicit demands and possessiveness.

Now that she was vulnerable as an unattached woman, Mary was shy and afraid of men in sexual relationships. She had been insulated for ten years by her union with Shelley and having dedicated herself to him at sixteen had had little experience of coping alone in society. She therefore turned the blaze of her emotional needs on Jane, with whom she felt safe, with whom she held in common Italian memories, the summer tragedy and the subsequent hardship and loneliness, to whom she felt attracted and protective. Ten years later, when she knew herself better, she wrote, '[Then] I was so ready to give myself away, and being afraid of men, I was apt to get *tousy-mousy* for women.... I am now proof, as Hamlet says, both against man and woman.'[14] It was the neglect and abuse of both man and woman which cornered her in that defensive self-sufficiency.

When Mary had first come to England she had met an ailing young poet, Bryan Waller Proctor. He was kind to her, reminded her fleetingly of Shelley and was finely tuned and physically effete, a perfect candidate for Mary's love-starved heart. 'I have always a sneaking kindness for these delicately healthed Poets',[15] she admitted to the Hunts. As she grew older this susceptibility for young men of talent and her generosity towards them, giving freely of her affection and meagre finances, made her vulnerable to the unscrupulous. However, it also brought her a sense of being needed and loved. But with Proctor it was never remotely serious; it had been a nice romantic diversion during the winter months. Nevertheless, when in October 1824 she heard that he had married she felt inevitably rejected and despondent; 'so much for my powers of attraction'[16], she sulked.

Percy was the one constant male presence in her life and in an unspectacular way, despite her own fleeting disappointments at his lack of Shelleyan brilliance, he was faithfully and finally to bring her the happy family, the love and appreciation she had always craved.

But in the winter of 1824–5 he was a tall, ruddy-cheeked schoolboy of six, a sweet-tempered lad who played with Jane Williams's children, taking Dina as his wife. He amused and warmed Mary's heart with his childish chatter and curiosity for the world she felt she had long outgrown.

Mary was in the middle of writing her third novel, *The Last Man*, a particularly popular theme at the time. Mary's, the most ambitious, was set in the twenty-first century when England was a republic discomposed by the rumblings between republican and royalist factions.

The three main characters are particularly interesting in that they are clear portraits of Shelley (Adrian, son of the last and deceased king of England), Byron (Lord Raymond, becoming Lord Protector of England) and Mary herself (Lionel Verney, son of an old favourite of Adrian's father and eventually the Last Man). With Sir Timothy Shelley so touchy over any publicity surrounding his son's name, and with Mary's own reservations about attempting a veracious biography of Shelley, she set out deliberately in *The Last Man* to portray in fiction the Ariel face of Shelley:

> 'Adrian, the matchless brother of my soul, the sensitive and excellent Adrian, loving all, and beloved by all, yet seemed destined not to find the half of himself, which was to complete his happiness. He often left us, and wandered by himself in the woods, or sailed in his little skiff, his books his only companions ... his slender frame seemed overcharged with the weight of life, and his soul appeared rather to inhabit his body than unite with it.'[17]

In the more forcefully characterized Raymond, she expressed also her admiration and shrewd summing of Byron, her feelings made all the more poignant by his recent death; 'that strange & wondrous creature, whom one regrets dayly more – who here can equal him?'[18]

In *The Last Man* her affection and perceptive understanding of the poet made Raymond an interesting and complex character:

> '"I appear to have strength, power, victory; standing as a dome-supporting column stands; and I am – a reed! I have ambition, and that attains its aim; my nightly dreams are realised, my waking hopes fulfilled; a kingdom awaits my acceptance, my enemies are overthrown. But here," and he struck his heart with violence, "here is the rebel, here the stumbling-block; this over-ruling heart, which I may drain of its living blood; but, while one fluttering pulsation remains, I am its slave."'[19]

Raymond was in many ways her memorial to Byron.

Despite the biographical interest in the first volume, the story really gained power and momentum in the second and the third where the plague that inexorably advanced across the inhabited world drew from Mary some forceful passages and images evoking well the menace and decay. In an accumulative nightmare, the ravages of the plague destroyed everything of civilized life, penetrating to the heart of family and home. The survivors were not a unified band, but a miserable disparate crew who meekly accepted their fate. It could be argued that this was an expression of Mary's undoubted emotional conservatism, her instinctive fear of rapid and radical change. That she had written a parable of the dehumanizing threat of unchecked industrialization is possible, living as she did through the Industrial Revolution, well aware of the Cobbetts of the land who feared the ravages and neglect of the countryside, the destruction of the people. But more it was an expression of her own desolation of spirit and disillusionment with her fellows. During the time she was writing it Mary felt acutely isolated and alone, at times so out of place in London society, so much an alien, that surely she was the last relic of her beloved race. Deprived by death of those whom she had so loved, she was the Last Man, 'girded, walled in, vaulted over, by seven-fold barriers of loneliness'.[20]

Mary's story defied categorization. Full of horror, it nevertheless did not belong to the Gothic tradition. It in no way relied on supernatural agencies but rather was given substance and credence with its realism and domestic detail. Mary's imagination was always spun from experience, giving her writing an intensity of emotion that sliced through her inevitably prolix style. The unflinching and accumulative exploration in *The Last Man* of the utter desolation of civilization and of human life gave it something of the mesmerizing force of *Frankenstein*. It is as interesting as that first remarkable novel but lacks the basic originality of concept, its symbolic power and compactness of design.

19
Some Clever Men

> 'I know some clever men, in whose conversation I delight, but this is rare, like angels' visits. Alas! having lived by day with one of the wisest, best, and most affectionate of spirits, how void, bare, and drear is the scene of life!'
>
> Mary Shelley's journal

During the summer of 1824 Mary had made the acquaintance of two Americans, John Howard Payne, the actor-manager, and his clever literary friend, Washington Irving. She was attracted by Irving in whom she thought she recognized something of the genius of a Shelley. Thereafter her interest was only partially returned, but it was Payne, with more prosaic devotion, who proved a long-time friend and consolation.

Payne had immediately found Mary interesting and appealing and, sensing that he could easily fall in love with her, resolved to keep himself from her company. Their desultory correspondence since then led in the spring of 1825 to Payne's abandoning circumspection and meeting Mary again.

He did fall in love with her. 'You are perpetually in my presence, and if I close my eyes you are still there, and if I cross my arms over them and try to wave you away, still you will not be gone.'[1] Mary was flattered and mildly alarmed by his increasing ardour but liked him as a useful and good friend, diligent in providing opera and theatre tickets for her and Jane, and easy, attentive company for a night out. They inevitably discussed Washington Irving. Payne was effusive about his friend and Mary listened and daydreamed of her romanticized version of the man. She was encouraged in her intermittent fancies by Payne himself, who lent her Irving's letters and perpetuated the idealization of his friend, partly due to his own enthusiasm and wish to please and partly perhaps to enhance his own status in Mary's eyes.

In the midst of Payne's obvious courtship Mary wrote to the Hunts who were at last returning to England, '... the hope & consolation of my life is the society of Mrs W[illiams]. To her, for better or worse I am wedded – while she will have me & I continue in the love-lorn state that I have since I returned to this native country of yours....'[2] Her love-lorn state was an exaggeration, but to Leigh Hunt who had so hurtfully criticized her as Shelley's wife she would deny any opportunity to criticize her role as Shelley's widow. Despite what she implied to the Hunts, Mary's life was busy and certainly far from unhappy. She saw Jane Williams every day; she knew that her passion for Jane was not reciprocated but she was kind and warm and that seemed to suffice. Percy was at an interesting age; a cheerful, affectionate little boy who, by his existence and enthusiasm, forced her to live each day as it came. She allowed herself the occasional romantic fancy about Washington Irving, but in the real world she was gratified by Payne's earnest attentions and scarcely-contained affection. After three years in the desert, it was good to be cherished by a man, to be sexually desired once again. During 1825 and 1826 she seldom had to resort to the comfort of her journal which had become since Shelley's death a record of her most despairing days, interleaved with loneliness and stained with self-pitying tears. For the time being, life for Mary was too fleeting and full to allow time for any prolonged self-analysis and anguish. She only picked up her pen to put the finishing touches to *The Last Man* and to write numerous affectionate letters to her faithful hound, Payne.

However, when at the end of June 1825 Payne was moved to declare his passion for her, Mary with priggish honesty not only refused his offer of marriage but added that having been Shelley's wife she could only ever marry someone endowed with the rare quality of genius; perhaps someone like Washington Irving, she suggested archly. Payne was hurt and dispirited but his natural magnanimity prompted an extraordinary plan. He loved Mary but was obviously not good enough for her, whereas his great friend Irving most obviously was; to his troubled mind there appeared the perfect and simple answer. He would 'act the hero'[3] and be the agent to bring his two talented friends together in friendship, perhaps even love. Mary knew from Payne's letter that he intended to further what had been for her a purely vicarious relationship with Irving. The prospect appealed. 'As to friendship with him – it cannot be – though everything I hear &

know renders it more desirable – How can Irvine surrounded by fashion rank & splendid friendships pilot his pleasure barque from the gay press into this sober, sad, enshadowed nook?'[4] The sexual symbolism, subconscious as it almost certainly was, nevertheless revealed her covert longings for just such an invasion.

However, Mary would have been humiliated and angered if she had known that Payne intended to effect this navigation by bundling up copies of every one of her letters that he had kept and giving them to Irving to read. It was done with the best of motives. In his accompanying letter to his friend he explained that Mary 'was too much out of society' for Irving to have met her easily and made his own approaches of friendship to 'a woman of the highest and most amiable qualities'.[5] Mary would have been crippled with embarrassment to think that every hasty scrawl, every coquettish phrase and impulsive whimsy was to be coolly appraised by 'my favourite I', her dream lover, a virtual stranger.

Luckily for Mary she never did find out. Irving read the letters and chose not to pursue the matter. Her friendship with Payne continued warmly until he returned to America in 1832. By then the light of reality had seeped through to dispel her dreams of friendship, and possibly even marriage, with Washington Irving. This wishful thinking illustrated how certainly she was amenable to the possibility of remarriage, as long as her suitor had the necessary intellectual status. At this youthful stage of her life, she did not necessarily mean to stay Shelley's widow for ever.

Too soon summer was fading and autumn blew in on a broomstick. The leaves on the trees outside Mary's modest house were golden and then gone in a few days' flurry. She dreaded winter. The darkness closed in and Italy and those hazy, leisured days receded further into memory and dream. She nursed Percy through the measles. She discussed and planned with Jane a summer holiday to give the children fresh air and some fun at the seaside. Calais caught her imagination. She felt starved of travel and foreign faces, and Calais, ugly as it was, would give an impression of both.

The Last Man was published in February 1826 to unenthusiastic reviews. She had not put her name directly to the book but distinguished it with the implicit and promising 'by The Author of Frankenstein'. Nevertheless this did not protect her from the choler of her father-in-law, old Sir Timothy. The sight of his disreputable son's name being bandied about in unfavourable mention sent him rapping out orders to his solicitor Whitton to withdraw Mary's modest allowance.

Once again Peacock dutifully employed himself as Mary's negotiator and, after a battery of diplomatic letters, managed to get the decision reversed. But the whole episode emphasized to her how precarious were her finances, dependent on the whim of any unsympathetic old man, and how essential it was to make herself as self-sufficient as possible. Writing was her only means of earning a living and bringing a little more security to her own and Percy's future.

This was possibly one of the reasons why *The Last Man* was her last novel of any real merit. Her first three fictions exhibited to varying degrees a grandness of concept and imaginative power, a unity and effective characterization that her subsequent three novels merely glanced.

Doubtless she felt pressurized into writing popular fiction. The sales of her books were a critical influence on the security and freedom of her own and her son's immediate future. But when in September of 1826 Charles Shelley, Harriet's son, died tragically at the age of eleven, Percy as Shelley's sole surviving son became heir to the family estates. Sir Timothy was seventy-three and was not expected to last much beyond the coming year – in fact tenacious and obdurate as ever he lived on to a remarkable ninety-one – but Mary, along with other beneficiaries of Shelley's will, looked forward to an easier life in the not too distant future.

The decline in her creative powers was more clearly an expression of her own life's recession from the vivid days with Shelley. Then, although her life was distinguished more by its tragedy than its joy, she had been continually bombarded with stimuli, from the intensity and unpredictability of the Italian experience to the companionship and love of an inspired intellect such as Shelley's. She had been lucky enough to share the unique intellectual fireworks of speculation and debate in the long evenings at Byron's Villa Diodati. Her own abilities were less spectacular. However, acutely perceptive and unfailingly intelligent she sat in the shadows appraising, pondering and remembering. Her life with Shelley had had all the ingredients of high drama; a comic tragedy with extremes of fortune and bold, prodigious characters whose essences vitalized her early fiction.

She was now denied by death and distance such breadths of experience and inspiration. Her world had contracted to a sequestered corner of disenchanted London, and her spirit, her passions were slowly fading for want of impulse. Under pressure and ill at ease, writing from this barrenness, missing the critical encouragement of someone intimate and able, it was little wonder that Mary's creative efforts disintegrated.

However, a further and equally powerful reason was to be found in the nature of Mary's abilities. Her natural inclination and Godwin's influence ensured her a keenly academic approach to work. Widely read, she was a good and diligent researcher. And with her insight, her clarity of judgement and understanding of human needs and motives, she was steered more readily towards biography than fiction. Here her occasionally leaden touch and deficient sense of humour lay less ponderously.

Certainly biography attracted Mary and she managed it particularly well. *Valperga* was essentially biographical, as was, though less effectively, *Perkin Warbeck*. By 1826 she had written reminiscences of Lord Byron and later was to help Thomas Moore substantially with his biography of the poet. She had written notes on Shelley's life and after Godwin's death in 1836 she prepared herself to write his biography, making lucid and sympathetic notes on Mrs Gisborne and her own mother, amongst others.

But apart from familial biography, her breadth of interest and enterprise was illustrated by an impressive list of subjects for projected books that she offered to John Murray, the publisher. From the end of 1829 and into 1830 she suggested, amongst other wide-ranging subjects, 'a history of the Earth in its earlier state',[6] and a 'history of manners and literature of England from Queen Anne to the French Revolution, from Pope to H Walpole',[7] biographies of the Empress Josephine, Madame de Staël, Mahomet, the English Philosophers and Celebrated Women.

Although Murray did not immediately take up any of these suggestions Mary's abiding interest in Madame de Staël might have been instrumental in prompting her prestigious part as one of the biographers on Lardner's *Cabinet Cyclopaedia*, written and published during the 1830s.

It was a measure of her intellectual status at the time that she was commissioned to do so comprehensive and immense a task, alongside such distinguished writers as Sir Walter Scott, Sismondi and Thomas Moore. The only woman amongst the contributors, she was responsible for five volumes embracing French, Italian, Spanish and Portuguese lives, totalling more than half a million words.

She enjoyed writing the *Lives* and maintained an impressive standard of scholarship with few lapses into near-sightedness and sentimentality. Her finely-balanced prose covered a mileage that encompassed such diverse personalities as Machiavelli, Cervantes and Dante.

Mary had lost the extraordinary impulse of Shelley's presence. She could no longer converse with Byron and the band of expatriat eccentrics. She had moved on from the acute stimuli of such concentrated experience. Mary's new life was quieter, industrious, circumscribed and favoured her steadier qualities of intelligence and appraisal, which found happy and highly effective expression in such biography. Years later, in 1843, she wrote to the publisher Edward Moxon, 'Is it a novel or a romance you want? – I should prefer quieter work, to be gathered from other work – such as my lives for the Cyclopedia – & which I think I do *much* better than romancing.'[8]

The screw was turned on Mary's faltering spirit by the traumatic failure of her relationship with Jane Williams. Fate had united them arbitrarily with their mutual widowhood, memories and loss. Their dependent friendship should have ended after the recovery of each, as it would have done if it had been solely in Jane's hands. Although Mary's was the stronger personality, she became the dependent partner, emotionally bound to Jane by their past. Perhaps this domesticated, light-hearted woman, in becoming a confidante with an intimacy of shared experience that made it seem to Mary that they had known each other all their lives, assumed something of the emotional roles of mother, sister, lover. Whatever elements might have compounded the attraction, Mary invested a reservoir of love in her friend, knowing full well that her passion was recklessly bestowed.

Mary had always liked women. As a girl she had keenly felt the need of a mother, especially her own idealized and beatified brand. Isabel Baxter had been her first real friend but had failed her badly when she was most needed. Mary was always generous and loving towards Claire in her absence, although through bitter experience she had learned to eschew her presence. In Italy Mrs Gisborne was a motherly figure for whom Mary felt great affection and loyalty. Mary was kind and later immensely sympathetic to Teresa Guiccioli, Byron's most permanent mistress. Even to Emilia Viviani she had been free with her time, her books and appreciation, although the latter eventually wore a little thin.

In August 1826, on a month's holiday in Brighton with Percy, Jane and her children, Mary wrote a happy letter to the Hunts, explaining something of her feelings for Jane: 'I cannot express to you the extreme gratitude I feel towards this darling girl, for the power she has over me of influencing me to happiness.... She is in truth my all – my sole delight – the dear azure sky from which I – a sea of bitterness beneath – catch alien hues & shine reflecting her loveliness – This excessive feeling towards her has grown slowly, but is now a part of myself....'[9]

Despite the possessive ring in this expression of devotion, Mary had no intention of keeping her solely for herself. Ever since Jane had first returned to England with an introduction from Mary to Hogg, Hogg had been dogged in his attentions. Jane had encouraged him, loath as she was to put up with the deprivations of widowhood for long. Little did Mary guess but those deprivations for Jane lasted less than a year; she and Hogg had been engaged in a stealthy love affair since spring 1823. Mary did all she could to foster this apparently tentative relationship, although ever since her adolescent flirtation with Hogg all those years back she had felt an unease about him, fearing the coldness in his heart.

Given this generosity and her willingness to share Jane's love, something she had never been happy to do with Shelley, it is likely that her feelings for Jane owed less to sexual passion than to a deep affection and identification of experience, exaggerated by Mary's peculiarly solitary state and emotional intensity. As always she was vulnerable. At the end of the month's holiday in Brighton when her affection and gratitude towards Jane were running high, her fragile good spirits were crushed by Jane's cruel denigration: 'I have lived to hear her thank God that it is over ...',[10] she wrote pathetically in her journal. If she had learnt something of self-preservation, she would have donned her breastplate then and there, for the thrust at the heart was yet to come.

In the spring of 1827 Jane had finally gone to live with Hogg. Mary was delighted, hoping that it would bring happiness to both of them.

But Jane, away from Mary's daily influence, began to capitalize on her intimacy with the Shelleys at Spezia. She gossiped about the breakdown in Mary and Shelley's relationship, exaggerating conflicts and enhancing her own seductive role. Inevitably the tales got back to Mary.

The realization that someone she had loved so unreservedly could betray her was a cold stiletto in her heart. That Jane, in betraying her, defiled the past, destroying the most precious thing left to her, was almost too much to bear. It left a wound which never fully healed. Her memories and the distillation of her life with Shelley were profaned, her private life was held up to ridicule and censure, reviving her own deep-rooted remorse. Predictably constrained and solitary in suffering, she turned to her journal and only there spilt a drop of the bitterness that engulfed her: 'Not for worlds would I attempt to transfer the deathly blackness of my meditations to these pages. Let no trace remain save the deep bleeding wound of my lost heart, of such a tale of horror and despair ... what deadly cold flows through my veins; my head weighed down; my limbs sink under me. I start at every sound as the messenger of fresh misery....'[11] And Mary was just thirty years old.

Mary kept her feelings hidden from Jane. Imprisoned by the horror and shame of Jane's revelations, by her own sense of privacy and solitariness, Mary suffered that winter a form of mental breakdown which she explained briefly to Jane the following spring: 'When I first heard that you did not love me – every hope of my life deserted me – the depression I sunk under, and to which I am now a prey, undermines my health – how many hours this dreary winter, I have paced my solitary room driven nearly to madness, as I could not expell from my mind the memories of harrowing import that one after another intruded themselves....'[12]

Fortunately that autumn she left town on a visit to Arundel with Percy to stay with Isabel Robinson, for whom she felt an enthusiastic affection. Still shocked and wounded by Jane's treatment, Mary had decided that, although longing for love, she was destined rather to the less committed ties of friendship.

At the end of June she had met Tom Moore, the Irish songwriter and poet, who charmed her thoroughly. He had known Byron and had been entrusted with his *Memoirs*, the controversial manuscript that was ritually destroyed by John Murray, Byron's publisher.

Summer was Mary's best season, when she felt most reconciled to life and at ease with herself. Her characteristically warm enthusiasm for her friends had increased with her need of them. But unfortunately those easily kindled affections were less easily expressed. Her life-long self-consciousness and the circumspection that she was learning through disillusion and experience conspired in her frequently cool and remote manner. Occasional glimpses of the intensity of her emotional life disconcerted acquaintances and friends who would withdraw their whole-hearted support, suddenly uncertain as to the true nature of a woman whose social style was distinctive for its serenity, grace and understatement.

She was gradually learning to depress the high hopes and expectations of friends who had let her down so painfully in the past. But instinctively her heart flowed out to Moore. 'I never felt myself so perfectly at my ease with any one. I do not know why this is, he seems to understand and to like me.' Moore's talk of the Italian past delighted Mary, his language and his strange singing of wild Irish melodies intrigued her. With newly-acquired pragmatism she tried to content herself with the present – 'it is an evanescent pleasure, but I will enjoy it while I can',[13] – and all too soon he was gone. It was the beginning of a long and rewarding, if intermittent friendship.

By the beginning of 1828 Mary felt her relationship with Moore was secure enough to confide to him the corrosive secret of Jane's betrayal. He, too, had heard relations of that gossip and advised Mary to confront Jane with her discoveries. This she did only to have Jane promptly burst into tears and, full of contrition, beg not to lose her friendship. Mary ended up consoling her, but grimly reminding herself how Jane had heedlessly stained the past, 'taking the sweetness from memory and giving it instead a serpent's tooth'.[14] Her affection and sympathetic care for Jane through pregnancy and an unsatisfactory union with Hogg continued for years but the passion and trust were dispelled for ever.

In the midst of heartbreak over Jane and despair for the future Mary received an interesting letter from an extraordinary woman. Frances Wright was a vigorous and independent lady, enthusiastically committed to her own brand of Robert Owen's socialism. She had turned her reforming gaze towards the plight of the slaves in America and with admirable zeal had travelled to the United States and bought a plot of land on the Nashoba river in Tennessee as a settlement for freed slaves. Here she hoped to set up a community based on self-help, co-operation and freedom, intending the experiment to be a microcosm on which could be based a worldwide social reorganization.

She wrote to Mary as the daughter of the radicals Wollstonecraft and Godwin and as the wife of Shelley. As she pointed out, 'my active pursuits and engagements in distant countries' had denied her 'occasion to peruse your works'.[15] However resistible Mary might have found Fanny's brash reforming zeal, the warmth of the woman towards her, the intimations in those first letters that in losing one 'bosom intimate' she was in need of another: 'I do want one of my own sex to commune with, and sometimes to lean upon in all the confidence of equality of friendship',[16] roused Mary's affections.

When she finally met Fanny and learnt the details of the Nashoba colony, much burnished by her optimism, she knew that she and Fanny could be friends from afar but never comrades-in-arms. For Mary, to live alongside her in a rude log cabin in the woods, amongst wild black men, wilder animals and the vagaries of the elements, would be as spiritually destructive as bringing the Noble Savage into London society.

However much she loved to travel, Mary was never a woman of action. Her pursuits were intellectual, her pleasures domestic; individual relationships sustained and rewarded her, the large issues of political and social reform were not her platform. Although liberal in her sympathies, her clear-sighted veracity and insistence on weighing both sides of every question meant she would never make an effective proselytizer. She believed strongly in the importance of domestic happiness, affairs of the heart, and the delusion of personal ambitions outside that sphere. This theme was mainstream to all her novels, particularly coming to the fore in *Frankenstein*, *Valperga* and *Perkin Warbeck*: ' "This" I thought "Is power! Not to be strong of limb, hard of heart, ferocious and daring; but kind, compassionate and soft." ',[17] Verney declared in *The Last Man*. Added to this belief, her own timidity and obsession with the necessity for keeping her name and life from public gaze meant she would never willingly take a political stand. For this reluctance she suffered much criticism, particularly since she was so often judged, by those who did not know her well, in terms of her liberal parents and radical spouse. Stung to uncharacteristic retort, she committed to her journal an apologia for her political backwardness which, in its frequent and surprising forcefulness, belied something of the content of her justification. Nevertheless it is revealing and worth quoting:

> 'I am much of a self-examiner. Vanity is not my fault, I think; if it is, it is uncomfortable vanity, for I have none that teaches me to be satisfied with myself; far otherwise, – and, if I use the word disdain, it is that I think my qualities (such as they are) not appreciated from unworthy causes.
>
> 'In the first place, with regard to "the good cause" – the cause of the advancement of freedom and knowledge, of the rights of women, &c. – I am not a person of opinions. I have said elsewhere that human beings differ greatly in this. Some have a passion for reforming the world; others do not cling to particular opinions. That my parents and Shelley were of the former class, makes me respect it. I respect such when joined to real disinterestedness, toleration, and a clear understanding. My accusers, after such as these, appear to me mere drivellers. For myself, I earnestly desire the good and enlightenment of my fellow-creatures and see all, in the present course, tending to the same, and rejoice; but I am not for violent extremes, which only bring on an injurious reaction. I have never written a word in disfavour of liberalism; that I have not supported it openly in writing, arises from the following causes, as far as I know: –
>
> 'That I have not argumentative powers: I see things pretty clearly, but cannot demonstrate them. Besides, I feel the counter-arguments too strongly. I do not feel that I could say aught to support the cause efficiently; besides that, on some topics (especially with regard to my own sex), I am far from making up my mind. I believe we are sent here to educate ourselves, and that self-denial, and disappointment, and self-control, are a part of our education; that it is not by taking away all restraining law that our improvement is to be achieved; and, though many things need great amendment, I can by no means go so far as my friends would have me. When I feel that I can say what will benefit my fellow-creatures, I will speak: not before.
>
> 'Then, I recoil from the vulgar abuse of the inimical press. I do more than recoil: proud and sensitive, I act on the defensive – an inglorious position.

'To hang back, as I do, brings a penalty. I was nursed and fed with a love of glory. To be something great and good was the precept given me by my Father: Shelley reiterated it. Alone and poor, I could only be something by joining a party; and there was much in me – the woman's love of looking up, and being guided, and being willing to do anything if any one supported and brought me forward – which would have made me a good partisan. But Shelley died, and I was alone. My Father, from age and domestic circumstances, could not *"me faire valoir"*. My total friendlessness, my horror of pushing, and inability to put myself forward unless led, cherished and supported, – all this has sunk me in a state of loneliness no other human being ever before, I believe, endured – except Robinson Crusoe. How many tears and spasms of anguish this solitude has cost me, lies buried in my memory.

'If I had raved and ranted about what I did not understand; had I adopted a set of opinions, and propagated them with enthusiasm; had I been careless of attack, and eager for notoriety; then the party to which I belonged had gathered round me, and I had not been alone. But since I had lost Shelley I have no wish to ally myself to the Radicals – they are full of repulsion to me – violent without any sense of Justice – selfish in the extreme – talking without knowledge – rude, envious and insolent – I wish to have nothing to do with them.

'It has been the fashion with these same friends to accuse me of worldliness. There, indeed, in my own heart and conscience, I take a high ground. I may distrust my own judgement too much – be too indolent and too timid; but in conduct I am above merited blame.

'I like society; I believe all persons who have any talent (who are in good health) do. The soil that gives forth nothing, may lie ever fallow; but that which produces – however humble its product – needs cultivation, change of harvest, refreshing dews, and ripening sun. Books do much; but the living intercourse is the vital heat. Debarred from that, how have I pined and died!

'My early friends chose the position of enemies. When I first discovered that a trusted friend had acted falsely by me, I was nearly destroyed. My health was shaken. I remembered thinking, with a burst of agonizing tears, that I should prefer a bed of torture to the unutterable anguish a friend's falsehood engendered. There is no resentment; but the world can never be to me what it was before. Trust, and confidence, and the heart's sincere devotion, are gone.

'I sought at that time to make acquaintances – to divest my mind from this anguish. I got entangled in various ways through my ready sympathy and too eager heart; but I never crouched to society – never sought it unworthily. If I have never written to vindicate the rights of women, I have ever befriended women when oppressed. At every risk I have befriended and supported victims to the social system; but I make no boast, for in truth it is simple justice I perform; and so I am still reviled for being worldly.

'... Enough of this! The great work of life goes on. Death draws near. To be better after death than in life is one's hope and endeavour – to be so through self-schooling. If I write the above, it is that those who love me may hereafter know that I am not all to blame, nor merit the heavy accusations cast on me for not putting myself forward. I *cannot* do that; it is against my nature. As well cast me from a precipice and rail at me for not flying.'[18]

Mary's son was growing up. It was the spring of 1828 and Percy Florence was eight and a half, that tender age when sons of the nobility and gentry were expected to put aside warm domesticity and childish things. Little Percy's disenchantment came in the form of Mr Slater's school in Kensington. Mary had chosen carefully and hoped it would teach him well and treat him kindly. The school fees were £45 per annum and, with the extra incidentals like books and clothes, she feared she would not be able to manage on her meagre allowance. She wrote once again to the Shelley family's crabbed old solicitor, Whitton, and asked him to pass on to Sir Timothy her respectful request for a slight increase in funds. She had to wait increasingly anxiously for more than a year to have the £300 annuity confirmed.

Mary was usually short of money, sometimes afraid that she would be unable to meet her bills. But despite her financial worries she was always generous with any money she had to hand; her ageing and troubled father and Claire, now remote and overworked in Moscow, were helped out as often as possible. Possessions mattered very little to her. Money was only ever important in that it brought freedom from practical cares, security and the opportunity to travel. To Mary it seemed that foreign travel was life's silver lining, a prism for her imagination. For five years she had been confined, almost exclusively, to London; now in the spring of 1828 she received an invitation to join her friend Julia, the sister of Isabel Robinson, in Paris.

Percy was happy enough at school so she decided to go for a two-to-three-week holiday. Mary left London on 11 April. She felt surprisingly low-spirited and unwell, suffering throughout the journey, and regretfully taking to her bed the moment she arrived in Paris. Unbeknown to her she had contracted smallpox and Julia Robinson, who devotedly nursed her, at times feared for her life. Only when she was recovering was Mary told the nature of her illness. She would certainly have guessed, for her lifeless hair and pock-marked skin was evidence enough of the ravages of the disease.

Due in part to the attentions of Julia, Mary was restored to perfect health within three weeks but was still disfigured. Shy as she was and valuing her looks especially among strangers she nevertheless overcame her reticence and went into society. Her courage was amply rewarded with Gallic charm and genuine interest wherever she went. 'It was rather droll to play the part of an ugly person for the first time in my life, yet it was very amusing to be told – or rather not to be told but to find that my face was not all my fortune.'[19]

Amongst her interesting company in Paris was the young writer Prosper Mérimée who seemed to have been greatly impressed by Mary. 'What will you say also the imagination of one of the cleverest men in France; young and a poet, who could be interested in me inspite of the marks I wore',[20] she wrote in the same letter to Jane Williams. Mérimée had apparently been so carried away by Mary's charms that he wrote a letter in a rush of enthusiasm, possibly even proposing marriage, which elicited this sensible response from an older and wiser Mary: 'It is because I am not a coquette that I return your letter. I should not like to keep the expression of sentiments which you will probably repent of later.... You ask for my friendship – It is yours.... You will find in me a friend sympathetic – tender – true.'[21] She was certainly flattered and the general attention and kindness shown to her during her Parisian stay put her into the best of spirits.

The pock-marks were only temporary and she was advised to take up sea-bathing to hasten their going. Mary's hair was still sadly thin and dull and she had to keep it cut short to encourage the new growth. She spent the summer by the sea at Dover and then at Hastings, where Percy joined her. She had her father down to stay for a few days and then Joshua Robinson, Isabel and Julia's father. Trelawny had returned to England and was in town demanding her presence, but she was afraid of facing friends, and especially him, until she was looking more like her old self again.

Summer with its warmth, the long days and open skies, always kept her black dog of despair at bay. But in a sense she was merely treading water, all her energies spent in surviving, getting through each day, making do with compromises; 'I shut my eyes and enjoy – but a restless spirit stirring in my heart whispers to me that this is not life, & youth flies the while....'[22]

Undoubtedly to Mary love was life. The love of a man, preferably a great one, certainly comforting, protecting, exhilarating, was the greatest fulfilment that she had known. She attracted men with her gentleness and sweet nature. Her unusual looks had improved with age. She was highly cultured and interesting to talk to, an excellent and sympathetic listener, yet few acquaintances perceived the ravelled web of emotions that in private disquieted her. Robert Dale Owen, the famous socialist and Fanny Wright's friend, was one who recognized, beyond Mary's social grace and serenity, the lonely and unconfident woman within: 'In person she was of middle height and graceful figure. Her face, though not regularly beautiful, was comely and spiritual, of winning expression, and with a look of inborn refinement as well as culture. It had a touch of sadness when at rest. She impressed me as a person of warm social feelings, dependent for happiness on living encouragement, needing a guiding and sustaining hand.'[23] Whereas the idiosyncratic Lord Dillon, having asked Mary's opinion on a poem of his, confided to her that she puzzled him; from her writing she appeared just the sort of woman he liked, passionate, 'rather indiscreet, and even extravagant', but in person she was rather disappointing, 'cool, quiet, and feminine to the last degree – I mean in delicacy of manner and expression'.[24] To some extent Lord Dillon was misled, as many others, by that controlled, self-sacrificing public face. Mary could be intensely passionate about people and had been, and would be again, wildly indiscreet.

Trelawny knew Mary better. Although both were so different in temperament he was an important fixture in her life; the feelings between them always ran high, whether with love and admiration, or irritation and pique. Trelawny was Mary's last powerful link with the past. He was the only one left who in his bold and maverick ways, seeming too large for England and the orthodoxy for which she had settled, conjured once again memories of those distant vagabond days.

By the time he had returned on a fleeting visit to England in 1828 he was thirty-six. Grizzled with the long years fighting for Greek freedom with the guerilla commander Odysseus, wounded with him, surviving him, Trelawny was increasingly aware that his quixotic days were numbered. Age was leaving its mark, and, like Mary, he felt strangely at odds with the world, 'like an old patriarch who has outlived his generation'.[25]

His letters to Mary had ever been enthusiastic and forceful, and hers back, affectionate, full of news and encouragement. Trelawny's letter to her from Southampton, having arrived in England and finding the strictures of parochial society hard to bear, reverberated with his muzzled roar:

> 'I love you sincerely, no one better. Time has not quenched the fire of my nature; my feelings and passions burn fierce as ever, and will till they have consumed me. I wear the burnished livery of the sun.
>
> 'To whom am I a neighbour? and near whom? I dwell amongst tame and civilised human beings, with somewhat the same feeling as we may guess the lion feels when, torn from his native wilderness, he is tortured into domestic intercourse with what Shakespeare calls "forked animals", the most aborrent to his nature. You see by this how little my real nature is altered....'[26]

This outburst highlighted the disparity of their natures. Where Trelawny was feral, Mary was domesticated, civilized; it was amongst those very 'civilised human beings' and in 'domestic intercourse' that she was most happy. Although she was hardly parochial or prudish, and seldom censorious, she enjoyed companionship and society and needed to belong, albeit with the licence of being a minor literary celebrity with a scandalous past. She was always interested in people, sympathetic and tolerant of their problems and inadequacies, and eternally curious as to the motives and conflicts in their personalities and relationships.

Mary was never fully at ease in Trelawny's presence. He was restless and resentful of London life. He could be gloomy and temperamental too. Age's reckoning and increasing dissatisfaction with himself were beginning to affect his dashing and passionate spirit. He found fault with Mary and her friends, and was boorish and petulant at having to share her affections. He criticized Mary for valuing the friendship of such narrow and bigoted minds when she had loved and lived with the freest soul of all.

Mary felt this long-awaited visit destroyed a little more of their ease and intimacy with each other:

> 'Once you loved me sufficiently to confide in me – that time I know and feel to be gone – at least such was the case in the winter. You distorted my motives – did not understand my position, and altogether I lost in your eyes during your last visit – You were quite wrong – I never was more worthy of your love and esteem – but blind miserable beings thus we grope in the dark we depend on each other yet we are each a mystery to the other....'[27]

Claire, too, had come back to England during the end of the year of 1828 on a brief visit to Mary and her own family, now ensconced at 195 Strand and as troubled as ever by lack of money and a surfeit of work.

She had escaped the considerable trials of governessing in Russia and the tribulations of conserving her necessarily unblemished professional reputation against even a whisper of irregularity in her past relationships with Shelley and Byron. Still volatile in her emotions but more valiant in spirit, Claire, too, found her friends and family older and, to her eyes, set on a compromise course with life.

She had always been in awe of Mary's talents and her apparent composure but, like Trelawny, she was less admiring of Mary's complicity in a literary society which had cruelly neglected Shelley in his lifetime, and now diademed her with a cosy respectability that ill became the Shelley name. Neither did Percy escape the critical auntly gaze. He was the last surviving child of those Italian days whose dark force had claimed not only her own pathetic Alba but Mary's baby Clara and the beloved William too. Percy was also Shelley's only surviving son, linking his genius with the future; for these reasons alone he was to Claire a special child. But in addition, on the survival of this sturdy nine-year-old boy rested the hopes of many whose legacies under Shelley's generous will would be realized on the demise of the intractable old Sir Tim. Claire was particularly reliant on Shelley's £6,000 bequest to buy her freedom from a life of playing governess and nurse to spoiled children and companion to crotchety old maids.

At first she was disappointed with her nephew, expecting an immediate rapport, despite the fact that to Percy she was a stranger whose name belonged to the unknown past and to his mother's letters. However, she ended up liking the lad although there was little in him of the eccentric genius and waywardness that had characterized the youth of his father.

After her visit, she wrote rather tactlessly to Mary, 'When I first saw him [Percy] I thought him cold, but afterwards I discovered so much intellect in his speeches, and so much originality in his doings, that I willingly pardoned him for not being interested in anything but himself.'[28]

Claire's old friend Trelawny was also a bit of a disappointment. Turbulent, insubstantial relationships such as theirs more easily flourished with distance where infrequent letters were the only communication: consoling, affectionate, full of good intentions and vigour, but allowing romantic illusions and impractical hopes to grow unchecked by reality. In person, Claire, like Mary, found this handsome, restive man unsettling. In the same letter to Mary she explained why a permanent relationship with Trelawny was impossible:

'I admire, esteem and love him; some excellent qualities he possesses in a degree that is unsurpassed, but then it is exactly in another direction from my centre and my impetus. He likes a turbid and troubled life, I a quiet one; he is full of fine feelings and has no principles, I am full of fine principles but never had a feeling; he receives all his impressions through his heart, I through my head. *Que voulez-vous? Le moyen de se recontrer* when one is bound for the North Pole and the other for the South?'[29]

It was a poignant reunion for everyone. How sad it was to see friends, who had been in youth so full of promise, growing older, dissatisfied with themselves and thwarted by personal inadequacy and circumstance. Trelawny, never liking to admit the encroachments of age on his powers and personality, mocked Claire, with whom he had once been in love, for being so oldmaidish, although only thirty:

'... nothing gives me so much pleasure as your letters – I prefer them infinitely to oral communication – particularly as you are becoming so horribly prudish – and sister-like insensible.

'I consider you very fish-like – bloodless – and insensible – you are the counterpart of Werter – a sort of bread butter and worsted stockings – like Charlotte fit for "suckling fools and chronicling small beer." Adieu old Aunt.'[30]

Before the year was out Claire was back to her thankless work, this time in Germany as companion and maid.

Mary was busy researching and writing her third novel, *The Fortunes of Perkin Warbeck*. She had already been working on it for a year, diligently tracking down the best reference books, reading, sifting and collating her material. Set in the fifteenth century, like *Valperga*, it was a fiction based securely on fact. Perkin Warbeck, pretender to Henry VII's throne, was postulated by Mary to be in fact the legal heir to the throne, 'Richard IV'.

Again, *as in Valperga*, she depicts the conflict of worldly ambition. Having eventually discovered that all he needed was love, Warbeck nevertheless wearily continued with his ill-fated quest out of loyalty to his supporters. He was, of course, duly captured and executed. Although so well researched and with the advantage of a strong story line, Mary's telling was tedious and lack-lustre. Her characters lacked dimension and vitality. She did, however, include the requisite romantic hero, this time modelled on Trelawny in the swashbuckling guise of Herman de Faro, a Spanish sailor. Also, perhaps goaded by Trelawny's critical tongue during his last turbulent visit. Mary ended her novel with a long monologue from Katherine, Warbeck's widow, seeking to justify her courting of society. She explained that, although always faithful to her dead husband's memory, to survive she needed affection and the company of others:

'... human affections are the native, luxuriant growth of a heart whose weakness it is, too eagerly and too fondly, to seek objects on whom to expend its yearnings.... I quarrel not with – I admire – those who can be good and benevolent, and yet keep their hearts to themselves, the shrine of worship of God, a haven which no wind can enter. I am not one of these, and yet take no shame therefore: I feel my many weaknesses, and know that some of these form a part of my strength.... My reason, my sense of duty, my conscientious observance of its dictates you will set up as the better part; but I venerate also the freer impulses of our souls. My passions, my susceptible imagination, my faltering dependence on others, my clinging to the sense of joy – this makes an integral part of Katherine, nor the worst part of her.... I must love and be loved. I must feel that my dear chosen friends are happier through me. When I have wandered out of myself in my endeavour to shed pleasure around, I must again return laden with the gathered sweets on which I feed and live. Permit this to be, unblamed – permit a heart whose sufferings have been, and are, so many and so bitter, to reap what joy it can from the strong necessity it feels to be sympathised with – to love.'[31]

That was just as surely Mary, rather woodenly, justifying her own need for society and friends, however shrunken they might appear to her cantankerous and uncompromising old friend Trelawny, who lived for ever in Shelley's shadow.

The Fortunes of Perkin Warbeck was published in 1830 but was both a financial and to some extent a critical disappointment. As Percy was growing up and Mary was always short of money, her earnings from writing became an increasingly indispensable part of the family income. She maintained this income as best she could with short stories for periodicals, especially the *Keepsake*. In the main these stories were unexceptional but well-executed romances aimed directly and successfully at the growing market of bored and captive daughters of the increasingly literate middle classes. These young women liked undemanding reading as they whiled their time away, in waiting for marriage: a Charybdis for many, for in being sprung from parental bondage they too often found themselves in the life-long grip of husband as master, enforced domesticity, endless childbearing and an early grave. Mary's romances, with Byronic heroes, beautiful, noble heroines and true self-sacrificing love were for her readers an escape, an evasion of reality. Few were likely to live, as did Mary, a youth which approached the condensity and colour of her romantic fantasies.

20
Love's Sacrifice

> 'Do you mark my words; I have learned the language of despair....'
>
> *Mathilda*, Mary Shelley

Mary's friendship with Trelawny was more deeply fractured by her refusal to collaborate with him in an attempt to write a life of Shelley: 'Do you approve of this? Will you aid in it? Without which it cannot be done. Will you give documents? Will you write anecdotes? Or – be explicit on this, dear – give me your opinion; if you in the least dislike it, say so, and there is an end of it',[1] he wrote in March 1829. She did dislike the idea but in fact that was not the end of it.

Trelawny had felt that Mary would contribute even more invaluable information than she had done for Moore in his life of Byron. But Mary refused for reasons interpreted by Trelawny as personal reticence, false modesty and fear of upsetting the status quo:

> '... to be in print – the subject of *men's* observations – of the bitter hard world's commentaries, to be attacked or defended! – this ill becomes one who knows how little she possesses worthy to attract attention – and whose chief merit – if it be one – is a love of that privacy which no woman can emerge from without regret – Shelley's life must be written – I hope one day to do it myself, but it must not be published now ....'.[2]

was her reply to him.

Mary's horror of being once again the centre of controversy, of opening old sores in public, of thrusting her past life before her friends and enemies, to be gossiped about, her conduct and Shelley's upbraided or defended, was all reasonable enough and even reason enough for opposing a biography of Shelley at that time. But there were other considerations which just as surely reinforced that decision. Mary did in fact intend to write Shelley's biography herself, however daunting this prospect might seem and however impossible the truth. She was afraid of incurring Sir Timothy Shelley's displeasure, especially now that the old man was showing signs of interest in his grandson, visiting Percy occasionally at his school, but still resolutely refusing to see Mary. She also felt protective of Percy and did not wish to disturb his happy life at school with any of the speculation and aspersions that a biography might engender.

Mary was also justifiably uncertain of Trelawny's ability to do Shelley justice; although his instinct was unerring, he was untutored and at times unsubtle and lacking in insight. He had never tackled a book before and although she knew well enough from his letters what naturally vigorous language flowed from his pen, Mary might well have been suspicious of such an incorrigible romancer and mythmaker, who was to carry his hero-worship of Shelley to the grave. She could not have known how vividly and essentially he was to capture the quixotic, other-wordly, 'poetic' side of Shelley's character in his *Recollections of the Last Days of Shelley and Byron*, finally published after Mary's death in 1858.

At first Mary heard nothing from Trelawny in answer to her refusal. He did, however, vent some of his spleen on Claire. 'Mary has written me a letter which I have just received, – with a good deal of mawkish cant – as to her love of retirement – opinion of the world – and a deal of namby-pamby stuff – as different from her real character and sentiments as Hell is from Helicon.'[3]

Although frustrated for the time being in his wish to write Shelley's life, Trelawny embarked vigorously on writing his own life. Finally on 20 October he raised the matter of the Shelley biography with Mary who had been anxiously awaiting a letter: 'I am anything but satisfied with your reply to my request – regarding Shelley – and I must say your reasons for not doing so – are most unsatisfactory – mere evasion – had Shelley's *detractor* and your very good *friend* Tom Moore – made the request, I feel confident he would not have been so fobbed off. . . .'[4] The prospect of losing Trelawny's friendship chilled Mary. She wrote back addressing him, 'My very dear Trelawney ... my spirits are depressed by care and I have no resource save in what sunshine my friends afford me – afford me you a little, Dearest friend – seal up words sweeter than vernal breezes – flatteries if you will – warm tokens of kindliness – I need them – I have been so long accustomed to turn to you as the spot whence distant, but certain good must emanate that a chill from you is indeed painful....'[5] She herself was a generous friend to anyone in need, writing affectionate, cheering letters to Trelawny, Leigh Hunt, Claire, all her friends when they were down-hearted. She could not bear to feel that Trelawny would not console her in turn.

It was nearly Christmas 1829. Mary was now living in lodgings at 33 Somerset Street, off Portman Square, with the grass and trees of Hyde Park just a short walk to the south. London was then a far larger and more pleasant place in which to live than when she had been a child growing up in the cramped, noisy quarters at Skinner Street. Streets were cleaner, wider, lighter. They were grander, too, with John Nash's theatrical terraces adding symmetry and sublimity to the London skyline. Slums still existed in the sprawling overcrowded alleys and courtyards of the city and East End. But even here wooden shacks and rickety tenements were being razed to make way for more substantial brick-built houses. The Paving and Improvement Acts were slowly being enforced and drained roads, paved and illuminated, gradually pushed their civic orderliness into the obscurity of dockland and the rookeries of St Giles.

Mary was living through a period of rapid social change, the effects of which disquieted her as they did most thinking people. Industrialization had become a Frankenstein's monster grown too powerful, its effects so widespread and inexorable that mere men, their livelihoods and lives were being sacrificed to the machine. The industrial oligarchy reaped the riches while poverty and hardship yoked the factory workers in their urban ghettos and hit hardest the country labourers, dispossessed of their land and livelihood. There was increasing economic and social unrest with Europe on the verge of revolution. In England this took the form of a mass movement of labouring poor, supported in part by middle-class radicals, demanding, amongst other things, reform of the out-dated and ludicrous electoral system. Conservatism was being forced to yield in the face of overwhelming public opinion to a more liberal, popular government. The old King George IV was sinking while the great age of the railway was gloriously dawning. There was a sense of impermanence and insecurity, everything was in flux. Although ever liberal in her sympathies and whole-hearted in her disavowal of oppression and injustice, Mary's personally beleaguered state exaggerated her emotional conservatism. Alone and insecure she feared the overthrow of the old order, she feared the nightmare of chaos and disunity prophesied so tellingly in *The Last Man*. In her blackest hours Mary's thoughts seemed to be yet again portentous of tragedy. 'How dark – how very dark the future seems – I shrink in fear from the mere imagination of coming time',[6] she confided to her journal.

To Trelawny, in the agitated letter of justification quoted earlier, her apprehension was more specific and less dramatic:

'... while fog and ennui possesses London, despair and convulsion reign over the country – some change some terrible event is expected – rents falling – money not to be got – every one poor and fearful – Will any thing come of it – Was not the panic and poverty of past years as great – Yet if Parliament meet as they say it will in January – something is feared – something about to be done – besides fishing in Virginia Water and driving about in a pony phaeton.'[7]

Mary survived the dread winter quite well. Her social life expanded modestly with her courage in organizing her own soirée repaid with a successful party. Percy flourished. As he grew older he became an increasingly good friend to his mother. News of the July revolution in France and the overthrow of the Bourbons crossed the Channel disseminating excitement and disquietude.

The breach with Trelawny was spanned by his need for a good agent in London to see his autobiography through publication. He could not have picked a better person than Mary and he knew it; she was immensely conscientious in everything she undertook for her friends and was to show her mettle on Trelawny's behalf. By the end of the year 1830 she had the manuscript in her hands and had read it with care and discrimination. She thought it 'full of passion, energy and novelty',[8] but jibbed at a certain coarseness of phraseology and violence of incident. Book publishing was in a parlous state. The unrest, the riotings, the scarcity of ready money meant that most firms had to publish books with as wide a popular appeal as possible. Mary bravely and forthrightly pointed out to Trelawny that in wishing to be published he would have to bow to current taste in the few instances she outlined. Coarseness was 'now wholly out of date',[9] she firmly pronounced.

Sure enough Trelawny promptly replied with a list of eminent men and women who had read his life and offered no such squeamish criticism. 'My life, though I have sent it to you, as the dearest friend I have, is not written for the amusement of women; it is not a novel.'[10]

Mary might well have been his dearest friend, but she was also his most honest and attentive. Colburn, the publisher chosen by her as the most likely bet, objected to much the same passages and expressions, but Trelawny had decreed that Horace Smith was to be the one to decide what had to be expunged.

Mary ended her detailed business letter to Trelawny with some news of mutual friends who married, adding a little self-reflecting badinage:

'If Clare and I were either to die or marry, you would be left without a Dulcinea at all, with the exception of the sixscore new objects for idolatory you may have found among the pretty girls in Florence. Take courage, however, I am scarcely a Dulcinea, being your friend and not the Lady of your love, but such as I am, I do not think that I shall either die or marry this year, whatever may happen the next; as it is only spring you have some time before you.'[11]

This provoked Trelawny's teasing suggestion of marriage which was gratifying to Mary, although she realized it was mere banter.

'Do not you, dear Mary, abandon me by following the evil examples of my other ladies. I should not wonder if fate, without our choice, united us; and who can control his fate? I blindly follow his decrees, dear Mary.'[12] Mary's light-hearted refusal came bouncing back, her daring typically withdrawn with a hasty parry: 'You tell me not to marry, – but I will, – any one who will take me out of my present desolate and uncomfortable position. Any one, – and with all this do you think that I shall marry? Never, – neither you nor anybody else. Mary Shelley shall be written on my tomb, – and why? I cannot tell, except that it is so pretty a name that though I were to preach to myself for years, I never should have the heart to get rid of it.'[13]

Trelawny bowed out with a parting shot, 'I was more delighted with your resolve not to change your name than with any other portion of your letter. Trelawny, too, is a good name, and sounds as well as Shelley; it fills the mouth as well and will as soon raise a spirit.'[14] This earned him a rapid riposte from Mary, cutting clean through the raillery to the heart of the matter: 'My name will *never* be Trelawny. I am not so young as I was when you first knew me, but I am as proud. I must have the entire affection, devotion, and, above all, the solicitous protection of any one who would win me. You belong to womenkind in general, and Mary Shelley will *never* be yours.'[15]

And there ended the Trelawny proposal incident. Although never really a serious proposal of marriage, it was interesting in that it showed how Mary, in her idealistic moments, felt that a wholehearted relationship with the right exceptional man might solve her financial and social problems and, most of all, the emotional deprivation that oppressed her. She had certainly fathomed Trelawny. She knew he would never be the sort of man she needed. She longed for someone to look up to, to lean on, a comfort and protector. She also felt drawn to young men of talent who needed her patronage and help. Crusty old Trelawny fitted neither of these comfortable roles; she would lean and find him gone, extend a helping hand only to have it bitten.

Nevertheless she had done her best for his book. It was being printed. Trelawny's title, *A Man's Life*, had been categorically rejected by his publishers and it fell to Mary to find a new one quickly. *Adventures of a Younger Son* was what she chose although, predictably, it did not please the awkward younger son himself.

Other friends, both Mr and Mrs Gisborne, her father and Claire, did not hesitate to make use of her literary connections and generosity; Claire with a short story seeking publication and Godwin for help negotiating with publishers, supplying money and the occasional idea for a book. Trelawney, never one to be grateful for unspectacular sacrifices in friendship, did not think to thank Mary for her labours. Rather did he complain to Claire at how much money the publisher was making out of his book, all because certain authors undervalue every work but their own. He proceeded to billet his elder daughter, Julia, on Mary during the trying summer of 1832.

Percy had reached twelve years old and Mary wanted to send him to a public school in keeping with Shelley's wishes and her own desire to give him a good start in life. Shelley's old school, Eton, was vetoed by the family so Mary chose Harrow, Byron's school, then enjoying a good reputation and having no great tradition of fagging, the bane of Shelley's school days and considered by Mary to be the greatest evil of the public school system.

She was already in straitened circumstances and she spent a very anxious few months trying to negotiate with Sir Timothy, through Whitton and then his successor, John Gregson, for a small loan to tide her over, followed eventually by a permanent increase in her allowance, all of which was due to be paid back to the estate on realization of Shelley's will. The frustrations and perturbation in having to communicate by proxy, waiting for letters which never came, fearing a refusal, dreading the consequences as her debts mounted however frugally she lived, all compounded Mary's anxiety; for to whom could she turn for money? John Gregson was in fact a more benign influence on Sir Timothy than his dour predecessor and he did much to ease something of Mary's burden. An increase in her allowance to £400 was finally agreed to by the old man and Percy was due to start at Harrow in the autumn term.

That summer the dreaded cholera crossed the channel and entered the noisome heart of London. Claire, at a distance, was shaken with terrible forebodings. The juxtaposition of the year – 1832 was the tenth anniversary of Shelley's death – with Harrow – Allegra was buried in the churchyard there – and the outbreak of cholera was enough to raise an hysterical fear in her heart for everyone, not least Percy, the heir in whom so much material relief ultimately resided.

Mary was less concerned. With the commencement of Percy's holidays she did remove him first to Southend and then to Sandgate. There Trelawny and his daughter joined her, although she found Julia wildly gay and silly and Trelawny gloomy and opinionated. Safe from the cholera themselves, it was a shock to hear that William Godwin, her half-brother, had succumbed to the disease and died. This was a heavy blow to Godwin, although while William had lived he had burdened the lad with his didactic expectations and evident disapproval. Mrs Godwin suffered cruelly the loss of her youngest child. Mary for once was not the victim of arbitrary tragedy.

Percy delighted her more and more. He learnt to swim, he grew ruddy-cheeked and fair-haired. Mary had relaxed into accepting him as he was and, in appreciating his affectionate easy-going nature instead of mourning his lack of genius, she was constantly surprised by his perceptive intelligence and humour. He was to become increasingly the light of her life and although at times she was fearful that, in investing so much love and hope in him, she was courting disappointment and rejection, Percy never once let her down.

However, the expense of his education at Harrow alarmed her. She had to apply to Sir Timothy for help in paying the first term's bill of £75. Mary determined at once that in order to maintain him at a school both he and she liked she had to move to Harrow so that Percy could become a day boy. This removal to such a 'dull inhospitable place'[16] away from her hard-won friends and acquaintances was a sacrifice, but one she willingly made in order to keep her son's life tranquil and happy. She felt particularly sad at leaving her old father who was nearly eighty.

In April 1833 she made the move. Everything cost much more than she had estimated and once again caused her anguished anxieties over her bills and how she was going to live in the coming months. Poverty was her prison. It prevented her travelling to London to see friends and console her father, it immured her in solitariness, reduced to shabby lodgings without the wherewithal to furnish them comfortably. Her son and her work were her only entertainment and consolation. 'I live in a silence and loneliness – not possible any where except in England where people are so *islanded* individually in habits – I often languish for sympathy – and pine for social festivity.'[17]

Mary was nearing the end of her novel *Lodore*, parts of which were strongly autobiographical. She was anxious as to its fate, for both her and her father's financial ease rested on the success of this latest literary offering. It had little merit, was weak and rambling in plot, with Lodore once again based firmly on Byron, but it was to be a considerable popular success. She worked with much greater pleasure and enthusiasm on her *Lives* for Lardner's *Cabinet Cyclopaedia* which were to occupy her throughout her exile at Harrow. The pattern of her solitary but productive days was recorded in her journal:

> 'Routine occupation is the medicine of my mind. I write the "Lives" in the morning. I read novels and memoirs of an evening – such is the variety of my days and time flies so swift, that days form weeks and weeks form months before I am aware ... my heart and soul is bound up in Percy. My race is run. I hope absolutely nothing except that when he shall be older and I a little richer to leave a solitude, very unnatural to anyone and peculiarly disagreeable to me....'[18]

Godwin had been awarded a minor government post by Lord Grey which entitled him to a small income and lodgings in New Palace Yard. Despite the much-needed security it was a sad comedown for the old rebel who had so denounced and worried governments in the past. Her much-beloved friend, Maria Gisborne, was ill at her home in Devon and Mary, unable to afford the fare to see her, wrote her long affectionate letters, sometimes slipping into the old lament of loneliness and despair. For days, even weeks, she saw no one, spoke to no one from Percy's early morning departure until his return at evening. Mary became so confined in solitude that at one time she was unable to go beyond the gate by herself without unbearable agitation. The twilight of mental illness was warded off by her own resilience, her pleasure in and application to her work and the rewards of Percy's sunny disposition.

However, she was more often ill. When she first moved to Harrow she had succumbed to influenza, the debilitating effects of which lingered for three months. Holidays away by the sea or in London revived her. Then in the summer of 1835 she suffered a further prolonged illness. She was cared for by Jane Williams Hogg and even Mrs Godwin came to her aid. The kindness of both these women when she most needed their help and affection was an important contribution to her recovery. But she had to earn her living and, weak and confined to her sofa, she drove herself to work on with her second volume of the Italian *Lives*.

Mary decided to leave Harrow in the Easter of 1836. She had done her bit for Percy's public education and now felt it would help him more, and relieve her infinitely, if he had a tutor for his final year before going up to university.

Lodore's success brought financial benefit as well as a request for another novel. Claire, who since Allegra's death had nursed an obsessive hatred for Byron, burst out against yet another Byronic characterization:

> 'Good God! to think a person of your genius, whose moral tact ought to be proportionately exalted, should think it a task befitting its powers to gild and embellish and pass off as beautiful what was the merest compound of vanity, folly, and every miserable weakness that ever met together in one human being. As I do not want to be severe on the poor man, because he is dead and can-

not defend himself, I have only taken the lighter defects of his character....'[19]

Poor Claire, as she grew older and more cantankerous her fantasies of Byron as evil genius grew to such absurd proportions that Trelawny, who had never really liked the man, was moved to blurt out when Claire was nearly eighty: 'Your relentless vindictiveness against Byron is not tolerated by any religion that I know of.'[20]

Apart from the request for another novel Mary had been offered £600 by Edward Moxon for an edition of Shelley's works with his life and notes written by her. An orthodox biography, as long as Sir Timothy was alive, was out of the question, but she began to collect letters and other writings together, which painful and arduous labour was to result in her edition of the *Poetical Works* published in 1839 and followed the next year by his collected prose.

But she had more immediate problems. Her old and dear friends. Maria and John Gisborne died in 1836 in rapid succession. Maria had been in many ways a mother-figure to Mary, warm and generous with her affections, sensible in her advice. Mary's indomitable old father, too, died in the spring of 1836. He was eighty. Mary and Mrs Godwin, once sworn enemies, nursed him together through his short illness. Both were present at his peaceful death. Mary was exhausted from her night vigils but accepted his death with equanimity.

Godwin had requested in his will that his remains be buried 'as near as may be, to those of the author of *A Vindication of the Rights of Woman*'.[21] In a quiet simple ceremony Mary's father was buried beside her mother, under the tombstone where she and Shelley had first declared their love.

Godwin had been to Mary as a child and young woman an object of intense passion and admiration. Remarkably her loyalty and love for him survived his emotional abandonment of her and his insensitive and persistent worrying of Shelley for money. Even in the financial hardship and loneliness of her widowhood, Godwin expected what spare money she could offer. But he had mellowed with age and Mary's passion, too, had settled into a more realistic concern and affection. His death was not the fateful blow that it would have been fifteen years previously. Her forty long years marked by wild extremes of fortune, and appreciation of her own beloved son, were teaching her slowly to expect less of life, to enjoy more serenely its everyday pleasures and be less dispirited by adversity.

With her usual willingness and generosity she set about petitioning the government for a small pension for Godwin's widow. Mrs Godwin had worked hard all her life and, although she and Mary could never be sympathetic friends, age and suffering had brought to both greater tolerance and understanding.

Mary was struggling, too, with her last novel, *Falkner*, her pen driven more by necessity than inspiration. Better constructed and more enjoyable reading than *Lodore*, it was still an unambitious and unimportant work. Once again its theme was Mary's own song: the essential futility of worldly ambition; the absolute value of love. However, with her penchant for Byronic heroes, and aware of the truth of Claire's criticisms, she made Falkner a wandering adventurer whose childhood bore close resemblance to Trelawny's harsh upbringing, as described in his *Adventures of a Younger Son*.

Trelawny, of course, was delighted and keen to propagate the merits of the book. He wrote to Claire for support:

> 'Assist me!! Lend me your hand!!! don't fob me off with excuses of its weakness, its engagements – an iron will can force a way anywhere. I must get written or write myself a review of Mary's new work – will you do it – or failing in that will you write me one of your long flighty fanciful beautiful letters commentating on the peculiarities – and individuality of the Godwin School in which Mary is saturated with the admixture of a little of Shelley's bland and softening balm – penetrating and making the hair grow?'[22]

But Trelawnyesque buccaneers and Byronic heroes had had their heyday. In the year of *Falkner*'s publication, 1837, Queen Victoria began her influential reign and with her star rose a young man's, Charles Dickens, whose serialized *Pickwick Papers* and *Oliver Twist* burst upon the reading public with vigorous reality and humour, bold characters and grim social commentary. The retreat from Romanticism had been sounded.

Further literary burdens fell on Mary's shoulders. She certainly felt duty-bound to attempt a biography of her father, 'whose passion was posthumous fame'.[23] Trelawny, with the years and his own growing discontent, was becoming more truculent and critical of Mary's need of and pleasure in society, of her self-protective compromises. He was never slow to judge and criticize, he had scorned Mary's friends the Robinsons and the Hares and now upbraided her for tardiness in immortalizing Godwin, for lack of muscle in the Liberal Cause.

It was spring 1837 and Mary had chosen to put her father's life by until she had managed to get Percy into university. She feared most 'further delapidation on his ruined prospects ... when a cry was raised against his Mother – and that not on the question of *politics* but *religion*....' Trelawny's aggressive letter had caught Mary in a vulnerable state. 'I am obliged to guard against low spirits as my worst disease – and I do guard – and usually I am not in low spirits – Why then do you awaken me to thought and suffering by forcing me to explain the motives of my conduct – could you not trust that I thought anxiously – decided carefully – and from disinterested motives – not to save myself but my child from evil....' Not only was her reply a painful justification of her conduct, it was also an attack on the double standards of a society which could not really accept her, yet lionized Trelawny whose youth had been as as irregular as Mary's own. Her bitterness was barbed with truth: 'You may pick and choose those from whom you deign to receive kindness – You are a man at a feast – champagne and comfits your diet – and you naturally scoff at me and my dry crust in a corner – often you have scoffed and sneered at all the aliment of kindness or society that fate has afforded me – I have been silent – the hungry cannot be dainty – but it is useless to tell a pampered man this....'[24]

Mary's other literary labour was one she did not neglect, 'my most sacred duty',[25] though at times the effort and the emotional stress seemed too much to bear. She had been gathering and copying out Shelley's poems, together with his descriptive letters, essays and other prose fragments for the edition of his poetry and the separate one of his prose. This task brought many difficulties. She had to find first editions of his published poems to send to the printer; those she owned were too precious, inscribed and thumbed as they were, every well-read page imprinted with unique associations. The remaining unpublished material had to be pieced together largely from scrawled pages, crossed and re-crossed, blotted and blurred; '... the wonder would be how any eyes or patience were capable of extracting it from so confused a mass, interlined and broken into fragments, so that the sense could only be deciphered and joined by guesses, which might seem rather intuitive than founded on reasoning.'[26] Mary felt the burden of bringing Shelley before a generally unsympathetic and uninterested public. She laboured alone, all decisions rested on her. To help resolve her dilemma as to whether to omit the 'atheistical' sections, as requested by Moxon the publisher, she asked the advice of Hunt, Hogg and Peacock, all of whom offered no objection. She also left out *Queen Mab*'s dedication to Harriet because Shelley had expressed approval when a pirated version had done just that, but regretting all the while the mutilation.

Reading the poems and writing her explanatory biographical notes was physically and emotionally exhausting. The emotions and incidents which crowded her extraordinary years with Shelley claimed her once again. 'Every impression is as clear as if stamped yesterday',[27] she wrote in her preface. Mary's memory was always excellent and in her solitary labours she suffered once more the agony of regret for what had been lost and remorse at her own and others' obtusity, inadequacies and omissions: 'I am torn to pieces by memory.'[28]

This labour of suffering love sapped her energy until, declined in spirits and health, she was forced to admit to a kind of defeat: 'Days of great suffering have followed any attempts to write, and these again produced a weakness and langour that spread their sinister influence over these notes. I dislike speaking of myself, but cannot help apologising to the dead, and to the public, for not having executed in the manner I desired the history I engaged to give of Shelley's writings.'[29]

Despite all these problems and overlooking certain inaccuracies, her notes to the *Poetical Works* were compassionate and perceptive, genuinely elucidative of some of the historical and spiritual sources for much of Shelley's writing. Idiosyncratic, and surprisingly free of sentimentality, they implicitly reflected the generous and intelligent woman who had lived in Shelley's shadow during his life and after his death had toiled to bring his genius before the world.

Volume one was published in January 1839 and Mary was rewarded with a broadside of criticism for her omission in *Queen Mab*, from the press and from Hogg, and Trelawny who promptly sent his copy back to Moxon in a rage.

'How very much he must enjoy the opportunity thus afforded him of doing a rude and insolent act! It was *almost* worth while to make the omission, if only to give him this pleasure',[30] she wrote in her journal. But she was aware of having made the wrong decision over *Queen Mab* and wrote to Moxon to ask if the omitted verses could be reinstated. As she pointed out to her friends, poems like *Epipsychidion*, which were far more personally damaging, she had included without hesitation.

Mary's mammoth task was completed with the publication in 1839 (dated 1840) of Shelley's prose with notes, under the title *Essays, Letters from Abroad, Translations and Fragments*.

With that duty done, Mary's days grew brighter and more peaceful. Her son, Percy, had just celebrated his twentieth birthday when she wrote in her Journal, at last learning to replace melancholic contemplation of the past with the substantial virtues of the present: 'A hope gleams through the clouds of my life – will it break forth into sunshine? Never! I do wrong to write thus. With Percy I enjoy perpetual sunshine – and he spreads a warm glow over my life that, when not ill, penetrates every portion of it.'[31]

Percy Florence had not had an easy youth. He had had to endure alone his mother's concentrated company, he had been the butt for much of her depression and despair and he had suffered too the constant and deprecatory comparisons with the sanctified genius of his father. Crabb Robinson's attitude to the young man probably echoed the thoughts, at least, of most of those who had known Shelley: 'A loutish-looking boy, quite unworthy of his intellectual ancestors in appearance. If talent descended, what ought not to be the issue of Mrs Wollstonecraft, Godwin, Shelley, and Mrs Shelley!'[32]

Yet Percy obstinately remained himself, facing his mother and the world with good nature and generosity. It is of the greatest credit to Mary's mothering and to Percy himself that, despite the extraordinary disadvantages of being Shelley's sole surviving son, separated from him by the impenetrable barriers of death and genius, he nevertheless grew up to excel in a pursuit quite removed from his father's – by living a good, long and happy life.

21
Counting the Blessings

'... though I no longer soar, I repose. Though I no longer deem all things attainable, I enjoy what is, and while I feel that whatever I have lost of youth and hope, I have acquired the enduring affection of a noble heart....'

Mary Shelley's journal

With the new year 1840, Mary's life began at last to expand and brighten into a more benign middle age. Her successful editions of Shelley's works meant that for the first time in her life she did not have to worry herself over money.

Percy was at Trinity College, Cambridge, due to take his finals in the following January. He and two friends had decided to spend their long summer vacation by the shores of Lake Como and, much to Mary's delight, had asked her to go too. That three young men should desire her company she considered as the greatest compliment. With a little more money at her disposal she could now reward herself with travel, a prescription which had always lifted her spirits and restored her powers.

They were due to leave in mid-June. Meanwhile Mary was spending a few weeks at Brighton where she recorded a rare tranquillity in her journal, so often a history of pain, misery and blighted hopes:

'I must mark this evening, tired as I am, for it is among few – soothing and balmy. Long oppressed by care, disappointment, and ill health, which all combined to depress and irritate me, I felt almost to have lost the spring of happy reverie. On such a night it returns – the calm sea, the soft breeze, the silver bow new bent in the western heaven – nature in her sweetest mood, raised one's thoughts to God and imparted peace.

'Indeed, I have many, many blessings, and ought to be grateful, as I am, though the poison lurks among them; for it is my strange fate that all my friends are sufferers – ill health or adversity bears heavily on them, and I can do little good, and lately ill health and extreme depression have even marred the little I could do. If I could restore health, administer balm to the wounded heart, and banish care from those I love, I were in myself happy, while I am loved and Percy continues the blessing that he is. Still, who on such a night must not feel the weight of sorrow lessened? For myself, I repose in gentle and grateful reverie, and hope for others. I am content for myself. Years have – how much! – cooled the ardent and swift spirit that such hours bore me freely along. Yet, though I no longer soar, I repose. Though I no longer deem all things attainable, I enjoy what is, and while I feel that whatever I have lost of youth and hope, I have acquired the enduring affection of a noble heart, and Percy shows such excellent dispositions that I feel that I am much the gainer in life.'[1]

This was an appropriate creed for the remaining years of Mary's life. There were fewer vicissitudes, greater equanimity and no longer a necessity to write to live. Her continued caring for friends and family and contentment with her lot gave her the inner serenity that her pacific expression for so long had misleadingly implied.

She and Percy set off for Paris. Mary, remembering her dreadful seasickness as a young woman, feared the same prostration but in fact managed the passage very well. They then met up with Percy's two undergraduate friends and travelled by diligence down through France, along the Moselle into Germany, from there up the Rhine through Switzerland and on to Lake Como. Here at Cadenabbia they stayed for nearly two months. Mary was delighted to be once again speaking Italian in a country that she loved and considered her spiritual home. The scent of the air, the peculiar light, the sounds and its people, 'dear, courteous, lying, kind inhabitants',[2] were poignantly familiar. But in Mary's present mood, elated by travel and variety, the memories were happy ones.

Percy immediately found the local boat-builder and ordered a sailing skiff for excursions on the lake. Shelley's sea tragedy, never far from her mind, was brought into the present by the sight of his son's pleasure in this fragile boat and in afternoons spent tacking to and fro across the fickle waters. Mary realized she had to silence her fears and admonitions, but nevertheless found herself too often gazing out across the lake to catch a sight of the flickering flag of Percy's sail dipping and skimming in the distance.

Too soon it was September and they had to return to England. Mary, having stayed behind in Milan for over a fortnight awaiting the arrival of a letter containing money, returned via the lake of Geneva which, on the dull, chilly day she crossed it, raised irresistible memories of the idyllic summer with Shelley and William and the late-night speculations with Byron at the Villa Diodati:

> 'At length, I caught a glimpse of the scenes among which I had lived, when first I stepped out from childhood into life. There, on the shores of Bellerive, stood Diodati; and our humble dwelling, Maison Chapuis, nestled close to the lake below. There were the terraces, the vineyards, the upward path threading them, the little port where our boat lay moored; I could mark and recognise a thousand slight peculiarities, familiar objects then – forgotten since – now replete with recollections and associations. Was I the same person who had lived there, the companion of the dead? For all were gone: even my young child, whom I had looked upon as the joy of future years, had died in infancy – not one hope, then in fair bud, had opened into maturity; storm, and blight, and death, had passed over, and destroyed all.'[3]

With the coming of age and some ease and contentment, even her most painful memories had been lanced and the emotion seeped away.

Instead of returning straight to London, she stopped off in Paris, to stay a while and see Claire and other old friends. This summer trip was to be written up by Mary in epistolary form, constituting part one of her two volumes, *Rambles in Germany and Italy*, to be published in 1844 by Moxon. Mary's next excursion abroad was planned to span from the summer of 1842 to the following year. Percy, on attaining his degree, was awarded a non-repayable allowance of £400 by grandfather Timothy who, rather late in the day, had taken quite a liking to his heir.

This time Mary and Percy took another undergraduate with them. He was Alexander Knox, a motherless and ailing young man who wanted to write. These were qualifications enough to merit Mary's charity. He had been ordered to a warmer climate for health reasons and it seemed only right to Mary that she should take him with them, paying some of his expenses if need be.

Departing on 12 June for Antwerp, Mary, Percy and Knox spent most of the summer in drought-stricken Germany. They wintered in Italy and from mid-March they spent two spring months in Rome then went on south for two further months at Sorrento, until 10 July and their return home. Once again Mary stopped off for a few days with Claire in Paris.

For part of the summer and autumn of 1842 Mary sheltered in her party a distinguished young musician, Henry Hugh Pierson. He, too, was suffering from ill health and, although his musical abilities filled Mary with admiration and gratitude, especially since he set some of Shelley's poetry to music, his quick irritability, constant malaise and child-like irresponsibility were very trying. Neither was Knox a particularly cheerful companion. Debilitated by a heart condition, he was writing poems for a slim volume, *Giotto and Francesca and Other Poems*, to be published later that year. When his poetizing was not going well he was prone to histrionic despair. Mary, however, liked him a great deal and sympathized and encouraged him, no doubt recognizing some shades of the youthful Shelley.

Percy was as stolidly affectionate and commonsensical as ever; not even beginning to attempt to learn German, constitutionally incapable of rhapsodizing over ruins and foreign scenery, he preferred more concrete pastimes and bought himself a trumpet to toot in accompaniment to Pierson's playing. However, he was far less tolerant of egoists than was his mother and had little sympathy with either young man. He also lacked his mother's sociability and, much to her chagrin, shrank from going out in society and making friends.

Mary's time was taken up with mothering her three 'sons', two of whom were particularly temperamental and demanding. Pierson became more unpleasant and an increasing liability. Her money was certainly running out faster than she had planned and it was with the greatest relief that she and Percy managed to cast off the disruptive musician, while in Florence for the winter.

From spring 1843 onwards Percy was longing to return to England. He did not care for ruins and architecture, pictures and statues, which gave Mary so much pleasure, and said he would die if kept from his homeland any longer. He was lonely through want of a friend, or as his mother put it, '... he is dull from not being in love – but how & when that will happen – & whether more ill will not thence arise, who can tell!'[4]

Mary had been disappointed in Percy's lack of enthusiasm for the sights and experiences of travel which so sustained her. Once again she was falling into her old trap of spoiling her enjoyment of what was in contemplation of what could never be. In a rare outburst she expressed her discontent to Claire: 'He is happy – I believe that he is utterly free from vice – he has a thousand precious virtues – he has good sense, a clear understanding a charming temper. Ought I not to be blest? Yet you know well what disquiets me – He will live at Clarkes see Med – go on the river & except an idea of music, which he will never follow up to any real study – there is no aim – no exertion – no ambition.'[5] Poor Mary, her misguided hopes were only self-destructive; Percy, too, was obstinate and continued on his course of phlegm and good-natured philistinism for the rest of his happy life.

She had, however, just met in Paris on her return journey a young Italian, Gatteschi, a political exile. He had none of Percy's plain virtues but an abundance of those desirable qualities of ambition and drive which, combined with a ruthless opportunism, were to lead him to exploit Mary's generosity and flay her spirit.

When Mary first met him and his fellow members of the Carbonari, he was handsome, zealous and poverty-stricken with vivid tales to tell of a blighted youth. He immediately appealed to Mary's ever-sympathetic heart. She had barely enough money to return to England but borrowed 200 francs from Claire to give to Gatteschi to relieve his immediate hardship. She pondered on other ways to help him without wounding his manly pride; would he provide her with information on the Carbonari and other political matters which she could incorporate in her *Rambles*? For that Mary was prepared to donate the proceeds of her book to help him pay his debts. Gatteschi was a charming opportunist who had little trouble extracting favours from lonely and love-lorn ladies. Mary was an ideal candidate: soft-hearted and gullible, immediately warmed by the affectionate attentions of anyone attractive, particularly susceptible to young, talented men who, assuming the ill-fated stance, appealed to her for help and support.

Although Mary's greatest attraction was ultimately her open purse, perhaps Gatteschi, despite his roguery, was charmed too, by this unusually intelligent and generous woman who spoke Italian colloquially and well and was extremely knowledgeable about and sympathetic to his country and its struggles. Mary was certainly an extraordinary English tourist, utterly lacking in chauvinism, widely read and well informed over a breadth and depth of European culture that few could match.

Claire reported that Gatteschi was 'quite in despair at your departure'.[6] He continued to write Mary passionate, miserable and bitter letters and Mary, as always longing to be of use to friends in need, sent money, encouragement and affection. Claire, in Paris, gave her highly-coloured accounts of the plight and behaviour of Gatteschi and his fellow exiles there. Mary's own inflammatory enthusiasms were fanned by the young man's apparent devotion, there was even talk of him marrying her, and she responded with a series of frank, over-ardent letters, full of details of her own life and hopes, her search for love, the betrayal of friends, the extremes of inscrutable fate. Perhaps she felt that at last there was someone uncritical and caring to whom she could freely reveal a little of herself. Perhaps she recognized in Gatteschi something of her own intense and melancholy personality. Or her letters may well have been merely flirtatious and silly. In any event she was uninhibited from English conventions by writing them in Italian, a language which lent itself to exaggeration and superlatives. And they were certainly written for Gatteschi's eyes alone. Their correspondence probably continued for two years, during which time the *Rambles* was published in July 1844.

The friendship began to turn sour when Mary heard that Gatteschi was having an affair with the pathetic and unstable Lady Sussex. She was greatly hurt and jealous; once again someone she had trusted and opened her heart to had rejected and betrayed her. She no doubt expressed some of her disillusionment to Gatteschi who retaliated by writing fierce, threatening letters. Mary's agitation increased; she answered them kindly, conciliatingly, but the threats continued: 'hideous letters... they act like poison'.[7] Mary was by now thoroughly frightened, for she knew well 'revenge is justifiable to an Italian',[8] and feared most of all having her indiscreet letters published, holding her up to ridicule and destroying Percy's chances of entering Parliament, society or any of the other establishment roles she wished for him.

Mary was nervous with anxiety and remorse. Once again she was weighed upon by an overwhelming sense of how solitary and vulnerable she was in a hostile world. Percy did not know and could not be told. Claire was in Paris. What would her already critical and middle-aged friends, like Trelawny and Leigh Hunt, think of such vain stupidity ... and when she was nearly fifty? She was quicker to blame herself than the young man, and her agitated regrets and self-reproaches tumbled out in emotional letters to Claire: 'I am indeed humbled – & feel all my vanity & folly & pride – my credulity I can forgive in myself but not my want of common sense ... at my age too....'[9] Yet I meant no ill – I thought I was doing so kind so good an action – comforting an angel – till I found he was not one.... Still I wish him good not evil....'[10]

There was one friend who came to her aid. One friend, out of the many to whom she had extended her kindness and generosity, repaid her handsomely. Alexander Andrew Knox was let in on the secret in September 1845. Indignant and horrified at Gatteschi's betrayal, he set off for Paris with a good deal of Mary's money in his pocket. By some means, probably bribery, he managed to persuade the chief of police there to seize the young man's papers on some political pretext and then allow Knox to extract Mary's letters.

Mary was in Brighton awaiting the outcome, not daring to believe that Knox could find a way, yet unable to believe he would fail. On 13 October she was told the good news. Her relief was boundless: 'Is not Knox a darling ... how clever – how more than clever he is ... my letters my stupid nonsensical letters really rescued from such villainous hands.'[11] The moment her nonsensical letters were in her hands again they were consigned to the fire and Mary's folly, fears and a good deal of money went up in flames. It was a high price to pay for her genuine concern for someone worse off than herself.

Despite the rescue of the incriminating letters there were still rumbles from Paris that Gatteschi and Lady Sussex planned to expose both Mary and Claire's early lives and loves, but Mary was unperturbed. Claire, although still very agitated by the threat, was soothed by Mary's reasoning and a visit to her new house at 24 Chester Square in early 1846.

22
Dust Claims Dust

> 'First our pleasures die – and then
> Our hopes, and then our fears – and when
> These are dead, the debt is due,
> Dust claims dust – and we die too.'
>
> *Death*, Percy Bysshe Shelley

Some months before the Gatteschi incident had reached such ugly proportions, Mary was informed that the grand old man Sir Timothy Shelley was finally, at ninety-one, on the brink of death; '. . . falling from the stalk like an overblown flower',[1] was her image in a letter to Hogg. He had steadfastly refused to meet her, yet had been a constant throughout her life, an ogre become with the years the family mascot, a symbol of continuity, permanence and obstinacy absolute. Although Sir Timothy's intransigence, particularly during Mary's early widowhood, had made life all the more miserable and fraught, his presence and her poverty had largely protected her from opportunists, leeches and blackmailers.

The estate passed to Percy, heavily encumbered with, amongst other things, Mary's years of allowance due to be repaid with interest When mortgages had been arranged, the legacies were finally doled out to Leigh Hunt, to Claire, who received £12,000, twice what it should have been through a slip of the pen, and to Hogg who, in his acceptance of the money, included a backhander at Mary which owed something to truth but more to dissatisfaction and malice: 'I daresay you wish that you were a good deal richer – that this had happened and not that – and that a great deal, which was quite impossible, had been done, and so on! I should be sorry to believe that you were quite contented; such a state of mind, so preposterous and unnatural, expecially in any person whose circumstances were affluent, would surely portend some great calamity.'[2] Not only had Mary to put up with the dissatisfactions of legitimate beneficiaries, but she became fair game for bounty-hunters too.

Gatteschi may have been partially spurred to blackmail, rather than mere abuse, by her elevation from woman of limited means to the mother of a baronet with far grander sums to hand. Mary's agitation over this affair had hardly settled and excitement at Knox's bold success was still running high when in October 1845 a stranger, calling himself G. Byron, approached Thomas Hookham with what he claimed were original Shelley letters for sale. Hookham passed the information on to Mary who was excited and intrigued; were they Shelley's early love letters that had been lost when her precious box of manuscripts had been stolen at Paris on their elopement in 1814? She was very keen to repossess them for many reasons, not least the fact that she did not want such early ardent letters published by anyone else.

Hookham and she both thought G. Byron a rogue but Mary wished to buy all the material, letters, copies of poems, private papers, but was loath to pay exorbitantly for them. Finally by November with Hookham's help she had acquired possibly eight letters for thirty pounds, but was certain there were more. Although G. Byron seemed to have disappeared, Mary expected him eventually to reappear and try and sell the remainder. Return he did. In the autumn of 1846, while Mary was taking the cure in Baden-Baden for her nervous debility, G. Byron contacted Hookham with a further offer of letters, and a threat of selling them to a rascally bookseller Memon. Mary had all along insisted that these Shelley papers were her property, stolen from her, and with this claim Hookham managed to extract the letters from Mr Thomas Holcroft, the solicitor with whom Mr Byron had deposited them.

Mary was still sure that this was not the sum total of the letters in G. Byron's possession. Certainly these repossessed letters were most likely to be genuine, not copies. Mary would have been aware of the possibility of forgery and would have immediately recognized anything irregular in handwriting or content. She had worked so closely on Shelley's manuscripts, as recently as 1840 for her editions of his works, and as a highly perceptive and critical woman she knew his writing, his style, his inflexions and idiosyncrasies, almost as well as her own.

Although G. Byron became notorious for his forgeries of Shelley letters sold to William White two years later, some of which were published by Moxon in an edition of Shelley's letters in 1852, it would seem particularly unlikely that any of the letters Mary obtained were forgeries. The haggling over money, the unease as to whether he had any other letters and whether he would offer them to her or otherwise dispose of them, preyed on Mary's already fragile health. She probably never met him and, possibly because of this, his sinister shadow grew in her imagination, his insidious notes alarmed and distressed her. Mary's health declined over the winter of 1845 and she was once again quite seriously ill during the spring. But she was not to be allowed much respite.

Between the two appearances of Mr Byron, while she was still immobile, her 'neuralgia' only slowly retreating, she was visited by another more threatening scrounger. Thomas Medwin, Shelley's cousin, from being 'infinitely commonplace'[3] in their young days was now that and worse, a blustering Germanophile. He wrote to Mary in May 1846, informing her that his life of Shelley was in progress. He wished for details of the Chancery case which had deprived Shelley of custody of his first children, Ianthe and Charles.

Mary was surprised and a little disturbed. She still intended to be the one who decided when and what of Shelley's life should be committed to public view. Mary had never liked Medwin, his crass opportunism was anathema to her and the idea of someone so antipathetic blundering around in such sacred territory filled her with indignation. He had already fed off his acquaintance with Lord Byron with his long and spurious book, *Conversations of Lord Byron*.

But more than the possible damage to Shelley's memory and her own reputation she feared that Ianthe, then Mrs Esdaile, would suffer, particularly if details of her mother's decline and suicide and of the Chancery suit were once again thrust before the public. Claire, too, was especially vulnerable to scandal having kept well hidden the grand secrets of Byron and Allegra and of her part in Shelley's life. Mary wrote a reasonable and civil reply. 'In modern society there is no injury so great as dragging private names and private life before the world ... the account of the Chancery Suit above all, would wound and injure the living – especially Shelley's daughter, who is innocent of all blame and whose peace every friend of Shelley must respect. I must therefore in the most earnest manner deprecate the publication of particulars and circumstances injurious to the living.'[4]

Medwin's answer, amongst the abuse of England and her writers, was that publication of the book was due in four to six weeks and going ahead as planned. Mary wisely said nothing. This letter was closely followed by another explicit in its blackmail: 'I have found in the Record Office and made extracts of the proceedings in Chancery regarding Shelley's children, which I have deemed an indispensable passage in his life. There are also other passages, I fear, whose discussion you would not approve of, but which justice to his memory has obliged me to dilate on....' With mention of his expenses and the £250 he claimed to have been offered for the book, he promised to forget it all and 'sacrifice my own fame',[5] if Mary would reimburse his losses.

Mary was still suffering from her nervous illness, but was learning forbearance. She did nothing. Shrewd and experienced author as she was, she admitted to Jane Williams Hogg that she very much doubted he had obtained in such arid times as much as £250 for his book. She certainly hoped and half-believed that Medwin would be unable to find anyone to publish his 'trash'.[6]

Medwin's treachery had further disillusioned her and the anxieties his threats had engendered threatened her precarious health. Nevertheless, this time Mary was able to dismiss the depressed forebodings to which, as a younger woman, she would have succumbed. She determinedly convinced herself that the book was unlikely ever to be published and, even if it was, she could not really care. Increasing age, adequate money and secured status protected her from the vagaries of fate and the vulnerability of the solitary. The months passed and nothing more transpired.

In the spring of 1847 Mary and Percy moved into 24 Chester Square in Pimlico, a new five-storey house overlooking the square gardens just to the south of the King's Garden itself. Mary was still unwell and often confined to bed, at times happy and grateful for recovery, at others welcoming the death that had been her desideratum during the agony of her early widowhood.

If not death, certainly a spiritual tranquillity anaesthetized the keenness of sensation. She allowed Percy to embark on a summer yachting expedition to Norway which meant he was away at sea for well over two months. Her tranquillity momentarily trembled with a further note from Medwin saying he was correcting his last proof, followed the next day by an advertisement in the *Examiner* for the book. She wrote appealing for Leigh and Thornton's help in suppressing the book. This had been a hasty and nervous reaction; on reflection she had to agree with Hunt 'that pushing the matter is only to awaken attention ... I shall dismiss the whole affair from my mind & shall only be too grateful if it is not dragged before my eyes by articles in the newspapers. I will not read a line – I will not look at the book if I can help it.'[7]

In the spring of 1848 Percy was canvassing in Horsham in the hopes of winning a seat in Parliament. These hopes turned out to be vain ones, although Mary never deluded herself that his future in Parliament would have been distinguished by anything other than personal integrity and dogged service.

By April both Mary and Percy had made the acquaintance of a young widow, Jane St John, who was living across the square from them. She had already been recommended to marry Sir Percy by a mutual friend: 'such an awfully nice fellow. You would suit each other capitally; you would be so happy with him.'[8] In Jane's own words it would appear that she liked Mary from the moment she first set eyes on her:

> 'I had been resting one afternoon in my bedroom, after having suffered from one of my bad headaches. Feeling better towards the late afternoon, I wandered down to the drawing-room to find my book, not knowing that the maids had let in a visitor. As I opened the door I started back in surprise, for someone was sitting on the sofa, and I said to myself, "who are you – you lovely being?" She must have seen my start of surprise, for rising gently from the sofa, she came towards me and said very softly, "I am Mary Shelley".'[9]

By the middle of June, Percy, with characteristic determination, had wooed and married her.

Jane St John was the best thing that had happened to Mary in twenty-six years. She was not only 'the sweetest wife to Percy', which would have been reward enough to Mary, bound up as she was in her son, desiring his happiness and glad to effect his emotional independence of herself. But Jane was also very special to Mary. 'She is in herself the sweetest creature I ever knew – so affectionate – so soft – so gentle with a thousand other good qualities – she looks what she is all goodness and truth.'[11] She was the woman for whom Mary had been searching all her life. She was as devoted, patient and self-sacrificing as a mother, as bright and loving as Mary's lost and longed-for daughter, as honest and open as a sister. At last Mary had found a woman with as great a capacity for affection and for constancy as herself.

After Percy and Jane's honeymoon in the Lake District Mary was to move with them to Field Place, the Shelley country house in Sussex, with the idea of living there the lives of country landowners: improving the property, husbanding the land and caring for the retainers. It was to be a rural seclusion in peace and modest prosperity.

Mary's own poor health and concern for Jane's spasmodic bronchitic attacks were all that overcast her days. She found Claire's increasing irritability and hysteria exhausting and with the help of Percy and Jane could evade at last her demanding visits.

The damp winters at Field Place, which was set low in heavy, plashy land, forced Mary, Percy and Jane abroad to Nice for the winter of 1849. She longed to settle with them in a permanent home but Jane's health was her priority and she was happy with them anywhere. Mary's own pleasure in Jane's company, 'the sunshine of our house',[12] her gratitude for her own and Percy's happiness, suffused her last years with the quiet glow of familial love. For twenty-six years Mary had been the reluctant head of her family, the sole provider and protector. She had had to be independent and strong. Now within the benign circle of Percy's happy marriage and the Shelley inheritance she could relinquish at last that burden, and with it the spur to life. Percy with his marriage had assumed manhood and Jane, her daughter-in-law, was infinitely capable and loving; both were assured an easy and happy life. Mary, relieved of responsibility, was free to die in peace.

She wrote from Nice to Trelawny's long-suffering wife for whom she felt a great affection:

'The spring has come on us like a sudden leap to summer, so bright and warm.... Jane is now much better and we begin to hope – what we long despaired of – that she will entirely throw off her illness. She and Percy amuse themselves by painting and sketching, and are as happy as possible. They suit so entirely – both being absolutely devoid of every tinge of worldliness and worldly tastes – both having cheerful tempers and affectionate hearts – Indeed Jane is the very ideal of woman, gentle, soft – yet very vivacious – when well even to high lively spirits – both wearing the heart upon the sleeve – but both having the precious instinct of avoiding pecking daws – and of keeping off ill conditioned wasps. I never deserved so much peace and happiness as I enjoy with them....'[13]

Jane did recover with the help of a homoeopathic doctor who also managed to ease much of Mary's pain and get her back on to her feet again, despite her own scepticism.

Mary's last two unfulfilled wishes were that Field Place was situated in dry soil preferable in the Vale of Usk, in Monmouthshire, amongst the mountains and streams, and that with Jane's improved health she and Percy would have a baby. Mary had had a lifetime of wishes, a few dramatically and unexpectedly fulfilled, the rest neglected, regretted and eventually dispelled. Set against past blighted hopes, these last two hardly rippled her contentment with her lot.

Her last winter was spent in Chester Square where the spasmodic attacks on her nervous system, the pain and debility of which she had suffered for years, took its inexorable course. Her old familiar head pains returned with a vengeance, then numbness crept up from her left leg and paralysed the whole of that side of her body. Her doctors ordered her not to read or write. Percy and Jane were in constant attendance, reading to her, reminiscing once again about the sunny days of her youth with Shelley, and the days with them, so much nearer in time. Mary was not afraid of dying. Twice in her life she had believed herself to be near death, during her miscarriage at Lerici and her acute illness in 1839, after editing Shelley's poems. She believed that she would pass from life through to something reassuringly familiar; 'as there is beauty and love here, such is there, and I felt as if my spirit would when it left my frame be received and sustained by a beneficent and gentle Power',[14] she wrote in her journal for 1839.

In the January of 1851, although Percy and Jane could only hope and work towards Mary's recovery, she knew herself to be dying. She handed over to her beloved Jane the care of all her Shelley papers and relics and the responsibility for preserving and furthering his reputation as an angelic and inspirational poet, a misunderstood philanthropist and simple genius. The complexity, the darker side of his nature, she kept locked in her memory, for she alone understood; who else, not knowing him, would see his single-minded pursuit of ideals, his self-centredness and occasional callousness as she did, an essential part of his rare genius? She had always been convinced that loving and living with Shelley for those crowded eight years repaid many times all her suffering. Her faith only faltered once and that after the trauma of William's death.

To Jane, Mary also confided her wish to be buried next to her mother and father under the gravestone in St Pancras churchyard that had witnessed the momentous pledge of undying love between herself and her own Shelley. Although she left no will, Mary remembered, too, Isabel Baxter, the old and special friend of her Scottish youth, who became a less happy Mrs Booth, but to whom Mary had remained faithful despite insult, rejection and neglect. She wished that Isabel have £50 per annum for life and money enough for a suit of mourning.

The paralysis increased its stealthy grip. In the last week of January Mary had a series of strokes which left her semi-conscious. She was free from pain, unable to move or speak yet unafraid. She had always believed that her soul at the last would flee its corporeal prison for the light. Having reluctantly had to struggle for most of her life, having many times longed to give up the fight, now at last she could peacefully acquiesce to death. While she was in this transitory state, Percy and Jane, whom she loved most in the world, sat in vigil by her small, impassive frame. Perhaps with her, too, were 'the beloved dead', Shelley, William, her two babies, her sister Fanny, her mother and father: 'Such surely gather round one ... and make part of that atmosphere of love, so hushed, so soft, on which the soul reposes and is blest.'[15]

On 1 February 1851, at the age of fifty-three, Mary Shelley's spirit slipped gratefully away.

Afterword

Mary's body was not buried beneath her mother's gravestone in St Pancras churchyard. The area had declined with the years and her daughter-in-law, Jane, could not allow 'her loveliness to wither in such a place'. So Mary was laid to rest, as she had requested, between the remains of her mother and father in St Peter's churchyard, Bournemouth, to be near Boscombe Manor, the Shelleys' new country home.

At this house Percy Florence and Jane continued to live the predictable and happy lives which Mary had so briefly shared. They remained childless but adopted a baby niece of Jane Shelley's, Bessie Gibson. Percy continued the shy, affectionate, easy-going man who had so exasperated his mother with his lack of cultural aspirations and ambition. Theatricals, painting and sailing gave him the greatest pleasure. He built a private theatre at Boscombe and painted the scenery for the entertainments there that delighted his family and friends.

Lady Shelley was particularly diligent in her safeguarding of the Shelley manuscripts and relics that Mary had relinquished to her. These were displayed in a part of a room at Boscombe Manor known as the 'Sanctum', and here under a ceiling painted with stars were hung the Curran portrait of Shelley, the miniature of William, the Rothwell portrait of Mary, and locks of hair of the children and the precious manuscripts were stored in special cases. Sir Percy died in 1889 at the age of seventy. Lady Jane lived on a further ten years, having witnessed and fostered the ascent of Shelley reputation that

Mary had initiated so doggedly with her collections of his poetical and prose works, half a century before.

Claire in eccentric old age finally settled, with adequate comfort, in Florence, attended by her niece Paula. She had been converted to the Roman Catholic faith and, unlikely as it may have seemed in her youth, she doubtless found it a solace as she approached the end of her life. She wrote to Trelawny – most probably horrifying him with the sentiment: 'My own firm conviction after years and years of reflection is that our Home is beyond the Stars, not beneath them. Life is only the prologue to an Eternal Drama as a Cathedral is the Vestibule of Heaven.' Claire died peacefully in 1879 at the grand age of eighty-one.

Only Trelawny remained from those Pisan days and he continued to be a law unto himself. He published in 1858 *Recollections of the Last Days of Shelley and Byron*, a distinctively dramatic and romantic reminiscence that was not entirely exact in detail although vivid and accurate in spirit. Twenty years later he published *Records of Shelley, Byron, and the Author*, a coloured and elaborated version of the *Recollections*, and which, because of his harsh treatment of Mary Shelley, drew dignified disapprobation from Lady Jane.

Unrepentant, and as obdurate as ever, he spent the last twelve years of his life living in a cottage near Worthing with a young lady whom he called his niece. To the end he was tough and remarkable; every day in all weathers he would ride to the beach for a swim, he attacked the domestic tasks of digging his garden or chopping wood with the same vigour and aggression that had ensured that his life, although curiously unfulfilled, had never been dull. As an old man he sat for John Millais' painting *North-West Passage*, in which his powerful, grizzled looks and his adventurer's mien live on, however tamely. He finally succumbed to age and after a short illness died in 1881 in his eighty-ninth year.

Jane Williams had also lived on into her eighties, a sweet and faded old lady. Her union with Hogg had been less than idyllic and he, having grown increasingly crotchety, had died seventeen years previously. Leigh Hunt too was long gone, having continued his amiable journalism until he died at seventy-four in 1859.

Of all the Pisan friends only Shelley and Byron had managed, by dying young, to secure their genius against the disillusionment and distemper of age. Mary's survival of Shelley's death and her painful progression into an ultimately fearless and serene middle-age marked a character more resilient and remarkable than that of any of the other survivors of that youthful band. Her plea in her novels, and the example of her life, was for the value of love over all worldly ambitions. *Frankenstein* had brought her extraordinary acclaim, but this mattered little to her, having endured the domestic tragedies of the deaths of her beloved children and finally of Shelley. It was the love of family and friends which she sought all her life, and rediscovered just in time in the modest persons of her own son and his wife.

Notes

ABBREVIATED REFERENCES

Letters
The Letters of Mary W. Shelley edited by F. L. Jones, 2 volumes, University of Oklahoma Press, 1944
Professor Jones's editions of Mary's and Shelley's Letters, and of Mary's Journal contain a wealth of information in the notes. In the editions of the Letters, both the letters and the notes are numbered and in my Notes I give both letter and page numbers for easy reference.

Journal
Mary Shelley's Journal edited by F. L. Jones, University of Oklahoma Press, 1947
This edition of the journals is not complete. It was based on Lady Jane Shelley's transcription of them for *Shelley and Mary*, printed privately in 1882. In fact the entries up to Shelley's death are published here largely intact and complete. However, much of the journals after 1822 remain unpublished, despite Professor Jones's use of the unpublished entries included by Rosalie Glynn Grylls in her *Mary Shelley*. Although these later journals are full of repetitive lamentation, there is still a great deal that is of interest. I have indicated in my notes when entries are taken from the unpublished manuscripts in the Bodleian. Fortunately a complete edition of the journals is in the process of being edited by Diana Pugh and Paula Feldman for publication in 1979.

Shelley's *Letters*
The Letters of Percy Bysshe Shelley edited by F. L. Jones, 2 volumes, Oxford University Press, 1968

Claire's *Journals*
The Journals of Claire Clairmont edited by Marion Kingston Stocking, Harvard University Press, 1968

This too is an excellent edition, sympathetic and full of essential and incidental information. It is particularly useful in giving Claire's view of Mary and Shelley and her life with them.

Chapter 1

1. Robert Southey, *Life and Correspondence*, 1849, Vol. 1, page 306
2. William Godwin, *Enquiry Concerning Political Justice*, 1792, Vol. 2, page 849
3. C. Kegan Paul, *William Godwin: his friends and contemporaries*, 1876, Vol. 1, page 240
4. ibid., page 237
5. ibid., page 239
6. Quoted from Claire Tomalin, *The Life and Death of Mary Wollstonecraft*, 1974, page 215
7. Kegan Paul, op. cit., Vol. 1, page 235
8. ed. Ralph M. Wardle, *Letters of William Godwin & Mary Wollstonecraft*, 1967, no. 53
9. ibid., no. 119
10. ibid., no. 120
11. For a full and sympathetic account of Mary's life see Claire Tomalin, op. cit.
12. William Hazlitt, *The Spirit of the Age*, 1824, Essay on William Godwin
13. Letters of Godwin and Wollstonecraft, op. cit., no. 129
14. ibid., no. 128
15. ibid., no. 130
16. ibid., no. 134
17. ibid., no. 158
18. ibid., no. 160
19. Claire Tomalin, op cit., page 21. For a full account of Mary's labour and last days see Claire Tomalin, pages 219-26
20. Kegan Paul, op. cit., Vol. 1, page 283
21. ibid., pages 275-6
22. ibid., pages 280-1

Chapter 2

1. C. Kegan Paul, *William Godwin: his friends and contemporaries*, 1876, Vol. 1, pages 289–90
2. ibid., page 298
3. William Hazlitt, *The Spirit of the Age*, 1824, Essay on William Godwin
4. Kegan Paul, op. cit., Vol. 1, page 139. Part of Mrs Inchbald's enthusiastic report while the novel was still in proof
5. Hazlitt, op. cit.
6. Kegan Paul, op. cit., Vol. 1, page 332. Mary Shelley's account
7. ibid., page 333
8. ed. Ralph M. Wardle, *Letters of William Godwin & Mary Wollstonecraft*, 1967, no. 135
9. Kegan Paul, op. cit., Vol. 1, page 335
10. ed. Earl Leslie Griggs, *Collected Letters of Samuel Taylor Coleridge*, 1956, Vol. 1, no. 305, page 553
11. Kegan Paul, op. cit., pages 364–5
12. ibid., page 367
13. ibid., page 374
14. ed. Earl Leslie Griggs, *Collected Letters of Samuel Taylor Coleridge*, 1956, Vol. 1, no. 333, page 588
15. ibid., no. 367, page 653
16. Kegan Paul, op. cit., Vol. 2, page 58
17. ed. Charles E. Robinson, *Mary Shelley Collected Tales and Stories*, 1976, page 244
18. Winifred Gérin, *Elizabeth Gaskell*, 1976, page 17
19. Kegan Paul, op. cit., Vol. 2, page 75
20. ibid., page 133
21. Mary Shelley, *Lodore*, 1835, Vol. 1, page 29
22. Kegan Paul, op. cit., page 188
23. Mary Shelley, *Frankenstein; or, The Modern Prometheus*, 1818. Penguin English Library edition, *Three Gothic Novels*, 1968, page 259. Mary Shelley's introduction to the Standard Novels edition, 1831
24. Dorothy George, *London Life in the Eighteenth Century*, 1925, Peregrine edition 1966, page 113
25. Kegan Paul, op. cit., Vol. 2, page 186

26 ibid., page 185
27 ibid., page 184
28 *Letters*, Vol. 1, no. 3, page 4
29 Aaron Burr, *Private Journal*, 1903, Vol. II, page 271
30 ibid., page 326
31 Kegan Paul, op. cit., Vol. 2, pages 213–14
32 R. Glynn Grylls, *Claire Clairmont, Mother of Byron's Allegra*, 1939, page 254
33 Edward John Trelawny, *Records of Shelley, Byron and the Author*, 1878, Penguin English Library edition, 1973, page 68
34 *Gilfillan's Literary Portraits*, 1856, Vol. 1, page 304
35 *Frankenstein*, op. cit., page 259
36 ibid., page 260
37 ibid., page 259

Chapter 3

1 William Hazlitt, *The Spirit of the Age*, 1824. Essay on William Godwin
2 Shelley's *Letters*, Vol. 1, no. 157, pages 210–20
3 ibid., no. 159, page 227
4 *Letters*, Vol. 1, no. 225, page 317
5 Shelley's *Letters*, Vol. 1, no. 67, page 80
6 ibid., no. 97, pages 122–3
7 ibid., no. 114, page 145, note 2
8 ibid., no. 139, page 182
9 ibid., no. 149, page 203
10 ibid., no. 144, page 193
11 Edward John Trelawny, *Records of Shelley, Byron, and the Author*, 1178, Penguin English Library edition, 1973, pages 68–9
12 Mrs Julian Marshall, *The Life and Letters of Mary Wollstonecraft Shelley*, 1889, Vol. 1, page 34
13 Shelley's *Letters*, Vol. 1, no. 199, note 6, page 320
14 Mrs Marshall, op. cit., Vol. 1, page 29

15 Shelley's *Letters*, Vol. 1, no. 202, note 8, page 327
16 ibid., no. 197, note 1, page 313
17 ibid., note 3, page 216
18 ibid., no. 207, note 3, page 331
19 ibid., no. 211, page 336
20 ibid., no. 213, page 337
21 ibid., no. 173, note 6, page 270
22 Mary Shelley, *Mathilda*, ed. Elizabeth Nitchie, 1959, page 60
23 *Journal*, page 124
24 Shelley's *Letters*, Vol. 1, no. 221, note 2, page 350
25 ibid., no. 242, note 1, page 372
26 ibid., no. 219, page 347
27 For an excellent exposition of all arguments, see Richard Holmes, *Shelley, The Pursuit*, 1974, chapter 7
28 Shelley's *Letters*, Vol. 1, no. 253, page 384
29 ibid., page 383
30 Quoted from Richard Holmes, op. cit., page 227
31 Shelley's *Letters*, Vol. 1, no. 265, page 402
32 ibid.

Chapter 4

1 From an unpublished letter in Lord Abinger's collection, quoted in Elizabeth Nitchie, *Mary Shelley: Author of Frankenstein*, 1953, page 89
2 *Letters*, Vol. 2, no. 440, page 88
3 Mary Shelley, *Mathilda*, ed. Elizabeth Nitchie, 1959, page 17
4 Shelley's *Letters*, Vol. 1, no. 216, note 3, pages 340–1
5 C. Kegan Paul, *William Godwin: his friends and contemporaries*, 1876, Vol. 1, page 231
6 Shelley's *Letters*, Vol. 1, no. 265, page 402
7 ibid.
8 Thomas Jefferson Hogg, *The Life of Percy Bysshe Shelley*, 1858, Vol. 2, pages 537–8
9 R. Glynn Grylls, *Claire Clairmont, Mother of Byron's Allegra*, 1939, pages 14–15

10 Shelley's *Letters*, Vol. 1, no. 265, page 403
11 Kegan Paul, op. cit., Vol. 2, page 215
12 R. Glynn Grylls, *Mary Shelley*, 1938, pages 29–30
13 Edward Dowden, *The Life of Percy Bysshe Shelley*, 1866, Vol. 2, Appendix A, page 544
14 Shelley's *Letters*, Vol. 1, no. 258, page 390
15 *Journal*, page 207
16 *Letters*, Vol. 2, no. 440, page 89

Chapter 5

1 Shelley's *Letters*, Vol. 1, no. 265, page 403
2 ibid.
3 *Journal*, page 3
4 ibid., page 4
5 ibid.
6 ibid., page 6
7 ibid., page 5
8 ibid.
9 Claire's *Journals*, page 441
10 *Journal*, page 7
11 Claire's *Journals*, page 24
12 Shelley's *Letters*, Vol. 1, no. 259, page 392
13 ibid., pages 391–2
14 Claire's *Journals*, page 26
15 *Journal*, page 9
16 ed. K. N. Cameron, *Shelley and his Circle*, 1961, Vol. 3, page 350
17 Claire's *Journals*, page 26
18 ibid., page 27
19 *Journal*, page 10
20 Claire's *Journals*, pages 27–8
21 *Journal*, page 11
22 ibid.

23 ibid.
24 Claire's *Journal*, page 30
25 ibid., page 31
26 ibid.
27 *Journal*, page 12
28 ibid.
29 ibid., page 13
30 Claire's *Journals*, page 37
31 *Journal*, page 14
32 ibid.
33 Nothing further is known of this early work, all fragments presumed lost
34 Claire's *Journals*, page 41

Chapter 6

1 Shelley's *Letters*, Vol. 1, no. 260, page 395
2 ibid., no. 262, page 397
3 ibid.
4 *Journal*, page 15
5 ibid., page 17
6 Claire's *Journals*, page 49
7 *Journal*, page 20
8 Shelley's *Letters*, Vol. 1, no. 265, page 403
9 *Journal*, page 21
10 Claire's *Journals*, page 53
11 Shelley's *Letters*, Vol. 1, no. 268, page 407
12 *Letters*, Vol. 1, no. 3, pages 4–5
13 Shelley's *Letters*, Vol. 1, no. 269, page 408
14 ibid. no. 273, pages 412–13
15 ibid., page 413
16 ibid.
17 *Journal*, page 23

18 ibid., page 24
19 Claire's *Journals*, page 58
20 Shelley's *Letters*, Vol. I, no. 276, page 416
21 *Letters*, no. 4, page 5
22 *Journal*, page 24
23 *Letters*, no. 4, page 5
24 *Journal*, page 25
25 ibid.
26 Claire's *Journals*, page 59
27 *Journal*, pages 25–6

Chapter 7

1 *Journal*, page 26
2 ibid., page 27
3 ibid.
4 ibid.
5 ibid., page 29
6 ibid., page 28
7 ibid.
8 ibid., page 30
9 ibid.
10 Percy Bysshe Shelley, *Epipsychidion*, lines 160–1
11 Shelley's *Letters*, Vol. I, no. 283, page 423
12 ed. W. S. Scott, *New Shelley Letters*, 1948, no. 34, page 80
13 ibid., no. 35, page 81
14 ibid., no. 37, page 82
15 *Journal*, page 35
16 *New Shelley Letters*, op. cit., no. 38, page 83
17 Shelley's *Letters*, Vol. I, no. 287, page 426
18 ibid., no. 284, note 3, page 424
19 *Journal*, page 36
20 ibid., page 37

21 ibid., page 38
22 ibid., page 39
23 ibid.
24 ibid.
25 *New Shelley Letters*, op. cit., no. 40, pages 84–5
26 *Journal*, page 40
27 ibid.
28 ibid., page 41
29 ibid., page 44
30 ibid., page 41
31 *New Shelley Letters*, op. cit., no. 41, page 85
32 ibid., no. 42, pages 86–7
33 Shelley's *Letters*, Vol. 1, no. 287, page 426
34 *New Shelley Letters*, op. cit., no. 44, page 89
35 ibid., no. 44, page 88
36 *Journal*, page 46
37 ibid.
38 ed. Leslie A. Marchand, *So Late into the Night,* Byron's Letters, Vol. 5, page 162
39 *Journal*, page 47

Chapter 8

1 R. Glynn Grylls, *Claire Clairmont, Mother of Byron's Allegra*, 1939, page 51
2 ibid.
3 *Letters*, Vol. 1, no. 17, page 8
4 ibid.
5 Shelley's *Letters*, Vol. 1, no. 291, pages 429–30
6 ed. Charles E. Robinson, *Mary Shelley, collected tales and stories*, 1976, The Mourner, pages 81–3
7 Mary's note on *Alastor, The Poetical Works of Percy Bysshe Shelley*, 1839, Vol. 1, pages 141–2
8 *Alastor*, Stanza 16, op. cit., page 127

NOTES

9   Shelley's *Letters*, Vol. 1, no. 313, page 443
10 ibid., no. 315, page 447
11 ibid., no. 324, page 459
12 Grylls, *Claire Clairmont*, op. cit., page 55
13 Claire's *Journals*, page 71
14 Grylls, *Claire Clairmont*, op. cit., page 60
15 *Journal*, page 194
16 George Paston and Peter Quennell, '*To Lord Byron*': Feminine Profiles Based on Unpublished Letters, 1807–1824, 1939, page 208
17 Shelley's *Letters*, Vol. 1, no. 346, page 472

Chapter 9

1   *Letters*, Vol. 1, no. 18, page 9
2   ibid., page 10
3   ibid.
4   ibid., page 11
5   ibid.
6   Shelley's *Letters*, Vol. 1, no. 348, page 475
7   ed. Leslie A. Marchand, *So Late into the Night: Byron's Letters and Journals*, 1976, Vol. 5, page 162
8   Mary Shelley, *The Last Man*, 1826, Vol. 1, pages 82–3
9   Thomas Moore, *Letters and Journals of Lord Byron*, 1830, Vol. 2, page 24
10 Mary Shelley, *Frankenstein; or, The Modern Prometheus*, 1818. Penguin English Library edition, *Three Gothic Novels*, 1968. Mary Shelley's introduction to the Standard Novels edition, 1831, page 261
11 *Letters*, Vol. 1, no. 68, page 70
12 *Frankenstein*, introduction, op. cit., page 262
13 ed. W. Rossetti, *The Diary of William Polidori*, 1911, page 127
14 *Journal*, page 184
15 *Frankenstein*, introduction, op. cit., pages 263–4
16 *Frankenstein*, op. cit., chapter 5, page 318
17 Christopher Small, *Ariel Like a Harpy: Shelley, Mary and 'Frankenstein'*, 1972, explores these sources in detail

18 *Frankenstein*, op. cit., page 296

19 Percy Bysshe Shelley, *Alastor*, Stanza 2

20 *Frankenstein*, op. cit., page 364

21 ibid., page 497

22 *Frankenstein*, introduction, op. cit., page 262

23 *Frankenstein*, preface by Shelley, op. cit., page 267

24 *Diary of Polidori*, op. cit., page 128

25 ibid.

26 Shelley's *Letters*, Vol. 1, no. 353, page 483

27 Mary Shelley, *Valperga*, 1823, Vol. III, pages 261–2

28 *Journal*, page 205

29 Shelley's *Letters*, Vol. 1, no. 354, page 491

30 ibid.

31 *Journal*, page 53

32 *Frankenstein*, op. cit., pages 362–3

33 *Journal*, page 54

34 ibid., page 55

35 ibid.

36 ibid., page 63

Chapter 10

1 Shelley's *Letters*, Vol. 1, no. 363, page 508

2 *Journal*, page 65

3 C. Kegan Paul, *William Godwin: his friends and contemporaries*, 1876, Vol. 2, page 242

4 R. Glynn Grylls, *Mary Shelley*, 1938, pages 70–1

5 Mary Shelley, *Lodore*, 1835, Vol. III, page 309

6 Percy Bysshe Shelley, 'On F. G.'

7 *Letters*, Vol. 1, no. 21, page 16

8 *Journal*, page 6

9 Mary Shelley, *Frankenstein: or, The Modern Prometheus*, 1818. Penguin English Library edition, *Three Gothic Novels*, 1968, pages 447–8

10 *Letters*, Vol. 1, no. 20, page 14

11 ibid., page 15
12 Shelley's *Letters*, Vol. 1, no. 374, page 520
13 ibid.
14 *Letters*, Vol. 1, no. 21, page 16
15 ibid., Vol. 2, no. 387, page 47
16 Shelley's *Letters*, Vol. 1, no. 378, page 525
17 ibid.
18 ibid., no. 380, page 528
19 *Journal*, page 71
20 ibid., pages 74–5
21 ibid., page 75
22 Shelley's *Letters*, Vol. 1, no. 400, page 546
23 *Letters*, Vol. 1, no. 24, page 19
24 ibid., no. 26, page 21
25 ibid., no. 29, pages 25–6
26 ibid., no. 28, page 24
27 Shelley's *Letters*, Vol. 1, no. 398, pages 542–3
28 *Journal*, page 79
29 ibid., page 80
30 ibid., page 83
31 *Letters*, Vol. 1, no. 34, page 32
32 ibid., no. 37, pages 37–8
33 ibid., no. 43, page 45
34 ibid., no. 44, page 45
35 Shelley's *Letters*, Vol. 1, no. 441, page 587
36 *Letters*, Vol. 1, no. 46, page 46
37 *Journal*, page 186

Chapter 11

1 *Letters*, Vol. 1, no. 49, page 48
2 *Journal*, page 95

NOTES

3 Shelley's *Letters*, Vol. 2, no. 463, page 11
4 *Journal*, page 97
5 Claire's *Journals*, page 92
6 *Journal*, page 98
7 ibid.
8 *Letters*, Vol. 1, no. 53, page 54
9 ibid., no. 52, page 52
10 ibid., page 53
11 Shelley's *Letters*, Vol. 2, no. 472, pages 26–7
12 *Blackwood's Edinburgh Magazine*, March 1823
13 *Quarterly Review*, January 1818
14 *Edinburgh Review*, March 1818
15 Shelley's *Letters*, Vol. 2, no. 476, page 31
16 Edward John Trelawny, *Records of Shelley, Byron, and the Author*, 1878. Penguin English Library edition, 1973, page 190
17 Shelley's *Letters*, Vol. 2, no. 471, page 22
18 *Letters*, Vol. 1, no. 54, page 56
19 Shelley's *Letters*, Vol. 2, no. 478, page 33
20 *Journal*, page 105
21 ibid.
22 *Letters*, Vol. 1, no. 55, page 58
23 Shelley's *Letters*, Vol. 2, no. 481, page 40
24 ibid., page 39
25 Mary Shelley, *Rambles in Germany and Italy in 1840, 1842, and 1843*, 1844, Vol. 2, page 79
26 ibid., page 78
27 ibid., page 79
28 Shelley's *Letters*, Vol. 2, no, 482, page 41
29 ibid., no. 483, page 42
30 ibid., no. 479, page 38
31 *Journal*, page 109
32 Shelley's *Letters*, Vol. 2, no. 482, note 2, page 41

33 ibid., no. 488, page 58
34 *Journal*, page 110
35 Shelley's *Letters*, Vol. 2, no. 487, page 55
36 *Journal*, page 110
37 ibid., page 111
38 ibid.
39 ibid.
40 Mary Shelley, *The Last Man*, introduction, 1826, pages iii–iv
41 Shelley's *Letters*, Vol. 2, no. 488, page 61
42 Mary Shelley, *Frankenstein; or, The Modern Prometheus*, 1818. Penguin English Library edition, *Three Gothic Novels*, 1968, page 360
43 Mary's notes on poems of 1818, *The Poetical Works of Percy Bysshe Shelley*, 1839, Vol. 3, page 163
44 Percy Bysshe Shelley, 'Stanzas, Written in Dejection, Near Naples', Stanza 3, op. cit., Vol. 3, page 153
45 Mary's notes on poems of 1818, op. cit., Vol. 3, page 162
46 ed. Leslie A. Marchand, *Between Two Worlds: Byron's Letters and Journals*, 1977, Vol. 7, pages 174–5
47 Shelley's *Letters*, Vol. 2, no. 650, note 5, page 318
48 Byron's *Letters*, op. cit., page 191
49 *Letters*, Vol. 1, no. 128, page 149
50 Shelley's *Letters*, Vol. 2, no. 575, page 211
51 ibid., no. 650, page 319
52 *Letters*, Vol. 1, no. 128, page 148
53 ed. Leslie A. Marchand, *The Flesh is Frail: Byron's Letters and Journals*, 1976, Vol. 6, page 92
54 *Letters*, Vol. 1, no. 64, page 64
55 ibid., no. 128, page 148

Chapter 12

1 *Letters*, Vol. 1, no. 64, page 63
2 *Journal*, page 116
3 *Letters*, Vol. 1, no. 64, page 63

4 ibid., no. 65, page 65
5 Claire's *Journals*, page 100
6 *Letters*, Vol. 1, no. 67, page 69
7 ibid., no. 65, pages 66–7
8 ibid., no. 70, page 72
9 ibid., no. 73, page 76
10 Mary Shelley, *The Last Man*, 1826, Vol. 3, page 273
11 Claire's *Journals*, page 113
12 Mary's notes on poems of 1819, *The Poetical Works of Percy Bysshe Shelley*, 1839, Vol. 3, page 207
13 ibid., page 194
14 *Letters*, Vol. 1, no. 72, page 75
15 Mary's note on 'The Cenci', op. cit., Vol. 2, page 275
16 ibid.
17 *Letters*, Vol. 1, no. 71, page 73.
18 Unpublished entry in Mary Shelley's Journal in Bodleian, Vol. 4, Oct. 27, 1822, page 20
19 *Journal*, page 122
20 *Letters*, Vol. 1, no. 177, page 224
21 Mary Shelley, *Mathilda*, ed. Elizabeth Nitchie, 1959, page 54
22 ibid., page 66
23 Shelley's *Letters*, Vol. 2, no. 508, page 109
24 ibid., no. 526, page 134
25 *Letters*, Vol. 1, no. 75, page 81
26 ibid.
27 *Journal*, page 126
28 *Letters*, Vol. 1, no. 78, page 84
29 Shelley's *Letters*, Vol. 2, no. 529, page 151
30 *Letters*, Vol. 1, no. 80, page 88
31 Shelley's *Letters*, Vol. 2, no. 534, note 1, page 159
32 Helen Rossetti Angeli, Shelley and His Friends in Italy, 1911, page 97

Chapter 13

1. Shelley's *Letters*, Vol. 2, no. 545, page 170
2. Unpublished entry in Mary Shelley's Journal in Bodleian, Vol. 4, Nov. 10th 1822, pages 21-2
3. *Letters*, Vol. 1, no. 91, page 105
4. ed. Frederick L. Jones, *Maria Gisborne and Edward E. Williams, Shelley's Friends: Their Journals and Letters*, 1951, page 27
5. ed. Leslie A. Marchand, *Between Two Worlds: Byron's Letters and Journals*, 1977, Vol. 7, page 80
6. Shelley's *Letters*, Vol. 2, no. 567, page 198
7. *Letters*, Vol. 1, no. 96, page 108
8. Shelley's *Letters*, Vol. 2, no. 571, page 207
9. Claire's *Journals*, page 153
10. Shelley's *Letters*, Vol. 2, no. 577, page 217
11. ibid., no. 576, page 214
12. ibid., no. 577, page 215
13. ibid., no. 592, page 245
14. ibid.
15. *Letters*, Vol. 1, no. 98, page 112
16. Shelley's *Letters*, Vol. 2, no. 577, page 216
17. ibid., page 217
18. *Letters*, Vol. 1, no. 101, page 116
19. Shelley's *Letters*, Vol. 2, no. 579, page 220
20. *Letters*, Vol. 1, no. 99, page 113
21. Mary's note on poems of 1820, *The Poetical Works of Percy Bysshe Shelley*, 1839, Vol. IV, page 53
22. ibid., page 51
23. ibid., page 52
24. Claire's *Journals*, page 170, note 9
25. Shelley's *Letters*, Vol. 2, no. 582, page 224
26. *Journal*, page 136
27. ibid., page 138

28 ibid., page 139
29 ibid., page 199
30 Shelley's *Letters*, Vol. 2, no. 588, note 4, page 238
31 ibid., no. 591, page 243
32 Mary's note on poems of 1820, op. cit., page 54

Chapter 14

1 *Journal*, page 141
2 Thomas Medwin, *The Life of Percy Bysshe Shelley*, 1847, page 169
3 *Letters*, Vol. 1, no. 101, page 117
4 Leslie Marchand, *Byron: A Biography*, 1957, Vol. 2, page 844n
5 *Letters*, Vol. 1, no. 111, page 134
6 ibid., no. 101, page 118
7 Medwin, op. cit., page 279
8 Percy Bysshe Shelley, 'Epipsychidion', Stanza 17
9 Newman Ivy White, *Shelley*, 1947, Vol. 2, Appendix II, Letter 11, page 479
10 ibid., Letter 7, page 474
11 *Letters*, Vol. 1, no. 109, page 129
12 ibid., no. 107, page 124
13 Percy Bysshe Shelley, 'Epipsychidion', Stanza 21
14 Shelley's *Letters*, Vol. 2, no. 676, page 374
15 ibid., no. 592, pages 244–5
16 Mary Shelley, *Rambles in Germany and Italy in 1840, 1842, and 1843*, 1844, Vol. 2, page 81
17 Shelley, 'Epipsychidion', Stanza 15
18 Shelley's *Letters*, Vol. 2, no. 606, note 3, page 263
19 ibid., pages 262–3
20 *Letters*, Vol. 1, no. 135, page 161
21 Shelley's *Letters*, Vol. 2, no. 715, page 44
22 *Letters*, Vol. 1, no. 110, page 130
23 ibid.

24 ibid., no. 109, page 130
25 ibid., no. 116, page 137
26 ibid., page 136
27 Edward Dowden, *The Life of Percy Bysshe Shelley*, 1886, Vol. 2, page 399
28 Shelley's *Letters*, Vol. 2, no. 620, note 2, page 280
29 *Letters*, Vol. 1, no. 118, page 138
30 Shelley's *Letters*, Vol. 2, no. 624, page 228
31 Mary's note on poems of 1821, *The Poetical Works of Percy Bysshe Shelley*, 1839, Vol. IV, page 152
32 ibid.
33 *Letters*, Vol. 1, no. 126, page 145
34 Shelley's *Letters*, Vol. 2, no. 634, page 302
35 *Journal*, page 159
36 Shelley's *Letters*, Vol. 2, no. 651, page 322
37 ibid., page 324
38 ibid., no. 653, pages 330–1
39 ibid., page 331
40 ibid., no. 651, page 324
41 ibid., no. 660, page 344
42 *Letters*, Vol. 1, no. 129, page 150
43 ibid.

Chapter 15

1 *Letters*, Vol. 1, no. 132, page 155
2 *Journal*, page 165
3 Edward John Trelawny, *Records of Shelley, Byron and the Author*, 1878. Penguin English Library edition, 1973, page 68
4 ibid., page 69
5 *Letters*, Vol. 1, no. 163, page 212
6 ibid., no. 132, page 156
7 ibid., no. 135, page 158

348 NOTES

8 In part unpublished, Mary Shelley's Journal in Bodleian, Vol. 5, pages 54–5
9 ibid., page 202
10 ibid., pages 169–70
11 Claire's *Journals*, note 91, page 276
12 *Letters*, Vol. 1, no. 133, page 157
13 *Journal*, note 9, pages 170–1
14 *Letters*, Vol. 1, no. 136, page 162
15 Mary's notes on poems of 1822, *The Poetical Works of Percy Bysshe Shelley*, 1839, Vol. IV, page 229
16 ibid.
17 *Letters*, Vol. 1, no. 139, page 170
18 Mary's note on poems of 1822, op. cit., page 231
19 *Letters*, Vol. 1, no. 139, page 171
20 Shelley's *Letters*, Vol. 2, no. 709, page 427
21 ibid., no. 715, page 435
22 ibid., no. 719, page 443
23 ibid., no. 715, page 435
24 *Letters*, Vol. 1, no. 144, page 179
25 *Journal*, page 208
26 *Letters*, Vol. 1, no. 144, page 180
27 ibid.
28 ibid.

CHAPTER 16

1 Mary's note on poems of 1822, *The Poetical Works of Percy Bysshe Shelley*, 1839, Vol. IV, page 235
2 *Letters*, Vol. 1, no. 140, page 172
3 ibid., no. 260, page 241
4 ibid., no. 144, page 181
5 Shelley's *Letters*, Vol. 2, no. 720, page 444
6 ibid., no. 721, page 445
7 Mary's note on poems of 1822, op. cit., page 233

8   *Letters*, Vol. 1, no. 144, page 182
9   ibid.
10 ibid.
11 ibid., page 184
12 ibid.
13 ibid.
14 ibid., page 185

Chapter 17

1   *Letters*, Vol. 1, no. 145, page 186
2   Mary Shelley, *The Last Man*, 1826, Vol. 3, page 301
3   *Letters*, Vol. 1, no. 145, page 189
4   Edward John Trelawny, *Records of Shelley, Byron, and the Author*, 1878. Penguin English Library edition, 1973, page 172
5   *Journal*, page 189
6   R. Glynn Grylls, *Mary Shelley*, 1938, Appendix D, page 298
7   ed. Frederick L. Jones, *Maria Gisborne and Edward E. Williams, Shelley's Friends: Their Journals and Letters*, 1951, Letter 6, page 166
8   *Journal*, page 186
9   *Letters*, Vol. 1, no. 144, page 145
10 Percy Bysshe Shelley, 'Adonais', Stanza 26
11 *Letters*, Vol. 1, no. 150, page 194
12 ibid.
13 *Journal*, page 182
14 *Letters*, Vol. 1, no. 153, page 198
15 ed. Peter Gunn, *Byron: Selected Prose*, Penguin English Library, 1972. Letter from Byron to Mary Shelley, 6 October 1822, page 486
16 *Journal*, page 184
17 *The Last Man*, op. cit., Vol. 1, page 89
18 ibid.
19 *Journal*, page 184
20 *Letters*, Vol. 1, no. 162, page 208
21 *Gisborne and Williams*, op. cit., page 93

22 *Letters*, Vol. 1, no. 159, page 205
23 *Journal*, page 188
24 *Letters*, Vol. 1, no. 168, page 216
25 ed. W. S. Scott, *New Shelley Letters*, 1948, no. 80, page 141
26 ibid., pages 141–2
27 *Letters*, Vol. 1, no. 177, page 222
28 ibid.
29 ibid., no. 185, page 231
30 ibid., no. 186, page 232
31 ibid., page 233
32 ibid., no. 193, page 255
33 *Gisborne and Williams*, op. cit., page 391
34 *Letters*, Vol. 1, no. 194, page 258

Chapter 18

1 *Journal*, page 193
2 *Letters*, Vol. 1, no. 194, page 259
3 ibid.
4 ibid., no. 195, page 265
5 ibid., no. 196, page 272
6 ibid.
7 Henry Crabb Robinson, *On Books and their Writers*, 1938, Vol. 1, page 299
8 *Journal*, page 192
9 ibid., page 194
10 ibid., page 203
11 ibid., page 194
12 ibid.
13 ibid., page 195
14 *Letters*, Vol. 2, no. 456, page 104
15 ibid., Vol. 1, no. 199, page 279

NOTES

16 Unpublished entry in Mary Shelley's Journal in Bodleian, Vol. 4, page 82
17 Mary Shelley, *The Last Man*, 1826, Vol. 1, pages 189–90
18 *Letters*, Vol. 1, no. 224, page 316
19 *The Last Man*, op. cit., Vol. 1, pages 126–7
20 ibid., Vol. 3, page 339

Chapter 19

1 *Letters*, Vol. 1, no. 230, note 1, page 322
2 ibid., no. 243, page 330
3 ibid., no. 245, note 1, page 333
4 ibid., no. 245, page 333
5 *Letters*, Vol. 2, Appendix II, page 349
6 ibid., no. 369, page 34
7 ibid., no. 367, page 34
8 ibid., no. 560, page 200
9 ibid., Vol. 1, no. 265, page 347
10 *Journal*, page 197
11 ibid., page 199
12 *Letters*, Vol. 1, no. 297, pages 369–70
13 *Journal*, page 198
14 ibid., page 202
15 Mrs Julian Marshall, *The Life and Letters of Mary Wollstonecraft Shelley*, 1889, Vol. 2, page 169
16 ibid., page 173
17 Mary Shelley, *The Last Man*, 1826, Vol. 1, pages 46–7
18 *Journal*, pages 204–6
19 *Letters*, Vol. 1, no. 309, page 377
20 ibid.
21 ibid., no. 304, page 374
22 ibid., Vol. 2, no. 312, page 3
23 Marshall, op. cit., Vol. 2, page 178

24 ibid., page 197
25 ibid., page 184
26 ed. H. Buxton Forman, *Letters of Edward John Trelawny*, 1910, no. XLIV, pages 111–12
27 *Letters*, Vol. 2, no. 336, page 18
28 Marshall, op. cit., Vol. 2, page 199
29 ibid., page 202
30 Trelawny's *Letters*, op. cit., no XLVIII, page 116

CHAPTER 20

1 Mrs Julian Marshall, *The Life and Letters of Mary Wollstonecraft Shelley*, 1889, Vol. 2, page 192
2 *Letters*, Vol. 2, no. 329, page 13
3 ed. H. Buxton Forman, *Letters of Edward John Trelawny*, 1910, no. LII, page 126
4 R. Glynn Grylls, *Mary Shelley*, page 217
5 *Letters*, Vol. 2, no. 346, page 23
6 *Journal*, page 199
7 *Letters*, Vol. 2, no. 346, page 25
8 ibid., no. 372, page 36
9 ibid.
10 Trelawny's *Letters*, op. cit., no. LX, page 141
11 *Letters*, Vol. 2, no. 379, pages 41–2
12 Trelawny's *Letters*, op. cit., no. LXIII, page 162
13 *Letters*, Vol. 2, no. 387, page 46–7
14 Trelawny's *Letters*, op. cit., no. LXIV, page 166
15 *Letters*, Vol. 2, no. 389, page 49
16 ibid., no. 437, page 82
17 ibid.
18 *Journal*, page 203
19 Marshall, op. cit., Vol. 2, pages 265–6
20 Trelawny's *Letters*, op. cit., no. CIX, page 246

21 *Letters*, Vol. 2, no. 465, note 1, page 114
22 Trelawny's *Letters*, op. cit., no. LXXVII, page 205
23 *Letters*, Vol. 2, no. 472, page 119
24 ibid., pages 119–20
25 Mary's preface to *The Poetical Works of Percy Bysshe Shelley*, 1839, Vol. 1, page xvi
26 Mary's note on poems of 1822, op. cit., Vol. IV, page 226
27 Mary's preface, op. cit., Vol. I, part xvi
28 *Journal*, page 207
29 Mary's note on poems of 1822, op. cit., Vol. IV, page 226
30 *Journal*, page 207
31 Unpublished entry in Mary Shelley's Journal in Bodleian, Vol. 5, Nov. 27, 1839
32 Henry Crabb Robinson, *On Books and their Writers*, 1938, Vol. II, March 4, 1839

Chapter 21

1 *Journal*, pages 208–9
2 *Letters*, Vol. 2, no. 523, page 147
3 Mary Shelley, *Rambles in Germany and Italy in 1840, 1842, and 1843*, 1844, Vol. 1, pages 139–40
4 *Letters*, Vol. 2, no. 546, page 183
5 ibid., no. 554, page 192
6 R. Glynn Grylls, *Claire Clairmont, Mother of Byron's Allegra*, 1939, page 208
7 *Letters*, Vol.2, no. 614, page 256
8 ibid., no. 611, page 252
9 ibid.
10 ibid., no. 613, page 254
11 ibid., no. 616, page 258

Chapter 22

1 ed. W. S. Scott, *New Shelley Letters*, 1948, no. 95, page 169
2 Mrs Julian Marshall, *The Life and Letters of Mary Wollstonecraft Shelley*, 1889, Vol. 2, page 304

3 *Letters*, Vol. 1, no. 110, page 131
4 ibid., Vol. 2, no. 643, pages 288–9
5 ibid., no. 643, note 2, page 288
6 ibid., no. 645, page 290
7 ibid., no. 671, page 310
8 Maud Rolleston, *Talks with Lady Shelley*, page 26
9 ibid., pages 27–8
10 *Letters*, Vol. 2, no. 699, page 333
11 ibid., no. 681, page 316
12 ibid., no. 704, page 339
13 ibid., no. 701, pages 335–6
14 *Journal*, page 208
15 ibid., page 209

Bibliography

Considering the vast field of Shelley literature, this bibliography is inevitably extremely limited and selective. I have included only those books which gave me particular insight into Mary's background, her relationships, character and motives.

MARY SHELLEY'S WORKS – FICTION

1 *Frankenstein; or, The Modern Prometheus*, London: Lackington, Hughes, Harding, Mayor & Jones, 1818
Published in many more recent editions, I have chosen to use probably the most readily available: Penguin English Library, *Three Gothic Novels*, 1968

2 *Valperga: or, the Life and Adventures of Castruccio, Prince of Lucca* London: G & W. B. Whittaker, 1823

3 *The Last Man*, London: Henry Colburn, 1826

4 *The Fortunes of Perkin Warbeck*, London: Henry Colburn and Richard Bentley, 1830

5 *Lodore*, London: Richard Bentley, 1835

6 *Falkner*, London: Saunders & Otley, 1837

7 *Mary Shelley, Collected Tales and Stories*, ed. Charles E. Robinson, Baltimore & London, 1976.

8 *Prosperine and Midas: Two unpublished Mythological Dramas*, ed. A. Koszul, London: Humphrey Milford, 1922

9 *Mathilda*, ed. Elizabeth Nitchie, Chapel Hill: University of North Carolina Press, 1959

10 *The Choice*, her long poem written after Shelley's death, is published in *Mary Shelley*, R. Glynn Grylls, London: Oxford University Press, 1938

NON-FICTION (INCLUDING HER JOURNAL AND LETTERS)

11 with P. B. Shelley: *History of Six Weeks' Tour through a Part of France, Switzerland, Germany and Holland: with Letters Descriptive of a Sail Round the Lake of Geneva, and of the Glaciers of Chamouni*, London: T. Hookham and C. & J. Ollier, 1817

12 *Lives of the Most Eminent Literary and Scientific Men of France*, London: Longman, Orme, Brown, Green, Longmans, & John Taylor, 1838–9. Two volumes, nos. 105, and 117 in Lardner's *Cabinet Cyclopedia*

13 *Lives of the most Eminent Literary and Scientific Men of Italy, Spain and Portugal*, London: Longman, Brown, Green, & Longmans, 1835–7. Three volumes, nos. 63, 71 and 96 in the *Cyclopedia*

14 Preface and Notes to *The Poetical Works of Percy Bysshe Shelley*, London: Edward Moxon, 1839; Oxford University Press edition edited by Thomas Hutchinson, 1968

15 *Rambles in Germany and Italy in 1840, 1842, and 1843*, London: Edward Moxon, 1844

16 *The Letters of Mary W. Shelley*, ed. Frederick L. Jones, Norman: University of Oklahoma Press, 1946

17 *Mary Shelley's Journal* ed. Frederick L. Jones, Norman: University of Oklahoma Press, 1947

18 *New Shelley Letters*, ed. W. S. Scott, London: The Bodley Head, 1948

BIOGRAPHIES

1 Kenneth Neill Cameron, ed. of *Shelley and His Circle*, Volumes I–IV, Harvard University Press, 1961
Subsequent volumes of this projected 10-volume edition of letters, and other miscellaneous Shelleyana in the Carl H. Pforzheimer Library, New York, have been edited by Donald H. Reiman. So far 6 volumes have been published

2 *The Journals of Claire Clairmont*, ed. Marion Kingston Stocking, Cambridge: Harvard University Press, 1968

3 Edward Dowden, *The Life of Percy Bysshe Shelley*, London: Kegan Paul, Trench & Co., 1886

4 *Maria Gisborne and Edward E. Williams, Shelley's Friends: Their Journals and Letters*, ed. Frederick L. Jones, Norman: University of Oklahoma Press, 1951

BIBLIOGRAPHY

5 M. Dorothy George, *London Life in the Eighteenth Century*, 1925, Harmondsworth: Peregrine, 1966

6 William Godwin, *An Enquiry Concerning Political Justice*, London: 1793; Oxford University Press, 1971

7 R. Glynn Grylls, *Mary Shelley: A Biography*, London: Oxford University Press, 1938

8 R. Glynn Grylls, *Claire Clairmont, Mother of Byron's Allegra*, London: John Murray, 1939

9 E. J. Hobsbawm, *The Age of Revolution*, 1962, London: Cardinal, Sphere, 1973

10 Richard Holmes, *Shelley, The Pursuit*, London: Weidenfeld & Nicolson, 1974

11 Leslie A. Marchand, *Byron: A Biography*, London: John Murray, 1957

12 Leslie A. Marchand, *Byron's Letters and Journals*, Volumes 1–7 so far completed, London: John Murray, 1973–7

13 Mrs Julian Marshall, *The Life and Letters of Mary Wollstonecraft Shelley*, London: Richard Bentley & Son, 1889

14 Elizabeth Nitchie, *Mary Shelley: Author of Frankenstein*, New Brunswick: Rutgers University Press, 1953

15 Sylva Norman, *The Flight of the Skylark: The Development of Shelley's Reputation*, Norman: University of Oklahoma Press, 1954

16 C. Kegan Paul, *William Godwin: His Friends and Contemporaries*, London: Henry S. King & Co., 1876

17 Percy Bysshe Shelley, *The Letters* ..., ed. Frederick L. Jones, London: Oxford University Press, 1964

18 Christopher Small, *Ariel Like a Harpy: Shelley, Mary and 'Frankenstein'*, London: 1972

19 Muriel Spark, *Child of Light: A Reassessment of Mary Wollstonecraft Shelley*, Hadleigh, Essex: Tower Bridge Publications, 1951

20 Claire Tomalin, *The Life and Death of Mary Wollstonecraft*, London: Weidenfeld & Nicolson, 1974

21 Edward John Trelawny, *The Letters* ..., ed. H. Buxton Forman, London: Oxford University Press, 1910

22 Edward John Trelawny, *Records of Shelley, Byron, and the Author*, 1878, Harmondsworth: Penguin New English Library, 1973

23 Newman Ivey White, *Shelley*, London: Secker & Warburg, 1947

24 Mary Wollstonecraft, *A Vindication of the Rights of Woman*, 1792, London: Dent, 1970

Acknowledgements

My acknowledgements and thanks to the staff of the British Library, the Bodleian Library, the London Library, the National Portrait Gallery, Nottingham Museums and the Carl H. Pforzheimer Library, New York, for access to their various and invaluable materials. My particular thanks for permission to quote from copyright material to: Lord Abinger; Constable & Co., London; David Higham Associates; Harvard University Press; John Murray (Publishers); University of Oklahoma Press; Oxford University Press; the Carl and Lily Pforzheimer Foundation, Inc.

My warmest thanks for the help and generosity of: Lord Abinger; Walter Armytage; Dr Bruce Barker-Benfield of the Department of Western Mss; the Bodleian; Mrs Gee of Keats House; Lady Mander (R. Glynn Grylls); Miss Pamela Wood of Newstead Abbey (Nottingham Museums); and to my long-suffering editor Alex MacCormick.

Finally my thanks for the invaluable support and enthusiasm of family and friends, with particular mention of my parents and parents-in-law; of Karen Thesen, who has typed and indexed and been far more than even the best sister should be; of Sheila Murphy, whose discriminating eye was the first, other than mine, to fall on my manuscript; of Angela Nicholas, who has been a good friend to me and a second mother to my children. And finally my most grateful thanks to Philip, Benjamin and Lily Dunn, who uncomplainingly have shared me with Mary Shelley, who like a demanding and rather querulous old aunt came to visit and stayed and stayed and stayed.

The author and publishers are grateful to the following for permission to reproduce illustrations: the National Portrait Gallery, nos. 1, 2, 3, 4, 5, 10 and 11; Lord Abinger, no. 6; the Carl H. Pforzheimer Foundation Inc., no. 7; Newstead Abbey (Nottingham Museums), no. 8; the Bodleian Library, no. 9; *Illustrated London News*, no. 12.

Index

Adventures of a Younger Son, The, 303, 308
Alastor, 73, 118, 121, 133, 148, 154
Albion House, Marlow, 152-4, 157-8, 160-61, 163-4
Alderson, Amelia, 7
Antonio, 22
Ariel (Shelley's boat), 139
Assassins, The, 76-8, 81

Ballechy (money-lender), 86, 92, 97
Baxter, Christy, 43, 44, 49
Baxter, Isabel, 33-5, 157, 283, 326; breaks friendship with Mary, 96-7, 164; illness, 272
Baxter, William, 30, 31, 164
Blake, William, 134
Blenkinsop, Mrs, 11-13
Boinville family, 51, 57, 62; Shelley's passion for Cornelia, 51; family denounces Shelley, 67
Boscombe Manor, 327
Brunnen, 75-8
Brunswick Square, 272
Burr, Aaron, 30

Byron, G., 320-21
Byron, Lord George Gordon, 35, 48, 113, 127, 128, 132, 134, 136, 142, 143, 157, 168, 208, 223, 238, 246, 251, 252, 257, 262, 263; and Shelley's relationship with Claire, 113; Claire's approaches to, 121-2; and Augusta, 122, 125-6; to Switzerland, 123; attitude to local community abroad, 123; indifference to Claire, 125; in Geneva, 126; first meeting and friendship with Shelley, 126; character in comparison to Shelley's, 126-7, 276; Mary's admiration for, 126-7, 276; moves to Villa Diodati, 127; on Lake Geneva, 137-8; adored by Claire, 139; and Claire's pregnancy, 141, and paternal responsibility, 141-2; rejection of Claire, 148; birth of daughter Allegra (Alba), 151; daughter christened, 165; his life in Venice, 168, 173, 175, 177-9, 186, 189; Allegra returns to, 179; puts Allegra into convent, 231; invites Shelley to Ravenna, 233;

INDEX

and Countess Guiccioli, 234, 241, 243, 254, 262, 263; reaction to Trelawny, 239; in Pisa, 235–6, 242–3; incident with soldier, 243; death of Allegra, 244; at Shelley's cremation, 256; helps Mary, 267; to Greece, 268; death in Greece, 273–4; characterization in *The Last Man*, 126–7, 276; characterization in *Lodore*, 306 Works: *Childe Harold*, 139, 143, 144, 155, 172; *Don Juan*, 263; *Lara*, 106; *Mazeppa*, 177; *Memoirs*, 285; *The Prisoner of Chillon*, 139

Caleb Williams, 18, 85, 132
Casa Bertini, 173–4
Cenci, The, 199, 203
Chesser, Dr Eustace, 39
Childe Harold, 139, 143, 144, 155, 172
Choice, The, 259
'Christabel', 136
Church Terrace, 86–8, 90–93, 96
Clairmont, Charles (Claire's brother), 91, 93, 96, 98; schooling, 26; Ramsgate, 29; visits Mary and Shelley, 85; visit to Windsor, 117; boat trip, 117; Claire joins, 262
Clairmont, Claire (originally Jane), 2, 22, 27, 30, 31, 48, 55, 152, 162, 321; changes name, 55, 101; confidante of Mary, 62; goes to Continent, 64; mother follows, 66; journal, 70, 71, 73, 75, 76, 80, 88, 98, 187; attitude to Swiss, 73, 76; and French, 73; and Germans, 79; resentful of Mary, 74; imagination, 78, 87–8; *The Ideot*, 81; return to London, 81–3;

despondency, 88, 93, 98; temperamental, 101; relationship with Shelley, 101, 106, 108, 112, 158, 160; departure for Lynmouth, 112, 115; re-enters Shelleys' life, 121; approaches Byron, 121–2; letters to Byron, 122–3; pregnancy, 123, 125, 138, 141, 145, 147; in Geneva, 123–5; renews affair with Byron, 138–9; visits Chamonix, 139–41; letter to Trelawny, 141; return to England, 143–4; in Bath, 144–7; and Fanny's suicide, 145; rejected by Byron, 148; birth of Allegra, 151; Albion House, 154; daughter christened, 165; leaves for Italy, 165; in Milan, 167–8; Allegra sent to Byron, 168; in Tuscany, 172; to Venice with Shelley, 173; and Allegra, 172–4; Allegra returns to Byron, 179; visits Vesuvius, 182–3; Elena affair, 186–7; to Rome, 193–9; and Masons, 206–207, 211–12; distress over Byron and Allegra, 211; to Florence, 218; to Pisa, 222; meets Emilia Viviani, 224; Allegra to convent, 231, 233; and Trelawny, 242–3; death of Allegra, 244–5; plans to join Charles in Vienna, 258–9; to Vienna, 262; in Moscow, 290; to England, 294–5; and Percy Florence, 294–5; vindictiveness, 306–307; letters from Trelawny, 308; in Paris, 314–17; Shelley's legacy, 319; old age, 328; death, 328
Clairmont, Clara Allegra (Alba), 151–2, 154, 157, 161–2, 166, 172–4, 179, 187, 191, 207, 209, 211, 233, 242; christening, 165; sent to

INDEX

Clairmont, Clara Allegra (Alba)—*contd.*
  Byron, 168; sent to convent, 231; death, 244–5
Clairmont, Mrs Mary Jane, *see* Godwin, Mrs
Colburn (publisher), 302
Coleridge, Samuel Taylor, 48, 134; visits Polygon, 19; and Godwin, 21; Skinner Street, 27–8; influence of *The Ancient Mariner* on *Frankenstein*, 132; 'Christabel', 136
Conversations of Lord Byron, 321
Curran, Amelia, 194–5, 200, 256

'Declaration of Rights', 45
Dickens, Charles, 308
Dillon, Lord, 292
Don Juan, 263

Elder Son, The, 23
Elise Foggi, 130, 140, 143, 144, 152, 157, 165, 168; marries Foggi, 185; and Elena affair, 185–9; story about Elena, 234
Enquiry Concerning Political Justice, An, 5, 6, 10, 18, 21, 22, 36, 44, 58
Epipsychidion, 95, 224, 226, 227, 228, 261, 311
Essays, Letters from Abroad, Translations and Fragments, 311
Evesham Buildings, 6, 7, 12, 16

Falkner, 242, 308
Fenwick, Mrs, 20
Field Place, 37, 38, 41, 50, 103, 104, 323

Fields of Fancy, see Mathilda
Foggi, Paolo, 170, 173, 180; marries Elise, 185; blackmail, 185, 188, 210, 214, 216, 218
Fortunes of Perkin Warbeck, The, 282, 287, 296–7
Frankenstein, 2, 28, 30, 34, 73, 124, 131–6, 139, 141, 153, 154, 155, 158, 162, 170, 171, 173, 208, 236, 241, 270, 271, 273, 277, 287, 329; influence of *Ancient Mariner* and *Paradise Lost*, 132; Shelley's preface to, 136; rejection by Murray, 156; critical reaction to, 170–72
Fuseli, Henry, 8, 9, 10, 11

Gamba, Count, 241, 243, 268; and incident with soldier, 243
Gatteschi, 316–18, 319, 320
Gisborne, Maria (as Maria Reveley), 7, 13, 16, 18; Godwin's courtship of, 18–19; (as Maria Gisborne), 19, 56, 169, 173, 174, 200, 202, 205, 212; and Mary Wollstonecraft, 169; letter from Shelley, 187; letters from Mary, 195, 196, 248, 257, 261, 265, 267–8; missed by Mary, 207–208; visit to Shelleys, 230; reunion with Mary, 272; illness, 306; death, 307
Godwin, Fanny, 6, 7, 9, 10, 13, 19, 25, 31, 33, 55, 85, 93, 96; and mother's death, 16; education, 21, 32; and Mrs Godwin, 23; domesticity, 26, 29, 30, 43, 48, 94; parentage, 43; and Shelley and Harriet, 45, 47; warns of bailiffs, 90–91; visits Mary and daughter,

INDEX

107; chronic melancholy, 115; letter from Claire, 115; despair, 142; responsibilities, 145; letter to Mary, 145; suicide, 145, 146

Godwin, Mary Wollstonecraft, *see* Wollstonecraft, Mary

Godwin, William, 2, 48, 53–4; marriage to Mary Wollstonecraft, 5, 6, 7; and correspondence with, 7, 8, 10–12; early life, 10; Mary's death, 14–15; parenthood, 15, 19, 20, 31–2; reasons for remarriage, 17–18; wooing of Maria Reveley, 18–19; fame, 18, 23, 36; financial worries, 18, 22, 24, 57, 145, 162, 205, 210–11, 213; letters to Marshall, 20; and Coleridge, 21; remarriage to Mrs Clairmont, 22; financial demands on Shelley, 22, 98, 101, 114, 119, 120, 137, 165, 203, 208, 216; publishing firm and bookshop, 25, 30; theories on education, 26–7; and Mary, 27, 31; letters to Mrs Godwin, 29; letters to Baxter, 31–3; first contact with Shelley, 36, 37, 42; remoteness, 43; enthusiasm for Shelley, 46; advice about books, 54; censure of Mary and Shelley, 60, 63, 84, 92, 97, 98, 121; attempt to mend Shelley and Harriet's relationship, 62; utilitarianism, 77; letter to Mary and Shelley at Church Terrace, 90; arrogant and selfish, 98, 120, 203; hardheartedness towards Mary, 107; rejection of Mary, 119, 120; Fanny's suicide, 145–6; first letter to Mary after elopement, 146; softening towards Mary, 150–51; on Clara's death, 178; Mary's feelings for, 203; leaves Skinner Street, 248; on Shelley's death, 262; Mary's return to England, 271; minor government post, 306; death, 307; burial, 307
Works: *Antonio*, 22; *Caleb Williams*, 18, 85, 132; *Enquiry Concerning Political Justice*, 5, 6, 10, 18, 21, 22, 36, 44, 58, 98; *Mandeville*, 163; *Memoirs*, 43

Godwin, Mrs (2nd wife), wooing of Godwin, 22; Fanny's and Mary's reaction to, 23; antipathy to Mary, 24, 152, 269; at Polygon, 24–5; publishing firm and bookshop, 25, 30; to Skinner Street, 30; pursuit to Calais, 66; letter to Mary, 95; and Fanny's suicide, 146; and Gisbornes, 219; tolerance towards Mary, 308

Godwin, William (Jnr), 29–30, 48, 304

Gregson, John, 304

Grove, Harriet, 39

Guiccioli, Countess Teresa, 234, 235, 238, 241, 243, 254, 262, 263, 284

Hans Place, 106

Hanway Street, 25

Hate, 81

Hazlitt, William, 18, 152, 155, 269

History of a Six Weeks' Tour, 157

Hitchener, Elizabeth, 40–41, 45, 46, 47, 50, 57

Hobhouse, John, 189

Hogg, Thomas Jefferson, 98–9, 128, 137, 154–6, 267, 310, 319; meets Shelley, 31; in Scotland and York, 40–41; letters from Shelley,

INDEX

Hogg, Thomas Jefferson—*contd.*
  46, 50, 51, 52, 89–90, 116; visits Skinner Street, 58; meets Mary, 99; visits Nelson Square, 100–101; attentions to Mary, 101–102, 103, 105; letters from Mary, 102–103, 104, 110; affair with Mary, 103–12; visits Hans Place, 106, 107; moves into household, 108; irritation with Shelleys, 110; farewells, 114; visits Shelleys at Windsor, 117, 118; to Switzerland, 123; reunion with Mary, 273; and Jane Williams, 284–5; Shelley's legacy, 319
Holcroft, Thomas, 6, 14, 18, 269, 320
Hookham, Thomas, 82, 86, 96, 101, 149, 320; denounces Shelley, 67; betrays Shelley, 90–91, 93
Hoppner, Mr and Mrs Richard Belgrave, 173, 178, 190, 209; help Shelleys, 176–7; and Elena affair, 185–92, 234
Hunt, Leigh and Marianne, 153, 163, 195, 204, 235, 247, 257, 263, 271, 272, 279, 300, 310, 318, 323; and Shelley, 148–52; letters to Marianne, 190, 198; coldness to Mary, 259, 265; softening towards Mary, 268; legacy, 319; death, 328

Ideot, The, 81
Imlay, Fanny, *see* Fanny Godwin
Imlay, Gilbert, 9, 10
Inchbald, Mrs, 7
Irving, Washington, 278–9, 279–80

Johnson, Mr, 8
Jones, Louisa, 16, 18, 20

Keats, John, 134, 152, 163, 213; Shelley meets, 148
Kenney, James and Louisa, 269
Keswick, 41
Kinnaird, Douglas, 189
Knox, Alexander Andrew, 314–15, 318

Lackington Allen & Co., 156
Lake Lucerne, 75–8
Lamb, Charles, 27
Laon and Cythna, 156, 158
Lara, 106
Last Man, The, 56, 126, 182, 196, 241, 263, 272–3, 275–7, 279–81, 287, 301
Lechlade, 118
Lee, Harriet, 17
Letters from Norway, 79
Lewis, Matthew Gregory (Monk), 142
Lodore, 26, 97, 146, 263, 306, 308
Longdill, Mr, 149, 156

Maison Chapuis, Geneva, 127, 137, 141, 143, 155, 314
Mandeville, 163
Marlow, 147, 148, 152, 158, 162; Shelley's visit to Peacock, 144, 148; Hunts stay with Shelleys, 154–6
Marshall, Mr, 20
Mary, 71

Mason, Mrs (Lady Mountcashell), 206–207, 212, 214, 215, 218, 220, 240; and Mary Wollstonecraft, 206
Mathilda, 48, 54, 56, 119, 201, 207
Mavrocordato, Prince Alexander, 223–4, 227, 229, 233, 238
Medwin, Thomas, 220; description of Claire, 222, and of Emilia Viviani, 224; and Shelleys, 222, 226, 228, 238; *Conversations of Lord Byron*, 321
Mérimée, Prosper, 291
Misery, 184
Moore, Tom, 282, 283, 285, 298, 299
Moxon, Edward, 283, 307, 310, 314, 321
Murray, John, 144, 282; rejects *Frankenstein*, 156; destroys Byron's Memoirs, 285

Necessity of Atheism, The, 39
Nelson Square, 97, 98–9, 100–103
Nicholson, William, 16–17
Novello, Vincent, 272
Nugent, Mrs, 48, 105

Ode to the West Wind, 206
Ollier, Charles, 156, 227, 236
Owen, Robert Dale, 286, 292; and Mary, 292
Oxford, 39, 117

Pacchiani, Francesco, 222–3, 229
Payne, John Howard, 278–9; courtship of Mary, 278–80
Peacock, Thomas Love, 86–7, 90, 91, 92, 96, 114, 128, 140, 152–3, 156, 158, 164, 203, 281, 310; in debtor's prison, 104; visits Shelleys at Windsor, 117; letters from Shelley, 125, 170, 172, 176, 179, 182, 226; with Shelley in Marlow, 148; and Sir Timothy Shelley, 281
Peter Bell the Third, 204
Petman, Mrs, 29
Pierson, Henry Hugh, 315
Pisa, 236
Poetical Works, Shelley's, 307; Mary's notes to, 310
Polidori, Dr William, 126, 127, 129, 136, 137, 142, 143; and Mary, 129, 138
Political Justice, 5, 6, 10, 18, 21, 22, 36, 44, 58, 98
Polygon, the, 6, 7, 10, 12, 16, 19, 20, 24
Prisoner of Chillon, The, 139
Proctor, Bryan Waller (Barry Cornwall), 275
Prometheus Unbound, 73, 174, 183

Queen Mab, 50, 60, 80, 121, 157, 310

Rambles in Germany and Italy, 314, 316, 317
Ramsgate, 29
Recollections of the Last Days of Shelley and Byron, 299, 328
Records of Shelley, Byron and the Author, 328
Reveley, Henry, 207, 229–30

Reveley, Maria, *see* Maria Gisborne
Revolt of Islam, The, 156, 172
Rime of the Ancient Mariner, 27, 132
Roberts, Captain, 251, 253–4
Robinson, Henry Crabb, 273, 311
Robinson, Isabel, 285, 291
Robinson, Joshua, 292
Robinson, Julia, 291

St Irvyne, or The Rosicrucian, 39
St John, Jane, *see* Lady Jane Shelley
St Pancras churchyard, 15, 28, 55, 59, 326, 327
Sgricci, Tommaso, 223
Shelley, Charles, 101, 149–52, 155, 156, 281
Shelley, Clara, 157–8, 165, 174–6
Shelley, Elena Adelaide, 185–92
Shelley, Harriet (née Westbrook), 48, 82, 86–7, 115, 137; marriage to Shelley, 40; and Godwin family, 43–5; and Miss Hitchener, 46; letters to Mrs Nugent, 49, 105; birth of daughter, 49; and Shelley's love for Mary, 62; Shelley's letter from Troyes, 69–70; visited by Shelley, 82; birth of son, 101; dependence on Shelley, 105; suicide, 149
Shelley, Ianthe, 49–51, 149–52, 155, 156, 321
Shelley, Lady Jane, 323–4, 325, 327–8
Shelley, Mary, birth, 11–13; early character reading by Nicholson, 16–17; early childhood, 19–21, 25–8; education, 21, 26, 32; reaction to 2nd Mrs Godwin, 23; at Ramsgate, 29–30; to Dundee, 31; first meeting with Shelley, 44–5; first impressions of Shelley, 47–8, 49; leaves Baxters, 53; reunited with father, 53–4; Shelley's impression of, 57; early meetings and falling in love with Shelley, 58–9; emotional commitment to Shelley, 61–2; feelings towards Harriet, 63–4; elopement, 65; in Europe, 67; first pregnancy, 67, 75, 84, 87, 100–101; first sight of Alps, 72–3; relationship with Shelley, 74, 89, 104, 118, 125; and Shelley's ideal community, 75, 77; Shelley's lack of money, 78; Shelley pursued by bailiffs, 91–3, 97; father's coldness towards, 92; love for Fanny, 94; move to Nelson Square, 97; meets Hogg, 99–100; Hogg's attentions, 101–102; Hogg's sexual advances, 102–103, 105; letters to Hogg, 102–103, 104, 108, 110, 112; affair with Hogg, 103–12; premature birth of daughter, 106; death of daughter, 108; Hogg's inclusion in household, 108; holiday near Windsor, 110; fears concerning Shelley and Claire, 112–13, 115; to Devon, 114; second pregnancy, 114, 115, 119; letters to Shelley from Bristol, 115–16; father's rejection, 119, 120; father's demands, 119, 121, 205, 210–11; birth of William, 120; first impression of Byron, 122–3; to Geneva, 123–4; insularity while abroad, 123; at Hôtel d'Angleterre, 124–5; delight in William, 125; admiration for Byron, 126–7, 276; Maison Chapuis, 127; Polidori infatuated with, 129; nightmare, 130; begins

Frankenstein, 131–3; to Chamonix valley, 139–41; and Claire's pregnancy, 141–2; letter from Fanny, 142; to England, 143–4; in Bath, 144–7; Fanny's suicide, 145; Harriet's suicide, 149; marriage to Shelley, 150–51; birth of Allegra, 151; restores relationship with father, 152; third pregnancy, 152, 155, 156; move to Albion House, 153; correspondence with Hunts, 153; revises *Frankenstein*, 154; submits *Frankenstein* to Murray, 155; manuscript rejected, 156; accepted by Lackington Allen, 156; birth of Clara, 157; dedication to in *Laon and Cythna*, 158; anxiety over Shelley's prolonged absence in London, 161–2; pestered by creditors, 162; joins Shelley in London, 162–3; return to Marlow and sale of Albion House, 163–4; social activities in London, 164; William and Clara christened, 165; leaves London, 165; arrives at Calais for third time, 166; and pistol incident at Lake Como, 167; in Milan, 167, 168; Allegra goes to Byron, 168; meets Gisbornes in Tuscany, 169; at Casa Bertini, 169–70; publication of *Frankenstein*, 170–71; reaction of critics, 170–72; Shelley and Claire to Venice, 173; Clara's illness, 174–6; departure for Este, 174; Clara's death, 176–7; transcribes Byron's *Mazeppa*, 177; return to Este, 177; William's illness, 177; letter from father on Clara's death, 178; to Naples, 180–81; to Vesuvius, 182–3; withdrawal from Shelley, 184; and Elena affair, 185–92, 210; letters to Marianne Hunt from Italy, 190, 198; to Rome, 193; fourth pregnancy, 193, 197, 203; and Amelia Curran, 194–5, 200, 256; letters to Maria Gisborne, 195, 196; William's illness and death, 195–9; discusses *The Cenci*, 199; at Monte Nero, 199–204; withdrawal from Shelley, 200, 202; emotional breakdown, 200–201; Godwin's demanding letters, 203; to Florence, 204; birth of Percy Florence, 204; Sophia Stacey's visit, 205; baptism of Percy Florence, 206; and friendship with Masons, 206–207, 212; missing Maria Gisborne, 207–208; and blackmail by Foggi, 210, 214, 216, 218; to Casa Ricci, 210; and Percy's illness, 210–11; estrangement from Gisbornes, 212–13; at Casa Prinni, Bagni di Pisa, 214–21; and peaceful life, 217–18; Claire to Florence, 218; break with Gisbornes, 219; visit from Medwin, 220; at Casa Galetta in Pisa, 222; meets Pacchiani, 222–3; meets Sgricci, 223; meets Taaffe, 223; meets Mavrocordato, 223; meets Viviani, 224; meets Edward and Jane Williams, 228; Claire returns to Pisa, 222; pride hurt by *Epipsychidion*, 226; Greek lessons, 227, 229; first impressions of Edward and Jane Williams, 228; enthusiasm for Greek liberation movement, 229; visit by Gisbornes at Pisa, 230; Byron

Shelley, Mary—*contd.*
sends Allegra into convent, 231; peaceful time again, 231–3; working on *Valperga*, 232; sitting for Williams, 232–3, 235; social activity in Pisa, 238; arrival of Trelawny, 239; impression of Trelawny and his impression of her, 240; bases hero of *Falkner* on Trelawny, 242; and incident with soldier on road to Pisa, 243; death of Allegra, 244–5; fifth pregnancy, 244, 246–7; to Lerici, 244; presentiment of evil at Lerici, 247–8; letter to Maria Gisborne from Lerici, 248; anxiety over Godwin's finances, 248; miscarriage, 248–9; and Shelley's nightmare, 249–50; against Shelley sailing to meet Hunts, 251; last contacts with Shelley, 251–3; letter to Leigh Hunt from Lerici, 252; feelings of foreboding, 252; Shelley's last letter to, 252; Shelley's death, 253–5; support from Trelawny, 255; and portrait of Shelley, 256; letters to Maria Gisborne on Shelley's death, 257, 261, 265, 267–8; reminiscences with Trelawny, 257; cremation and burial of Shelley, 257–8; Hunt's coldness to, 259; letter from Godwin after Shelley's death, 262; to Genoa, 262; transcribes *Don Juan*, 263; Sir Timothy Shelley demands she relinquish Percy Florence, 266; softening of Leigh Hunt towards, 268; leaves Genoa, 268–9; first social contact after Shelley's death, 269–70; return to England, 271; and Jane Williams, 271, 273, 274, 275, 279; sees dramatization of *Frankenstein*, 271; reunion with Gisbornes, 272; Isabel Baxter's illness, 272; into Brunswick Square, 272; friendship with Novello, 272; meets Hogg again, 273; work on Shelley's unpublished poems, 273; Robinson's description, 273; Byron's death, 273–4; into Bartholomew Place, 274; reawakening of creative powers, 274; alone in society, 274–5; meets Proctor, 275; characterization of herself in *The Last Man*, 276–7; and Payne, 278–80; and Irving, 278; and publication of *The Last Man*, 280; forced to write, 281; and Charles Shelley's death, 281; decline of creative powers, 281–2; contribution to *Cabinet Cyclopaedia*, 282, 305; new life in London, 282, 283; and failure of relationship with Jane Williams, 283, 284–5; holiday in Brighton, 284; and Hogg's relationship with Jane, 284–5; reaction to Jane's betrayal, 285; meets Moore, 285–6; letter from Wright, 286–7; Percy at Slater's school, 290, 291; financial worries, 290, 297; Claire in Moscow, 290; contracts smallpox, 291; meets Mérimée, 291; Owen's impression of, 292; and Trelawny, 292–4, 298–300, 302–303, 308–309; Claire's return to England and reaction to Percy, 294–5; refusal to collaborate with Trelawny, 298–9; in Somerset Street, 300; and friendship with Percy, 301, 304–305, 312–13, 315;

publication of Trelawny's autobiography, 301–303; and Trelawny's proposal, 302–303; Percy goes to Harrow, 303–305; moves to Harrow, 305; financial worries, 303–305; Maria Gisborne's illness, 306; Percy and university, 306, 309, 312; Maria and John Gisborne's deaths, 307; father's death and burial, 307; tolerance towards Mrs Godwin, 308; biography of father, 308; work on Shelley's poetry and prose, 309–310; notes to the *Poetical Works*, 310; publication of vol. 1 of *Poetical Works*, 310; publication of *Essays, Letters from Abroad, Translations and Fragments*, 311; financial situation, 312; to Lake Como, 312–14; visit to Claire, 314, 315, 316; hopes for Percy, 316; and the Gatteschi incident, 316–18; Knox to the rescue, 318; Sir Timothy's death and Percy's inheritance, 319; and repossesses Shelley letters, 320–21; and the Medwin incident, 321–2; moves to Chester Square, 322; Percy marries, 323; her love for Jane, 323; moves to Field Place, 323; to Nice, 324; prepared for death, 324–6; death, 326; burial, 327
Character: affinity to women, 283–4; antipathy to Mrs Godwin, 24, 29, 34, 35, 59, 92, 95, 152, 219, 269; anxiety, 161–2, 174, 195, 248, 251–3; appreciation of loved ones, 148, 274, 286, 297, 329; attitude to French, 68–9, 166; attitude to Holland, 80; attitude to Italians, 169, 190, 222, 245; attitude to Swiss, 78; belief in God, 249, 274; burdened by responsibility, 162; confidence, 118, 125; conscience about Harriet, 160; conservatism, 273–4; consideration for Claire, 109–110, 233, 242, 259, 283; constraint, 285; contentment, 117, 215, 217, 313–14, 324; creativity, 132, 161; desire for knowledge, 21, 26, 27, 33, 34; despair and despondency, 97, 108, 109, 162, 195, 200, 204, 246–7, 257, 273, 292; domesticity, 2, 120, 287, 293; emotional dependency, 207, 283; emotional intensity, 108, 208, 284; fear of radical change, 277; feeling for mother, 55–6; generosity, 208, 232, 275, 284, 290, 308; good health, 118; happiness, 217; high spirits, 33, 55, 74, 110, 117, 125, 145, 153, 273, 284; homesickness, 199; humility, 261; ill health, 100–101, 111, 162, 306, 320–25; imagination, 42; independence, 114, 118; insecurity, 34, 115; intellect, 42, 54, 55, 127, 247, 281–2, 287; intuition, 232, 241; irritation with Claire, 74, 75, 78, 84, 87, 90, 98, 101, 108, 112, 138, 148, 160, 209–211, 323; isolation, 23, 26, 27, 30, 101, 273, 277; lack of confidence, 34; lack of humour, 74; lack of political fervour, 287–90; liberality, 75; loneliness, 115, 158, 264; low spirits, 291; maternity, 107, 109, 120, 125, 151, 196, 214–15; melancholy, 33, 55, 135, 147, 153, 157, 184, 246–7, 264, 272; modesty, 1, 34, 43, 71, 72; and the moon (recurring

370

INDEX

Shelley, Mary—*contd.*
theme), 226–7, 261, 274; need to be loved, 24, 30, 109, 208, 274, 286, 297, 329; optimism, 79; perception, 231–2, 241, 281; relationship with father, 27, 31, 53–4, 59, 61, 75, 162, 203, 205, 290, 307; remorse, 247, 259–60; seasickness, 30–31, 65, 81; sensitivity, 160; shy, 153, 286; solitariness, 274, 275, 277, 284–5, 305; studious, 84, 116, 118, 125, 131, 144, 147, 177, 239, 266; and travel, 287, 290–91, 312; undomesticated, 23, 87, 161, 246, 263; vulnerability, 147, 266, 284–5; and water (recurring theme), 125, 127, 138, 139, 167, 199, 201–202, 220–21, 231, 241, 251, 254, 313–14; weakness for young men, 275, 278–80, 286, 291, 303, 314–15, 316–18; wisdom, 225
Works: The Choice, 259; *The Elder Son,* 23; *Falkner,* 56, 242, 308; *Frankenstein,* 2, 28, 30, 34, 73, 124, 131–6, 139, 141, 153, 154, 155, 158, 162, 170, 173, 208, 236, 241, 270, 271, 273, 277, 279, 287, 329; *Hate,* 81; *History of a Six Weeks' Tour,* 157; *Journal,* 79, 80, 95, 98, 103, 104, 105, 108, 112, 113, 139, 140, 145, 151, 157, 180, 217, 241, 273, 279, 284–5, 287–8, 305; missing pages, 103, 106, 110, 112; gave up journal, 196; resumed, 201; *The Last Man,* 56, 126, 182, 196, 241, 263, 272, 273, 275–7, 279–81, 287, 301; *Lodore,* 26, 97, 146, 263, 305, 306, 308; *Mathilda,* 48, 54, 119, 138, 201, 207; *Perkin Warbeck,* 282, 287, 296–7; *Rambles in Germany and Italy,* 314, 316, 317;
Valperga, 139, 212, 215, 218, 232, 235–6, 263, 265, 282, 287, 296
Shelley, Percy Bysshe, first correspondence with Godwin, 36, 37, 42; childhood, 37–9; at Eton, 38–9; at Oxford, 39; meets Hogg, 39; and expulsion from Oxford, 39; marriage to Harriet, 40; letters to Elizabeth Hitchener, 40–41; separation from Hogg, 41; meets Godwin family, 44; in Dublin, 45, 50; visits to Skinner Street, 46, 57, 58; letters to Hogg, 46, 50, 51, 52, 59, 89–90, 112, 116; defection from Miss Hitchener, 46; letter to Fanny, 47; disenchantment with Godwin, 49; dislike of Eliza Westbrook, 51; passion for Cornelia Boinville, 51; feelings about Harriet, 51, 59, 62; letters to Godwin, 55; demands by Godwin, 22, 57, 101, 137, 165, 203, 205, 208, 216; impression of Mary, 57; early meetings with and falling in love with Mary, 58–9; tells Harriet of love for Mary, 62; elopes with Mary, 65; crossing of Channel, 65–6; in Paris, 67–8; letter to Harriet from Troyes, 69–70; and Mary, 74, 89, 104, 118, 125; ideal community, 75, 77, 102; financial difficulties, 78, 81, 84, 86, 87, 90, 97, 111; visit to Harriet, 82; letters to Harriet, 84–5; plan to rescue younger sisters, 86–7; moves to Church Terrace, 86; flight from bailiffs, 90–92; letters to Mary during separation, 92, 93, 94–5, 96; moves to Nelson Square, 97; relationship with Claire, 101, 106, 108, 112, 113, 158; birth of a son by Harriet,

101; and Hogg's advances to Mary, 102; Harriet's dependence on, 105; and Mary's confinement, 106–108; holiday near Windsor, 110; financial freedom, 114, 118; to Devon, 114; return to Oxford, 117; correspondence with Godwin, 119; birth of William, 120; in London, 121; financing of Claire, 112, 121; Shelley's circle, 122; Geneva, 123–4; at Hôtel d'Angleterre, 124–5; commitment to Mary, 125; first meeting with Byron, 126; in comparison with Byron, 126–7, 276; move to Maison Chapuis, 127; and Byron's friendship, 127–8, 174–5; hallucinations at Villa Diodati, 137; to Chamonix valley, 139–41; Claire's pregnancy, 141; and *Childe Harold*, 143–4; return to England, 143–4; in Marlow with Peacock 144, 145; in Bath, 144–7; effect of Fanny's suicide on, 145; help for Godwin, 145; and Leigh Hunt, 148–52; meets Keats, 148; Harriet's suicide, 149; seeks custody of Harriet's children, 149–52, 155, 156; marriage to Mary, 150–51; birth of Allegra, 151; move into Albion House, 153; preface to *Frankenstein*, 156; writes *Laon and Cythna (The Revolt of Islam)*, 156; in London, 158; dedication to Mary in *Laon and Cythna*, 158; return to Marlow, 163; laudanum hallucinations, 163; Sale of Albion House, 164; social activities in London, 164; christening of William and Clara, 165; leaves London for Italy, 165; pistol incident at Lake Como, 167; in Milan, 167, 168; Allegra goes to Byron, 168; at Casa Bertini, 169, 170; letters to Peacock from Italy, 170, 172, 176, 179, 182; publication of *The Revolt of Islam*, 172; to Venice, 173; stay at Villa d'Este, 174; Clara's death, 176; return to Este, 177; to Naples, 180–81; to Vesuvius, 182–3; reaction to Clara's death, 184; and Elena affair, 185–92, 210; blackmail by Foggi, 185, 188, 210, 214, 216, 218; to Rome, 193; in Rome, 193–9; William's illness and death, 195–9; at Monte Nero, 199–204; Mary's withdrawal, 200, 202; intercepts Godwin's letters to Mary, 203, 248; to Florence, 204; birth of Percy Florence, 204; Sophia Stacey's visit, 205; baptism of Percy Florence, 206; friendship with Masons, 206–207, 212; and Percy's illness, 210–11; moves to Casa Ricci, 210; at Casa Prinni, Bagni di Pisa, 214, 215–21; peaceful life with Mary, 218; break with Gisbornes, 219; visit from Medwin, 220; at Casa Galetti in Pisa, 222; meets Pacchiani, 222–3; meets Sgricci, 223; meets Taaffe, 223; and Mavrocordato, 223; and Emilia Viviani, 224, and Edward and Jane Williams, 228; relationship with Emilia Viviani; 224–7; missing Claire's presence, 226; sends *Epipsychidion* to the printer, 227; to Leghorn, 229; peaceful time with Mary again, 231–3; to Ravenna to visit Byron, 233–4; gathering in Pisa, 236; arrival of

Shelley, Percy Bysshe—*contd.*
Trelawny, 239; Trelawny's feelings for, 239–40; and incident with soldier on road to Pisa, 243; death of Allegra, 244–5; attentions to Jane Williams, 246–7; nightmare, 249–50; sails to meet Hunts, 251; last letter to Mary, 252; death, 253–5; cremation and burial, 257–8; characterization in *The Last Man*, 276

Character: arrogance, 38; atheism, 239, 249; attitude to children, 119; contentment, 89, 120, 218, 231–3; creative vitality, 118; disappointment at lack of public appreciation, 235; dissatisfaction, 226; fugitive from society, 133; good health, 118, 229, 246, 252; high spirits, 154, 252; homesickness, 125, 170, 184, 199; hypochondria, 157; ill-health, 111, 157, 158, 160, 163, 174, 184, 206, 217, 226, 238; imagination, 37, 38, 42; insularity while abroad, 123; irritation with Claire, 88–9; liberal views, 85; love for Mary, 125, 158–60; melancholy, 96, 116, 184; and the moon (recurring theme), 226–7; paternity, 154; philosophical ideal as revealed in Victor Frankenstein, 132; physical appearance, 36–7; political awareness, 42, 85, 126, 190; practical in crises, 106, 249; quick temper, 38; revolutionary, 126; self-centred, 175, 176–7; studious, 116, 126; unstable, 63; and water (recurring theme), 125, 127, 137, 138, 154, 157, 167, 170, 220–21, 229–30, 231, 240–41, 246, 250, 251; vulnerability, 62

Works: Alastor, 73, 118, 133, 148, 154; *The Assassins*, 76–8, 81; *The Cenci*, 199, 203; *Epipsychidion*, 95, 224, 226, 227, 228, 261, 311; *Essays, Letters from Abroad, Translations and Fragments* – Shelley's prose with Mary's notes, 311; 'Misery', 184; *The Necessity of Atheism*, 39; 'Ode to the West Wind', 206; 'Peter Bell the Third', 204; *Poetical Works*, 307; *Prometheus Unbound*, 73, 174, 183; *Queen Mab*, 50, 60, 80, 121, 157, 310; *The Revolt of Islam (Laon and Cythna)*, 156, 158, 172; *St Irvyne, or The Rosicrucian*, 39; 'Stanzas Written in Dejection, Near Naples', 184; 'A Summer-Evening Church-Yard, Lechlade', 118; 'To William', 197–8; *The Witch of Atlas*, 215; *Zastrozzi*, 39

Shelley, Percy Florence, 1, 258, 279, 280, 285, 286, 294–5; 299, 301; birth, 204; baptism, 206; childhood at Bagni di Pisa, 214–15, 218; in England, 271, 273, 275; at Slater's school, 290–91; at Harrow, 303–305; at university, 306, 309, 312; twentieth birthday, 311; his generosity and good nature, 311; to Lake Como, 312–14; character, 315; inherits, 319; moves to Chester Square, 322; marries Jane St John, 323; nurse Mary, 325–6; Mary's death, 326; domesticity, 327; death, 327

Shelley, Sir Bysshe, 103

Shelley, Sir Timothy, 230, 262, 265, 266, 267, 275–6, 280–81, 290, 294,

304, 305; demands Mary relinquish Percy Florence, 266; orders recall of volume of Shelley's poems, 273; interest in Percy, 299; liking for Percy, 314; death, 319

Shelley, William, 152, 155, 173, 174; birth, 120; early childhood, 125, 130, 131, 137, 140–41; in Bath, 144–7; ill in Este, 177; illness and death, 195–7

Shields, Milly, 165, 168, 173, 193

Skinner Street, 25, 27–8, 30, 40, 47, 49, 53, 55, 60, 64, 84, 85–6, 90, 91, 95, 98, 101, 106, 107, 112, 114, 115, 119, 147, 151, 152, 155, 205, 300; Shelley's visits to, 46, 57, 58

Smith, Horace, 230, 233, 246, 269, 302

Somers Town, 5, 6, 20, 28, 86, 90, 97, 155

Southey, 5, 42, 134

Stacey, Sophia, 205

'Stanzas Written in Dejection, near Naples', 184

'A Summer-Evening Church-Yard, Lechlade', 118

Sussex, Lady, 317–18

Taaffe, John, 223, 232, 238, 239, 243

Tan-yr-allt, 45, 46, 50

'To William', 197–8

Trelawny, Edward John, 150, 172, 253–4, 265, 267, 292–4, 295–6, 310, 318, 328; first impressions of Mary, 33, 42, 240; Claire's letter to, 141; arrival in Pisa, 239; and Shelley, 239–40; relationship with Shelleys, 239–42, 243; Mary's first impression of, 240; relationship with Claire, 242–3; hero of *Falkner*, 242; supportive role, 255, 257; reminiscences after Shelley's death, 257; generosity, 267–8, 271; to Greece, 268; to England, 292; letter to Mary from Southampton, 293; characterized in *The Fortunes of Perkin Warbeck*, 296–7; seeks publication of autobiography, 301–303; proposal to Mary, 302–303; letters to Claire, 308; and Mary, 308–309; old age and death, 328 Works: *Adventures of a Younger Son*, 303; *Recollections of the Last Days of Shelley and Byron*, 299, 328; *Records of Shelley, Byron and the Author*, 328

Trelawny, Julia, 303, 304

Utilitarianism and William Godwin, 77, 98

Valperga, 212, 215, 218, 232, 235–6, 263, 265, 282, 287

Villa Diodati, 127–30, 132, 136–7, 139, 141–3, 263, 274, 281, 314

Vindication of the Rights of Woman, A, 5, 9, 307

Vivian, Charles, 253

Viviani, Emilia, 224–7, 284

Wedgwood, Thomas, 7, 10

Westbrook, Eliza, 39–40, 41, 48, 50, 105, 149

Westbrook, Harriet, *see* Harriet Shelley
Whitton, Mr, 39, 104, 262, 265, 281, 290, 304
Williams, Edward, and the Shelleys, 228–9, 231, 232, 233, 235, 238, 239, 241, 242, 243, 244, 246, 247, 249; to Lerici, 244; to meet Hunts, 251; death, 253–5
Williams, Jane, 54, 103, 139, 262, 273–5, 279, 291, 322; and the Shelleys, 228–9, 231–3, 235, 238–9, 241–4, 246–7, 249; to Lerici, 244; death of Williams and Shelley, 253–5; Mary united with, 271; failure of relationship with Mary, 283–5; lives with Hogg, 284–5; old age, 328
The Witch of Atlas, 215

Wollstonecraft, Mary, marriage to Godwin, 5, 6, 7; correspondence with Godwin, 7, 8, 10–12; childhood and early life, 8, 9; birth of Mary, 12–13; death, 13–14; burial, 15; Mary and Shelley's feelings for, 55–6; Maria Gisborne's observations of, 169; Mrs Mason's memories of, 206; Mrs Kenney's impression of, 270
Works: Letters from Norway, 79; *Mary*, 71; *A Vindication of the Rights of Woman*, 5, 9, 307
Wordsworth, William, 134, 269
Wright, Frances, 286–7, 292

Zastrozzi, 39